Court Mediation Reform

When perfect justice reigns in every country of the Eastern and Western World, then will the earth become a place of beauty. The dignity and equality ... [and] the ideal of the solidarity of the human race ... will be realized.
Abdu'l-Bahá, *Paris Talks* (2012) p. 154

Court Mediation Reform

Efficiency, Confidence and Perceptions of Justice

Shahla F. Ali

Faculty of Law, University of Hong Kong

Cheltenham, UK • Northampton, MA, USA

© Shahla F. Ali 2018

All rights reserved. No part of this publication may be reproduced, stored in a retrieval system or transmitted in any form or by any means, electronic, mechanical or photocopying, recording, or otherwise without the prior permission of the publisher.

Published by
Edward Elgar Publishing Limited
The Lypiatts
15 Lansdown Road
Cheltenham
Glos GL50 2JA
UK

Edward Elgar Publishing, Inc.
William Pratt House
9 Dewey Court
Northampton
Massachusetts 01060
USA

A catalogue record for this book
is available from the British Library

Library of Congress Control Number: 2017955169

This book is available electronically in the **Elgar**online
Law subject collection
DOI 10.4337/9781786435866

ISBN 978 1 78643 585 9 (cased)
ISBN 978 1 78643 586 6 (eBook)

Typeset by Servis Filmsetting Ltd, Stockport, Cheshire
Printed and bound in Great Britain by TJ International Ltd, Padstow

Contents

List of figures and tables vi
Overview viii
Acknowledgements ix

Introduction: balancing the scales: assessing the efficacy of global court mediation reform   1

PART I AIMS AND OBJECTIVES OF COURT MEDIATION REFORM

1. Court mediation reform aims in a global context   25
2. Voluntary and mandatory mediation programme design   49

PART II VOLUNTARY MEDIATION PROGRAMMES

3. Mediation in the UK courts   65
4. Mediation in the Hong Kong courts   85
5. Mediation in the French courts   99
6. Mediation in the Dutch courts   111
7. Mediation in the Malaysian courts   125

PART III MANDATED COURT MEDIATION PROGRAMMES

8. Mediation in the United States federal courts   143
9. Mediation in the Australian federal courts   158
10. Mediation in the Italian courts   170
11. Mediation in the Chinese courts   186
12. Mediation in the Indian courts   206

PART IV EMPIRICAL FINDINGS ON COURT MEDIATION

13. Insights and recommendations from a global mediation survey   221
14. Conclusions   249

Select bibliography   260
Index   273

Figures and tables

FIGURES

I.1	Percentage of regions experiencing positive change over a five-year period in efficiency, confidence and perceptions of justice by voluntary/mandatory programme type	14
13.1	Percentage of practitioners rating very high/high perceptions of efficiency, confidence and fairness in court mediation by programme type	222
13.2	Region of practice	225
13.3	Experience with court mediation	226
13.4	Court mediation cost coverage	227

TABLES

3.1	Mediation outcomes under the Small Claims Mediation Scheme	80
3.2	Success rates of ADR in cases involving government departments and agencies	82
3.3	UK rankings: developments in efficiency, confidence and perceptions of justice, 2011–2016	83
4.1	Hong Kong rankings: developments in efficiency, confidence and perceptions of justice, 2011–2016	97
5.1	France's rankings: developments in efficiency, confidence and perceptions of justice, 2011–2016	109
6.1	The Netherlands' rankings: developments in efficiency, confidence and perceptions of justice, 2011–2016	122
7.1	Successful mediated cases in various courts of Malaysia in 2011	136
7.2	Malaysia's rankings: developments in efficiency, confidence and perceptions of justice, 2011–2016	138
8.1	Programme features of specific mandatory mediation programmes in 12 US federal districts	148

Figures and tables vii

8.2	United States' rankings: developments in efficiency, confidence and perceptions of justice, 2011–2016	156
9.1	Australia's rankings: developments in efficiency, confidence and perceptions of justice, 2011–2016	168
10.1	Italy's rankings: developments in efficiency, confidence and perceptions of justice, 2011–2016	184
11.1	Breakdown by types of disputes of judicial-mediated civil cases at the first instance level of the PRC courts	201
11.2	Breakdown of civil cases closed at the first instance level of the PRC courts	203
11.3	China's rankings: developments in efficiency, confidence and perceptions of justice, 2011–2016	204
12.1	India's rankings: developments in efficiency, confidence and perceptions of justice, 2011–2016	217
13.1	Rationale for court mediation by programme type, 2015–2017	228
13.2	Confidence in mediation programme by programme type, 2015–2017	230
13.3	Fairness of mediation programme by programme type, 2015–2017	231
13.4	Efficiency of mediation programme by programme type, 2015–2017	233
13.5	Key achievements in mandatory and voluntary programmes, 2015–2017	235
13.6	Key challenges in mandatory and voluntary programmes, 2015–2017	238
13.7	Suggestions for improvement of mandatory and voluntary mediation programmes	242

Overview

As judicial systems advance, evolving conceptions of justice are reflected in varying emphasis on the role, place and practice of mediation in civil courts. How such programmes provide opportunities for party directed reconciliation, on the one hand, while ensuring access to formal legal channels, on the other, remains an area of continued inquiry. Drawing on an 83 person survey, case studies of 10 mediation jurisdictions, and time-series analysis of aggregate civil justice indicators, this book explores comparative empirical findings examining the association between judicial mediation structure and perceptions of justice, efficiency and confidence in courts. Variation among such programmes reflects, to a large extent, distinct approaches to individual and collective responsibility for the financial, social and temporal resources required for resolution. Given the highly contextual nature of court mediation programmes, the book highlights achievements, challenges and lessons learned in the implementation of mediation programmes for general civil claims. Programme achievements largely depend on the functioning of the civil litigation system, the qualities and skill of the mediators, safeguards against bias, participant education, and cultural and institutional support.

Acknowledgements

The research for this book has been made possible by funds from the Government of Hong Kong's Research Grants Council (HKU 17603215). Without the valuable observations from court mediation officials and practitioners, the practical insights in this book would not be possible. Special thanks go to members of mediation centres and associations, including members of the ABA Section of Dispute Resolution, the Asia Pacific Mediation Forum, the Mediator Network, CPR Institute, National Centre for State Courts, Mediators Beyond Borders, Hong Kong Mediation Network, Resolution Systems Institute, the Court Annexed and Judicial Mediation Network and the Collaborative Justice Institute. In addition, valuable input was received from the Asia-Pacific UNCITRAL Conference on Legal Harmonization, UC Hastings Centre for Negotiation and Conflict Resolution, the Singapore International Arbitration Forum, the Centre for International and Comparative Law, the Peace Chair at the University of Maryland, the UC Berkeley Centre for the Study of Law and Society, the World Bank Group, the Centre for Understanding Conflict, Shanghai Law School, Pepperdine Strauss Institute for Dispute Resolution, the Dubai International Court and the Japan Mediation Centre.

Many people have helped with this book. Laura Mann and Luke Adams, editors at Edward Elgar, expertly oversaw the review and publication of this project. Anonymous reviewers provided extremely valuable input at the early stages of the project. Jennifer Lee, Elizabeth Clack and Sue Sharp provided valuable oversight of production and distribution. Special thanks go to an outstanding team of research assistants, including Tong Lok Hei, Emily Chan, Nicholas Chu, Florence Tse, Thomas Leung, Kate Chan and Jennifer Hui.

Numerous colleagues have provided valuable insights that have improved this book. I am grateful for fruitful exchanges with Thomas Stipanowich, Lola Akin Ojelabi, Deborah Hensler, Judge Dorothy Nelson, Moti Mironi, Ota Shozo, Martin Krygier, Malcolm Feeley, Sheila Purcell, Heather Anderson, Luigi Cominelli, Carrie Menkel-Meadow, Diane Desierto, Nancy Welsh, Setsuo Miyazawa, Cynthia Alkon, Richard Reuben, Dorcas Queck, Mark Feldman, Hiroshi Takahashi, Hiro

Aragaki, Michelle LeBaron, Mark Feldman, Jill Gross, Aya Yamada, Hiro Aragaki, Nadja Alexander, Stacie Strong, Sharon Press, Fu Hualing, Eric Feldman, Lisa Blomgren-Amsler, Susan Franck, Loukas Mistelis, Michael Palmer, Eric Feldman, Robert Ahdieh, Rosmary Howell, Anna Koo, Katherine Lynch, Elayne Greenberg, David Caron, Peer Zumbansen, Sherna Deamer, Jack Coe, Dale Bagshaw and Robert Moberly. I am also thankful to our Law Faculty Dean Michael Hor, Associate Dean for research Simon Young and Department Head Zhao Yun for providing a supportive research environment at the University of Hong Kong. I am also grateful to participants who shared valuable feedback at the following conferences: the Law and Society Association Annual Conference (Mexico City), the ABA Section on Dispute Resolution (San Francisco, CA), the International Association of Conflict Management (Berlin, Germany), the ITA Academic Council Works in Progress (Washington, DC), the UNCITRAL Working Group II (Dispute Resolution) commission meeting at the United Nations (New York), AALS (San Francisco, CA), CASS/IGC Conference (Macau SAR), the Asia-Pacific Mediation Forum (Lombok, Indonesia), the Mixed-Mode Dispute Resolution Summit Strauss Institute Pepperdine (Malibu, CA), IBA Conference (Shanghai, PRC) and UNCITRAL Emergence Conference (Macau SAR).

This book is dedicated to Victor and my two girls, Martha and Agnes, the youngest of whom was born during this project. All that is positive in this book reflects the support and generosity of colleagues, research participants, family, friends and associates. All errors and omissions are my own.

Introduction: balancing the scales: assessing the efficacy of global court mediation reform

OVERVIEW

Since the mid-twentieth century, the question of achieving procedural and substantive justice in the context of judicial mediation has received significant attention beginning with the work of Owen Fiss and Lon Fuller. Recent work has highlighted the growing inefficiencies of civil litigation in economically advanced countries, while at the same time, cautioning judiciaries to ensure that justice is safeguarded in extra-judicial procedures.[1] Building on a growing body of empirical cross-jurisdictional research examining mediation reform and policy,[2] this book explores

---

[1] See M. Galanter, 'Why the "Haves" Come Out Ahead: Speculations on the Limits of Legal Change' (1974) 9(1) *Law and Society Review* 95; M. Feeley, *The Process is the Punishment: Handling Cases in a Lower Criminal Court* (New York: Russell Sage Foundation, 1979); C. Albiston, 'The Rule of Law and the Litigation Process: The Paradox of Losing by Winning' (1999) 33(4) *Law and Society Review* 869; H. Genn, *Judging Civil Justice* (Cambridge University Press, 2010); A.J. Cohen, 'Revisiting Against Settlement: Some Reflections on Dispute Resolution and Public Values' (2009) 78 *Fordham Law Review* 101.

[2] See F. Steffek et al., *Regulating Dispute Resolution: ADR and Access to Justice at the Crossroads* (Oxford: Hart, 2013); Schonewille & Schonewille, *Variegated Use of Mediation: A Comparative Study of Mediation Regulation and Practices in Europe and the World* (The Hague: Eleven International Publishing, 2014); D. Stienstra, T.E. Willging and Federal Judicial Center, *Alternatives to Litigation: Do They Have a Place in the Federal District Courts?* (Washington, DC: Federal Judicial Center, 1995); R.L. Wissler, 'Mediation and Adjudication in the Small Claims Court: The Effects of Process and Case Characteristics' (1995) 29 *Law and Society Review* 323; C. Menkel-Meadow, 'Regulation of Dispute Resolution in the United States of America: From the Formal to the Informal to the "Semi-formal"' in F. Steffek et al. (eds), *Regulating Dispute Resolution: ADR and Access to Justice at the Crossroads* (Oxford: Hart, 2013); T. Stipanowich, 'The International Evolution of Mediation: A Call for Dialogue and Deliberation' (2015) 46 *Victoria University of Wellington Law Review* 1191; S.I. Strong, 'Realizing Rationality: An Empirical Assessment of International Commercial Mediation' (2016) *Washington*

initial comparative findings examining the association between judicial voluntary and mandatory mediation structure and perceptions of justice, efficiency and confidence in courts. It suggests that variation among such programmes reflects distinct approaches to individual and collective responsibility for the financial, social and temporal resources required for resolution. As many such civil mediation programme reforms have been underway for more than a decade, it is timely to examine lessons learned in the implementation of such programmes. In doing so, the book highlights positive lessons learned from selected jurisdictions, analyses local circumstances, and distils best practices.

In numerous jurisdictions worldwide, civil justice reform has advanced rapidly in recent years since the early days of the 'multi-door courthouse'.[3] In response to what has been described as 'a sharp increase in the number, rapidity and complexity of transactions'[4] characterized by 'cumbersomeness, costliness and legal unpredictability',[5] reform proposals have been advanced, including the introduction of mediation in civil case administration.[6] Existing scholarship has examined the varying intrinsic and extrinsic rationales motivating courts to introduce mediation programmes,[7]

---

and Lee Law Review, forthcoming; H. Genn et al., *Twisting Arms: Court Referred and Court Linked Mediation Under Judicial Pressure* (Ministry of Justice Research Series, 2007); L. Blomgren Amsler (formerly Bingham), J.K. Martinez, S.E. Smith and C. Merchant, 'The State of Dispute System Design' (2015) 33 *Conflict Resolution Quarterly* S7; A. Kupfer Schneider, 'Foreword: The Future of Court ADR: Mediation and Beyond' (2012) 95(3) *Marquette Law Review* (Spring); T. Sourdin and A. Zariski, *The Multi-Tasking Judge: Introduction to Comparative Judicial Dispute Resolution* (Sydney: Thomson Reuters, 2013); D. Quek Anderson and J. Lee, 'The Global Pound Conference: A Conversation on the Future of Dispute Resolution' (2016) *Asian Journal on Mediation* 70.

[3] See F.E.A. Sander, 'Varieties of Dispute Processing' in A. Levin and R. Wheeler (eds), *The Pound Conference: Perspectives on Justice in the Future* (West Publishing, 1979) pp. 65–87.

[4] Civil Justice Reform, *Interim Report and Consultation Paper* (2001) p. 3, para. 9.

[5] Citing D. Bok, 'A Flawed System of Law Practice and Training' (1983) 33(4) *Journal of Legal Education* 570; R. Kagan, *Adversarial Legalism: The American Way of Law* (Cambridge, MA: Harvard University Press, 2001).

[6] See e.g., C.J. Alkon. 'The Modern Problem-Solving Court Movement: Taking Stock After 25 Years', paper presented at Association of American Law Schools (AALS) Annual Conference 2016; and R. Fisher and W. Ury, *Getting to Yes: Negotiating an Agreement Without Giving In* (2nd edn, New York: Random House Business Books, 1991) pp. 10–11.

[7] D.R. Hensler, 'Our Courts, Ourselves: How the Alternative Dispute Resolution Movement is Re-Shaping Our Legal System' (2003–2004) 108 *Pennsylvania State Law Review* 165.

including reduction of caseloads,[8] private and public sector efficiency,[9] as well as extrinsic factors including relational,[10] societal[11] and process-based[12] considerations. Examining the impact of such programmes is critical, since 'with little . . . information about the process or outcomes of dispute resolution, citizens' abilities to use the justice system effectively to achieve social change' is limited.[13]

Significant variation in the implementation of court mediation reforms currently exists. In some jurisdictions, mediation is mandated for particular civil case types, whereas in others, parties are encouraged to engage in voluntary mediation with cost consequences being attached in some jurisdictions to unreasonable refusal to engage in mediation. At the individual level, such programmes reflect distinct applications of individual rights suggesting self-determination and party choice in regulatory practice.[14] On the other hand, notions of collective responsibility place importance on reducing the costs of litigation on society as a whole. Avenues toward voluntary or mandatory mediation reflect varying underlying normative conceptions of individual and collective justice. Given that 'public means available for financing dispute resolution are not unlimited',[15] a balancing of individual process choices and social efficiency requires careful investigation.

In responding to calls for expanded empirical research exploring the operation[16] and implementation[17] of civil justice reforms, and building on

---

[8] H. Foo Chee, *Civil Case Management in Singapore: Of Models, Measures and Justice* (ASEAN Law Association, 2016), available at www.aseanlawassociation.org/11GAdocs/workshop2-sg.pdf (accessed 14 January 2016).

[9] W. Maclons, *Mandatory Court Based Mediation as an Alternative Dispute Resolution Process in the South African Civil Justice System* (University of Western Cape, 2014) p. 85.

[10] Y. Shamir, *Alternative Dispute Resolution Approaches and Their Application* (UNESCO, 2003) p. 24.

[11] Mediate.com, *Engineering Peace: Achieving the Promise of Mediation in the World's Most Difficult Conflicts*, available at www.mediate.com/articles/engpeace.cfm#_edn7 (accessed 19 January 2016).

[12] R. Zeinemann, 'The Characterisation of Public Sector Mediator' (2003) 24(2) *Environs Law* 51, available at http://environs.law.ucdavis.edu/volumes/24/2/articles/zeinemann.pdf.

[13] Hensler, 'Our Courts Ourselves' (n. 7 above).

[14] Steffek et al., *Regulating Dispute Resolution* (n. 2 above).

[15] *Ibid.*

[16] See M. Heise, 'Justice Delayed? An Empirical Analysis of Civil Case Disposition Time' (2000) 50(4) *Case Western Reserve Law Review* 813; C. Tobias, 'Civil Justice Delay and Empirical Data: A Response to Professor Heise' (2000) 51(2) *Case Western Reserve Law Review* 235.

[17] See T. Stipanowich, 'The International Evolution of Mediation: A Call for Dialogue and Deliberation' (2015) 46 *Victoria University of Wellington*

an important foundation of rich scholarship examining the extension[18] and usage[19] of court mandated mediation; experience of procedural justice;[20] investigation of efficiency claims;[21] impacts on the quality and means[22] of access;[23] social justice and minority impacts;[24] settlement outcomes;[25] and cultural factors,[26] this book presents a set of 10 longitudinal country case studies supplemented by survey research about the per-

---

Law Review 1191; Pepperdine University Legal Studies Research Paper No. 2016/1.

[18] C. Menkel-Meadow, 'Pursuing Settlement in an Adversary Culture: A Tale of Innovation Co-opted or the Law of ADR' (1991) 19 *Florida State Law Review* 1; J. Resnik, 'Many Doors? Closing Doors? Alternative Dispute Resolution and Adjudication' (1995) 10 *Ohio State Journal of Dispute Resolution* 211; E.E. Deason, 'Procedural Rules for Complementary Systems of Litigation and Mediation: Worldwide' (2004) 80 *Notre Dame Law Review* 553.

[19] See T.C.W. Farrow, *Civil Justice, Privatization and Democracy* (2011), available at http://papers.ssrn.com.eproxy1.lib.hku.hk/sol3/papers.cfm?abstract_id517 95407 (accessed 28 November 2011).

[20] J. Thibaut and L. Walker, 'A Theory of Procedure' (1978) 66(3) *California Law Review* 541; D. Stienstra, M. Johnson, P. Lombard and M. Pecherski, *Report to the Judicial Conference Committee on Court Administration and Case Management: A Study of Five Demonstration Programs Established Under the Civil Justice Reform Act of 1990* (Washington, DC: Federal Judicial Center, 1997).

[21] D.R. Hensler, *A Research Agenda: What We Need to Know About Court-Connected ADR* (Santa Monica, CA: RAND Corporation, 2000), available at www.rand.org/pubs/reprints/RP871.html; T.J. Stipanowich, 'ADR and the 'Vanishing Trial': The Growth and Impact of Alternative Dispute Resolution' (2004) 1(3) *Journal of Empirical Legal Studies* 843; K. Kressel and D.G. Pruitt, 'Themes in the Mediation of Social Conflict' (1985) 41 *Journal of Social Issues* 179; J. Kakalik et al., *Just, Speedy and Inexpensive? An Evaluation of Judicial Case Management Under the Civil Justice Reform Act* (Santa Monica, CA: RAND, 1997).

[22] See H. Genn, *Paths to Justice* (Oxford: Hart, 1999); Genn, 'Judging Civil Justice' (n. 1 above).

[23] H. Genn, 'What is Civil Justice For? Reform, ADR, and Access to Justice' (2013) 24 *Yale Journal of Law and the Humanities* 397.

[24] R. Delgado et al., 'Fairness and Formality: Minimizing the Risk of Prejudice in Alternative Dispute Resolution' (1985) *Wisconsin Law Review* 1359; G. LaFree and C. Rack, 'The Effects of Participants' Ethnicity and Gender on Monetary Outcomes in Mediated and Adjudicated Civil Cases' (1996) 30 *Law and Society Review* 767; S. Press, 'Court-Connected Mediation and Minorities: Has Any Progress Been Made?' (2013) *ABA Dispute Resolution Magazine* 36 (Summer).

[25] J.M. Brett, Z.I. Barsness and S.B. Goldberg, 'The Effectiveness of Mediation: An Independent Analysis of Cases Handled by Four Major Service Providers' (1996) 12(3) *Negotiation Journal* 259; M. Galanter and M. Cahill, 'Most Cases Settle: Judicial Promotion and Regulation of Settlements' (1994) 46 *Stanford Law Review* 1339.

[26] See Heise, 'Justice Delayed?' (n. 16 above).

ceptions, observations and experiences of court mediation practitioners from diverse regions in order to gain insight into the dynamics, strengths and challenges of mandatory and voluntary court mediation programmes. It aims to respond to calls for 'empirical studies of the effectiveness of ADR' especially outside of North America, including comparative studies within and between mediation programme types, including mandatory and voluntary programmes.[27] In particular, this book contributes to a growing body of empirical scholarship on the experience of civil justice in countries that have implemented mediation reforms, including the United Kingdom, Hong Kong, France, the Netherlands, Malaysia, the United States, Australia, Italy, China and India.

The degree of movement along the voluntary or mandatory mediation spectrum varies from one jurisdiction to another. Such variation exists with respect to the 'initiation control'[28] of mediation[29] where approaches range from mandatory assignments for all cases under a particular monetary amount or case type, compelled orders to mediation (characterized in some cases as 'case settlement'[30]) to more informal party directed initiation of mediation.[31] As described by Menkel-Meadow, the intermediaries facilitating judicial mediation sessions vary from judges provided by the courts, to private mediators.[32] In addition, parties' duties concerning engagement in mediation may also differ. Some states use 'opt-out' rules where parties to a particular case type are automatically subjected to mediation unless there is a good reason for opting out,[33] while other programmes use an 'opt-in' mechanism by which adverse cost consequences are imposed if parties unreasonably refuse to participate

---

[27] L. Bingham et al., 'Dispute Resolution and the Vanishing Trial: Comparing Federal Government Litigation and ADR Outcomes' (2009) 24(2) *Ohio State Journal of Dispute Resolution* 1.

[28] Steffek et al., *Regulating Dispute Resolution* (n. 2 above).

[29] C. Menkel-Meadow, 'Variations in the Uptake of and Resistance to Mediation Outside of the United States' in A. Rovine (ed.), *Contemporary Issues in International Arbitration and Mediation: The Fordham Papers 2014* (Leiden: Brill-Nijhoff, 2015) p. 197.

[30] M. Mironi, 'Mediation v. Case Settlement: The Unsettling Relations Between Court and Mediation, A Case Study' (2014) 19 *Harvard Negotiation Law Review* 173; the distinction outlined by Mironi between 'mediation' and 'case settlement' is helpful, noting that mediation is characterized by an interest-based, party focused process rather than a 'settlement' oriented rights-based positional discourse.

[31] Menkel-Meadow, 'Variations in the Uptake of and Resistance to Mediation' (n. 29 above) p. 197.

[32] *Ibid.*

[33] *Ibid.*

in mediation or behave unreasonably. As has been well documented by Stipanowich's extensive meta-survey of court connected mediation in the United States, even within a common court mandated mediation programme, differential levels of judge-directed encouragement may lead to widely differing user experiences of the process.[34] Existing empirical work examining mandatory and voluntary programme outcomes has found that selection and uptake of diverse programme structures is largely dependent on domestic factors, including the level of cooperation by the Bar,[35] mediation awareness, socio-cultural context and harmonizing legislation.[36] At the global level, soft-law-making bodies such as UNCITRAL have generally left open the question of mediation programme design to be inclusive of both voluntary and mandatory modalities depending on domestic circumstances.[37]

For purposes of this project, voluntary mediation jurisdictions are characterized as those requiring formal party-agreement prior to commencement,[38] while mandatory mediation jurisdictions are classified, following Sander's definition, as consisting of both 'categorical'[39] automatic referral programmes for certain categories of cases[40] and 'discretionary' such that judges have authority to order mediation where there is no consent from the parties. In jurisdictions where mixed methods of voluntary and mandatory resolution options co-exist, reference is made to the primary mechanism employed in non-family civil trials. In cases of varying federal and state programmes, reference is made to federal programme features. Despite efforts to achieve accurate groupings, limitations exist in such broad characterizations and future studies will no doubt further refine such categorizations and improve upon them.

---

[34] T.J. Stipanowich, 'ADR and the 'Vanishing Trial': The Growth and Impact of Alternative Dispute Resolution' (2004) 1(3) *Journal of Empirical Legal Studies* 843.

[35] See generally, P. Taivalkoski and A. Pynnä, 'The Courts and Bar Association as Drivers for Mediation in Finland' in *New Developments in Civil and Commercial Mediation* (New York: Springer, 2015) pp. 275–89.

[36] *Ibid.*

[37] United Nations (ed.), *UNCITRAL Model Law on International Commercial Conciliation with Guide to Enactment and Use 2002* (New York: United Nations, 2002) p. 55, Art. 3.

[38] See H. Anderson and R. Pi, *Evaluation of the Early Mediation Pilot Programs* (Judicial Council of CA Administrative Office of the Courts, 2004).

[39] F.E.A. Sander, 'Another View of Mandatory Mediation' (2007) 13(2) *Dispute Resolution Magazine* 16.

[40] M. Hanks, 'Perspective on Mandatory Mediation' (2012) 35(3) *University of New South Wales Law Journal* 929.

DATA COLLECTION METHODS

Contemporary scholars have acknowledged the challenges of obtaining sound empirical data on diverse ADR mechanisms, especially on court-annexed mediation.[41] On the one hand, aggregated data from surveys and interviews provide the basis for comparisons yet may lack interpretive consistency.[42] On the other hand, qualitative, in-depth analysis of a particular mediation event[43] may afford rich insights, yet may not be representative. Useful insights have been drawn from studies disaggregating perceptions of attorneys, clients and mediators within the same mediation process and across regions of practice.[44] Given such challenges, scholars have suggested that, to the extent possible, suitable quantitative and qualitative metrics should be examined in combination.[45]

In response to such observations, the research methodology employed here triangulates the exploration of judicial mediation reform by drawing on a combination of 10 voluntary and mandatory mediation country case studies coupled with longitudinal analysis of changes to judicial efficiency,

---

[41] C. Menkel-Meadow, 'The Baseline Problem of What ADR is and What It is Compared To' in P. Cane and H. Kritzer (eds), *Oxford Handbook of Empirical Legal Research* (Oxford University Press, 2010); T.J. Stipanowich, 'ADR and the "Vanishing Trial": The Growth and Impact of Alternative Dispute Resolution' (2004) 1(3) *Journal of Empirical Legal Studies* 843; C. Menkel-Meadow et al., 'Thinking Critically about Nonadjudicatory Processes' in *Dispute Resolution: Beyond the Adversarial Model* (Aspen, 2005) pp. 875–6; M. Galanter et al., 'How to Improve Civil Justice Policy' (1994) 77 *Judicature* 185; D.R. Hensler, *Why We Don't Know More About the Civil Justice System – and What We Could Do About It* (USC Law, 1994); B. McAdoo, 'All Rise, the Court is in Session: What Judges Say About Court-Connected Mediation' (2006) 22(2) *Ohio State Journal on Dispute Resolution* 337.

[42] Menkel-Meadow et al., 'Thinking Critically about Nonadjudicatory Processes' (n. 41 above).

[43] *Ibid.*

[44] See: T.J. Stipanowich, 'Beyond Arbitration: Innovation and Evolution in the United States Construction Industry' 31 *Wake Forest L. Rev.* 169 (1996); T.J. Stipanowich, 'ADR and the "Vanishing Trial": The Growth and Impact of Alternative Dispute Resolution' (2004) 1(3) *Journal of Empirical Legal Studies* 843; T.J. Stipanowich, 'Insights on Mediator Practices and Perceptions' (2016) *Disp. Resol. Mag.*, Winter 2016, at 4.

[45] *Ibid.*; see also D.R. Hensler and M.A. Gasperetti, 'The Role of Empirical Legal Studies in Legal Scholarship, Legal Education and Policy-Making: A U.S. Perspective' in R. van Gestel, H.-W. Micklitz and E.L. Rubin (eds), *Rethinking Legal Scholarship: A Transatlantic Dialogue* (New York: Cambridge University Press, 2017); see also T. Ginsburg, P.G. Monateri and F. Parisi, *Classics in Comparative Law: An Introduction* (Cheltenham: Edward Elgar, 2014).

perceptions of justice and overall confidence in the court system over a five-year time period since the implementation of such programmes. It supplements such findings with comparative examination of global court user experience data,[46] and analysis of survey data from 83 practitioners, including judges, attorneys, administrators, mediators and participants practising in the area of court mediation reform. The aim is that through a process of triangulation the selected research techniques can, to some extent, compensate for inherent deficiencies in any one method alone, and provide a broader foundation for critical analysis.[47] Country case studies are selected from a non-random sample of 10 countries consisting of five regions in a 'mandatory mediation regions' group and five in a 'voluntary mediation regions' tracking intra-regional changes, if any, to levels of efficiency, confidence and perceptions of justice following the implementation of court mediation reforms over a five-year time-frame.[48] Within each group of five, at least two common law and two civil law jurisdictions are selected, with at least two in each group being from an economically

---

[46] Judicial and governance indicators are selected from survey databases including the World Bank Group's Worldwide Governance Indicators (WGI) (World Bank Group, 2016), available at http://info.worldbank.org/governance/wgi/index.aspx#home; the World Economic Forum's Global Competitiveness Report (GCR) and the World Justice Project's Rule of Law Index (ROI). This data was analysed by country and coded according to judicial mediation approach. The WGI is based on more than 30 individual data sources produced by various survey institutes, think tanks, non-governmental organizations, international organizations and private sector firms. Indicators in GCR are derived from the International Monetary Fund, the World Economic Forum and the Executive Opinion Survey. Indicators in the ROI are derived from a general public polling (GPP) and qualified respondent questionnaires (QRQs) (see World Justice Project, *Rule of Law Index 2016*).

[47] D.T. Campbell and D.W. Fiske, 'Convergent and Discriminant Validation by the Multitrait–Multimethod Matrix' (1959) *Psychology Bulletin* 56, 81; N.K. Denzin, *The Research Act: A Theoretical Introduction to Sociological Methods* (New York: McGraw-Hill, 1978); J.A. Cook and M.M. Fonow, *Beyond Methodology: Feminist Scholarship as Lived Research* (Bloomington, IN: Indiana University Press, 1991).

[48] On small-n sampling methodology, see J. Gerring, *Case Study Research: Principles and Practices* (Cambridge University Press, 2007); R. Hirschl, 'The Question of Case Selection in Comparative Constitutional Law' (2005) *American Journal of Comparative Law* 53. For countries in which divergent court mediation programmes exist at the federal and state level, categorization is made with reference to court practice at the federal level. This research background is also discussed in S. Ali, *Nudging Civil Justice: Examining Voluntary and Mandatory Court Mediation Experience in Diverse Regions*, forthcoming.

advanced (OECD) country. Within the civil law groupings, both primary and secondary civil law jurisdictions are selected.

With respect to measures of efficiency, confidence and perceptions of justice, civil justice indicators and court opinion data are selected from survey databases including the World Bank Group's Worldwide Governance Indicators (WGI)[49], the World Economic Forum's Global Competitiveness Report (GCR)[50] and the World Justice Project's Rule of Law Index (ROI).[51] In particular, efficiency is measured through an aggregation of indicators measuring operational cost in civil justice, accessibility and affordability and lack of delay in resolution.[52] Confidence is examined in relation to the overall ranking of the civil justice system, ease of enforcement and impartial and effective ADR.[53] Finally, perceptions of justice are assessed through measures of rule of law and levels

---

[49] See n. 46 above.

[50] See 'Technical Notes and Sources' in *Global Competitiveness Report 2014–2015* pp. 537–45 for a detailed description of sources for individual indicators. Indicators in the GCR are derived from the International Monetary Fund, the World Economic Forum and the Executive Opinion Survey.

[51] World Justice Project, *Rule of Law Index 2015* p. 15. It is conducted by leading local polling companies using a representative sample of 1,000 respondents in the three largest cities of each country. Indicators in the ROI are derived from a general public polling (GPP) and qualified respondent questionnaires (QRQs).

[52] For purposes of the study, efficiency is measured through an aggregation of the following indicators: *Efficiency of Legal Framework in Settling Disputes*: this indicator appears in the *Global Competitiveness Report*. It measures the efficiency of the legal framework in settling disputes. Data was collected from the Executive Opinion Survey where participants rate the efficiency of the legal framework in their countries on a 1 to 7 scale. Data from the World Economic Forum was also used in generating the results. *Accessibility and Affordability*: this indicator appears in the World Justice Project Rule of Law Index. It indicates people's awareness of available remedies and the accessibility and affordability of courts, legal advice and representation. It also examines the extent to which court procedures and costs affect the accessibility and affordability of civil justice. *No Unreasonable Delay*: this indicator appears in the World Justice Project Rule of Law Index. It indicates the level of delay in adjudicating disputes and general perception of delay.

[53] For purposes of the study, confidence is measured through an aggregation of: *Overall Civil Justice Ranking*: this ranking is included in the World Justice Project's Rule of Law Index and measures the overall ranking of civil justice systems. *Impartial and Effective ADR*: this indicator appears in the World Justice Project Rule of Law Index. It measures the accessibility, impartiality, efficiency and the effectiveness in enforcing decisions reached through mediation. It also examines whether mediation is free of improper influence. *Effective Enforcement*: this indicator appears in the World Justice Project Rule of Law Index. It indicates levels of effectiveness in enforcing judgments and the delays in enforcing decisions.

of reported discrimination.[54] Indicator analysis, while providing useful insights, reflects inherent limitations, including challenges associated with the existence of intervening and exogenous variables, and therefore is supplemented by contextual case investigation of civil justice dynamics and survey data.

To provide comparative analysis, case studies and longitudinal data are supplemented by survey data collected from 83 mediation practitioners working in five regions. The survey was conducted between September 2015 and January 2017. A total of 120 surveys were distributed in person and initiated via a weblink portal and 83 surveys were completed. The aim of the survey was to gain insight into the dynamics, challenges and lessons learned in the context of mandatory and voluntary court mediation programmes and the impact of programme type, if any, on perceptions of confidence, fairness and efficiency. Given the small sample size (n=83) the survey data cannot be considered generalizable.

The aim is that the multiple research methods employed here, while limited, together can contribute insights to an evolving understanding of the efficacy of diverse civil mediation policy approaches from the perspective of those directly engaged in the work of civil justice administration.

LIMITATIONS

The question of voluntary or mandatory programme design is highly context dependent. As noted in an earlier study of mandatory and voluntary

---

[54] Perceptions of Justice are examined through the following indicators: *Level of Discrimination*: this indicator appears in the World Justice Project Rule of Law Index. It indicates the extent to which a person's economic and social status, e.g. sex, race, religion, place of origin or sexual orientation, affect one's access to civil justice. *Rule of Law*: the Worldwide Governance Indicators defines rule of law as the 'perceptions of the extent to which agents have confidence in and abide by the rules of society, and in particular the quality of contract enforcement, property rights, the police, and the courts, as well as the likelihood of crime and violence'. With respect to rule of law, legal scholars have argued that the rule of law can co-exist beyond the formal boundaries of courts to include more informal procedures such as mediation and traditional conciliation methods. See e.g. R.C. Reuben, 'ADR and the Rule of Law: Making the Connection' (2010) 16(4) *Dispute Resolution Magazine* 4; R.C. Reuben, 'How ADR Can Foster the Rule of Law: Beyond the Fundamental Tension', paper presented at Symposium on ADR and the Rule of Law: Making the Connection, Missouri School of Law, 15 October 2010; and M. Krygier, 'Legal Pluralism and the Value of the Rule of Law', paper presented at HKU-UNSW Research Symposium, Sydney, Australia, 4–5 December 2015.

programmes, 'the differences in the structure and court environments ... mean that each program ... is unique: they cannot simply be lumped together and viewed generically'.[55] While the study reports on the programme's correlation with the same measures including efficiency, confidence and perceptions of justice, the results must be seen as reflecting the unique conditions of each particular programme and 'any cross-program comparisons must therefore take into account the impact of ... environmental differences on these results'.[56] In addition, given the small sample size of the country case studies (n=10) and survey research (n=83), lack of policy uniformity in some cases, and the fact that in some regions, elements of voluntary and mandatory systems may co-exist, the results cannot be considered generalizable but rather aim at offering initial insights into the dynamics of diverse civil mediation policy approaches in the selected regions. The aim is that future studies will continue to refine and develop increasingly more accurate approaches to the analysis of such relationships. Insights from practice will no doubt assist in outlining directions for further study with the wider objective of developing a court system responsive to user needs. This being the case, several key insights may be drawn from the study as follows.

SUMMARY OF FINDINGS

The principal findings of the 10 country case studies, survey research and analysis of civil justice indicators indicate that overall, while both voluntary and mandatory mediation programmes demonstrate unique programmatic strengths and are associated with positive gains in the advancement of civil justice quality over a five-year period since implementation, sampled voluntary mediation programme regions are associated with a slightly higher proportion of longitudinal advancement in levels of efficiency, and perceptions of justice with a nearly equal proportion of advancement in levels of confidence, and an identical proportion of voluntary and mandatory regions experiencing positive advancement in the sub-categories of impartial and effective ADR (see Figure I.1). Comparative t-test analysis of a non-generalizable small-n 12 country comparison of 2016 civil justice indicators similarly suggest that sampled countries implementing voluntary court mediation programmes on average are associated with

---

[55] Anderson and Pi, *Evaluation of the Early Mediation Pilot Programs* (n. 38 above).
[56] *Ibid.*

statistically significantly higher jurisdictional scores for efficiency and non-discrimination with higher, though non-significant difference with respect to the quality of civil justice, effective enforcement, accessibility and affordability and impartiality and effectiveness between voluntary and mandatory mediation systems.[57] To some extent, such findings correspond with insights from 'nudge theory' suggesting that positive reinforcement is at least as effective as directions issued through court rules.[58] At the same time, encouragement of mediation coupled with high quality mediators and supportive infrastructure can, in appropriate contexts, assist individuals, the wider community and judiciaries to achieve high quality outcomes.

While such statistical findings may be informative in a limited sense, correlation of changes in civil justice systems and perceptions of efficiency, justice and confidence over time or even in the aggregate are not a sign of a causal relationship. At the same time, it is clear that civil justice quality indicators in many cases mutually influence one another. For example, the quality of a given civil justice system may make it prone to select one form of court mediation over another. A diversity of external, exogenous and intervening variables including court financing, cultural factors and wider socio-political environment also impact programme outcomes and mediation programme design. Moreover, given the non-random, small-n sample, such findings cannot be considered generalizable. The aim is

---

[57] For complete discussion, see S. Ali, *Nudging Civil Justice: Examining Voluntary and Mandatory Court Mediation Experience in Diverse Regions*, forthcoming. Given the non-random, small n sample, as well as the influence of highly variable socio-economic contexts of the sampled countries, such findings cannot be considered generalizable.

Average Civil Justice Indicator Scores by Voluntary and Mandatory Mediation Program Type

	Vol. average	Std. dev.	Mand. average	Std. dev.
Percentile scores (out of 100)				
Accessibility and affordability*	62.40	10.62	48.8	12.25
Impartiality/effectiveness	79	5.7	70.8	13.29
No discrimination*	71.8	15.36	51.2	10.15
Effective enforcement*	74.4	11.7	57.2	17.9
Ranking				
Efficiency* [138 countries]	12.2	8.4	52.4	47.6
Quality of civil justice* [113 countries]	20.2	17.96	48.6	30.73

* Indicates statistically significant difference.

[58] *Ibid.*

that the examination of such relationships, rather than provide for generalizable findings, can provide insights suggesting directions for further analysis. Such relationships suggest, for example, that in environments of higher reported discrimination, safeguards including those aimed at addressing implicit bias[59] and lax civil[60] and procedural[61] justice compliance will be necessary to safeguard the integrity of the mediation process. The findings also echo insights from socio-legal scholars of civil mediation reform that in some contexts, 'facilitation and encouragement together with selective and appropriate pressure are likely to be more effective and possibly more efficient than blanket coercion to mediate'.[62] At the same time, the provision of high quality mediation coupled with contextual understanding will have a positive impact in increasingly complex forms of mediation.[63]

With respect to the analysis of 83 open-ended survey responses, the findings provide insights into the dynamics, challenges and lessons learned from the perspective of those directly engaged in the work of administering, representing and mediating civil claims. While slight variation exists such that practitioners report higher levels of confidence in mandatory mediation programmes (70 per cent) as opposed to voluntary programmes (64 per cent), and higher perceptions of efficiency with respect to voluntary programmes (77 per cent) as opposed to mandatory programmes (68 per cent), both regard voluntary (81 per cent) and mandatory (82 per cent) mediation programmes with relatively equal perceptions of fairness. It must be noted that varying judicial and cultural understandings of the concepts of 'confidence', 'efficiency' and 'fairness', may also influence results.

With respect to advancing programme quality, the survey findings provide insights into the dynamics, challenges and lessons learned from the perspective of those directly engaged in the work of administering,

---

[59] C. Izumi, 'Implicit Bias and the Illusion of Mediator Neutrality' (2010) 34 *Washington University Journal of Law and Policy* 71.

[60] See L. Edelman, 'Legal Ambiguity and Symbolic Structures: Organizational Mediation of Civil Rights Law' (1992) 97(6) *American Journal of Sociology* 1531; Feeley, *The Process is the Punishment* (n. 1 above); Albiston, 'The Rule of Law and the Litigation Process' (n. 1 above); Genn, *Paths to Justice* (n. 22 above); Genn, *Judging Civil Justice* (n. 1 above).

[61] Feeley, 'The Process is the Punishment' (n. 1 above); Albiston, 'The Rule of Law and the Litigation Process' (n. 1 above).

[62] Genn et al., *Twisting Arms* (n. 2 above).

[63] C. Menkel-Meadow, 'When Litigation is Not the Only Way: Consensus Building and Mediation as Public Interest Lawyering' (2002) 10 *Washington University Journal of Law and Policy* 37.

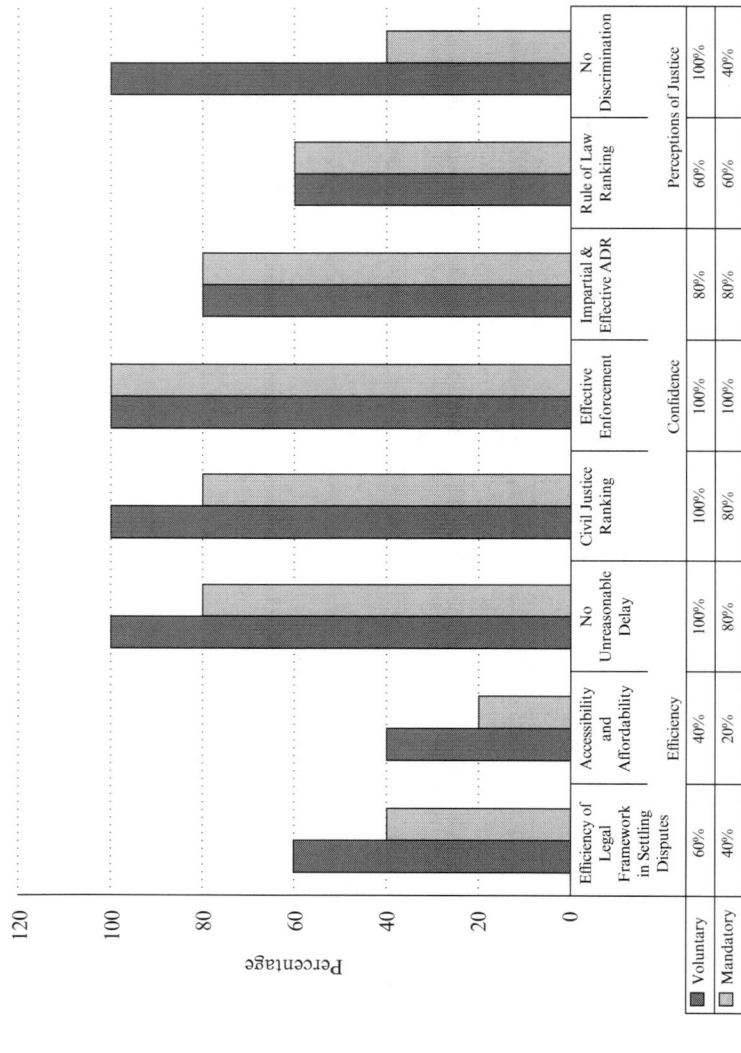

Figure 1.1 Percentage of regions experiencing positive change over a five-year period in efficiency, confidence and perceptions of justice by voluntary/mandatory programme type

representing and mediating civil claims. In particular, the findings indicate that practitioners working in mandatory court mediation programmes identify several key benefits, including normalizing party-driven resolution, enhanced efficiency in some cases through effective case screening and contributing to relational repair, while practitioners working in voluntary programmes identified the key strengths of such programmes as the development of simple procedures and self-determined engagement. With respect to programme challenges, mandatory mediation practitioners noted that key challenges included limited party understanding of the mediation process, lawyer conflicts of interest, lack of good faith, and the need for greater experience in managing power imbalances. Both programme types highlighted resource limitations as a significant challenge, while challenges within voluntary court mediation programmes included difficulties associated with encouraging party participation and limited resources. Practitioner suggestions for improving the overall court mediation process ranged from enhanced training, public education, organizational resources, to ongoing evaluation and greater flexibility in settlement arrangements.

THEORETICAL BACKGROUND

Relevant to the question of mandatory and voluntary mediation programme design is the broader question of the process and place of mediation generally within the context of systems of civil justice. As judicial systems advance, evolving conceptions of justice are reflected in varying emphasis on the role, place and practice of mediation in civil courts. Exploring how such programmes can provide opportunities for party directed reconciliation, on the one hand, while at the same time ensure access to formal legal channels remains an area of continued inquiry. Beginning in the late 1970s, Lon Fuller and Owen Fiss articulated early insights into the role, forms and limits of adjudication. Fiss argued that the purpose of adjudication is to provide a public forum to enact public values and not a forum for settlement proceedings.[64] Continuing this line of exploration, modern court mediation as a policy approach has not been without criticism. Chief among these arguments, similar to those raised by Fiss, is that such informal processes do not result in the development of public goods including rules of precedent, advocacy skills, publication of facts and enhanced authority of courts as

---

[64] See O. Fiss, *The Forms of Justice*, Faculty Scholarship Series Paper 1220 (1979); O. Fiss, 'Against Settlement' (1984) 93(6) *Yale Law Journal* 1073.

achieved through adjudication.[65] Accordingly, this view holds that adjudication is a central part of political life because it contributes to the articulation of public values[66] while at the same time acknowledging that only a small portion of disputes are occasions for structural transformation.[67] Out of court mediation has also been challenged[68] based on the view that such processes enlarge social disputes,[69] deformalize justice, diffuse legitimate indignation of parties,[70] are not suitable for high-conflict cases,[71] and pose an increased risk of outcomes coloured by prejudice.[72] Similarly, scholars have suggested that in some cases, absent proper safeguards, women's interests may be undermined in the mediation process[73] due to its absence of rules, and minimization of fault.[74]

In response to such criticisms, and consistent with Fuller's observations that alternative processes such as mediation are potentially appropriate in cases where adjudication has reached 'its limits',[75] while contributing toward the creation of relevant interpersonal norms rather than the conformity to such norms,[76] particularly when parties concerned are locked in a relationship of 'heavy interdependence', such that each is dependent on some form of collaboration with the other,[77] and the facilitation of a mediator can speed the discussion, reduce the likelihood of miscalculation and help parties reach an optimal agreement by adjusting the parties' divergent valuations,[78] modern day scholars of mediation have put

---

[65] D. Luban, 'Settlements and the Erosion of the Public Realm' (1995) 83 *Georgetown Law Journal* 2619.
[66] *Ibid.*
[67] *Ibid.*
[68] R. Delgado, 'ADR and the Dispossessed: Recent Books about the Deformalization Movement' (1988) 13 *Law and Social Inquiry* 145.
[69] *Ibid.*
[70] *Ibid.*
[71] O. Tjersland, W. Gulbrandsen and H. Haavind, 'Mandatory Mediation Outside the Court: A Process and Effect Study' (2015) 33 *Conflict Resolution Quarterly* 19.
[72] *Ibid.*
[73] T. Grillo, 'The Mediation Alternative: Process Dangers for Women' (1991) 100 *Yale Law Journal* 1545.
[74] *Ibid.*
[75] See L.L. Fuller, 'Forms and Limits of Adjudication' (1978) 92(2) *Harvard Law Review* 353; this occurred, Fuller argued, when adjudication attempted to resolve what he described as 'polycentric' type disputes (such as when there is no clear issue subject to proofs and contentions).
[76] L.L. Fuller, 'Mediation: Its Forms and Functions' (1970) 44 *Southern California Law Review* 308.
[77] *Ibid.* 310–12.
[78] *Ibid.* 318.

forward justifications for the continued support of 'process pluralism'[79] through court-connected mediation on moral, policy and process-based grounds. In particular, scholars note[80] that settlement can be justified on moral grounds consistent with fundamental values including participation, empowerment, dignity, respect, empathy, catharsis, privacy, efficiency, quality, equity, access and justice.[81] Privacy may be useful in some cases, providing greater possibilities for just results, and deeper and richer access to justice[82] and settlements absent consensus should not be enforced.[83] Others have questioned whether justice can be achieved through the court system,[84] and highlight the value of reconciliation of broken relationships through mediation.[85] In addition, participant satisfaction[86] and party self-determination[87] have been cited as important contributions.[88]

In all cases, as recent research has found, 'innovations intended to reduce costs and delay should not do so at the expense of those qualities of the judicial process that are more important to litigants',[89] most importantly the realization of justice.[90] Institutions involved in the provision of court mediation services must be mindful of benchmarking success beyond measures of 'settlement' to actual resolution of issues through an impartial, just and principle-based process.[91] The relative advantages of mediation in a given jurisdiction vary according to the functioning of the underlying national civil litigation system. Success largely depends on the

---

[79] C. Menkel-Meadow, 'Peace and Justice: Notes on the Evolution and Purpose of Legal Process' (2006) 94 *Georgetown Law Journal* 553.

[80] C. Menkel-Meadow, 'Whose Settlement is It Anyway? A Philosophical and Democratic Defense of Settlement (In Some Cases)' (1995) 83 *Georgetown Law Journal* 2663.

[81] *Ibid.*

[82] *Ibid.*

[83] *Ibid.*

[84] A.W. McThenia and T.L. Shaffer, 'For Reconciliation (1985) 94 *Yale Law Journal* 1660.

[85] *Ibid.*

[86] J. Thibaut and L. Walker, 'A Theory of Procedure' (1978) 66(3) *California Law Review* 541; J.D. Rosenberg and H.J. Folberg, 'Alternative Dispute Resolution: An Empirical Analysis' (1994) 46 *Stanford Law Review* 1487.

[87] K.K. Kovach and L.P. Love, '"Evaluative" Mediation is an Oxymoron' (1996) 14 *Alternatives to High Cost Litigation* (March).

[88] *Ibid.*

[89] E.A. Lind et al., *The Perception of Justice: Tort Litigants' Views of Trial, Court-Annexed Arbitration, and Judicial Settlement Conferences* (Santa Monica, CA: RAND, 1989).

[90] Genn, *Judging Civil Justice* (n. 1 above).

[91] See Genn, 'What is Civil Justice For?' (n. 23 above); Mironi, 'Mediation v. Case Settlement' (n. 30 above).

quality and skill of the mediators, institutional support, party education and preparation, and engagement with local needs and conditions.

OVERVIEW OF THE BOOK

This book is divided into four parts, each of which analyses the dynamics of mandatory and voluntary court mediation programmes in selected regions and the relationship between programme type, if any, on perceptions of confidence, fairness and efficiency.

Part I examines the contribution of existing research examining the aims and objectives of court mediation reform. These include existing intrinsic and extrinsic rationales for the introduction of court mediation programmes, including efficiency, reduction of caseloads, private and public sector cost reductions, as well as relational, societal and process-based considerations. Chapter 2 builds on this analysis by examining, at a broad level, rationales for mandatory versus voluntary mediation programme design. Varying national experiences in relation to the global development of civil justice reforms in Asia Europe and North America[92] seem to point mostly to the prominent influence of unique domestic factors in a country's eventual adoption of a particular mediation model, whether voluntary or mandatory.[93]

Following Part I, each of the voluntary and mandatory country case studies in Parts II and III systematically examines the policy background, programme features, practical implementation and achievements of court mediation programmes in 10 regions. In-depth case studies are supplemented by longitudinal research over a five-year time-frame, tracking changes (if any) to levels of efficiency, confidence and perceptions of

---

[92] See N.M. Alexander, 'What's Law Got to Do with It? Mapping Modern Mediation Movements in Civil and Common Law Jurisdictions' (2001) 13(2) *Bond Law Review* Article 5; N.M. Alexander, *International and Comparative Mediation: Legal Perspectives* (The Hague: Kluwer Law International, 2009); B. Clark, *Lawyers and Mediation* (Berlin/Heidelberg: Springer, 2012); Genn, *Judging Civil Justice* (n. 1 above); M. Hanks, 'Perspectives on Mandatory Mediation' (2012) 35(3) *University of New South Wales Law Journal* 929; C. Menkel-Meadow and B. Garth, 'Process, People, Power and Policy: Empirical Studies of Civil Procedure and Courts' in P. Cane and H. Kritzer (eds), *Oxford Handbook of Empirical Legal Research* (Oxford University Press, 2010); J.M. Nolan-Haley, 'Mediation Exceptionality' (2010) 78 *Fordham Law Review* 1247.

[93] See generally, E.E. Gordon, 'Why Attorneys Support Mandatory Mediation' (1998) 82 *Judicature* 224; Hanks, 'Perspectives on Mandatory Mediation' (n. 92 above) pp. 929–32.

justice within each region following the implementation of court mediation reforms. Overall, both voluntary and mandatory programmes demonstrate positive movement in all indicator areas, with slightly higher levels of positive change in regions implementing voluntary court mediation programmes.

Part II explores the dynamics of voluntary mediation programmes in five jurisdictions including the United Kingdom, Hong Kong, France, the Netherlands and Malaysia. While a variety of factors impact civil justice programme outcomes, overall in the jurisdictions examined, over a five-year time period since the introduction of such reforms, 60 per cent of these jurisdictions have experienced positive internal movement in rankings relating to efficiency of settling disputes; 40 per cent have experienced positive development with respect to improved accessibility and affordability; 100 per cent have advanced in relation to reduction of delay; 100 per cent improved in relation to overall ranking in the quality of civil justice; 100 per cent advanced in relation to effective enforcement; 80 per cent experienced positive movement with respect to impartial and effective ADR; and 100 per cent experienced a reduction in the level of reported discrimination.

Part III examines mandatory mediation programmes in the United States, Australia, Italy, China and India. In general, key findings over a five-year time-frame similarly indicate positive developments in many areas. In particular, 40 per cent of these jurisdictions have experienced positive internal movement in rankings relating to efficiency of settling disputes; 20 per cent have experienced positive development with respect to improved accessibility and affordability; 80 per cent have advanced in relation to reduction of delay; 80 per cent improved in relation to the overall quality of civil justice; 100 per cent advanced in relation to effective enforcement; 80 per cent experienced positive movement with respect to impartial and effective ADR; and 40 per cent experienced a reduction in the level of reported discrimination.

Building on country case studies presented in Parts II and III exploring relative longitudinal gains in civil justice quality over a five-year period in mandatory and voluntary mediation countries, Part IV presents survey findings of 83 court mediation practitioners regarding their insights into the dynamics, challenges and lessons learned from the perspective of those directly engaged in the work of administering, representing and mediating civil claims. In particular, building on existing research findings, the survey examines insights into effective design of court mediation policy. It finds that key to improving court mediation programmes is overcoming a number of challenges, including the need for greater party understanding of the mediation process; overcoming conflicts of interest;

enhancing mediator quality; developing greater capacity to manage power imbalances and overcome implicit and explicit biases and resource support through ongoing monitoring and evaluation. Such findings echo existing research suggesting that the formulation of mediation policy must respect party autonomy,[94] comply with principles of justice and cost efficiency,[95] and provide supportive infrastructure including financing, enforcement mechanisms and a reliable legal framework for mediation.[96] Given the important role of economic and cultural factors[97] in influencing the use of mediation in diverse regions,[98] including social, legal and historical factors,[99] mandatory or voluntary policy must be sensitive to such variation.[100]

The question of voluntary or mandatory programme design is highly context dependent and as such the book does not purport to offer a unitary conclusion as to which type of programme is most effective in the abstract, but rather aims to reflect on the achievements of such programmes and what has led to success. In some contexts, systems that reinforce principles of autonomy, volition and choice in dispute resolution may result in more enriched experiences of confidence and perceptions of justice. In other contexts, particularly in cases involving relationships of heavy interdependence, absent abuse or harassment, parties may be best served by a more systematic consideration of mediation opportunities. Given the primary focus of this study on general civil claims, it must be noted that court referral of family cases to well-trained mediation staff resulting in well documented benefits to parties, is not the focus of the study and therefore beyond the scope of interpretation. As noted in an earlier study, 'the differences in the structure and court environments of ... programs mean that each program ... is unique: they cannot simply be lumped together and viewed generically'.[101] While the study reports on the programmes' correlation with the same measures, including efficiency, confidence and perceptions of justice, the results must be seen as reflecting

---

[94] Steffek et al., *Regulating Dispute Resolution* (n. 2 above) p. 15.
[95] *Ibid.* 17.
[96] *Ibid.* 18.
[97] I. Macduff, 'Your Pace or Mine? Culture, Time and Negotiation' (2006) 22 *Negotiation Journal* 31.
[98] Menkel-Meadow, 'Variations in the Uptake of and Resistance to Mediation' (n. 29 above).
[99] *Ibid.* See also I. Macduff, 'The Role of Negotiation: Negotiated Justice?' (1995) 25 *Victoria University Wellington Law Review* 144.
[100] *Ibid.*
[101] Anderson and Pi, *Evaluation of the Early Mediation Pilot Programs* (n. 38 above).

the unique conditions of each particular programme and 'any cross-program comparisons must therefore take into account the impact of programmatic and environmental differences on these results'.[102]

On the whole, whether voluntary or mandatory, it can be suggested that at an early stage, small-scale pilot mediation programmes can provide a useful base of experience to develop culturally specific programmes and train a growing pool of capable mediators, engage in a collective process of learning and advance programme design. At the mid-stage as experience is gained, public information programmes can assist with the diffusion and expansion of such programmes in a given region. At an advanced stage, as high quality mediation services are developed and mediators receive adequate training in avoiding implicit bias, preventing the abuse of power imbalances, and institutional support and safeguards are in place to prevent discrimination and enhance access, then movement towards more targeted encouragement of mediation in appropriate cases can further enhance options for resolution. In all stages, ongoing learning through collaborative reflection on challenges and best practices will assist in the advancement of court mediation programmes and inform policy reform. Such ongoing learning, coupled with the provision of accessible public information on the mediation process, will contribute to enhanced efficacy. As recent research has found, 'innovations intended to reduce costs and delay should not do so at the expense of those qualities of the judicial process that are more important to litigants', including the realization of justice.[103] Institutions involved in the provision of court mediation services must be mindful of benchmarking success beyond measures of 'settlement' to actual resolution of issues through an impartial, just and principle-based process.[104] The relative advantages of mediation in a given jurisdiction will largely vary according to the quality and skill of the mediators,[105] the underlying quality of the civil litigation system, institutional and financial support,[106] party education and preparation, and engagement with local needs and conditions.

---

[102] *Ibid.*

[103] Lind et al., *The Perception of Justice* (n. 89 above).

[104] See Genn, 'What is Civil Justice For?' (n. 23 above); Mironi, 'Mediation v. Case Settlement' (n. 20 above).

[105] Empirical studies indicate that nearly 30 per cent of court mediators believe that further training is needed to effectively conduct mediations. See S. Purcell and J. Martinez, 'Mediators in the Field: Experiences Around the Globe' (2014) *Dispute Resolution Magazine* (Winter).

[106] See J. McHale and T.C.W. Farrow, 'Mandatory Dispute Resolution and the Question of Resources' (2013) *Slaw*; J. McHale, 'Access to Justice: A Government Perspective' (2012) 63 *University of New Brunswick Law Journal* 352.

Given the complexity of surrounding civil justice dynamics, much remains to be examined, including the need for more in-depth qualitative studies examining intra-mediation programme variation and how mediator and participant training including programmes directed toward the cultivation of relevant mediator capabilities including impartiality and equity interact with the development of surrounding mediation culture and the advancement of social justice, including the development of safeguards against bias and the promotion of enhanced cohesion. Future studies by a growing number of researchers will no doubt contribute insights to the advancement of such understanding.

PART I

Aims and objectives of court mediation reform

1. Court mediation reform aims in a global context

1.1 INTRODUCTION

In many countries, governments have taken a special interest in introducing mediation as a means of improving judicial performance.[1] Much of the world has undergone civil justice reform in the past few decades. Empirical studies of such reforms have focused on the increased usage of alternative dispute resolution in specific jurisdictions,[2] how individuals access justice,[3] and the role of local legal culture as an explanatory variable influencing the pace of civil case disposition.[4] While court-based mediation is generally recognised as an efficient and less complex alternative to litigation, questions remain regarding its efficacy, prompting calls for continued examination.[5]

---

[1] See N.M. Alexander, 'What's Law Got to Do with It? Mapping Modern Mediation Movements in Civil and Common Law Jurisdictions' (2001) 13(2) *Bond Law Review* Article 5; N.M. Alexander, *International and Comparative Mediation: Legal Perspectives* (The Hague: Kluwer Law International, 2009); B. Clark, *Lawyers and Mediation* (Berlin/Heidelberg: Springer, 2012); H. Genn, *Judging Civil Justice* (Cambridge University Press, 2010); M. Hanks, 'Perspectives on Mandatory Mediation' (2012) 35(3) *University of New South Wales Law Journal* 929; C. Menkel-Meadow and B. Garth, 'Process, People, Power and Policy: Empirical Studies of Civil Procedure and Courts' in P. Cane and H. Kritzer (eds), *Oxford Handbook of Empirical Legal Research* (Oxford University Press, 2010); J.M. Nolan-Haley, 'Mediation Exceptionality' (2010) 78 *Fordham Law Review* 1247.

[2] See T.J. Stipanowich, 'ADR and the "Vanishing Trial": The Growth and Impact of Alternative Dispute Resolution' (2004) 1(3) *Journal of Empirical Legal Studies* 843; T.C.W. Farrow, *Civil Justice, Privatization and Democracy* (2011), available at http://papers.ssrn.com.eproxy1.lib.hku.hk/sol3/papers.cfm?abstract_id 51795407 (accessed 28 November 2011).

[3] See H. Genn, *Paths to Justice* (Oxford: Hart, 1999); Genn, *Judging Civil Justice* (n. 1 above).

[4] See M. Heise, 'Justice Delayed? An Empirical Analysis of Civil Case Disposition Time' (2000) 50(4) *Case Western Reserve Law Review* 813.

[5] See T. Stipanowich, 'The International Evolution of Mediation: A Call for Dialogue and Deliberation' (2015) 46 *Victoria University of Wellington*

In this chapter, we examine the existing intrinsic and extrinsic rationales for introducing court-based mediation in civil justice systems. These include efficiency, reduction of caseloads, private and public sector cost reductions, as well as extrinsic factors including relational, societal and process-based considerations. In this regard, we examine a range of studies that have explored the contributions of court-based mediation to the performance of judiciaries in diverse regions, and how critiques of court-based mediation have influenced the design and implementation of reforms.

1.2 INTRINSIC POLICY JUSTIFICATIONS CONTRIBUTING TO THE RISE IN COURT-BASED MEDIATION

Several intrinsic factors have influenced the judicial design of court-based mediation programmes. These factors include aspirations toward reduction of caseloads and private and public sector cost reductions. In this regard, we examine a range of studies that have examined the contributions of court-based mediation to the performance of judiciaries in diverse regions. Initial findings suggest that the achievement of the above objectives is highly dependent on key factors including proper implementation and training.

1.2.1 Efficiency Factors Contributing to the Rise in the Use of Court-based Mediation in the Context of Civil Justice Reform

In both developing and emerging economies, the judiciary is often challenged with a large backlog of cases, which if left unaddressed, have the potential of 'eroding individual and property rights, stifling private sector growth, and, in some cases, even violating human rights',[6] since many consider access to an impartial tribunal as a basic human right.[7]

Law Review 1191; Pepperdine University Legal Studies Research Paper No. 2016/1, available at SSRN: http://ssrn.com/abstract52712457; see also S.I. Strong, 'Realizing Rationality: An Empirical Assessment of International Commercial Mediation' (2016) 73(4) *Washington and Lee Law Review* 1973; University of Missouri School of Law Legal Studies Research Paper No. 2016-07, available at SSRN: http://ssrn.com/abstract52737462.

[6] M. Dakolias, *Court Performance Around the World: A Comparative Perspective* (Washington, DC: World Bank, 1999) pp. 1–3.

[7] See European Convention for the Protection of Human Rights and Fundamental Freedoms 1950, Art. 6; American Convention on Human Rights 1969, Art. 8.

Traditional judiciaries continue to be challenged by the complexities of court procedures and lengthy hearings which often result in a costly, inefficient and sometimes unfair system of justice.

In recent years, researchers have explored the link between economic development and judicial efficiency. In Brazil, for instance, court delay has been linked with a decrease in foreign investment by 10 per cent and a 9 per cent drop in employment.[8] Similarly, in 2013, a study found that 32 million cases were pending in Indian courts, and out of these cases, 67,000 were pending in the Supreme Court. India ranks 178 out of 189 countries on 'the ease of enforcing contracts, an indicator measuring the effectiveness of national judicial systems' according to a World Bank Doing Business Report.[9] Italy[10] has faced similar challenges regarding the length of trial and overall judicial inefficiency. In 2013, a study by the Organisation for Economic Co-operation and Development (OECD) revealed that the total length of a trial in Italy approached 2,866 days.[11]

On the basis of such efficiency concerns, while contested,[12] court-annexed mediation has been implemented in many countries. Since the early 1980s, legislation in many countries has been introduced to promote the use of alternative dispute resolution such as mediation.[13]

Today, Singapore is often looked to as an example of a highly efficient

---

[8] See A.C. Pinheiro, 'The Hidden Costs of Judicial Inefficiency: General Concepts and Estimates for Brazil', Address at the seminar 'Reformas Judiciales en América Latina: Avances y Obstáculos para el Nuevo Siglo', Confederación Excelencia en la Justicia, Bogotá, 1998. See also Dakolias, *Court Performance Around the World* (n. 6 above).

[9] 'Enforcing Contracts – Doing Business – World Bank Group' (2015), available at www.doingbusiness.org/data/exploretopics/enforcing-contracts/ (accessed 14 January 2016).

[10] Italy along with Portugal, Greece and Malta have often been labelled as countries with inefficient justice. See 'European Justice Scoreboard' (2014) available at http://ec.europa.eu/justice/effective-justice/files/justice_scoreboard_2014_en.pdf (accessed 14 January 2016).

[11] G. Palumbo et al., *The Economics of Civil Justice: New Cross-Country Data and Empirics* (2013), available at www.oecd.org/officialdocuments/publicdisplaydocumentpdf/?cote5ECO/WKP(2013)52&docLanguage5En (accessed 14 January 2016).

[12] D.R. Hensler, 'Our Courts, Ourselves: How the Alternative Dispute Resolution Movement is Re-Shaping Our Legal System' (2003–2004) 108 *Pennsylvania State Law Review* 165.

[13] The introduction of mediation as an alternative method was introduced in the United States in 1983 when Rule 16 of the Federal Rules of Civil Procedure was amended. Since then up to 1994, the number of US States formally incorporating ADR methods grew to 27. See D. Quek, 'Mandatory Mediation: An Oxymoron? Examining the Feasibility of Implementing a Court-Mandated

and effective judicial system. As noted by the World Bank: 'the Singapore Judiciary is presently lauded for its efficiency, its technological sophistication, its accessibility and the confidence of ... citizens ... in the system'.[14] The World Economic Forum ranked Singapore 1st out of 142 countries in terms of the efficiency of its legal framework for settling disputes.[15] However, two decades ago the picture was not so positive. At that time scholars noted, 'the then-existing system of judicial administration was not designed with the fast-changing landscape in mind and it struggled to cope'.[16] By the end of September 1990, 'there were still 1,963 suits begun by writ and 108 admiralty suits which were awaiting hearing dates in the High Court ... some of these cases had been set down for hearing as early as 1982. It was then estimated that up to five years was needed before these cases could be disposed of'.[17] As a consequence, judicial reforms were implemented to improve the system. Among the solutions considered was the adoption of diversionary measures for civil disputes suited to alternative methods of resolution. Today in Singapore, 'court-based mediation takes place in the courts after parties have commenced legal proceedings. This type of mediation is mainly carried out by the State Courts for civil disputes and minor criminal offences and the Family Justice Courts'.[18]

Australia presents another useful example of a court-annexed mediation programme which has been described as 'one of the oldest and most successful mediation systems in the modern world'.[19] Mediation in Australia is practised through court-referred programmes and serves as the primary method of civil dispute resolution. Following challenges associated with inefficiency and high costs in New South Wales (NSW) and Victoria, a mandatory mediation programme was implemented in both States,[20]

Mediation Programme' (2010) 11(2) *Cardozo Journal of Conflict Resolution* 479, available at http://cardozojcr.com/vol11no2/479-510.pdf.

[14] W. Haider Malik, *Judiciary-Led Reforms in Singapore: Framework, Strategies and Lessons* (World Bank, 2007) p. 1. See also 17th PACI Task Force Meeting Executive Summary (2012)), available at http://reports.weforum.org/global-competitiveness-2011-2012/ (accessed 14 January 2016).

[15] *Ibid.*

[16] H. Foo Chee, *Civil Case Management in Singapore: Of Models, Measures and Justice* (ASEAN Law Association, 2016), available at www.aseanlawassociation.org/11GAdocs/workshop2-sg.pdf (accessed 14 January 2016).

[17] *Ibid.*

[18] 'Chapter 03 Mediation', available at www.singaporelaw.sg/sglaw/laws-of-singapore/overview/chapter-3 (accessed 14 January 2016).

[19] W. Maclons, *Mandatory Court Based Mediation as an Alternative Dispute Resolution Process in the South African Civil Justice System* (University of Western Cape, 2014) p. 85.

[20] *Ibid.* 91.

albeit only for certain types of cases.[21] Following the decision to promote mediation, the Law Society of NSW in 1991 initiated a 'Settlement Week'[22] during which time courts set aside 'their usual court rolls for a week and devoted the entire period to attempting to settle their civil matters through ... mediation while making use of the physical court facilities'.[23] This initiative helped to reduce the backlog of cases, with 235 cases pending litigation ultimately successfully mediated.[24]

Regional implementation of court mediation, even to address efficiency concerns, has largely been dependent upon public acceptance and support. In Hong Kong, many scholars and members of the judiciary[25] have considered court-encouraged mediation as a means of addressing concerns regarding extensive costs and delays. Despite the fact that mediation in general was introduced in Hong Kong in the 1980s, it hasn't yet 'been accepted widely among the public or even amongst professionals, such as business people, lawyers, clients and other stakeholders involved in disputes'.[26] As a consequence, when mandatory mediation was first introduced in Hong Kong, a public consultation report recommended that it not be adopted.[27] Rather, a system of voluntary mediation is currently in place and has resulted in growing familiarity with the process among the Hong Kong public.

The desire to make justice more efficient has encouraged countries to

---

[21] *Ibid.* 96.

[22] Inspired and based on a concept in the United States of an annual American (Washington, DC) Alternative Dispute Resolution Scheme.

[23] Maclons, *Mandatory Court Based Mediation* (n. 19 above) p. 96.

[24] *Ibid.*

[25] 'As a result, as pointed out by the Secretary for Justice of Hong Kong, Wong Yan Lung, legislators complained to the Judiciary Administrator about delays in court hearings. Wong Yan Lung therefore emphasised the application of mediation.' See S. Hilmer, 'Mandatory Mediation in Hong Kong: A Workable Solution Based on Australian Experiences' (2013) 1 *China-EU Law Journal* 62, available at http://dx.doi.org/10.1007/s12689-012-0016-y.

[26] *Ibid.*

[27] The Hong Kong Civil Procedure Rules were amended and came into force on 2 April 2009. However, the Mediation Practice Direction 31 (PD 31) came into force on 4 January 2010. This set of rules encouraged mediation and resulted in increasing mediation in Hong Kong, but still does not make mediation mandatory. It is important to highlight that when the topic of mandatory mediation was analysed and discussed, Proposal 64 of the Chief Justice's Working Group made the following recommendation: 'A rule should be adopted conferring a discretionary power on the judge to require parties to resort to a stated mode or modes of ADR, staying the proceedings in the meantime'. That recommendation was not successful and as a consequence was discarded. See Hilmer, 'Mandatory Mediation in Hong Kong' (n. 25 above).

create innovative solutions, including the growing integration of mediation in court processes. Consequently, many judicial systems have implemented mediation legislation 'in courts, government departments, businesses and [within] ... industries'.[28] However, mandatory mediation is still viewed with caution in many jurisdictions where discretionary or categorical referral of cases for mediation may imply differing levels of compulsion.[29]

1.2.2 Practical Justifications for the Use of Mediation

As discussed in the previous section, the rise in the use of mediation is based on several justifications. Key among them include: (1) enhanced accessibility through the provision of cost-effective alternatives, and (2) reduction of delays. However, 'some writers opine that these benefits are over-stated and have not been subject to rigorous empirical scrutiny'.[30] In the following

---

[28] 'Chapter 03 Mediation' (n. 18 above).
[29] There are different levels of imposition when mandating mediation: '1. Categorical or Discretionary Referral with No Sanctions A prime illustration of this kind of referral is the UK Automatic Referral to Mediation pilot scheme in Central London County Court, which took place from 2004 to 2005. Although cases were automatically being referred by the courts for mediation, the disputing parties had the option to express their objections. 2. Requirement to Attend Mediation Orientation Session or Case Conference This approach is employed in Queensland, Australia, where the court may require parties to appear before the court prior to assessing whether mediation is appropriate (Section 97 of the District Court Act 1967). Similarly, in the US state of Virginia, parties are required to attend mediation orientation sessions before they are allowed to decide whether they wish to attempt mediation. 3. Soft Sanctions The United Kingdom offers the best example of this approach. The courts encourage parties to attempt ADR, and take into account the party's conduct including any unreasonable refusal of ADR or uncooperativeness during the ADR process in determining the proper order of costs. 4. Opt-Out Scheme The mandatory mediation programme in Ontario, Canada refers all civil cases, except family cases, to mediation, but provides the parties the option of seeking exemption by way of motion. 5. No Exemptions Some Australian states, such as the courts in South Australia, Victoria and New South Wales, are empowered by legislation to refer parties to mediation with or without their consent. This continuum demonstrates how the extent of coercion into mediation can vary drastically across different programs. It is this paper's assertion that mandatory mediation only becomes an oxymoron at level five of the mandatoriness continuum, i.e., when cases are referred for mediation without any provision for exemption and are accompanied by sanctions for non-compliance. It is submitted that mediation is not necessarily a contradiction in terms in all other types of mandatory mediation programs'. See Quek, 'Mandatory Mediation: An Oxymoron?' (n. 13 above) p. 490.
[30] K. Dayton, 'The Myth of Alternative Dispute Resolution in the Federal Courts' (1991) 76 *Iowa Law Review* 889; R. Posner, 'The Summary Jury Trial

sections, we will analyse existing studies exploring the question of whether court-based mediation does in fact alleviate cost and inefficiency concerns.

(i) Reduction of cost: access to justice

When approaching the topic of costs, two perspectives must be acknowledged. The first perspective is that of the government which aims to reduce judicial costs, and secondly, that of the consumer which aims at reducing legal costs. On the one hand, when governments consider addressing costs savings they often focus on reducing judicial expenses. As such, from both a public and private perspective, governments commonly see alternative dispute resolution methods, and in particular, mediation, as a viable option for the purposes of promoting efficiency and accessibility.

With respect to the objective of costs savings, the example of the United Kingdom is noteworthy, given that the implementation of court-based mediation was highly motivated by the objective of reducing judicial costs. Since 1980, various government administrators have expressed deep concerns over the increasing costs of legal aid. Civil legal aid in the United Kingdom was established in 1949 with the primary purpose of moderating the monetary imbalances associated with accessing justice 'so that the weak and powerless are able to protect their rights in the same way as the strong and powerful'.[31] However, as the years passed the legal aid costs that had to be borne by the government were quickly increasing.

In 1990, through the Courts and Legal Services Act, a conditional fee arrangement was introduced with the purpose of reducing expenses in the civil justice system. In 1994 and 1996, the civil justice review aimed at reforming the judiciary, especially in matters related to civil legal aid.[32] This policy was justified by the observation that 'the problems of cost, delay and complexity in civil justice were linked together' given that 'the principal cause of the shortcomings of the civil justice system [were]

---

and Other Methods of Alternative Dispute Resolution: Some Cautionary Observations' (1986) 53 *University of Chichester Law Review* 366. Also see Quek, 'Mandatory Mediation: An Oxymoron?' (n. 13 above) pp. 481–2, available at http://cardozojcr.com/vol11no2/479-510.pdf.; T.J. Stipanowich, 'ADR and the "Vanishing Trial": The Growth and Impact of Alternative Dispute Resolution' (2004) 1(3) *Journal of Empirical Legal Studies* 843.

[31] H. Genn, 'What is Civil Justice For? Reform, ADR, and Access to Justice' (2013) 24(1) *Yale Journal of Law and the Humanities* 3, available at http://digital commons.law.yale.edu/cgi/viewcontent.cgi?article51392&context5yjlh.

[32] *Ibid.* 4, 5.

to be found in the behaviour of lawyers and their adversarial tactics'.[33] Therefore, 'the proposed solution involved judicial case management and measures to promote early settlement'.[34] As a consequence, a fundamental reform postulated that Alternative Dispute Resolution (ADR) methods should be tried before and after the initiation of court proceedings. The 1995 Interim Report encouraged parties to consider ADR. This position developed when mere encouragement transformed into a requirement on the part of courts to consider 'whether the parties have unreasonably refused to try ADR or behaved unreasonably in the course of ADR'.[35] Such policy direction in the United Kingdom was based primarily on public and private sector resource savings justifications.[36]

Similarly, in some States in the United States, financial difficulties brought about following the Financial Crisis of 2008 led to reductions in budgets allocated to the judiciary. Mediation was also seen as a method of costs savings and case management.[37]

However, despite the many efforts made by governments to reduce judicial costs, the question remains whether mediation is truly effective at reducing the overall costs associated with civil trials. From a global perspective, many studies have shown that the use of an alternative method such as mediation can reduce the costs of litigation. However, such findings are not conclusive and contradictory findings exist, with some

---

[33] Ibid. 5. See also Lord Woolf, *Interim Report on the Civil Justice System* (Department for Constitutional Affairs, 2016), available at http://webarchive.nati onalarchives.gov.uk/+/http:/www.dca.gov.uk/civil/final/contents.htm (accessed 17 January 2016).

[34] *Ibid.* 5.

[35] *Ibid.* 5, 6.

[36] 'In the wake of the civil justice reforms and following the lead provided by Lord Woolf, several enthusiastic judges in courts around England collaborated with mediation providers to set up mediation schemes offering no- or low-cost, time-limited mediation, held on court premises for litigants who had already commenced court proceedings. The first and largest of these court-based mediation schemes was established in a county court trial centre in central London (Central London County Court) in 1996. Although the courts administered the schemes, the mediations themselves were undertaken by trained mediators, initially on a pro bono basis by trained mediators keen to try out their newly acquired skills.' See Genn, 'What is Civil Justice For?' (n. 31 above) pp. 7–8. See also Woolf, *Interim Report on the Civil Justice System* (n. 33 above).

[37] From one perspective, 'The enthusiasm for mediation is inspired in large part by economics as the state's court system struggles with cutbacks and layoffs.' See further 'ACDR: State Hopes Mediation Can Ease Court Overload' (2011), available at www.alabamaadr.org/web/media/articles/111018_MA_Mediation_Week. php (accessed 17 January 2016).

studies including important work by Hensler showing that differences in costs savings may be negligible if they exist at all,[38] while others show some reduction in costs. At present, no unified view exists on the question of private sector costs savings.

With respect to the question of costs savings on the part of litigants, a study conducted after the introduction of mediation in the former Bosnia and Herzegovina showed that after a year of implementing the court mediation programme, associated costs were almost 50 per cent less than those associated with court litigation.[39] In North America, according to Barkai and Kassebaum, mediation 'saved about US$500 per party in the United States[40] and about US$6,000 per case in Canada'.[41] Research by Rosenberg and Folberg[42] reported that while about 40 per cent of parties believed that they saved money with mediation, 38 per cent of attorneys and parties believed that mediation added about US$4,000 on average to the cost of litigation. Stipanowich provides an extensive analysis of cost impacts of various forms of mediation in the US, finding that costs savings exist in some contexts and Wissler reports mixed results on general civil mediation costs savings.[43]

When examining mandatory court-based mediation, the story varies. A recent study found that 'many cases that attempt to use ADR, mainly

---

[38] D. Hensler, 'In Search of Good Mediation' in J. Sanders and V.L. Hamilton (eds), *Handbook of Justice Research in Law* (New York:, Springer, 2001); See: T.J. Stipanowich, 'ADR and the "Vanishing Trial": The Growth and Impact of Alternative Dispute Resolution' (2004) 1(3) *Journal of Empirical Legal Studies* 843 for a comprehensive meta-survey of mediation impact and experience in the US.

[39] In a year the direct costs of mediation had averaged US$225, about 50 per cent of the costs of litigation (c. US$470). See I. Love, 'Settling Out of Court: How Effective is Alternative Dispute Resolution?', available at www.openknowledge.worldbank.org/bitstream/handle/10986/11055/678050VP00PUBL0Setting0out0of 0court.pdf?sequence51 (accessed 17 January 2016).

[40] Ibid. See also, J. Barkai and G. Kassebaum, *Hawaii's Court-Annexed Arbitration Programme, Final Evaluation Report* (Peace Institute of Hawaii, 1992), available at www.peaceinstitute.hawaii.edu/resources/_epubs/Hawaiis-Court-Annexed-Arbitration-Programme-Final-Evaluation-Report.pdf (accessed 17 January 2016).

[41] R. Hann and C. Baar, *Evaluation of the Ontario Mandatory Mediation Programme (Rule 24.1): Executive Summary and Recommendations* (Ministry of the Attorney General, 2001), www.attorneygeneral.jus.gov.on.ca/english/courts/manmed/exec_summary_recommend.pdf (accessed 17 January 2016).

[42] J. Rosenberg and J. Forlberg, 'Alternative Dispute Resolution: An Empirical Analysis' (1994) *Stanford Law Review* 46.

[43] See: T.J. Stipanowich, 'ADR and the "Vanishing Trial": The Growth and Impact of Alternative Dispute Resolution' (2004) 1(3) *Journal of Empirical Legal Studies* 843; see also Love, 'Settling Out of Court' (n. 39 above); Hensler, 'In Search of Good Mediation' (n. 38 above).

under mandatory mediation, end up in court anyway', so the real cost saving is not clearly established.[44] Supporting this finding, it was reported that in the case of London's court-referred mediation programme, of the 1,232 cases referred to the programme, only 14 per cent were mediated; the rest went back to court. Overall, 'the settlement rate was 55 per cent in no-objection cases, and 48 per cent in cases where parties were persuaded to mediate. The study estimated that for cases that failed to reach settlement through ADR, total legal costs were US$2,000–4,000 higher than they would have been if no attempt had been made to use ADR'.[45] In North Carolina, a report measuring the outcomes of a court-sponsored mediation programme for civil claims showed that its programme did not meet its cost-saving goals as expected; and satisfaction with mediation was no greater than with conventional settlement, though those who settled, whether via mediation or otherwise, were more satisfied than those who went to trial.[46]

There is no doubt that in theory, mediation can reduce the costs of litigation. At the same time, 'mediation can save government money by resolving conflicts outside of or earlier in the court system. This allows court resources to be re-allocated to other matters. More indirectly, mediation saves civil litigants and families legal and court fees'.[47] Yet, given the mixed findings in terms of overall costs savings, particularly for mandated cases that require further litigation, questions still remain as to whether court-referred mediation does in fact reduce litigation costs. Studies thus far show mixed results and tend to show that voluntary mediation can be more successful than mandatory mediation in reducing costs, as will be discussed later in this chapter.

(ii) Reduction of caseload and delay

Court-centred case congestion contributes to the delay of justice. One of the principal justifications for reforming systems of civil justice is the

---

[44] See Love, 'Settling Out of Court' (n. 39 above). See also H. Genn et al., *Twisting Arms: Court Referred and Court Linked Mediation Under Judicial Pressure, Ministry of Justice Research Series 1/07 (2007)*, available at www.ucl.ac.uk/laws/judicial-institute/files/Twisting_arms_mediation_report_Genn_et_al_1.pdf (accessed 17 January 2016).

[45] See Love, 'Settling Out of Court' (n. 39 above). See also, Genn et al., *Twisting Arms* (n. 44 above).

[46] See Love, 'Settling Out of Court' (n. 39 above).

[47] S. Vander Veen, *A Case for Mediation: The Cost-Effectiveness of Civil, Family, and Workplace Mediation (Mediate BC, Dispute Resolution and Design, 2014)*, available at www.mediatebc.com/PDFs/1-52-Reports-and-Publications/The-Case-for-Mediation.aspx (accessed 17 January 2016).

reduction of caseloads. The story of India is particularly noteworthy in this regard. As discussed above, the Indian justice system has been struggling for the last 20 years with extensive delays due to a high volume of pending cases. A study conducted by the Ministry of Law in India found that 'at the current rate it will take 324 years to dispose of the backlogs of cases in Indian courts'.[48] Various justifications have been put forward to explain the source of the issue, including the population explosion, a lack of human resources in the judicial system, lack of adequate training and changes to the pattern of litigation.[49]

In 1987, at the trial court level, India promulgated the Legal Services Authorities Act by which court mediation was introduced. The Act came into effect in 1995 and was implemented through specialized courts called 'Lok Adalats'.[50] Mediation operated mostly on a consensual basis and according to Dr Adarsh Sein Anand, former Chief Justice of India, 'Lok Adalats' had settled over 97 lakh[51] legal matters throughout the country by 1999.[52] Due to this success, in 1999 the Indian Parliament passed the Civil Procedure Code requiring that trial courts refer disputes for settlement through mediation and other alternative means of solving conflict.[53] The passage of this Code alongside support from the Chief Justice of India B.N. Kirpal[54] has led to the proliferation of court-based mediation throughout India.[55] While the Indian legislature has made significant provision in law to facilitate the introduction of court-annexed mediation, nevertheless

---

[48] Indian Institute of Arbitration and Mediation (IIAM), Community Mediation Service, available at www.arbitrationindia.org/pdf/brochure_cms.pdf (accessed 17 January 2016).

[49] T. Hussain Jillani, 'Delayed Justice and the Role of ADR', p. 5, available at www.supremecourt.gov.pk/ijc/articles/7/1.pdf. (accessed 17 January 2016).

[50] People's Court: 'Lok' refers to 'people' and 'Adalat' means court. India has a long tradition and history of such methods being practised in the society at grass roots level.

[51] Lakh = 100,000.

[52] Hussain Jillani, 'Delayed Justice and the Role of ADR' (n. 49 above) p. 5.

[53] Supreme Court of India, Manual for Training Mediation, available at http://supremecourtofindia.nic.in/MEDIATION%2520TRAINING%2520MANUAL%2520OF%2520INDIA.pdf (accessed 17 January 2016).

[54] Bhupinder Nath Kirpal (B.N. Kirpal) was appointed Chief Justice of the Gujarat High Court in 1995 and later on he was appointed as Judge of the Supreme Court of India, and became Chief Justice of India in May 2002, serving from 6 May 2002 until his retirement on 7 November 2002.

[55] Justice M. Shah, 'Study of the American Legal System for Procedural Reforms in Civil Courts in India, available at http://gujarathighcourt.nic.in/Articles/msshah.pdf (accessed 17 January 2016).

implementation of such legislation in practice has been limited.[56] Scholars believe that systematic training of mediators is required in order to achieve the legislative objectives. At present, existing challenges include the minimal availability of effective court-annexed mediation services, the lack of training to handle complex commercial and civil cases, and the lack of systems to monitor and evaluate the disposition of cases sent for mediation.[57]

The Netherlands likewise presents a useful illustration of a judiciary seeking to address case backlog. During the 1990s, in an effort to address court delay, the judiciary promoted court-annexed mediation. A study analysing the effects of the programme found that 'about 5% of the cases suitable for mediation were resolved and concluded by court-referred mediation'.[58] The study showed that while a small number of cases proceeded to mediation, each successful mediation decreased the work of the courts given 'the time saved that the court would otherwise have to spend drawing up a judgement, hearing testimony and reviewing written exchanges of statements'.[59]

Many studies have shown that mediation can save time for courts and parties, ranging from several months to several years. In Colombia, a study examining its court mediation programme[60] showed that in 2001 tenant eviction cases took 15 months on average in court but only four months in mandatory conciliation.[61] A study by Hann and Baar[62] analysing the

---

[56] Justice S.B. Sinha has stated the following: 'The currently available infrastructure of courts in India is not adequate to settle the growing litigation within reasonable time. Despite the continual efforts, a common man may sometimes find himself entrapped in litigation for as long as a life time, and sometimes litigation carries on even to the next generation. In the process, he may dry up his resources, apart from suffering harassment. Thus, there is a chain reaction of litigation process and civil cases may even give rise to criminal cases. Speedy disposal of cases and delivery of quality justice is an enduring agenda for all who are concerned with administration of justice. In this context, there is an imminent need to supplement the current infrastructure of courts by means of Alternative Dispute Resolution (ADR) mechanisms'.

[57] N. Bhatt, *Legislative Initiative for Court Annexed Mediation in India* (2003), available at www.mediate.com/articles/bhattn.cfm (accessed 17 January 2016).

[58] B. Niemeijer and M. Pel, 'Court-Based Mediation in the Netherlands: Research, Evaluation and Future Expectations' (2005) 110(2) *Pennsylvania State Law Review* 365.

[59] *Ibid.*

[60] A. Alvares de la Campa, The Private Sector Approach to ADR: Commercial ADR Mechanism in Colombia (Investment Climate Department, World Bank Group, 2009) pp. 5–10, available at www.wbginvestmentclimate.org/uploads/Private%20Sector%20Approach%20to%20Commercial%20ADR_%20the%20case%20of%20Colombia%20.pdf (accessed 19 January 2016).

[61] *Ibid.*

[62] Hann and Baar, *Evaluation of the Ontario Mandatory Mediation Programme* (n. 41 above).

effects of court-referred mediation in Canada found that mandatory mediation programmes resulted in more cases being settled sooner. At 'six months, for example, 25 per cent of cases under the mandatory mediation rule were disposed, compared with only 15 per cent of control cases'.[63] Similarly, Wissler[64] reported that 'in five studies of appellate cases, the time to disposition was one to three months shorter for cases assigned to mediation than for other cases'.[65]

In addressing court delay, pilot programming followed by the introduction of legislation, as exemplified in Canada, has been considered an effective model for designing court-based programmes. In 1999, in Toronto and Ottawa, a two-year pilot rule was introduced in the Ontario Court Rules for the Ontario Superior Court of Justice[66] making mediation mandatory. According to a study examining 3,000 mediated cases alongside a control group, the study concluded that mandatory mediation under the rule resulted in significant reductions in the time taken to dispose of cases, decreased costs to litigants, a higher proportion of cases (roughly 40 per cent overall) being completely settled, and a larger further group partially settled, early in the litigation process.[67] The same study also reported other benefits to litigants in cases that did not end up settling. The same study also found that 'lawyers estimated their clients' cost savings to be $10,000 or more per case in 38% of mediated cases, [and] less than $5,000 in 34% of them, and from $5,000–$10,000 in 28% of mediated cases'.[68] As a result of the pilot programme, further legislation was developed, further integrating mediation into the civil justice system.

Additional findings from studies in Australia likewise suggest that court-based mediation programmes have contributed to reduction in delays. A study of the mandatory court-referred mediation programme in New South Wales found that at least half of the cases referred to mediation successfully resulted in settlement, thereby significantly reducing the

---

[63] See Love, 'Settling Out of Court' (n. 39 above).

[64] R. Wisler, 'The Effectiveness of Court-Connected Dispute Resolutions in Civil Cases' (2004) 22(1–2) *Conflict Resolution Quarterly*, available at http://onlinelibrary.wiley.com/doi/10.1002/crq.92/abstract.

[65] See Love, 'Settling Out of Court' (n. 39 above).

[66] Rule 24.1: this Rule provides for mandatory mediation in specified actions, in order to reduce costs and delay in litigation and facilitate the early and fair resolution of disputes. See 'Law Document, English View', available at www.ontario.ca/laws/regulation/900194 (accessed 19 January 2016).

[67] Hann and Baar, *Evaluation of the Ontario Mandatory Mediation Programme* (n. 41 above).

[68] Ibid.

courts' remaining caseload.[69] In Australia, a 2008 study reported that mandatory civil mediation for cases under AUS$10,000 showed a settlement rate of 86 per cent, and of those cases, 32 per cent settled before mediation and 12 per cent settled shortly thereafter. The overall effect was a significant reduction in judicial and administrative workload.[70]

While, as noted above, several studies have established the existence of a considerable time reduction through court-referred mediation programmes, other reports have established no significant reduction in duration of cases. In 1996, a study conducted by RAND reported that there was 'no strong statistical evidence that the mediation or neutral evaluation programs significantly affected time to disposition, litigation costs or attorney view of fairness and satisfaction'.[71] However, later studies have suggested a wider base of programmes be examined to provide additional insights.[72] Bergman and Bickerman[73] noted that in the case of court-mediation programmes, well-run ADR programmes can reduce cost and time. Therefore, success and achievement of goals in mediation largely depend on implementation and training efforts.

Given mixed results regarding the overall impact of mediation in reducing cost and duration of civil cases, additional questions must be addressed. These include how efficacy in mediation can be measured and what might define success and efficiency. A study conducted by the National Alternative Dispute Resolution Advisory Council (NADRAC) and Australian Institute of Judicial Administration (AIJA) in Australia provides a number of helpful insights in this regard noting, 'success can have a range of possible meanings and be measured in many different ways ... Even with ... relatively narrow measures [i.e. settlement rates, party satisfaction], there are substantial limits on the ability of empirical research to establish clear referral criteria'.[74] Many view success as most

---

[69] Maclons, *Mandatory Court Based Mediation* (n. 19 above) pp. 101–2.
[70] Vander Veen, *A Case for Mediation* (n. 47 above).
[71] T. Stipanowich, 'ADR and the "Vanishing Trial": The Growth and Impact of 'Alternative Dispute Resolution' (2004) 1(3) *Journal of Empirical Legal Studies* 852, available at http://papers.ssrn.com/sol3/papers.cfm?abstract_id51380922; D. Hensler, 'In Search of Good Mediation' (n. 38 above).
[72] The critiques of this report were based on the premise that the sampled programmes were not representative of other programmes in operation. See further, Stipanowich, 'ADR and the "Vanishing Trial"' (n. 71 above) p. 852.
[73] See E. Bergman and J. Bickerman, *Court-Annexed Mediation: A Critical Perspective on Selected State and Federal Programs* (Pike and Fischer, Inc., 1998).
[74] K. Mack, *Court Referral to ADR: Criteria and Research* (Attorney General Department of Australia 2003) pp. 2–3, available at www.ag.gov.au/LegalSystem/AlternateDisputeResolution/Documents/NADRAC%20Publications/Court%20

importantly measured through 'high client satisfaction' often resulting in high quality mediation programmes entailing 'highly trained, debriefed, problem-solving mediation services staffed by well-paid mediators, who use an intake process'.[75] Exploring these insights further, in the following sections, we will examine other justifications for the use of court mediation beyond mere costs savings and judicial efficiency.

1.2.3 Extrinsic Factors Contributing to the Use of Court-based Mediation

The following section examines key extrinsic considerations in implementing court-based mediation programmes beyond issues of time and costs savings. These factors include relational, societal and process-based contributions.

(i) Relational justifications

For disputing parties who hope to maintain a lasting relationship, mediation often presents an attractive approach. Many have discussed its efficacy in contributing toward both the health and positive transformation of relationships between individuals and in the context of deliberative participation in policy-making.[76] In some cases, mediation presents 'a special advantage when parties have on-going relations that must continue after the dispute is managed, since the agreement is by consent and none of the parties should have reason to feel that they are the losers'.[77] Relation-based justifications are particularly relevant to family disputes, conflicts between neighbours, workplace disputes and conflicts between business partners. Even in commercial cases where one party does not want to lose a client, 'mediation creates a foundation for resuming the relation after the particular issue has been resolved'.[78]

During the process of mediation, parties have an opportunity to gain an understanding of one another's motives, needs and interests. This understanding can often improve a given relationship going forward.[79]

Referral%20to%20ADR%20-%20Criteria%20and%20Research.PDF (accessed 19 January 2016).

[75] *Ibid.* 2–3.

[76] L.P. Love and E. Galton, *Stories Mediators Tell* (ABA Book Publishing, 2012); H.N. Aragaki, 'Deliberative Democracy as Dispute Resolution: Conflict, Interests, and Reasons' (2009) 24(3) *Ohio State Journal on Dispute Resolution* 406.

[77] Y. Shamir, Alternative Dispute Resolution Approaches and Their Application (UNESCO, 2003) p. 24.

[78] *Ibid.*

[79] R.E. Emery, D. Sbarra and T. Grover, 'Divorce Mediation: Research and Reflections' (2005) 43(1) *Family Court Review* 22; L.P. Love and E. Galton, *Stories Mediators Tell* (ABA Book Publishing, 2012).

Mediation has also been linked with improving workplace relations in appropriate circumstances. For example, in the case of the Canadian Public Service Staff Relations Board, which established an employee mediation service, '500 files had been mediated and reported at an 85% success rate'.[80] Later a 'modified version of the pilot programme . . . [became] a permanent part of the Board's dispute resolution processes'.[81] In addition, according to a 2011 Chartered Institute of Personnel and Development report examining conflict management in the workplace, mediation programmes were found to be beneficial in helping improve relationships between workers and colleagues.[82] Similarly, mediation in the workplace has been found to provide a 'cost-effective method for addressing the full economic consequences of conflict including lost productivity, absenteeism, employee turnover, and failed projects that translate into approximately $359 billion dollars a year in wages alone in the United States of America'.[83] Mediation for workplace conflicts involving civil rights issues is not without critiques, as will be discussed in the final section.

(ii) **Process considerations**

When it comes to process considerations, very often mediation is selected because of the opportunity it provides parties to design and contribute to the resolution of conflict. Parties tend to report higher levels of satisfaction when a settlement is reached through a participatory process. Underlying interests are often addressed, in contrast with judicial-based outcomes which must be based on strict legal principles that may ignore underlying needs.[84]

In general, mediation can be a flexible method of resolution 'adapted to meet the needs of . . . parties . . . in formulating a solution'.[85] The parties decide how to manage the process and agree on the relevant procedural

---

[80] *Ibid.* 22–3. See also, G. Baron, 'Public Service Staff Relations Board Mediation Programme' in Canadian Bar Association's Possibilities Newsletter (2003).

[81] Emery et al., 'Divorce Mediation: Research and Reflections' (n. 79 above) pp. 22–3. See also, Baron, 'Public Service Staff Relations Board Mediation Programme' (n. 80 above).

[82] Vander Veen, *A Case for Mediation* (n. 47 above) p. 25.

[83] *Ibid.*

[84] R. Zeinemann, 'The Characterisation of Public Sector Mediator' (2003) 24(2) *Environs Law* 51, available at http://environs.law.ucdavis.edu/volumes/24/2/articles/zeinemann.pdf.; T.J. Stipanowich, 'ADR and the "Vanishing Trial": The Growth and Impact of Alternative Dispute Resolution' (2004) 1(3) *Journal of Empirical Legal Studies* 843; L.P. Love and E. Galton, *Stories Mediators Tell* (ABA Book Publishing, 2012).

[85] Shamir, *Alternative Dispute Resolution Approaches and Their Application* (n. 77 above) pp. 24–5.

rules. This 'may involve the choice over location of the mediation, the time frame, the people who are to be involved, the selection of acceptable objective criteria, and many other choices related to the process'.[86] This approach appeals to parties who wish to be partners in the process of resolving their conflict and participate in crafting the resolution of their dispute. Moreover, given its flexibility, parties are enabled to present their arguments in an informal manner, not bound by legal procedures.[87] A study conducted in the Netherlands found that when parties are in control of the resolution process, they tend to reach agreement more easily. This applies to situations in which parties wish to craft their own outcomes, rather than 'follow the advice of the judge'.[88]

However, some researchers have noted that the increasingly formalized rules associated with court-based mediation have inhibited the key advantages of mediation, namely, its informality and flexibility. Some scholars have noted that formalized court mediation rules inhibit the potential of mediation since: 'case management, while important to the justice system, was never really the goal of mediation as a distinct social process. In effect, connection with the courts had distorted an incidental benefit of mediation into its primary goal'.[89]

(iii) Societal considerations

Mediation skills, applied both in a court-based context and at the community and international level, have the potential of transforming local and international conflicts into peaceful agreements, thereby in some contexts contributing towards greater social harmony. The skills learned in court-referred settings are similar to those relevant to both local and international conflict and thus have potential positive spill-over effects in the wider society.

Similar to the potentially positive interpersonal relational benefits of mediation discussed above, when examining the impact of mediation in addressing community-based conflicts, particular benefit has been associated with the opportunity for affected community members to participate in crafting relevant solutions. Through this process, community members take part in ensuring that key issues are appropriately addressed and resolved. The application of community-based mediation expanded in

---

[86] *Ibid.* 24–5.
[87] *Ibid.*
[88] Niemeijer and Pel, 'Court-Based Mediation in the Netherlands' (n. 58 above) p. 360.
[89] D. Della Noce, 'Mediation Theory and Policy: The Legacy of the Pound Conference' (2002) 17(3) *Ohio State Journal on Dispute Resolution* 554, 555.

Canada in the 1980s,[90] to the extent that by 1996, 26 jurisdictions across Canada had established such programmes. Similarly, the Indian Institute of Arbitration and Mediation (IIAM) established a mediation service to address the needs of community members by providing a localized resolution platform staffed by locally trained individuals.[91] In Hong Kong, the Mediation Council in Hong Kong introduced a mediation Pilot Scheme 2002 focused on addressing disputes involving neighbourhood, employment, contract, urban redevelopment and environmental issues.[92] Such programmes have proliferated in recent years, given the growing numbers of individuals who have been exposed to mediation skills training.

At the international level, mediation has, in some cases, contributed to the resolution of both armed and unarmed conflicts, thus advancing global peace and, as a consequence, alleviating suffering caused by war. Several notable examples demonstrate the efficacy of mediation in contributing to international peace. Most well documented was the Camp David mediation[93] in which former President Jimmy Carter facilitated a mediation process that resulted in achieving a resolution to the conflict engulfing Israel and Egypt.[94]

Mediation has been put forward as a key mechanism used by the United Nations in addressing global conflicts. In 2010, the governments of Finland and Turkey convened a Group of Friends of Mediation at the United Nations with the intention of raising 'awareness within the international community of the importance of mediation as a means of conflict prevention and resolution' and to 'help build mediation capacity and expertise both within the United Nations and also in regional organizations, which are often most well-placed to assume such a mediating role in their own area of responsibility'.[95] Today the initiative is supported by 37 United

---

[90] Church Council on Justice and Corrections, Restorative Justice (1996), available at www.johnhoward.ab.ca/pub/C26.htm#comm (accessed 19 January 2016).

[91] IIAM Community Mediation Service (n. 48 above).

[92] Government of the Hong Kong Special Administrative Region, Department of Justice, Report of the Working Group on Mediation (2010), available at www.gov.hk/en/residents/government/publication/consultation/docs/2010/Mediation.pdf (accessed 19 January 2016).

[93] J. Carter, *Keeping Faith: Memoirs of a President* (Fayetteville, AR: University of Arkansas Press, 1995) pp. 284–337.

[94] The Nobel Peace Prize for 2002 to Jimmy Carter, Press Release, available at www.nobelprize.org/nobel_prizes/peace/laureates/2002/press.html (accessed 19 January 2016).

[95] 'Engineering Peace: Achieving the Promise of Mediation in the World's Most Difficult Conflicts', available at www.mediate.com/articles/engpeace.cfm#_edn7 (accessed 19 January 2016).

Nations Member States in addition to seven regional multilateral organizations (the African Union, ASEAN, Arab League, Organisation of Islamic Cooperation, European Union, Organisation for Security and Co-operation in Europe and Organization of American States). Since that time, the initiative has brought international focus to the benefits of mediation in contributing to world peace. In 2011 'the United Nations General Assembly adopted a Resolution on Strengthening the Role of Mediation in the Peaceful Settlement of Disputes, Conflict Prevention and Resolution'.[96] A follow-up report on the implementation of this resolution was issued in 2012.[97]

Such initiatives have further promoted the use of mediation on a global level. As a result, the demand for mediation has increased, such that 'multilateral organizations now need to translate that interest . . . into the development of their capabilities as convenors, promoting understanding of what mediation is and how and why it works, and most critically developing a strong cadre of highly-trained, multi-talented, inter-cultural peace mediators whose skills are certified and who can be identified and valued easily'.[98] The group Mediators Without Borders has been working to develop mediation capacity around the globe. In one case, through the assistance of trained mediators in Nigeria, individuals have contributed to 'address[ing] 'ethnic and class conflict that have turned to violent confrontation and terrorist acts'.[99]

Therefore, beyond court backlog reduction and costs and time savings, it is clear that mediation has potentially wider extrinsic spill-over benefits at both the local and international levels in preserving relationships, engaging individuals in a process of crafting and implementing solutions, and developing long-term skills to address ongoing and future conflicts.

1.3 SCHOLARLY CRITIQUES OF THE RISE OF COURT-BASED MEDIATION

As discussed above, mediation has the potential to provide both direct and indirect benefits to judiciaries, individuals and society. It is not

---

[96] *Ibid.*
[97] Report on Strengthening the Role of Mediation in the Peaceful Settlement of Disputes, Conflict Prevention and Resolution, United Nations Res.A/66/811, available at http://peacemaker.un.org/node/79 (accessed 19 January 2016).
[98] 'Engineering Peace' (n. 95 above).
[99] International Sustainable Peace Alternative Dispute Resolution Center Initiative (Mediators Without Borders, 2012) p. 1, available at www.mediatorswithoutborders.org/wp-content/uploads/2012/02/Research-FindingsFinal.pdf (accessed 19 January 2016).

surprising, therefore, that mediation has become a major policy approach in civil justice reform programmes. However, court-based mediation is not without criticisms, principally those challenging its consistency within institutionalized settings, its potential to obstruct access to justice, and its inappropriateness to particular classes of cases.

1.3.1 Inconsistency with Institutionalized Court-based Settings

Given that one of the core principles of mediation is voluntariness, some scholars have observed that 'attempts to impose a formal and involuntary process on a party may potentially undermine the raison d'être of mediation'.[100] Further questions have been raised as to whether the 'full benefits of mediation [can] be reaped when parties are left to participate in it un-voluntarily'.[101] The argument against compulsory mediation is based on the view that 'mandatory mediation impinges upon parties' self-determination and voluntariness, thus undermining the very essence of mediation'.[102] Furthermore, it has been suggested that 'coercion into the mediation process invariably leads to coercion to settle within the mediation process, which leads to unfair outcomes' and therefore may be contrary to social justice.[103] Several studies have found that disputants are most satisfied with the mediation process when it is conducted in a non-coercive manner and attentive to parties' interests.[104]

There is no doubt that court-referred mediation increases usage rates. For example, in England prior to the introduction of its Civil Procedure Rules, mediation was selected in 160 out of 4,500 cases or 3.5 per cent of the time. Following the introduction of the Rules, 'which empowered the courts to encourage the use of ADR (with cost sanctions), the number of commercial disputes referred for mediation increased by 141 per cent'.[105] Some observers have established that despite the fact that court-based mediation might require parties to mediate, this does not contradict a parties' freedom to reach a voluntary agreement.

Some scholars have also challenged what is viewed as an over-extension

---

[100] Quek, 'Mandatory Mediation: An Oxymoron?' (n. 13 above) p. 481.
[101] *Ibid.* 484.
[102] *Ibid.*
[103] C. Guthrie and J. Levin, 'A Party Satisfaction Perspective on a Comprehensive Mediation Statute' (1998) 13(3) Ohio State Journal On Dispute Resolution 885, 892, 893, available at https://discoverarchive.vanderbilt.edu/bitstream/handle/1803/7392/Party_Satisfaction_Perspective.pdf?sequence51.
[104] *Ibid.*
[105] Quek, 'Mandatory Mediation: An Oxymoron?' (n. 13 above) p. 483.

of court-based mediation programmes based on the view that once the objective of public education has been fulfilled, court mediation should resume its voluntary character. In the United States, it has been suggested that 'mandatory mediation might have been appropriate in the United States as a remedial measure to get the ADR ball rolling in the 1970s and 1980s'.[106] However, with the passage of time, 'court compulsion is no longer needed since the ADR movement in the United States is more mature'.[107] Such scholars submit that 'court-mandated mediation should only be a short-term measure utilized in jurisdictions where mediation is relatively less well developed, and that this expedient should be lifted as soon as the society's awareness of mediation has reached a satisfactory level'.[108] This point is based on the claim that mandatory mediation could be contrary to the civil and human rights of the parties, which will be explored in greater detail in the following section.

1.3.2 Access to Justice

In addition to concerns regarding compulsion and over-extension, some scholars have suggested that mandatory mediation might hamper access to impartial justice. This view was adopted by the English courts in the case of *Halsey* v. *Milton Keynes General NHS Trust*, where it was held that 'to oblige truly unwilling parties to refer their disputes to mediation would be to impose an unacceptable obstruction on their right of access to courts'.[109]

While the right of access to court is guaranteed under Article 6 of the European Convention on Human Rights,[110] the passage of the EU Mediation Directive (2008/52) which provides for the implementation of either voluntary or mandatory court mediation for cross-border disputes and subsequent Court of Justice of the European Union (CJEU) litigation, have established that mandatory court mediation is not inconsistent with the right of access to a fair and impartial tribunal.[111] In defending the view that mandated mediation does not contradict basic human rights, some scholars have pointed out that:

---

[106] *Ibid.* 484.
[107] *Ibid.*
[108] *Ibid.*
[109] *Ibid.* 485.
[110] European Convention on Human Rights, Art. 6: Right to a Fair Trial, available at www.echr.coe.int/Documents/Convention_ENG.pdf (accessed 19 January 2016).
[111] See generally www.libralex.com/publications/the-impact-o-the-EU-mediation-directive.

an individual may be told to attempt the process of mediation, but that is not tantamount to forcing him to settle in the mediation. As the coercion in mandatory mediation only relates to requiring that parties try to reach an agreement to resolve their dispute. Therefore, the individual is not being denied access to court because mandatory mediation is not being ordered in lieu of going to court. Instead, the parties' access to court is only delayed; the parties have the liberty to pursue litigation once again if mediation fails.[112]

Taking up this view, the government of Hong Kong in its report on civil reform stated 'mandatory mediation does not deny access to justice, but merely defers it'.[113] Therefore:

only an order that the parties resort to ADR in lieu of having their case decided in court may run afoul of Article 35 of the Hong Kong Basic Law, which guarantees the right of access to the courts. A more significant issue with regard to this objection is ensuring that such access to justice is not unduly deferred (through, for instance, draconian sanctions), as well as ensuring that the quality of mandatory mediation is monitored closely so as not to unfairly compel parties to incur additional costs for mediation.[114]

While it can be argued that there exists a thin line separating compelled mediation from denial of court access, nevertheless, in general, given parties' subsequent right to proceed to trial, such concerns appear to have been largely addressed by recent court cases.[115]

1.3.3 Mediation and Public Policy

Modern court mediation as a policy approach has not been without critique. Chief among these arguments is that settlement does not result in the development of public goods, including rules of precedent, advocacy skills, publication of facts and enhanced authority of courts as achieved through adjudication.[116] This argument explicates Fiss's view that adjudication is a central part of political life because it contributes to the articulation of public values.[117] Unlike Fiss, some scholars such as Luban acknowledge that only a small portion of disputes are occa-

---

[112] Quek, 'Mandatory Mediation: An Oxymoron?' (n. 13 above) p. 486.
[113] *Ibid*. 498–9.
[114] *Ibid*.
[115] *Ibid*. 492–3.
[116] D. Luban, 'Settlements and the Erosion of the Public Realm' (1995) 83 *Georgetown Law Journal* 2619.
[117] *Ibid*.

sions for structural transformation,[118] and therefore endorses settlement approaches that are open to sunshine laws.[119] Others have noted that rather than a blanket challenge on policy grounds, court-mandated mediation may be unsuitable for particular case types. For example, when legal precedent is sought or a matter of public interest is raised, judicial determination may be more appropriate than mandatory court-referred mediation.[120] For example, some research has pointed to the dangers of civil rights employment mediation subsuming 'legal rights under managerial interests'.[121]

Out of court settlement[122] has also been challenged based on the view that such processes enlarge social disputes,[123] deformalize justice, diffuse legitimate indignation of parties[124] and pose an increased risk of outcomes coloured by prejudice.[125] Similarly, Grillo argues that women's interests may be undermined in the mediation process[126] due to its lack of context, absence of rules and minimization of fault.[127] Cases in which there is a clear power imbalance between parties, and where the mediator is not sufficiently trained to address such imbalance, some have suggested, may likewise raise procedural justice concerns.[128] In New South Wales and Victoria, for example, 'despite the long standing practice of mandatory court-referred mediation', due to the fact that courts have discretion in 'ordering appropriate cases to mediation, the court may select broad categories of cases as being amenable to mediation, thereby failing to take into consideration the unique circumstances of each case and vast divergences between disputes and parties, as well as the different needs of litigants'.[129]

---

[118] *Ibid.*
[119] *Ibid.*
[120] See O. Fiss, *The Forms of Justice*, Faculty Scholarship Series Paper 1220 (1979); O. Fiss, 'Against Settlement' (1984) 93(6) *Yale Law Journal* 1073.
[121] See L. Edelman, H. Erlanger and J. Lande, 'Internal Dispute Resolution: The Transformation of Civil Rights in the Workplace' (1993) 27(3) *Law and Society Review* 497.
[122] R. Delgado, 'ADR and the Dispossessed: Recent Books about the Deformalization Movement' (1988) 13 *Law and Social Inquiry* 145.
[123] *Ibid.*
[124] *Ibid.*
[125] *Ibid.*
[126] T. Grillo, 'The Mediation Alternative: Process Dangers for Women' (1991) 100 *Yale Law Journal* 1545.
[127] *Ibid.*
[128] Maclons, *Mandatory Court Based Mediation* (n. 19 above) p. 115.
[129] *Ibid.* 113.

1.3.4 Response to Critiques of Court Mediation

In response to such criticism, scholars have provided moral, policy and process-based responses to such critiques. On moral grounds, it has been suggested that[130] settlement can be justified on the basis of values including consistency, participation, empowerment, dignity, respect, empathy, catharsis, privacy, efficiency, quality, equity, access and justice.[131] From this perspective, settlement does not preclude the use or creation of precedent while secrecy may be useful in some cases, providing greater possibilities for just results, and deeper and richer access to justice.[132] In addition, settlements absent consensus should not be enforced.[133] Scholars have also examined whether justice can be achieved through the court system,[134] have highlighted the value of reconciliation of broken relationships through ADR,[135] and have[136] noted that facilitative mediation contributes to principles of self-determination.[137]

1.4 CONCLUSION

This chapter has examined the key intrinsic and extrinsic justifications for the development of court-based mediation, namely, efficiency, reduction of caseloads, private and public sector cost reductions, as well as extrinsic factors including relational, societal and process-based considerations. A range of studies have shed light on the contributions of court-based mediation to the performance of judiciaries in diverse regions. Critiques of court-based mediation likewise raise important considerations for court mediation design and implementation which will be examined through the various case studies and survey research presented in greater detail in the chapters that follow.

---

[130] C. Menkel-Meadow, 'Whose Settlement is It Anyway? A Philosophical and Democratic Defense of Settlement (In Some Cases)' (1995) 83 *Georgetown Law Journal* 2663; L.P. Love and E. Galton, *Stories Mediators Tell* (ABA Book Publishing, 2012).
[131] *Ibid.*
[132] *Ibid.*
[133] *Ibid.*
[134] A.W. McThenia and T.L. Shaffer, 'For Reconciliation' (1985) 94 *Yale Law Journal* 1660.
[135] *Ibid.*
[136] K.K. Kovach and L.P. Love, '"Evaluative" Mediation is an Oxymoron' (1996) 14 *Alternatives to High Cost Litigation* (March).
[137] *Ibid.*

2. Voluntary and mandatory mediation programme design

2.1 INTRODUCTION

The contemporary emergence from about the 1970s onwards of institutional and academic interest in mediation mechanisms generally and its proliferation and development has been extensively examined.[1] In particular, the interplay between mediation mechanisms and litigation have captured considerable attention.[2] Perhaps more than all other forms of alternative dispute resolution (ADR), mediation has been particularly highlighted.[3] Scholars and practitioners alike have suggested that mediated disputes tend to save disputants' time, accord them more control over their disputes and provide greater prospects of relationship preservation, especially in domestic and commercial disputes where the need for continued relationship tends to be critical.[4] Moreover, the apparent general adaptability of mediation across diverse dispute settings has contributed to its emergence as a preferred tool for conflict management.[5]

---

[1] See generally, V.A. Sanchez, 'Towards a History of ADR: The Dispute Processing Continuum in Anglo-Saxon England and Today' (1996) 11 *Ohio State Journal on Dispute Resolution* 1. Also discussed in S. Ali, 'To Nudge or to Compel: Examining Voluntary and Mandatory Court Mediation Civil Justice Outcomes' (forthcoming).

[2] See e.g., C. Menkel-Meadow, 'Introduction: What Will We Do When Adjudication Ends? A Brief Intellectual History of ADR' (1996) 44 *UCLA Law Review* 1613; T.J. Stipanowich, 'ADR and the "Vanishing Trial": The Growth and Impact of Alternative Dispute Resolution' (2004) 1(3) *Journal of Empirical Legal Studies* 843; J. Nolan-Haley, 'Mediation: The New Arbitration' (2012) 17 *Harvard Negotiation Law Review* 61. See most recently also T. Stipanowich, 'The International Evolution of Mediation: A Call for Dialogue and Deliberation' (2015) 46 *Victoria University of Wellington Law Review* 1191; Pepperdine University Legal Studies Research Paper No. 2016/1, available at SSRN: http://ssrn.com/abstract52712457.

[3] R.A. Baruch Bush and J.P. Folger, *The Promise of Mediation: The Transformative Approach to Conflict* (John Wiley & Sons, 2004).

[4] Ibid.

[5] Ibid.

Against this background, several jurisdictions, nationally and regionally, have taken steps to integrate mediation into their dispute settlement regimes.[6] However, an implicitly larger and somewhat rather overlooked component of this regulatory transformation has been the concurrent emergence of diverse mediation practices across jurisdictions in terms of adoption of either voluntary or mandatory (court-directed) mediation approaches for disputants. This chapter, therefore, surveys the global evolution of mediation across diverse jurisdictions in terms of both its voluntary and mandatory use prior to court proceedings. In this regard, the chapter not only delves into conceptual debates surrounding voluntary and mandatory mediation requirements but also examines rationales across jurisdictions justifying adoption of either model. Further, it interrogates the application of these mediation practices in regional and international dispute settlement frameworks and speculates as to possible future development.

2.2 CONCEPTUAL DIVIDE BETWEEN VOLUNTARY AND MANDATORY MEDIATION

At a conceptual level, the mediation process ordinarily presupposes participation of two (or more) consenting parties.[7] The idea and question of consent is, thus, central to mediation and arguably defines its unique place in dispute resolution. Whether through robust encouragement or voluntary selection, once parties engage in facilitative mediation, the final outcome rests in the hands of participants.[8] However, at a broader level, the momentum for adoption of various mediation practices across jurisdictions is also fuelled by a desire to address certain perennial public policy concerns. For instance, as identified above, many jurisdictions justify their movement towards mediation based on the need to identify innovative ways to reduce

---

[6] See generally, F. Steffek et al. (eds), *Regulating Dispute Resolution: ADR and Access to Justice at the Crossroads* (Oxford: Hart, 2013); J. Macfarlane and M. Keet, 'Civil Justice Reform and Mandatory Civil Mediation in Saskatchewan: Lessons from a Maturing Programme' (2005) 42(3) *Alberta Law Review* 677; R. Wissler, 'The Effects of Mandatory Mediation: Empirical Research on the Experience of Small Claims and Common Pleas Courts' (1997) 33 *Willamette Law Review* 565; A. Bruni, 'Mediation in Italy' (2010) 2 *Revista Forumul Judecatorilor* 96; D. Cornes, 'Mediation Privilege and the EU Mediation Directive: An Opportunity?' (2008) 74(4) *Arbitration: The Journal of the Chartered Institute of Arbitrators* 395.

[7] See J. Nolan-Haley, 'Consent in Mediation' (2007) 14 *Dispute Resolution Magazine* 4.

[8] *Ibid.*

case backlog and reduce costs.[9] Mediation is also seen in many countries as a potential platform for attainment of efficacy in the dispute management process.[10] Finally, some countries adopt mediation practices as a tool for facilitating the realization of their regional integration objectives.[11]

The inevitable result of this confluence of traditional normative and evolving public policy expectations of the mediation process has been the increasing proliferation of mediation practices integrating varying requirements on the question of consent. This essentially defines the current voluntary and mandatory mediation distinction. While in voluntary mediation, the assumption ordinarily is that the parties opt for mediation out of free will and without direct court supervision of the process,[12] mandatory mediation models tend to integrate direct court supervision into the mediation process.[13] This typically includes integration of supervisory measures, such as those requiring disputants to compulsorily attend or participate in mediation conferences prior to adjudication.[14] In addition, some jurisdictions impose 'good faith' requirements, thereby essentially setting a qualitative bar to courts in assessing disputants' participation in pre-adjudication mediation under mandatory mediation models.[15] This is often achieved through formal reporting obligations on the part of the

---

[9] N.M. Alexander, *Global Trends in Mediation* (The Hague: Kluwer Law International, 2006) vol. I, pp. 259–77; R.F. Peckham, 'Judicial Response to the Cost of Litigation: Case Management, Two-Stage Discovery Planning and Alternative Dispute Resolution' (1984) 37 *Rutgers Law Review* 253.

[10] See e.g., M.F. Radford, 'Advantages and Disadvantages of Mediation in Probate, Trust, and Guardianship Matters' (2000) 1 *Pepperdine Dispute Resolution Law Journal* 241; J. Folberg, *Resolving Disputes: Theory, Practice, and Law* (Aspen Law and Business, 2005) pp. 226–40.

[11] Nolan-Haley, 'Mediation: The New Arbitration' (n. 2 above) pp. 70–72; F. De Paolis, 'Italy Responds to the EU Mediation Directive and Confronts Court Backlog: The New Civil Court Mandatory Mediation Law' (2011) 4(1) *New York Dispute Resolution Lawyer* 44; J.M. Nolan-Haley, 'Is Europe Headed Down the Primrose Path with Mandatory Mediation?' (2011) 37 *North Carolina Journal of International Law and Commercial Regulation* 981.

[12] See generally, G. Smith, 'Unwilling Actors: Why Voluntary Mediation Works, Why Mandatory Mediation Might Not' (1998) 36(847) *Osgoode Hall Law Journal* 47; J. Nolan-Haley, 'Mediation: The Best and Worst of Times' (2014) 16 *Cardozo Journal of Conflict Resolution* 731, 737–8.

[13] M. Hanks, 'Perspectives on Mandatory Mediation' (2012) 35 *University of New South Wales Law Journal* 929; D.T. Saposnek, 'Clarifying Perspectives on Mandatory Mediation' (1992) 30/4 *Family Court Review* 490.

[14] D.S. Winston, 'Participation Standards in Mandatory Mediation Statutes: You Can Lead a Horse to Water' (1996) 11 *Ohio State Journal on Dispute Resolution* 187.

[15] *Ibid.* 189–91, 197–8; A. Zylstra, 'Road from Voluntary Mediation to

mediator.[16] Finally, in several instances courts have been empowered to impose penalties or costs on perceived non-cooperative disputants.[17]

Despite the above over-arching public policy basis for mediation, the eventual selection of either voluntary or mandatory mediation models varies from one jurisdiction to another. At present, there is no particularly discernible global pattern or trend towards adoption of either mandatory or voluntary mediation models. Instead, diverse national experiences seem to point mostly to the prominent influence of unique domestic factors in a country's eventual adoption of a particular mediation model, whether voluntary or mandatory.[18] For example, while Italy's mandatory mediation trial programmes have overcome significant opposition leading to eventual adoption of a mandatory mediation scheme in the country,[19] similar trial programmes in England have generally been phased out.[20] The Australian experience also points to successful mandatory mediation programmes across its diverse States.[21]

Several reasons have been advanced to explain this disparate pattern. First, in both mandatory and voluntary models, it has been argued that the level of cooperation by the Bar is critical as lawyers are often the most engaged in the dispute settlement process.[22] Therefore, this means that the extent to which lawyers are receptive to and engaged with trial mediation programmes is likely to impact its eventual uptake in a given jurisdiction.[23] Lawyers are for the most part the initial point of contact for most participants in the dispute resolution architecture and will most

---

Mandatory Good Faith Requirements: A Road Best Left Untraveled' (2001) 17 *Journal of American Academy Matrimonial Law* 69.

[16] Winston, 'Participation Standards in Mandatory Mediation Statutes' (n. 14 above) pp. 188–90, 197–8.

[17] Ibid. 195–6.

[18] See generally, E.E. Gordon, 'Why Attorneys Support Mandatory Mediation' (1998) 82 *Judicature* 224; Hanks, 'Perspectives on Mandatory Mediation' (n. 13 above) pp. 929–32.

[19] See A. De Luca, 'Mediation in Italy: Feature and Trends' in *New Developments in Civil and Commercial Mediation* (New York: Springer, 2015) pp. 345–65; Hanks, 'Perspectives on Mandatory Mediation' (n. 13 above) pp. 936–9.

[20] Hanks, 'Perspectives on Mandatory Mediation' (n. 13 above) pp. 939–44.

[21] T. Sourdin, 'Mediation in Australia: Impacts on Litigation' in *Global Trends in Mediation* (The Hague: Kluwer, 2006) pp. 37–63; A. Shea Hart, 'Child-Inclusive Mediation in Cases of Domestic Violence in Australia' (2009) *Conflict Resolution Quarterly* 3; Yang Zhang, 'Mediation Model Differences Between China and Australia and Their Possible Collaboration' (2015) 1(1) *Journal of Interdisciplinary Conflict Science* 46.

[22] Hanks, 'Perspectives on Mandatory Mediation' (n. 13 above) pp. 939–42.

[23] Ibid.

likely have earned a party's trust before mediation is even contemplated. Such unparalleled access accords them a significant role in shaping the success of any proposed mediation model. Besides the extent of reception by counsel, the use of either model in a jurisdiction also seems to be significantly influenced by the level of awareness about its existence amongst disputants and, in the case of low-income disputants, the cost implication on them. In this regard, empirical evidence suggests that this group of disputants will likely participate in mediation where there is a public subsidy on costs, mostly in the form of free or discounted mediator fees.[24] For example, arguments have been made that the Italian mandatory mediation regime achieved some demonstrated success following collaboration with the Bar.[25] Amendments, including those that were clearly designed to appease the legal fraternity by automatically qualifying all lawyers as mediators and requiring that they inform clients of mediation, undoubtedly put lawyers at the centre of the success of the mediation programme in Italy. In addition, considering that lawyers were also frustrated by prolonged litigation, a mandatory mediation option premised on their substantial involvement benefited from strong buy-in.[26]

The second factor that influences mediation programme design in a given jurisdiction relates to embedded cultural and societal approaches to dispute settlement.[27] It has been argued in this regard that English society, for example, has a deep and historically entrenched litigation culture informed by adversarial common law dispute settlement approaches.[28] The contention is that this has predisposed most disputants to prefer adjudication over other 'untested' alternatives such as mediation, something that seems to find credence in the generally low mediation uptake in trial programmes in London.[29] This contention, however, may find challenge in the fact that other Anglo-Saxon jurisdictions such as Australia and the United States with common legal roots have engaged in more direct integration of mediation. Similarly, the Danish informal mediation practice has historically been linked with monarchical influence, particularly King Christian V, who made it optional in civil cases 'with the aim of encouraging citizens

---

[24] Macfarlane and Keet, 'Civil Justice Reform and Mandatory Civil Mediation in Saskatchewan' (n. 6 above) p. 682.
[25] De Paolis, 'Italy Responds to the EU Mediation Directive' (n. 11 above).
[26] *Ibid.*
[27] See generally, R.R. Callister and J.A. Wall, 'Japanese Community and Organizational Mediation' (1997) 41(2) *Journal of Conflict Resolution* 311.
[28] Hanks, 'Perspectives on Mandatory Mediation' (n. 13 above) pp. 939–42.
[29] Nolan-Haley, 'Mediation: The New Arbitration' (n. 2 above) pp. 90–91.

to be less quarrelsome'.[30] A plausible explanation here lies in the fact that these jurisdictions have eventually developed their own legal environments that have significantly departed from the English tradition. Similarly, '*chotei*' (defined as both mediation and conciliation) has had a long tradition in Japan. Since the Tokugawa period, social and philosophical traditions, alongside a small population of lawyers, help account for the emphasis on relatively relational approaches to resolving conflict.[31] In 1922, the Japanese courts first introduced a 'landing and building leases mediation system' in order to address the increasing number of land and building disputes.[32] Other mediation systems were later introduced in 1940 to address various kinds of disputes, including tenant farmer, commercial, labour, family and environmental issues.[33] Such approaches are closely related to the pervasive practice of judicial settlement (*wakai*) which scholars have described as a dominant approach to in-court judicial resolution in Japan.[34] Given the pervasive deference accorded members of the judiciary, and the frequency with which civil mediation ('*minji chotei*') and judicial settlement (*wakai*) are encouraged, many regard such processes as integral to the civil litigation system in Japan.[35]

In sub-Saharan African countries such as Ghana, mediation practices date back to the existence of powerful governance structures[36] built around tribal kingdoms in which tribal chiefs, elders and the Queen Mother customarily mediated disputes.[37] Such practices have remained in effect in many remote regions.[38] Although the post-colonial order has generally weakened the place of tribal kingdoms in Ghana's political landscape,

---

[30] *Ibid.*

[31] K. Funken, *Court-Connected Mediation in Japan and Germany*, University of Queensland School of Law Working Paper No. 867 (March 2001), available at SSRN: http://ssrn.com/abstract5293495 or http://dx.doi.org/10.2139/ssrn.293495.

[32] A. Yasui, 'Alternative Dispute Resolution System in Japan', available at www.iadcmeetings.mobi/assets/1/7/18.2_-_Yasui-_ADR_System_in_Japan.pdf (accessed 12 January 2016).

[33] *Ibid.*

[34] E.A. Feldman, 'No Alternative: Resolving Disputes Japanese Style' in M. Bälz and J. Zekoll (eds), *Dispute Resolution: Alternatives to Formalization, Formalization of Alternatives* (Leiden: Brill, 2014); University of Pennsylvania Law School, Public Law Research Paper No. 15-9 (2014); T. Sourdin and A. Zariski, *The Multi-Tasking Judge: Introduction to Comparative Judicial Dispute Resolution* (Pyrmont: Thomson Reuters, 2013).

[35] Conversation on civil litigation and mediation with Professor Aya Yamada.

[36] J.M. Nolan-Haley and J.K. Annor-Ohene, 'Procedural Justice Beyond Borders: Mediation in Ghana' (2014) *Harvard Negotiation Law Review Online* 1.

[37] *Ibid.*

[38] *Ibid.*

its cultural influence remains strong.[39] Ghana developed comprehensive mediation legislation in 2010 when the Alternative Dispute Resolution (ADR) Act was promulgated.[40] As in many other countries, the eventual enactment of this legislation was based on a view of mediation's potential for addressing increasing case backlog and providing for greater party autonomy.[41] The ADR Act 2010 provides only for voluntary mediation and extends this to 'customary arbitration' which is essentially traditional mediation facilitated within tribal kingdoms, as described above.[42] Either of the parties may 'at any time before final judgement is given' by court also place a referral request for mediation.[43] The mediation standards envisaged under the Act are fairly similar to other global practices in that a party has the right to be represented by counsel and confidentiality of the proceedings is required.[44] The mediation trend across Africa is largely similar to that of Ghana. For example, in Kenya the use of mediation and 'traditional dispute resolution' mechanisms has been enshrined in the national constitution. The nature of the provision is aspirational in character lending itself to voluntary mediation practice,[45] while private mediation service providers have multiplied.[46]

The prevalence of particular dispute-types is also an important factor in the designation of mediation models across jurisdictions, which often expand alongside the growing skill base of mediators. Observers have noted that at the outset, communal disputes, especially those focusing on narrow but inclusive issue-areas like environmental protection and landfill reclamation, ought to be preferentially subjected to mediation.[47] In addition, relational and commercial disputes register higher settlement rates than other types of civil disputes.[48] For example, the mediation

---

[39] See generally, C.C. Reindorf, *History of the Gold Coast and Asante* (Ghana University Press, 2007); K. Akon Ninsin, *Ghana at 50: Tribe or Nation?* (Accra: Woeli Publishing Services, 2007).
[40] Alternative Dispute Resolution Act 2010 (Act 798, Ghana).
[41] *Ibid.*
[42] *Ibid.*
[43] *Ibid.* s. 64(2).
[44] *Ibid.* s. 71(1).
[45] B. Brainch, 'The Climate of Arbitration and ADR in Kenya', available at www.disputeresolutionkenya.org/pdf/The%20Climate%20of%20Arbitration%20 and%20ADR%20in%20Kenya.pdf (accessed 19 November 2015).
[46] Strathmore Dispute Resolution Centre (ed.), *Mediation Guidelines*.
[47] J.B. Stulberg, 'Theory and Practice of Mediation: A Reply to Professor Susskind' (1981) 6 *Vermont Law Review* 85, 110–13; S. Kaufman, 'Mediation in Environmental Disputes' (2002) *Conflict Resolution* 2.
[48] V.E. Solomon, 'Divorce Mediation: A New Solution to Old Problems' (2015) 16(4) *Akron Law Review* 5; N. Ver Steegh, 'Yes, No, and Maybe: Informed

practice in Canada's Saskatchewan province[49] was designed to be more responsive to disputes with a 'heavy emotional overtone' for which litigation was deemed increasingly inappropriate.[50] The acknowledgement of the prospects of mediation for such cases traces back to the success of a mandatory mediation programme for Saskatchewan farm foreclosures in the 1980s which enabled creative solutions for farmers facing foreclosure.[51] The scheme was seen to benefit both lenders and farmers while at the same time creating a pool of capable mediators in the province.[52] Since that time, and building off both the programme's success and the enhanced skills of domestic mediators, the scheme was extended to criminal cases.[53] The success of the farm programme created a wealth of knowledge and popular support that was crucial in overcoming misconceptions and resistance.[54] Its central aims of social welfare and judicial responsiveness inspired interest-based and transformative mediation practices.[55] Saskatchewan had a small pool of mediators who worked together regularly and shared learning and resources, all of which has contributed to improving the overall quality of the mediation process in the region.[56] Similarly, the development of mediation in Israel, according to Mironi, can be traced to the resolution of a series of labour disputes in the public healthcare sector.[57] The Prime Minister, in an unprecedented step, asked the parties to enter into mediation,[58] which resulted in innovative settlement terms.[59]

Decision Making About Divorce Mediation in the Presence of Domestic Violence' (2002) 9 *William and Mary Journal of Women and Law* 145; P.E. Bryan, 'Killing Us Softly: Divorce Mediation and the Politics of Power' (1992) 40 *Buffalo Law Review* 441.

[49] Macfarlane and Keet, 'Civil Justice Reform and Mandatory Civil Mediation in Saskatchewan' (n. 6 above).

[50] *Ibid.* 677–9.

[51] Macfarlane and Keet, 'Civil Justice Reform and Mandatory Civil Mediation in Saskatchewan' (n. 6 above).

[52] *Ibid.*

[53] *Ibid.*; J. Nuffield, *Evaluation of the Adult Victim-Offender Mediation Programme, Saskatoon Community Mediation Services* (Regina: Saskatchewan Justice, 1997).

[54] *Ibid.*

[55] M. Keet, 'The Evolution of Lawyers' Roles in Mandatory Mediation: A Condition of Systemic Transformation' (2005) 68(2) *Saskatchewan Law Review* 313.

[56] *Ibid.*

[57] M.M. Mironi, 'Experimenting with Alternative Dispute Resolution as a Means for Peaceful Resolution of Interest Labor Disputes in Public Healthcare: A Case Study' (20110 74 *Law and Contemporary Problems* 201.

[58] *Ibid.*

[59] *Ibid.*

Beyond the above domestic and cultural factors, rapid technological change has impacted mediation programme design in some jurisdictions.[60] The proliferation of online mediation platforms or 'e-mediation', particularly in North America, is notable in this regard.[61] In Israel, mechanisms of online dispute resolution facilitated through the Mediation Room or the Benoam System are emerging.[62] This has undeniably introduced additional conceptual complexities to the normative understanding of the mediation process. In the next section, national voluntary and court-directed mandatory mediation programmes are examined with the aim of determining the impact of domestic factors on mediation programme design.

2.3 REGIONAL AND INTERNATIONAL APPROACHES TO VOLUNTARY AND MANDATORY MEDIATION

Regionally and internationally, mediation policy has been integrated into disparate instruments with the objective of promoting regional integration. The most prominent instrument in this regard is the EU Mediation Directive (formally referred to as Directive 2008/52/EC of the European Parliament and of the Council of 21 May 2008 on certain aspects of mediation in civil and commercial matters) which came into effect in 2011.[63] The EU Directive principally focuses on cross-border mediation

---

[60] See generally, L.L. Fuller, 'Mediation: Its Forms and Functions' (1970) 44 *South California Law Review* 305; Stulberg, 'Theory and Practice of Mediation' (n. 47 above).

[61] See R. Birke and L.E. Teitz, 'US Mediation in 2001: The Path that Brought America to Uniform Laws and Mediation in Cyberspace' (2002) *American Journal of Comparative Law* 181, 206–8; J.W. Goodman, 'The Pros and Cons of Online Dispute Resolution: An Assessment of Cyber-Mediation Websites' (2003) 2(1) *Duke Law and Technology Review* 1; M. Lang, 'Cybersettle Secures $2m for Online Claims Settlement System' (2011) *Boston Business Journal*, available at www.bizjournals.com/boston/blog/mass-high-tech/2011/06/cybersettle-secures-2m-for-online-claims.html. Some of online mediation (e-mediation) platforms include onlinedebtsettlement.com and ussettle.com.

[62] O. Rabinovich-Einy, 'Reflecting on ODR: The Israeli Example' in *Proceedings of the 5th International Workshop on Online Dispute Resolution in Conjunction with the 21st International Conference on Legal Knowledge and Information Systems, Florence, Italy, 13 December 2008* (JURIX, 2008).

[63] C. Esplugues, 'Civil and Commercial Mediation in the EU after the Transposition of Directive 2008/52/EC' in *Civil and Commercial Mediation in Europe*, vol. II, *Cross-border Mediation* (2014).

with respect to civil and commercial disputes while excluding traditionally domestic and personal subject matter dispute areas.[64] The EU Directive was promulgated with the aims of reducing litigation costs and case backlog[65] as well as enhancing business transactions in the economic block.[66] Importantly, the EU Directive did not expressly provide for either mandatory or voluntary mediation, but a subsequent Court of Justice of the European Union (CJEU) decision clarified that its provisions do not restrict member countries from introducing either voluntary or mandatory schemes provided they do not unreasonably restrict a party's rights of access to the courts.[67] As a result, the EU Directive has resulted in a proliferation of many national schemes representing both voluntary and mandatory systems.[68]

Beyond the EU, other international organizations have increasingly embraced mediation as a preferred approach to dispute resolution. The WTO's Dispute Settlement Body, for instance, integrates a largely quasi-judicial framework which allows disputing parties' control over the determination of their dispute.[69] This includes provisions for referring cases to pre-adjudication consensus building that has actually resulted in most cases being settled before the adjudication stage.[70] Mediation has now been extended to international human rights matters, both the European and Inter-American Courts of Human Rights, and within hybrid and indigenous courts. In both cases, the approach is largely voluntary in nature.[71] In the European context, at any time during the proceedings, judges may direct

---

[64] *Ibid.*
[65] *Ibid.*
[66] Hanks, 'Perspectives on Mandatory Mediation' (n. 13 above) pp. 932–4.
[67] *Ibid.*
[68] *Ibid.*
[69] See generally, P. Michaud, *Experience from the Bilateral Fisheries Access Agreement: Impact on the Economy and Implications for Seychelles of the Outcome of the WTO Mediation on the Case of Tuna between the EU and Thailand and the Philippines* (2003), available at www.oceandocs.org/bitstream/handle/1834/194/Experience%20fisheries%20access%20agreement.pdf?sequence51; H.T. Pham, 'Developing Countries and the WTO: The Need for More Mediation in the DSU' (2004) 9 *Harvard Negotiation Law Review* 331.
[70] WTO, 'WTO Bodies Involved in the Dispute Settlement Process', www.wto.org/english/tratop_e/dispu_e/disp_settlement_cbt_e/c3s1p1_e.htm (accessed 19 November 2015).
[71] ECHR, Art. 39(1) states that 'at any stage of the proceedings, the Court may place itself at the disposal of the parties concerned with a view to securing a friendly settlement on the basis of respect for human rights'. Therefore the securing of amiable settlement requires willingness of the parties. Specifically, ECHR, Art. 38(1)(b) states that after determining that the case is admissible,

a friendly settlement of a matter[72] on the basis of respect for human rights as defined in the European Convention on Human Rights (ECHR).[73] If a friendly settlement is effected, the court will strike the case out of its list and hand down a brief statement of facts and of the solution reached.[74] Moreover, it permits friendly settlement negotiations even before the court declares a case to be admissible.[75] It codifies a pre-existing practice that friendly settlements are decided through 'judgments' instead of 'decisions'.[76] The enforcement of friendly settlements is also enhanced via the Committee of Ministers' direct supervision over the execution of 'judgment' remedies.[77] Similarly, with regard to the voluntary[78] friendly settlement procedure of the Inter-American Commission on Human Rights (IACHR), the Commission's Rules were amended in 2009[79] allowing the Commission to expedite the evaluation of a petition when the state formally expresses its readiness to enter into a friendly settlement procedure.[80]

At the United Nations level, the UNCITRAL Model Law on International Commercial Conciliation provides support for both

---

the Chamber then examines the case, and offers parties the option of friendly settlement.

[72] W.A. Schabas, *The European Convention on Human Rights: A Commentary* (Oxford University Press, 2015) p. 1622.

[73] ECHR, Art. 39(1).

[74] See n. 1 above.

[75] Explanatory Report to the CETS 194 (2009), s. IV, cl. 92, available at http://conventions.coe.int/Treaty/EN/Reports/Html/194.htm.

[76] See n. 4 above.

[77] Explanatory Report to the CETS 194 (2009), s. IV, cl. 94, available at http://conventions.coe.int/Treaty/EN/Reports/Html/194.htm.

[78] According to Comision Interamericana de Derechos Humanos, *Handbook on the Use of the Friendly Settlement Mechanism in the IACHR Petition and Case System*, p. 5 (available at www.oas.org/en/iachr/friendly_settlements/docs/handbook-fs-en.pdf), 'the friendly settlement procedure is voluntary', 'with or without direct involvement of the IACHR'. IACHR, *Impact of the Friendly Settlement Procedure Report* (18 December 2013) p. 1 (available at www.oas.org/en/iachr/friendly_settlements/docs/Report-Friendly-Settlement.pdf) also states that friendly settlement is a 'voluntary agreement reached by the parties'. But note that the rules of procedure authorize the IACHR to facilitate a friendly settlement at any time during the initial investigation phase. See M. Webster and S.B. Burke *Facilitating Friendly Settlements in the Inter-American Human Rights System: A Comparative Analysis with Recommendations* (1 May 2010) p. 23, available at SSRN: http://ssrn.com/abstract51676603.

[79] IACHR, *Impact of the Friendly Settlement Procedure* (n. 78 above) 17–18.

[80] IACHR Rules of Procedure of the Inter-American Commission on Human Rights, Resolution 1/2013, art. 29(2)(c).

mandatory and voluntary mediation.[81] The Model Law was developed given the high success rate of mediation with the aim of supporting its increased use both transnationally and domestically.[82] It also aimed at providing greater predictability and certainty in the use of conciliation to foster economy and efficiency in international trade.[83] While the Model Law principally addresses international and commercial cases, the drafters noted that states enacting the Model Law might consider extending it to domestic commercial disputes and to some non-commercial cases as well.[84] It was drafted with the view that while certain issues, such as the admissibility of evidence in subsequent judicial or arbitral proceedings or the role of the conciliator in subsequent proceedings, could typically be addressed by reference to rules such as the UNCITRAL Conciliation Rules, there were many cases in which no such rules were agreed upon. The conciliation process might thus benefit from the establishment of non-mandatory legislative provisions that would apply when the parties mutually desire to conciliate but have not agreed on a set of conciliation rules.[85]

The Model Law uses the term 'conciliation' to encompass all procedures, whether voluntary or mandatory, which are assisted by a third person to settle a dispute, such as conciliation, mediation, neutral evaluation or mini-trial.[86] Article 3, for instance, defines mediation as a process where 'parties request a third person or persons . . . to assist them in their attempt to reach an amicable settlement of their dispute'.[87] In Article 8, however, the scope of application of the law is expanded to all contexts 'irrespective of the basis upon which the conciliation is carried out, including agreement between the parties whether reached before or after a dispute has arisen, an obligation established by law, or a direction or suggestion of a court, arbitral tribunal or competent governmental entity'.[88]

---

[81] See generally, E. Van Ginkel, 'The UNCITRAL Model Law on International Commercial Conciliation' (2004) 21(1) *Journal of International Arbitration* 1; P. Binder and J. Sekolec, *International Commercial Arbitration and Conciliation in UNCITRAL Model Law Jurisdictions* (London: Sweet & Maxwell, 2005).
[82] UNCITRAL Model Law, commentary, para. 8.
[83] *Ibid.* paras. 15–16.
[84] See *ibid.* Art. 1, note 1.
[85] *Ibid.* para. 11.
[86] *Ibid.* para. 7.
[87] United Nations (ed.), *UNCITRAL Model Law on International Commercial Conciliation with Guide to Enactment and Use 2002* (New York: United Nations, 2002) p. 55, Art. 3.
[88] UNCITRAL Model Law, Art. 8.

The provisions in the Model Law governing mediation are designed to accommodate differences in procedure while leaving parties and conciliators free to carry out the conciliatory process as deemed appropriate. Essentially, the provisions seek to strike a balance between protecting the integrity of the conciliation process, for example, by ensuring that the parties' expectations regarding the confidentiality of the conciliation are met while also providing maximum flexibility by preserving party autonomy.[89]

As a tool for harmonizing legislation, the Model Law provides a legislative text that is recommended to states for incorporation into their national law.[90] Recent consultations have also focused on the development of an instrument for cross-border enforcement of mediated agreements.[91] In incorporating the text of the model legislation, a state may modify or leave out some of its provisions. This provides a great deal of flexibility to states. However, it also means that the degree of harmonization achieved through model legislation is likely to be lower than in the case of a convention.[92]

2.4 CONCLUSION

From the literature and examples of existing schemes discussed here, it is clear that domestic factors alongside harmonizing legislation such as the UNCITRAL Model Law have influenced mediation policy at the national level. The examination reveals the embedded involvement of lawyers and to a large extent courts, in most of the successful incidences mediation programmes, whether mandatory or voluntary.[93] In addition, socio-cultural background is an important complementary factor in the success of either mediation model. The UNCITRAL Model Law on conciliation as adopted by the UN General Assembly has accommodated voluntary and mandatory mediation policy design on the basis of unique domestic circumstances while at the same time contributing to further harmonization in mediation policy in the international sphere.

---

[89] *Ibid.* commentary para. 12.
[90] *Ibid.* para. 13.
[91] See generally S.I. Strong, 'Realizing Rationality: An Empirical Assessment of International Commercial Mediation' (2016) *Washington and Lee Law Review* 1973.
[92] UNCITRAL Model Law, commentary para. 14.
[93] See generally, P. Taivalkoski and A. Pynnä, 'The Courts and Bar Association as Drivers for Mediation in Finland' in *New Developments in Civil and Commercial Mediation* (New York: Springer, 2015) pp. 275–89.

PART II

Voluntary mediation programmes

3. Mediation in the UK courts

3.1 GENERAL INTRODUCTION

This chapter outlines the development of mediation in the United Kingdom from 1996 onwards. In the UK, the court encouraged mediation programme was developed on the basis of findings that heightened pressure to settle lowered the settlement rate,[1] while success hinged on parties' willingness to settle in good faith.[2] Civil mediation in the UK remains robust through the use of cost-sanctions encouraging participation and subsidized mediation programmes for select issue areas, including labour and employment, encouraging parties to consider the use of conciliation prior to civil trials. This chapter introduces the origins of mediation in the UK, including its policy background, ground rules and procedure. Recent cases that have significance for the practice of mediation are discussed, followed by an examination of the wider context of the UK judiciary's achievements in terms of efficiency, confidence and perceptions of justice. Results of a five-year analysis of relevant civil justice indicators suggest that since the implementation of its mediation programme, the UK has experienced positive developments in the areas of efficiency as measured by reduction in delay, confidence as measured by effective enforcement and impartial and effective ADR, and perceptions of justice as measured by its percentiles in rule of law and absence of discrimination.

---

[1] H. Genn, 'ADR and Civil Justice' in (2010) *Judging Civil Justice* 113, wherein it was stated that if the parties are forced to mediate, they may go through the motions yet without any intention to settle. Rather, parties may misuse the process as a venue for fishing information from or trying emotional tactics on the opponent.

[2] The *voluntary* nature of mediation is also reiterated in Lord Justice Jackson's *Final Report on the Review of Costs in Civil Cases* (December 2009) ch. 36, para. 3.4: 'In spite of the considerable benefits which mediation brings in appropriate cases, I do not believe that parties should ever be compelled to mediate'.

3.2 POLICY BACKGROUND

3.2.1 Historical Background

The contemporary development of civil mediation in the United Kingdom can be traced back to 1994 when Lord Woolf was appointed to review the rules and procedures of the civil courts in England and Wales. The aims of the review were to improve access to justice, to reduce costs and complexity of the rules, and to remove unnecessary distinctions of practice and procedure.[3] Lord Woolf then identified in the 1995 *Interim Report* on *Access to Justice* that the key issues facing the civil justice regime were 'cost, delay and complexity', with its principal shortcoming being the adversarial tactics and behaviour of lawyers.[4] He encouraged the use of alternative dispute resolution (ADR), including mediation, in the *Interim Report*. The 1996 *Final Report* on *Access to Justice* further encouraged mediation in civil trials based on its perceived advantage of saving strained judicial resources and its benefits to litigants in terms of lower costs and speedier results.[5,6] It was against this backdrop that some judges collaborated in establishing no- or low-cost mediation schemes for litigants. The Central London County Court (CLCC) voluntary mediation scheme (VOL) was the first court-based local VOL pilot scheme established in 1996.

The VOL scheme was established by the judges in the Central London County Court for non-family civil disputes.[7] The central aim of the scheme was to afford litigating parties the opportunity to have their case mediated and settled by a trained mediator at an early stage of the litigation process.[8] The scheme was entirely *voluntary* and *consensual* upon the litigation parties' acceptance of the court's personalized mediation offer. At the outset the scheme was scheduled to last for two years, but was made permanent in 1998 and was subsequently absorbed into the national county court mediation service, the National Mediation

---

[3] S. Moloney, 'A New Approach to Civil Litigation? Implementing the "Woolf Reforms" and Judicial Case Management' (2002) 2 *Judicial Studies Institute Journal* 98; Lord Woolf, *Access to Justice: Interim Report to the Lord Chancellor on the Civil Justice System in England and Wales* (June 1995).
[4] See *ibid.* ch. 3, para. 1 and ch. 4, para. 31.
[5] See *ibid.* ch. 18.
[6] Lord Woolf, *Access to Justice: Final Report to the Lord Chancellor on the Civil Justice System in England and Wales* (July 1996).
[7] H. Genn, *The Central London County Court Pilot Mediation Scheme Evaluation Report* (1998) pp. 3–4.
[8] *Ibid.*

Helpline (now replaced by the Civil Mediation Online Directory) in 2007.[9]

3.2.2 Rationale

The original rationale for setting up the VOL pilot scheme was the judicial concern regarding the lack of proportion between legal costs and recoveries in low-value claims, and a perception of a burgeoning number of litigants in person appearing in the county courts.[10] Mediation was introduced with the objectives of (i) *increasing access to justice* via reduced legal costs to litigants and more efficient resolution of disputes via an informal process; and (ii) *reducing the number of trials* which in turn could result in savings to the Legal Aid Board, and a reduction in the number of cases requiring trial and the attendant court costs.[11]

Nevertheless, it has been argued in contemporary literature that the major thrust behind the civil justice reforms (including the continued push for mediation) was 'simply about diversion of disputants away from the courts' instead of much-mentioned assertions regarding increased access and more justice.[12] Such diversion stemmed from the pressure on resources, which was substantiated by some members of the senior judiciary who 'publicize[d] the degradation of the civil courts and the problems facing the civil justice system'.[13] There was also copious evidence of declining standards in county court operational standards in the annual reports of Designated Civil Judges.[14] In light of the climate of scarce court resources, and the squeezing of resources for civil courts under a fixed justice budget caused by the strengthened demand for and increasing perceived importance of the criminal justice system, the endorsement of mediation aimed largely at removing cases from the judicial court system.[15]

Distinct court mediation schemes were introduced subsequent to the VOL scheme, including the Court of Appeal Mediation Scheme and Her Majesty's Courts Service (HMCS) Small Claims Mediation Scheme. In 1997, the Court

---

[9] K.J. Hopt and F. Steffek, *Mediation: Principles and Regulation in Comparative Perspective* (Oxford University Press, 2013) 427.

[10] H. Genn, *The Central London County Court Pilot Mediation Scheme* (n. 7 above); see also: L. Mistelis, 'ADR in England and Wales: a successful case of public private partnership' (2003) 6 (3) *ADR Bulletin* Article 6.

[11] *Ibid.*

[12] H. Genn, 'Civil Justice: How Much is Enough?' in (2010) *Judging Civil Justice* 69.

[13] *Ibid.* 48–51.

[14] *Ibid.*

[15] *Ibid.* 38–9, 49, 58.

of Appeal (Civil Division) established its own voluntary mediation scheme and several regional county courts (initially in Exeter and Bristol and later in Birmingham, Manchester, Guildford and Reading) followed suit and set up experimental mediation schemes.[16] In 1999, the new Civil Procedure Rules (CPR) were promulgated whereby judges could order a break in proceedings for parties to attempt to settle their dispute by mediation or other ADR methods and unreasonable refusal to engage in mediation could result in an imposition of costs penalties.[17] The Court of Appeal voluntary pilot mediation scheme was re-launched in 2003.[18] The HMCS Small Claims Mediation Scheme was rolled out in 2007 following the success of the in-house small claims mediation pilot scheme in the Manchester County Court.[19]

3.3 PROGRAMME FEATURES

3.3.1 Central London County Court Voluntary Mediation Scheme

The VOL and other county court mediation schemes 'offered no or low-cost, time limited mediation for litigants who had already commenced court proceedings'.[20] The VOL afforded an opportunity to parties in any defended case with a claim above £3,000 the opportunity to participate in a three-hour mediation session provided by trained mediators on a pro-bono basis. The mediation sessions generally took place after normal court hours.[21] Most of the schemes permitted flexibility and allowed a second session if a settlement could be reached with more time.[22] Each party initially paid a fee of only £25 in 1996 to cover administration costs. The fee was raised to £100 in 1998.[23]

---

[16] H. Genn et al., *Twisting Arms: Court Referred and Court Linked Mediation Under Judicial Pressure*, Ministry of Justice Research Series 1/07 (2007) p. 8, available at www.ucl.ac.uk/laws/judicial-institute/files/Twisting_arms_mediation_report_Genn_et_al_1.pdf (accessed 29 September 2015).
[17] See Civil Procedure Rules, Rules 1.4(2) and 26.4.
[18] UK Ministry of Justice, *The Court of Appeal's Mediation Scheme* (12 March 2015), available at www.justice.gov.uk/courts/rcj-rolls-building/court-of-appeal/civil-division/mediation (accessed 25 September 2015).
[19] S. Blake, J. Browne and S. Sime, *A Practical Approach to Alternative Dispute Resolution* (Oxford University Press, 2011) p. 255.
[20] Genn, 'ADR and Civil Justice' (n. 1 above) p. 97.
[21] *Ibid.* 109.
[22] *Ibid.*
[23] Blake, Browne and Sime, *A Practical Approach to Alternative Dispute Resolution* (n. 19 above) p. 254.

3.3.2 Court of Appeal Mediation Scheme

The Court of Appeal Mediation Scheme (CAMS) was first established on a voluntary basis in 1997 with a revised scheme rolled out in 2003[24] following the Court of Appeal's decision in *Dunnett* v. *Railtrack Plc*.[25] Except for family cases, CAMS is administered by CEDR Solve, a commercial mediation provider in the UK. It is usually used for civil disputes where the amount at dispute is higher than the limit for the small claims track, i.e. for multi-track claims with more complicated court procedures and heavier legal costs.

In non-family cases, the fixed fee per party is £850 plus VAT payable in advance. The fees cover four hours of preparation time and five hours of mediation.[26] An extension of time for the mediation meeting may be charged at a rate of £125 plus VAT per hour, per party.[27] The fixed fee does not, however, include the cost of a venue.[28]

(i) Pre-settlement

Upon parties' selection or the court's recommendation of mediation, CEDR Solve contacts the parties about scheduling mediation.[29] The court implemented a pilot scheme from 2 April 2012 to 31 March 2015 whereby it automatically referred appeals in personal injury, clinical negligence and contractual claims with an amount of up to £250,000 at stake to CAMS.[30]

With both parties' consent to mediation, three suitable mediators from the court-controlled mediatory panel are offered.[31] Upon failure to agree on a mediator, CEDR Solve makes a final selection.[32] Parties then identify and pay for a venue.[33] However, unlike the other county

---

[24] Centre for Effective Dispute Resolution, *CEDR Solve to Administer Court of Appeal's Relaunched Mediation Scheme* (6 March 2003), available at www.cedr.com/news/?item5CEDR-Solve-to-administer-Court-of-Appeal-relaunched-mediation-scheme (accessed 15 September 2015).
[25] *Dunnett* v. *Railtrack Plc* [2002] 2 All ER 850.
[26] CEDR, 'Court of Appeal Mediation', available at www.cedr.com/solve/courtofappeal/ (accessed 15 September 2015).
[27] *Ibid.*
[28] *Ibid.*
[29] Blake, Browne and Sime, *A Practical Approach to Alternative Dispute Resolution* (n. 19 above) p. 256.
[30] HMCS, 'The Court of Appeal's Mediation Scheme', available at www.justice.gov.uk/courts/rcj-rolls-building/court-of-appeal/civil-division/mediation (accessed 15 September 2015).
[31] See n. 25 above.
[32] Blake, Browne and Sime, *A Practical Approach to Alternative Dispute Resolution* (n. 19 above).
[33] See n. 26 above.

court mediation programmes, no witnesses are formally called in appeal mediations.[34] Given the scheme's voluntary nature, the mediation can be terminated at any time by the parties without providing reasons, subject to cancellation fees.[35] As a condition of participating in CAMS, the parties must agree not to make any claims regarding the mediation against the mediator, the court or its officials, or CEDR Solve.[36]

(ii) Post-settlement
Any settlement reached is normally placed on the court record, but the terms of settlement can be kept confidential if a party so desires. If no settlement is reached, the case is referred back to the Court of Appeal for determination.

3.3.3 HMCS Small Claims Mediation Scheme

The Small Claims Mediation Scheme is funded by HMCS and provides a free service for small claims cases operating in all court centres. Parties are referred to the scheme when the conditions in CPR Rule 26.4A are fulfilled,[37] yet party agreement is required prior to commencement. Since 1 April 2013, the small claims track ceiling has been raised from £5,000 to £10,000. This has resulted in a much higher number of cases being resolved under the scheme.[38] If the parties agree to mediate and elect not to opt-out of the service, a phone-based or face-to-face mediation session is arranged.[39] Telephone mediations are normally conducted through individual private discussions rather than a joint conference call.[40] The mediation session, by phone or meeting, generally lasts an hour.[41] If the mediation is successful, then the case is de-listed, or if not, parties have to attend the scheduled hearing date before a district judge.

---

[34] Blake, Browne and Sime, *A Practical Approach to Alternative Dispute Resolution* (n. 19 above).
[35] HMCS, *Court of Appeal Mediation Scheme (CAMS)* (April 2013) p. 4, available at www.cedr.com/docslib/56D_CA_Mediation_Scheme_rules_for_1_April_13_final.pdf (accessed 15 September 2015).
[36] Blake, Browne and Sime, *A Practical Approach to Alternative Dispute Resolution* (n. 19 above).
[37] *Ibid.* 300.
[38] *Ibid.* 301.
[39] *Ibid.*
[40] *Ibid.*
[41] *Ibid.*

3.3.4 Civil Mediation Online Directory

Since 2007, as part of the government's policy encouraging individuals and businesses to resolve civil disputes via ADR, a county court mediation programme was established via the National Mediation Helpline. From 1 October 2011, the National Mediation Helpline was replaced by the Civil Mediation Online Directory. The programme remains a low-cost method for settling a wide variety of disputes administered by the Ministry of Justice in conjunction with the Civil Mediation Council. Unlike the National Mediation Helpline, the Online Directory system requires that parties take the initiative in making referrals to the provider of their choice using the Directory.[42] In responding to the replacement of the National Mediation Helpline, a spokesman for the Ministry of Justice was quoted saying that 'over recent years, mediation referrals and settlements had continued to fall' and 'approximately two-thirds of all calls had nothing to do with mediation'. Hence the programme could no longer justify the annual £9,000 expense.[43]

Although the programme is not free of charge, it is still less costly than hiring lawyers and going to court, with fees ranging from £50 to £425 or above depending on the amount of the claim. For claims worth less than £5,000, mediation can be conducted by telephone with the parties' consent.[44]

3.4 GENERAL GROUND RULES

Mediation remains voluntary despite being robustly advocated by the court. Any party that unreasonably refuses to attempt mediation or acts unreasonably during the mediation session runs the risk of a costs penalty.

3.4.1 Consequences where Parties Acted Unreasonably in Mediation or Unreasonably Refused to Mediate

In *Dunnett* v. *Railtrack Plc*, the Court of Appeal deprived a successful defendant of its costs award after taking into account the defendant's rejection of the defeated plaintiff's earlier offer to mediate before appeal

---

[42] S. Blake, J. Browne and S. Sime, *A Practical Approach to Alternative Dispute Resolution* (3rd edn, Oxford University Press, 2014) p. 303.
[43] G. Slapper and D. Kelly, *The English Legal System: 2015–2016* (16th edn, Abingdon: Routledge, 2015).
[44] *Ibid.*

without providing explanations when mediation was suggested by the court.[45]

In *Halsey* v. *Milton Keynes General NHS Trust*, the Court of Appeal held that the costs award of a winning party could be forfeited if the losing party could show that its opponent had acted 'unreasonably' in refusing to agree to mediate.[46] When determining unreasonableness, the court would bear in mind the benefits of mediation over litigation and consider the surrounding circumstances of the case. Such factors include the nature of the dispute, whether the refusing party had a reasonable belief that it would prevail on the merits, previous attempts to settle via other ADR methods, proportionality of mediation costs, any likely delay of trial proceedings, and the prospect of success of mediation.[47] Consequently, there was no blanket presumption in favour of mediation. The *Halsey* principles have been endorsed, for instance in *Burchell* v. *Bullard*, where Ward LJ stated that '[t]he profession can no longer with impunity shrug aside reasonable requests to mediate'.[48]

In addition to unreasonable refusal, the court will take into account any unreasonable conduct by both the successful party and the losing party during mediation in making costs orders. In *Malmesbury and others* v. *Strutt & Parker (a Partnership)*, the party who agreed to mediation but then caused the mediation to fail due to its unreasonable position was deemed to be in the same position as a party who unreasonably refused to mediate.[49] When the failure to mediate is caused by the behaviour of both parties then neither can claim that failure should be taken into account in the final costs order.

3.4.2 Voluntary Nature of Mediation

The *voluntary* nature of mediation was reiterated in *Halsey*. The court can encourage parties to agree to mediation, even in the most robust terms, yet may not compel the parties to do so.[50] Nevertheless, questions have been raised, particularly by Lord Phillips, whether the use of sanctions to encourage participation in mediation may be seen as 'tantamount to compelling a party to [mediate]'.[51] The rationale behind this strong adher-

---

[45] *Dunnett* (n. 25 above).
[46] *Halsey* v. *Milton Keynes General NHS Trust* [2004] 1 WLR 3002.
[47] *Ibid.* 3009.
[48] See *Burchell* v. *Bullard* [2005] BLR 330, para. 43.
[49] *Malmesbury (James Carleton, Seventh Earl of Malmesbury) and others* v. *Strutt & Parker (a Partnership)* [2008] EWHC 424 (QB).
[50] *Halsey* (n. 46 above) p. 3007.
[51] Lord Phillips CJ, *Alternative Dispute Resolution: An English Viewpoint*

ence to the voluntary nature of mediation is twofold: first, compulsion of ADR would be deemed an unacceptable obstruction of the parties' right of access to the court system; secondly, such compulsion would not likely lead to effective settlement but would, nevertheless, increase the costs of the parties and delay the resolution of disputes, which would undermine the 'perceived effectiveness of the ADR process'.[52]

3.4.3 Timing of Mediation

Mediation theoretically can take place at any stage of a dispute, whether before, after, or at any time until trial.[53] However, in *Nigel Witham Ltd* v. *Smith*, the court held that *unreasonable delay* in consenting to mediation may result in adverse costs orders because such delay would have rendered its chances of success very poor.[54] Therefore, it is not sufficient that a party eventually consents to mediation. Nonetheless, the court also acknowledged that '[a] premature mediation simply wastes time and can sometimes lead to a hardening of the positions on both sides' since the responding party might sensibly want proper details concerning the case so as to gauge the commercial risks presented by the claim before committing itself to any meaningful mediation. Thus the key is to identify the 'happy medium'.[55]

Given the distinct contours and concerns raised in each case, the appropriate timing of mediation is an evolving concept. Having said that, *Bradford* v. *James*[56] provides some guidance in identifying an optimal time-frame for mediation. The 'happy medium' can be drawn from pertinent considerations including whether issues are well-defined, the clarity of the party's case and the progress of evidence-gathering.[57]

(India, 29 March 2008), available at www.google.com.hk/url?sa5t&rct5j&q5&esrc5s&source5web&cd51&cad5rja&uact58&ved50ahUKEwj_8Iftn4bXAhVPO7wKHSWQCzMQFggmMAA&url5http%3A%2F%2Fwww.civilmediation.org%2Fdownloads-get%3Fid%3D119&usg5AOvVaw063-2vSIrgpxhp25Zp1vr_

[52] *Halsey* (n. 46 above) p. 3007.
[53] Blake, Browne and Sime, *A Practical Approach to Alternative Dispute Resolution* (n. 19 above) pp. 186–8.
[54] *Nigel Witham Ltd* v. *Robert Lesley Smith and Jacqueline Isaacs* [2008] EWHC 12 (TCC).
[55] *Ibid.* para. 32.
[56] *Bradford* v. *James* [2008] EWCA Civ 837.
[57] Blake, Browne and Sime, *A Practical Approach to Alternative Dispute Resolution*, 3rd edn (n. 42 above).

3.5 CIVIL PROCEDURE OF THE UK COURTS

The objective of the UK ADR policy is embodied in the overriding objective of CPR Rule 1 – 'enabling the court to deal with cases justly'.[58] The court must further this cardinal objective by actively managing cases by 'encouraging the parties to use an [ADR] procedure if the court considers that appropriate and facilitating the use of [ADR]'.[59] The court has powers to adjourn hearings, stay proceedings and extend procedural timetables to facilitate the use of ADR.[60]

The CPR also provides that engagement in mediation is relevant in the assessment of costs by the court: the court will take into account 'the efforts made, if any, before and during the proceedings in order to try to resolve the dispute' when awarding costs.[61] Similar to the position in the common law, the court's discretion to impose costs penalties on parties who act unreasonably or unreasonably refuse to attempt mediation does not afford a positive incentive for parties to try ADR – rather, it imposes a threat of financial consequences on such parties.

The CPR is accompanied by 13 pre-action protocols setting out guidance on action to be taken by the disputants for a specific type of claim.[62] One of the objectives of the protocols is to encourage parties to 'try to settle the issues without proceedings'.[63] It is expressly recognized that there is a continuing duty to consider the possibility of reaching a settlement, even after the commencement of proceedings, notwithstanding that neither party should be compelled to mediate.[64]

3.5.1 Mediation Process

In preparation for mediation, each party must submit a position statement to the mediator setting out its own case. The position statement is not a formal document but merely aims to brief the mediator on the facts of the case.[65]

---

[58] Civil Procedure Rules, Rule 1.1(1).
[59] *Ibid.* Rule 1.4(2)(e).
[60] *Ibid.* Rules 3.1 and 26.4(1).
[61] *Ibid.* Rule 44.4(3)(a)(ii).
[62] UK Ministry of Justice, 'Pre-Action Protocols: Civil Procedure Rules', www.justice.gov.uk/courts/procedure-rules/civil/protocol (accessed 23 September 2015).
[63] UK Ministry of Justice, 'Practice Direction: Pre-Action Conduct and Protocols', paras 3 and 8, available at www.justice.gov.uk/courts/procedure-rules/civil/rules/pd_pre-action_conduct#3.1 (accessed 23 September 2015).
[64] *Ibid.* para. 9.
[65] Blake, Browne and Sime, *A Practical Approach to Alternative Dispute Resolution* (n. 19 above) pp. 203–12.

A pre-mediation meeting may be held to discuss practical logistics matters, identify attendees, set the timetable, form a view of the personalities of the parties and their interaction, and determine the structure of mediation.[66]

A typical mediation commences with a joint meeting.[67] The mediator makes a formal opening statement followed by the parties' opening statements. At the second stage (exploration phase), private meetings are held. The mediator meets with the parties privately to conduct 'reality checks' whereby the mediator assists the parties to evaluate the strengths and weaknesses of their own case and that of their counterparty.[68] The mediator then devises strategies and solutions to accommodate the parties' interests. When the parties consider putting forward proposals in the negotiating phase, the mediator sums up the offers and concessions.[69] The mediator may at some stage call the parties together for a joint meeting when he is of the view that face-to-face meetings will facilitate an agreement.[70] At the closing phase, if a settlement is reached, the mediator will confirm the terms and oversee the drafting, signing and implementation of the settlement agreement. If no settlement is reached, the mediator sets out the reasons for failure to settle.

3.5.2 Settlement Agreement

Settlement agreements reached following successful mediation must normally be in writing and signed by the parties. If the terms involve monetary payment, the amount of payment and any interest charged, together with the time, date and method of payment, should be stated. Provisions should be made for any penalty in the event of default and for enforcement mechanisms. The costs of the mediation should also be dealt with in the agreement.[71]

3.5.3 Enforceability

Mediation agreements usually provide that for any settlement to be binding, it must be in writing signed by the parties. Nonetheless, if a signed

---

[66] *Ibid.*
[67] *Ibid.* 219–33.
[68] *Ibid.*
[69] *Ibid.*
[70] *Ibid.*
[71] See Blake, Browne and Sime, *A Practical Approach to Alternative Dispute Resolution* (n. 19 above) pp. 239–40, para. 13.90 for more general concerns in contemplating the settlement terms to be included.

written settlement is not available, the court may still investigate whether the signed writing clause was varied or waived by the parties by an oral collateral contract, or subverted by estoppel.[72]

If litigation has not commenced, the settlement agreement usually operates as a contract between the parties, thereby requiring fresh proceedings to be issued for any breach. If proceedings have been issued, various forms of court order can be sought to give effect to the agreement: a Tomlin order staying the action on the terms of the settlement; a consent order dismissing the proceedings; or a consent order setting out the terms agreed at mediation. The Tomlin order is generally regarded as the most effective since, in case of default, it allows parties to apply to court for enforcement without having to issue fresh proceedings.[73] Further, the terms contained in the schedule attached to the Tomlin order remain confidential without forming part of the order. Settlements with relief restricted to money and delivery of goods, stay or dismissal of a case, and costs can be made as consent orders without involving a judge.[74]

3.6 IMPLEMENTATION IN PRACTICE

The recent body of case law in the UK addressing the scope of its voluntary mediation programme has provided further guidance regarding the circumstances and implications of a party's unreasonable failure to engage in mediation.

In *PGF II SA* v. *OMFS Company 1 Ltd*, the Court of Appeal held that as a general rule, silence in the face of an invitation to engage in mediation is unreasonable, irrespective of whether a refusal might have been justified.[75] Parties can reject mediation whenever they deem mediation inappropriate and they cannot be compelled into mediation,

---

[72] See *Brown* v. *Rice* [2007] EWHC 625 (Ch), para. 25, where Stuart Isaacs QC stated that, 'The absence of a written settlement signed by or on behalf of each of the parties does not necessarily mean that the parties may never have arrived at a concluded settlement. For example, it is possible in any given case that the parties may have expressly or impliedly agreed to vary or waive those provisions or that a party may be estopped from relying on them or that a collateral contract has arisen . . . with the consequence that a concluded settlement was or must be treated as having been made'.
[73] Blake, Browne and Sime, *A Practical Approach to Alternative Dispute Resolution* (n. 19 above) pp. 322–3.
[74] *Ibid.*
[75] *PGF II SA* v. *OMFS Company 1 Ltd* [2013] EWCA Civ 1288.

yet they have to engage with the idea. Some exceptions to this general rule include circumstances whereby the failure to respond is a result of an unintentional mistake or where mediation was so conspicuously unsuitable.[76] This case may be deemed as an extension of the *Halsey* approach to the extent that a refusal to mediate, even a refusal by silence, could be held unreasonable. This extension is essentially based on two grounds: first, in light of the time lag between the invitation and the costs hearing, it may pose forensic difficulties for the court to ascertain whether those belatedly advanced reasons to mediate were genuine or not; secondly, any difficulties or reasons to reject mediation should be advanced and discussed in a timely manner; conversely, failure to provide such explanations in time cripples the objective of encouraging positive engagement with mediation from the disputants.[77] In the *PGF II SA* case, the silence was in the face of (*a fortiori*) repeated requests to mediate, thereby such silence by itself was sufficient to warrant a costs penalty. Briggs LJ additionally commented that the costs sanction and its quantum were not an automatic result of a finding of an unreasonable refusal to mediate; rather they were ordered upon a discretionary and balancing exercise applied by the judge. The principles expounded in the case thus operate as guidelines for judges only to avoid unnecessary rigidity.[78]

In *Garritt-Critchley* v. *Ronnan*, a claimant's costs were ordered to be paid on an indemnity basis due to the defendants' unreasonable failure to mediate.[79] In refusing to mediate, the defendants cited their 'extreme confidence' in their case and their belief that the parties were too far apart, especially in light of considerable mistrust between them.[80] The court dismissed this rationale as the claim involved a question of fact which could have gone either way. The court further held that the parties would not know if they were actually too far apart unless they explored settlement.[81] Mistrust between parties should not be an impediment to mediation. This case reveals that refusing mediation is a risky strategy which ought not be pursued unless there are justifiable reasons likely to be accepted by the court. The court reiterated that a prompt response coupled with reasons in refusing mediation would not suffice if such reasons were 'misconceived'.[82]

---

[76] *Ibid.*
[77] *Ibid.*
[78] *Ibid.*
[79] *Garritt-Critchley* v. *Ronnan* [2014] EWHC 1774 (Ch).
[80] *Ibid.*
[81] *Ibid.*
[82] *Ibid.*

However, even a party's refusal to mediate based on a reasonable belief of having a strong case may not be sufficient to preclude cost penalties. In *Northrop Grumman Mission Systems Europe Ltd* v. *BAE Systems (Al Diriyah C4I) Ltd*, the defendant, being the successful party, had refused mediation as it reasonably believed that it had a watertight case.[83] Despite finding that the defendant's belief that it had a strong case was reasonable, the court ruled that its conduct in rejecting the mediation offer was unreasonable because of the reasonable prospects of success of mediation. On the face of the dispute, both parties seemed to have taken an irreconcilable position; yet the court stated that in such cases a mediator could find middle ground by analysing each party's expressed position and exploring other commercial arrangements or future opportunities.[84] Despite finding that the defendant's conduct was unreasonable, the court did not impose any sanctions as, according to CPR Rule 44.2(4)(c), the court had to take into account that the defendant had made a settlement offer which the claimant failed to beat. This case demonstrates the importance of making settlement offers to demonstrate to the court that rejection of a mediation invitation is not unreasonable. It also follows from *Northrop* that even if a party reasonably believes it has a watertight case, it should still be receptive to mediation to avoid costs penalties.[85]

In the recent case of *Murray* v. *Bernard*, the losing party in litigation argued that there should be no costs order in favour of the successful party due to the latter's initial refusal to mediate despite a change of mind one month later.[86] The court, however, made no costs sanctions as the successful party had subsequently and relatively speedily changed its mind to agree to mediation. Although this case confirms that a delay in agreeing to mediate will not automatically result in costs penalties, it would be risky to extrapolate a general rule that there would be no adverse costs consequences if one who initially refuses to mediate later changes his mind.[87]

---

[83] *Northrop Grumman Mission Systems Europe Ltd* v. *BAE Systems (Al Diriyah C4I) Ltd* [2014] EWHC 3148 (TCC).
[84] *Ibid.*
[85] *Ibid.*
[86] *Murray* v. *Bernard* [2015] EWHC 2395 (Ch).
[87] *Ibid.*

3.7 RESULTS OF THE UNITED KINGDOM'S VOLUNTARY MEDIATION PROGRAMME

3.7.1 Mediation-related Statistics: Number of Mediation Cases, Success Rates, Average Time-frame and Costs

(i) Paths to Justice Survey

In 1996, Professor Hazel Genn together with the National Centre for Social Research conducted a national study of the response of households in England and Wales to justiciable problems for a five-year period since January 1992.[88] The screening survey involved 4,125 individuals from which 1,134 adults were identified as having experienced a non-trivial justiciable problem.[89] Among the 1,134 weighted samples in the main survey, only 2 per cent of them stated that they had had or had planned for a mediation or conciliation session.[90] This finding reflected the 'trivial impact' that ADR had had in the dispute resolution regime in England and Wales.[91]

(ii) CLCC VOL: Court-based ADR Initiatives for Non-Family Civil Disputes

Despite its being under-used, the CLCC VOL scheme received favourable reviews by its participants. During the period between May 1996 and March 1998, 160 cases were mediated, representing 5 per cent of all cases.[92] The overall settlement rate was 62 per cent.[93]

The average time-frame for settled cases from date of entry of defence to date of conclusion was 158 and 176 days for personal injury (PI) and non-personal injury cases, respectively.[94] Even failing settlement at mediation, mediated cases that eventually settled at a later stage had shorter average case lengths than non-mediated settled cases.[95]

Under the CLCC VOL scheme, during the period from January 1999 to December 2004, a total of 865 cases were mediated. This came to an annual

---

[88] H.G. Genn and S. Beinart, *Paths to Justice: What People Do and Think About Going to Law* (Oxford: Hart, 1999) pp. 5–17.
[89] *Ibid.*
[90] Detailed outcomes are shown in Figure 1 in Appendix I.
[91] *Ibid.* 147, 215.
[92] See Figure 2-1 in Genn, *The Central London County Court Pilot Mediation Scheme* (n. 7 above) p. 16.
[93] See *ibid.* 44, para. 3.2.2.
[94] See *ibid.* 78, Tables 4-1 and 4-2.
[95] *Ibid.*

Table 3.1 Mediation outcomes under the Small Claims Mediation Scheme

Year	Number of cases referred to mediation	Mediation success rate
2007–08	3,745	67.5%
2008–09	9,240	72%
2009–10	10,174	69.5%
2010–11	10,622	69%

average of 144 cases as compared with the annual average of 83 cases in the previous two-year period.[96] The trend indicates that the use of the scheme had been gathering momentum following the judgment in *Dunnett*.[97] The overall settlement rate was 44 per cent.[98] Such figures reveal a steep rise in the rate at which cases have entered the scheme, yet a declining settlement rate.[99]

The average period between issue and date of mediation (for the 509 cases mediated between 1999 and 2003) was 448 days.[100]

(iii) Court of Appeal Mediation Scheme

When CAMS was first set up in 1997, it had a low take-up and a lower than 50 per cent success rate.[101] However, during the first year of its re-launch from May 2003, the scheme achieved a settlement rate at mediation of 68 per cent.[102]

(iv) HMCS Small Claims Mediation Scheme

As shown in Table 3.1,[103] between 2007 and 2011, an average of 69 per cent of cases referred to mediation under the Small Claims Mediation Service ultimately settled.

---

[96] Genn et al., *Twisting Arms* (n. 16 above) p. 134.
[97] *Ibid.* 135.
[98] *Ibid.* 143.
[99] See *ibid.* 139, Figure 4.3.
[100] *Ibid.* 142.
[101] Blake, Browne and Sime, *A Practical Approach to Alternative Dispute Resolution*, 3rd edn (n. 42 above).
[102] See n. 30 above.
[103] Blake, Browne and Sime, *A Practical Approach to Alternative Dispute Resolution*, 3rd edn (n. 42 above); HMCS, *Her Majesty's Courts Service Annual Report and Accounts* (2010–11) p. 10, available at www.justice.gov.uk/downloads/publications/corporate-reports/hmcs/annual-reports/hmcs-annual-report-2010-11.pdf (accessed 27 September 2015).

(v) Centre for Effective Dispute Resolution

Centre for Effective Dispute Resolution (CEDR) mediation audits were undertaken in conjunction with the Civil Mediation Council by means of an Internet-based survey open to all mediators in the UK. Included in the survey were ad hoc referrals to service providers and individual mediators through schemes such as the National Mediation Helpline and CAMS. The results from the six mediation audits in 2014 show that interest in UK mediation has expanded steadily by 9 per cent over the previous two years. The estimated size of civil and commercial mediation as of 2014 was in the order of 9,500 cases annually.

3.7.2 UK Government Mediation

In March 2001, the UK government pledged to use mediation to settle all suitable legal disputes involving government departments whenever agreed to by the opposing party. Since then, the Ministry of Justice has published annual pledge reports to review the effectiveness of this commitment. The figures in Table 3.2 are extracted from the annual pledge reports covering the period from 2001–02 to 2008–09.[104]

In a report published by the National Audit Office in 2007, the average cost of legal aid in mediated cases was £752, taking approximately 110 days to reach agreement,[105] as compared with £1,682 and 435 days for non-mediated cases.[106] In 2012, the average cost per client for mediation was reportedly £675 as compared to £2,823 for non-mediated cases.[107]

The costs provided under each scheme only account for the mediator's fees.[108] In addition to mediator's fees, other direct costs of mediation

---

[104] See UK Ministry of Justice, *Annual Pledge Report 2001–02: Monitoring the Effectiveness of the Government's Commitment to Using Alternative Dispute Resolution*, and the respective reports for 2002–03, 2003–04, 2004–05, 2005–06, 2006–07, 2007–08 and 2008–09.

[105] National Audit Office, *Legal Aid and Mediation for People Involved in Family Breakdown*, HC 256 Session 2006–2007 (2 March 2007) p. 5, available at www.nao.org.uk/wp-content/uploads/2007/03/0607256.pdf (accessed 15 September 2015).

[106] *Ibid.*

[107] National Family Mediation, 'How Much Does Mediation Cost', available at www.nfm.org.uk/index.php/family-mediation/cost-of-mediation (accessed 29 September 2015).

[108] Blake, Browne and Sime, *A Practical Approach to Alternative Dispute Resolution* (n. 19 above) p. 191.

82   *Court mediation reform*

Table 3.2   Success rates of ADR in cases involving government departments and agencies

Year	Number of cases referred to ADR	ADR settlement rate
2001–02	49	–
2002–03	163	83%
2003–04	229	79%
2004–05	167	75%
2005–06	336	72%
2006–07	331	68%
2007–08	374	72%
2008–09	314	82%

include the party's own costs of preparing for the mediation, any counsel's or expert's fees[109] and venue fees.[110]

3.7.3   United Kingdom's Civil Justice Rankings: Efficiency, Confidence and Perceptions of Justice

The voluntary mediation programme in the UK can be examined within the larger context of its achievements in the areas of efficiency, confidence and perceptions of justice over the past five years. In particular, efficiency not only implies questions of operational cost in civil justice, but related issues of accessibility and affordability of the courts and lack of delay in resolution. Confidence in court mediation systems can be examined in relation to the overall ranking of the civil justice system, ease of enforcement and impartial and effective ADR. Finally, perceptions of justice can be assessed alongside measures of rule of law, independence of the judiciary and levels of reported discrimination.

Table 3.3 shows relative movement over the past five years within the UK in relation to its rankings in the areas of efficiency, confidence and perceptions of justice. Areas highlighted in grey indicate a positive movement in the rankings. As can be seen, over the past five years, the UK has experienced positive development in the areas of efficiency, as measured by reduction in delay, confidence, as measured by effective enforcement and impartial and effective ADR, and perceptions of justice, as measured by its percentiles in rule of law and absence of

[109] *Ibid.*
[110] *Ibid.*

Table 3.3 UK rankings: developments in efficiency, confidence and perceptions of justice, 2011–2016*

	2011	2016
Efficiency		
• Efficiency of legal framework in settling disputes (rank)	13th/142	6th/138
• Accessibility and affordability (percentile)	0.56	0.56
• No unreasonable delay (percentile)	0.62	0.75
Confidence		
• Civil justice (rank)	10th/66	16th/113
• Effective enforcement (percentile)	0.68	0.76
• Impartial and effective ADR (percentile)	0.75	0.77
Perceptions of justice		
• Rule of law (percentile)	0.92	0.94**
• No discrimination (percentile)	0.56	0.66

* Greyed rows indicate a positive trend in the rankings.
** World Bank Group, *Worldwide Governance Indicators 2015*, available at http://info.worldbank.org/governance/wgi/index.aspx#home.

discrimination. This appears to indicate that the voluntary mediation programme as implemented in the UK has resulted in some positive successes in recent years.

In terms of overall efficiency in the civil justice system, according to the *Global Competitiveness Report 2016–2017*,[111] the UK ranks 6th out of 138 countries in the efficiency of its legal framework in settling disputes. The accessibility and affordability of the civil justice system is 0.56[112] on a 1 point scale, which is lower than the average for countries within the EU, EFTA and North America, as the problem of unpredictability of legal costs persists in English civil procedure.[113] Its score for 'no unreasonable delay' was 0.75[114] on a 1 point scale.

Confidence in court mediation systems can be examined in relation to the overall ranking of the civil justice system and ease of enforcement and impartiality and effectiveness of ADR. The overall rank for the UK's civil

---

[111] World Economic Forum, *The Global Competitiveness Report 2016–2017*, pp. 354–5.
[112] World Justice Project, *Rule of Law Index 2016*, p. 143.
[113] C. Hodges, S. Vogenauer and M. Tulibacka (eds), *The Costs and Funding of Civil Litigation: A Comparative Perspective* (Oxford: Hart, 2010) p. 302.
[114] See n. 112 above.

justice in the *Rule of Law Index 2016*[115] is 16 out of 113 countries. Its scores for effective enforcement and impartial and effective ADR were 0.76 on a 1 point scale and 0.77[116] on a 1 point scale, respectively, meeting the average of other OECD countries.

Finally, with respect to perceptions of justice, UK's rule of law percentile has steadily increased since 2011 and reached 94 on a 100 point scale in 2015.[117] The score for 'no discrimination' was 0.66 on a 1 point scale, which is below average.[118]

3.8 CONCLUSION

The United Kingdom's voluntary mediation programme presents a useful example of a well-established mediation system implemented through robust encouragement. Over the past five years, the UK has experienced positive developments in the areas of efficiency as measured by reduction in delay, confidence as measured by effective enforcement and impartial and effective ADR, and perceptions of justice as measured by its rankings in rule of law and absence of discrimination. Usage rates in the UK for most of its voluntary programmes have increased over the past 20 years. Likewise, the UK enjoys a strong reputation in the rule of law, civil justice and effective enforcement. Nevertheless, opinion poll rankings suggest that the issues of accessibility and affordability, as well as delay, remain major challenges facing its justice system.

---

[115] World Bank Group, *Worldwide Governance Indicators 2015*, available at http://info.worldbank.org/governance/wgi/index.aspx#home.
[116] *Ibid.*
[117] *Ibid.*
[118] *Ibid.*

4. Mediation in the Hong Kong courts

4.1 INTRODUCTION

Hong Kong introduced a robust court-encouraged mediation programme in 2009 through its Civil Justice Reform (CJR). Drawing on experiences in the United Kingdom, the reform includes judicial Practice Directions providing practitioners with guidance on the use of alternative dispute resolution (ADR) prior to civil trials. Modelled on the approach taken in England and Wales,[1] the CJR emphasizes cost effectiveness, the avoidance of delays, the facilitation of settlements and fair employment of the courts' resources.[2] In particular, Practice Direction 31 on Mediation (PD 31) was introduced to assist the court to discharge its duty of encouraging parties to use an ADR procedure.[3] PD 31 came into effect on 1 January 2010.[4] It applies to all civil proceedings in the Court of First Instance (CFI) and the District Court (DC) begun by writ (with some exceptions).[5]

To encourage mediation, the judiciary has adopted various measures including the imposition of costs on a party that unreasonably refuses to engage in mediation. Legal representatives are under an obligation to advise their clients of this possibility.[6] In addition, two Mediation Co-ordinators' Offices were set up in the High Court in 2010. Furthermore,

---

[1] See D. Ravenscroft, 'Mediation and Civil Justice Reform' (2008) *Hong Kong Lawyer*, available at http://law.lexisnexis.com/webcenters/hk/Hong-Kong-Lawyer-/Mediation-and-Civil-Justice-Reform (accessed 28 November 2011).

[2] See G. Soo, Y. Zhao and D. Cai, *Better Ways of Resolving Disputes in Hong Kong: Some Insights from the Lehman-Brothers Related Investment Product Dispute Mediation and Arbitration Scheme* (2010), available at http://law.hofstra.edu/pdf/academics/journals/jibl/jibl_vol9no1_soo_zhao_cai_hong_kong.pdf.

[3] Hong Kong Judiciary, Practice Direction 31 on Mediation (14 August 2014) paras 1–2. This Practice Direction supersedes the previous Practice Direction 31 on Mediation dated 12 February 2009.

[4] Hong Kong Judiciary, Practice Direction 31 on Mediation (12 February 2009) para. 21.

[5] Practice Direction 31, para. 2, Appendix A. The proceedings set out in Appendix A either have another direction to deal with the voluntary mediation part, or are related to discrimination or recovery of tax.

[6] *Ibid.* para. 4.

the judiciary established a mediation-dedicated webpage. The purpose of the website is to assist parties to understand the nature of mediation and how it might potentially assist parties in resolving their disputes.[7] In 2010, the Joint Mediation Helpline Office was also set up to promote the use of mediation and to provide mediation referral services.[8]

Prior to the implementation of the Civil Justice Reform, the Working Party on Mediation (Working Party) began in 2007 to facilitate the consensual and voluntary use of mediation for the resolution of civil disputes.[9] Over the past decade, pilot schemes for mediation were introduced across a range of litigation areas, including construction, building management and personal injury.[10] In ascertaining the true 'quality' of mediation services in Hong Kong after the CJR, it has been suggested that more in-depth and qualitative research should be carried out on topics such as user satisfaction,[11] as well as the extent to which robust encouragement of mediation provides parties with flexibility of choice in dispute resolution options. Results of a five-year analysis of relevant civil justice indicators suggest that since the implementation of its mediation programme, Hong Kong has experienced positive developments in the areas of efficiency, as measured by accessibility and affordability; reduction in delay and confidence, as measured by effective enforcement and impartial and effective ADR; and perceptions of justice, as measured by its percentiles in rule of law and reduction of discrimination.

4.2 LAW/POLICY BACKGROUND

The promotion of mediation in Hong Kong began five years prior to its formal introduction. In the *Final Report on Civil Justice Reform* in 2004, the judiciary recommended that, 'Proposal 68[12] should be adopted in conjunction with other appropriate measures to promote court-related

---

[7] Hong Kong Judiciary, 'Mediation: Welcome Message', available at http://mediation.judiciary.gov.hk/en/index.html (accessed 25 November 2015).

[8] Hong Kong Judiciary, 'Mediation: Working Party on Mediation', available at http://mediation.judiciary.gov.hk/en/working.html (accessed 25 November 2015).

[9] *Ibid.*

[10] *Ibid.*

[11] *Ibid.*

[12] See Chief Justice's Working Party on Civil Justice Reform, *Final Report on Civil Justice Reform* (March 2004) p. 424, Proposal 68: 'A scheme should be introduced for the court to provide litigants with information about and facilities for mediation on a purely voluntary basis, enlisting the support of professional associations and other institutions'.

mediation'.[13] The same report suggested that the court should have the power to make adverse costs orders in cases where mediation has been unreasonably refused, taking into account all relevant circumstances.[14] The Hong Kong Government's 2007–2008 Policy Address lent further support to the promotion of voluntary mediation in Hong Kong and outlined its rationale by noting that:

> To alleviate conflicts and foster harmony, we will promote the development of mediation services. On many occasions, interpersonal conflicts need not go to court. Mediation can reduce social costs and help the parties concerned to rebuild their relationship. This is a new trend in advanced regions around the world.[15]

The Policy Address expressly stated that mediation should be employed more extensively and effectively in Hong Kong. Subsequently, the Working Group on Mediation led by the Secretary for Justice was set up in 2008 to review the development of mediation and conduct studies regarding its use.[16]

Beginning in 2006, the judiciary introduced various pilot schemes for mediation including schemes addressing construction disputes, building management and bankruptcy. In September 2006, a two-year pilot scheme for mediation of construction disputes was introduced.[17] Pursuant to the review by the Working Party, this pilot scheme became permanent on 2 April 2009 under Practice Direction 6.1, which included encouragement and guidance for voluntary mediation between parties within the Construction and Arbitration List.[18] In January 2008, a similar one-year pilot scheme was introduced to promote mediation in building management cases in the Lands Tribunal.[19] Subsequently, the Lands Tribunal decided to adopt the Scheme as standard practice in July 2009.[20] In October 2008, a one-year pilot scheme was also introduced to encourage voluntary

---

[13] *Ibid.* 442.

[14] *Ibid.* 458.

[15] Hong Kong Government, *The 2007–08 Policy Address: A New Direction for Hong Kong* (10 October 2007) p. 85.

[16] Department of Justice, *Report of the Working Group on Mediation* (February 2010) p. 6.

[17] See n. 8 above.

[18] Hong Kong Judiciary, Practice Direction 6.1 on Construction and Arbitration List (12 February 2009) Part F.

[19] See n. 8 above.

[20] Hong Kong Judiciary, Direction Issued by the President of the Lands Tribunal Pursuant to Section 10(5)(a) of the Lands Tribunal Ordinance (Cap. 17) on Case Management and Mediation for Building Management Cases (21 May 2009).

mediation in winding up cases in October 2008.[21] Upon conclusion of the scheme, Practice Direction 3.3 made it a permanent practice in cases of the same nature, effective from 1 January 2010.[22] A New Insurance Mediation Pilot Scheme (NIMPS) was also introduced.[23]

The Civil Justice Reform was implemented on 2 April 2009, with underlying objectives of: (1) increasing the cost-effectiveness of civil proceedings; and (2) facilitating the settlement of disputes.[24] PD 31, initially issued in February 2009,[25] was later superseded by a new Practice Direction on 14 August 2014.[26] However, the difference between the two versions was minimal. Subsequent to the introduction of PD 31, various Practice Directions regarding mediation for land compulsory sale cases,[27] family mediation[28] and mediation on probate and administration of estate proceedings[29] were introduced or revised.

4.2.1 Initiating Legislation

As part of the Civil Justice Reform, the Rules of the High Court (Cap. 4A) (RHC) and the Rules of the District Court (Cap. 336H) (RDC) were amended to correspond to the objectives of the reform. 'Order 1A – Objectives' was included in the RHC and the RDC, through the Rules of the High Court (Amendment) Rules 2008 and the Rules of the District Court (Amendment) Rules 2008, respectively.[30,31] According to Order 1A Rule 1 in the RHC and the RDC, the underlying objectives of the Rules were:

---

[21] See n. 8 above.
[22] Hong Kong Judiciary, Practice Direction 3.3 on Voluntary Mediation in Petitions Presented under Sections 168A and 177(1)(f) of the Companies Ordinance, Cap.32 (2 December 2009).
[23] See n. 8 above.
[24] Hong Kong Judiciary, *Civil Justice Reform: An Overview* (2009) p. 1.
[25] See n. 4 above.
[26] See n. 3 above.
[27] Hong Kong Judiciary, Direction Issued by the President of the Lands Tribunal Pursuant to Section 10(5)(a) of the Lands Tribunal Ordinance (Cap. 17) on Mediation for Compulsory Sale Cases Under the Land (Compulsory Sale for Redevelopment) Ordinance (Cap. 545) (28 January 2011).
[28] Hong Kong Judiciary, Practice Direction 15.10 on Family Mediation (28 March 2012).
[29] Hong Kong Judiciary, Practice Direction 20.2 on Probate and Administration of Estate Proceedings (other than applications under the Non-Contentious Probate Rules (Cap.10A)) (2 July 2012).
[30] Rules of the High Court (Amendment) Rules 2008 LN 152 of 2008 (gazetted on 6 June 2008).
[31] *Ibid.*

(a) to increase the cost-effectiveness of any practice and procedure to be followed in relation to proceedings before the Court;
(b) to ensure that a case is dealt with as expeditiously as is reasonably practicable;
(c) to promote a sense of reasonable proportion and procedural economy in the conduct of proceedings; ...
(e) to facilitate the settlement of disputes.[32]

In the context of the Hong Kong judiciary, mediation is viewed as an effective means of enhancing the cost-effectiveness of case disposition.[33] Encouraging voluntary mediation is a mechanism used by the court to actively manage cases. Rule 4 of Order 1A states that the Court should actively manage cases by 'encouraging the parties to use an alternative dispute resolution procedure if the Court considers that appropriate, and facilitate[e] the use of such a procedure'.[34]

4.3 PROGRAMME FEATURES

Court-connected mediation in Hong Kong[35] is available in cases where all parties are legally represented.[36] Solicitors acting for their respective parties must file a Mediation Certificate stating (1) whether the party is

---

[32] Rules of the High Court (Cap. 4A) Order 1A Rule 1; Rules of the District Court (Cap. 336H) Order 1A Rule 1.

[33] See Hong Kong Judiciary, Practice Direction 15.10 on Family Mediation (28 March 2012) para. 1; Hong Kong Judiciary, Practice Direction 18.1 on the Personal Injuries List (12 February 2009) para. 26; Hong Kong Judiciary, Practice Direction 31 on Mediation (14 August 2014) para. 1; Hong Kong Judiciary, Direction Issued by the President of the Lands Tribunal Pursuant to Section 10(5)(a) of the Lands Tribunal Ordinance (Cap. 17) on Mediation for Compulsory Sale Cases Under the Land (Compulsory Sale for Redevelopment) Ordinance (Cap. 545) (28 January 2011) para. 3.

[34] Rules of the High Court (Cap. 4A) Order 1A Rule 4(e); Rules of the District Court (Cap. 336H) Order 1A Rule (e).

[35] Practice Direction 31, para. 2, Appendix A. Proceedings set out in Appendix A are: '(1) Court of First Instance: (a) Proceedings in the Construction and Arbitration List; (b) Proceedings in the Personal Injuries List; (2) District Court: (a) Proceedings in the Personal Injuries List; (b) Proceedings in the Equal Opportunities List under the Sex Discrimination Ordinance (Cap. 480), Disability Discrimination Ordinance (Cap. 487) and Family Status Discrimination Ordinance (Cap. 527); (c) Proceedings to recover tax under the Inland Revenue Ordinance (Cap. 112)'.

[36] Practice Direction 31, para. 8.

willing to attempt mediation; and (2) if the party is not willing to attempt mediation, the reasons for the party's unwillingness.[37] This should be done within 28 days after the submission of the pleadings.[38]

If the applicant wishes to attempt mediation, after filing the Mediation Certificate, he should serve a Mediation Notice on the respondent(s) and file it in court as soon as possible.[39] In the Mediation Notice, the applicant should propose the adoption of mediation rules;[40] the proposed mediator (with CV attached); the estimated costs and the proposal on payment; the venue for mediation; a specified minimum level of participation; the period of mediation; and any requests for an interim stay of legal proceedings.[41]

Within 14 days upon receipt of the Mediation Notice, the respondent must serve on the applicant a Mediation Response and file it in court.[42] The Mediation Response should include the respondent's indication as to whether or not he accepts the proposals by the applicant; and if not, the provision of alternative arrangements.[43]

If the parties reach an agreement, they must reduce it to a Mediation Minute signed by all parties and file it in court.[44] If no agreement is reached, either party may apply to the court for assistance in resolving their points of difference.[45] When an agreement on mediation is reached, the parties must proceed with the mediation as agreed, and may apply to court for an interim stay of proceedings.[46] The court may stay the proceedings, taking into account the importance of avoiding disruption to milestone dates and postponement of trial dates.[47] During the stay of proceedings, if a settlement is reached between the parties, the plaintiff

---

[37] *Ibid.* para. 9, Appendix B.
[38] *Ibid.* para. 9. Rules of the High Court (Cap. 4A) Order 25 Rule 1; Rules of the District Court (Cap. 336H) Order 25 Rule 1. See also Order 25 Rule 1 of both Ordinances: '(1) The pleadings in an action are deemed to be closed: (a) at the expiration of 14 days after service of the reply or, if there is no reply but only a defence to counterclaim, after service of the defence to counterclaim; or (b) if neither a reply nor a defence to counterclaim is served, at the expiration of 28 days after service of the defence'.
[39] *Ibid.* paras 10 and 15.
[40] The Hong Kong Mediation Code promulgated in 2010 is now widely adopted by mediation service providers.
[41] Practice Direction 31, para. 10, Appendix C.
[42] *Ibid.* paras 11, 15.
[43] *Ibid.* para. 11, Appendix D.
[44] *Ibid.* paras 12, 15.
[45] *Ibid.* para. 13.
[46] *Ibid.* para. 14.
[47] *Ibid.* para. 16.

must inform the court promptly, and the parties should formally conclude the legal proceedings.[48]

Where one or more parties of the proceedings are not legally represented, the Court may consider whether mediation is appropriate, and if so, it may give directions as to appropriate procedures.[49]

4.3.1 Ground Rules in the Hong Kong Mediation Code

Prior to the Civil Justice Reform, there were no uniform rules for the conduct of mediation in Hong Kong. The Hong Kong Mediation Code was promulgated by the Working Group on Mediation under Department of Justice in 2010, and is now used by different mediation bodies.[50]

The Hong Kong Mediation Code ('the Code') sets out ground rules for the conduct of mediation in Hong Kong. According to the Code, the mediator must maintain impartiality and avoid conflicts of interest. He must disclose to all parties any potential conflict, and obtain written consent from all parties before commencing the mediation.[51] The mediator must also explain the nature of mediation, the role of the mediator, and ensure that the mediation agreement is signed by all parties before proceeding with mediation.[52] The mediator must also uphold confidentiality.[53] She may encourage a party without legal representation to obtain independent advice where she deems it necessary.[54] Mediators are not permitted to charge contingent fees,[55] or give any legal or professional advice.[56]

The Hong Kong Mediation Ordinance (Cap. 620) (MO) was enacted in 2012, and effective from 1 January 2013.[57] Among its objectives is 'to protect the confidential nature of mediation communications'.[58] Section 8 of the MO expressly stipulates the confidentiality of mediation communications. According to section 8(1) of the MO, a person must not disclose a mediation communication, subject to some exceptions listed in

---

[48] *Ibid.* para. 17.
[49] *Ibid.* paras 18–20.
[50] Department of Justice, *Mediation* (24 February 2015), available at www.doj.gov.hk/eng/public/mediation.html (accessed 25 November 2015).
[51] Department of Justice, *The Hong Kong Mediation Code* (2010) para. 2.
[52] *Ibid.* para. 3.
[53] *Ibid.* para. 3. Confidentiality is further explored in the next sub-section.
[54] *Ibid.* para. 7.
[55] *Ibid.* para. 8.
[56] *Ibid.* sample Agreement to Mediate at para. 4.
[57] Mediation Ordinance (Cap. 620).
[58] *Ibid.* s. 3(b).

section 8(2) and (3).[59] Under section 8(3) of the MO, a person may disclose a mediation communication, with leave of the court or tribunal, to enforce or challenge a mediated settlement agreement;[60] to establish or dispute an allegation or complaint of professional misconduct;[61] or for any purpose considered justifiable by the court or tribunal.[62]

Practice Direction 31 clearly states that the court cannot compel disclosure of communications made during the mediation process since such communications are considered to be made without prejudice and protected by privilege.[63] This is of course subject to the circumstances listed in section 8(2) and (3) of the MO.

The Hong Kong Mediation Code requires that a mediator keep all information arising out of or in connection with a mediation confidential and that he not disclose such information without prior permission.[64] Disclosure can only be made when compelled on legal or public policy grounds, or when the information disclosed aims at protecting life or safety.[65]

4.3.2 Settlement Agreement and its Enforceability

Currently, there is no statutory mechanism for enforcing mediated settlement agreements.[66] Such agreements must be enforced as contracts through the commencement of legal proceedings if a party fails to comply. In *Champion Concord Ltd* v. *Lau Koon Foo (No. 2)*,[67] the Court of Final Appeal held that the settlement agreement between the parties constituted a contract and must be enforced according to the principles of contract law. Section 8(3)(a) of the MO states that disclosure of a settlement agreement may be allowed for purposes of enforcing a mediated settlement agreement.[68]

---

[59] *Ibid.* s. 8(1).
[60] *Ibid.* s. 8(3)(a).
[61] *Ibid.* s. 8(3)(b).
[62] *Ibid.* s. 8(3)(c).
[63] Practice Direction 31, para. 6.
[64] Hong Kong Mediation Code, para. 4(a), (b).
[65] *Ibid.* para. 4(a), (c).
[66] Mediation Ordinance (Cap. 620).
[67] *Champion Concord Ltd* v. *Lau Koon Foo (No. 2)* FACV16/2010; (2011) 14 HKCFAR 837.
[68] Mediation Ordinance, s. 8(3)(a).

4.4 IMPLEMENTATION IN PRACTICE

Subsequent to the implementation of the Civil Justice Reform and the issuance of PD 31, several court cases in Hong Kong have addressed the issue of the construction of mediation agreements and cost implications of unreasonable refusal to engage in mediation.

4.4.1 Court's Power to Resolve Points of Difference in Mediation Proposals

The question of the court's power to resolve points of difference in mediation proposals was addressed in *CY Foundation Group Ltd* v. *Leonora Yung and others*.[69] In this case, all parties were willing to seek mediation, but the plaintiff and the defendants could not reach an agreement on the mediation proposals.[70] Hence, they made a joint application to the court for directions on their points of difference. PD 31 allows the court to resolve differences between parties and facilitate mediation even if the parties are unable to reach consensus on the details of mediation. The court accordingly issued an order on the arrangement of costs and the commencement date of the mediation.

In an earlier case, *Resource Development Ltd* v. *Swanbridge Ltd*,[71] upon joint application of the parties, the court selected a mediator, determined the minimum level of participation, and ordered a stay of the proceedings. In the event that an application is made by only one party, the court can only decide on the timing of the Mediation Response, the venue of the mediation, the arrangement on costs, the minimum level of participation, and the commencement schedule.[72]

Hong Kong courts have also addressed the question of the minimum level of participation required of participants who agree to engage in mediation. In *Resource Development Ltd*, the court decided that the minimum

---

[69] *C Y Foundation Group Ltd* v. *Leonora Yung and others*, HCA933/2011.
[70] Practice Direction 31, para. 13: 'Where the parties are unable to reach agreement on certain proposals in the Mediation Notice and Mediation Response in relation to the mediation: (1) If the parties are willing to have their differences resolved by direction of the Court, they may make a joint application to the Court for directions resolving the points of difference between them; and (2) in the absence of such willingness, any party may apply to the Court for directions and the Court may give such directions as are appropriate to resolve differences between the parties regarding the proposals that they have each made in the Mediation Notice and the Mediation Response respectively'.
[71] *Resource Development Ltd* v. *Swanbridge Ltd*, HCA 1873/2009.
[72] See Practice Direction 31, para. 13(2), Appendix D, paras 4–7.

level of participation was 'agreement as to the terms of the appointment of the mediator and participation by the parties in the mediation up to and including one substantive mediation session (of a duration determined by the mediator)'.[73] This view was echoed in *Hak Tung Alfred Tang* v. *Bloomberg LP and another*, in which the court ruled that parties who agree to mediate must 'participate in the mediation up to and including at least one substantive mediation session'.[74] Participation in the mediation for at least one substantive mediation session at present satisfies the court's minimum requirement of participation.

4.4.2 Cost Implications for Unreasonable Failure to Engage in Mediation

An important implication of PD 31 is that an adverse costs order may be made against a party who unreasonably fails to engage in mediation.[75]

In *Golden Eagle International (Group) Ltd* v. *GR Investment Holdings Ltd*, the court provided a detailed discussion of what constitutes an 'unreasonable failure to engage in mediation' and the requisite burden of proof.[76] The court rejected the defence counsel's submission that the case (a simple contract dispute) was of a nature that could not easily be mediated,[77] and concluded that the defendant's reliance on the English case of *Halsey* v. *Milton Keynes General NHS Trust*[78] was inappropriate.[79]

The court nevertheless left open the question of whether the strength of a party's case could provide justifiable grounds for refusing mediation.[80] The court stated that a belief that one has a clear-cut strong case will be given little or no weight when considering whether refusal is reasonable.[81] In addition, the defendant could not rely on previous failed attempts to settle nor its own obdurate attitude to justify refusal to engage in mediation.[82]

As to the issue of burden of proof, the Hong Kong approach was distinguished from the position in *Halsey*. In *Halsey*, Dyson LJ held that

---

[73] *Resource Development Ltd*, n. 71 above, para. 8.
[74] *Hak Tung Alfred Tang* v. *Bloomberg LP and another*, HCA198/2010, paras 13, 15.
[75] Practice Direction 31, para. 5.
[76] *Golden Eagle International (Group) Ltd* v. *GR Investment Holdings Ltd*, HCA2032/2007; [2010] 3 HKLRD 273.
[77] *Ibid.* paras 22–3.
[78] [2004] 1 WLR 3002.
[79] *Golden Eagle International (Group) Ltd,* n. 76 above, para. 26.
[80] *Ibid.* para. 30.
[81] *Ibid.* paras 30–31.
[82] *Ibid.* paras 34–5.

the burden was on the willing party to show a reasonable prospect that mediation would have been successful.[83] However, Lam J interpreted paragraphs 4 and 5(2) of PD 31, and concluded that the burden of proof must fall on the refusing party to provide a reasonable explanation for not engaging in mediation.[84]

Golden Eagle International (Group) Ltd was adopted in *Wu Yim Kwong Kindwind* v. *Manhood Development Ltd*[85] and subsequent cases. *Wu Yim Kwong Kindwind* affirmed that the burden of proof must fall on the party refusing mediation. The court also rejected the defendant's argument that the dispute was of such a nature that it was not possible to come to a compromise.[86] Accordingly, it ordered costs against the defendant for violating the underlying objectives of Order 1A Rule 1 of the RHC.[87]

4.5 ANALYSIS OF RESEARCH RESULTS

Mediation Statistics in Hong Kong show a growing level of efficacy of the courts in relation to its mediation programme.[88]

From 2011 to 2014, 2,265 cases were mediated in the Court of First Instance (CFI), and 1,446 cases were mediated in the District Courts (DCs).[89] Among 2,265 mediated cases in the CFI, 938 of them reached full agreement, and 29 of them reached partial agreement.[90] Among 1,446 mediated cases in the DCs, 617 of them reached full agreement, and 18 of them reached partial agreement.[91] The percentage of mediation cases resulting in agreements increased from 38 per cent to 48 per cent during the period from 2011 to 2014.[92]

The average duration from the date of appointing a mediator to the date of completion for cases filed in the CFI was 39 days in 2012, 43 days in 2013, and 40 days in 2014.[93] In the DCs, the average duration was 27 days

---

[83] *Ibid.* para. 41.
[84] *Ibid.* paras 43–4.
[85] *Wu Yim Kwong Kindwind* v. *Manhood Development Ltd*, DCCJ3839/2012.
[86] *Ibid.* paras 15–20.
[87] *Ibid.* para. 36.
[88] Hong Kong Judiciary, 'Mediation Statistics for the Civil Justice Reform Cases', Annex B to the *Review of the Implementation of Civil Justice Reform* (2015).
[89] *Ibid.* 5, 7, 9, 11, 13, 15, 17, 19.
[90] *Ibid.* 5, 9, 13, 17.
[91] *Ibid.* 7, 11, 15, 19.
[92] *Ibid.* 4, 16.
[93] *Ibid.* 3.

in 2012, 29 days in 2013, and 33 days in 2014.[94] In both the DCs and CFI, an average of five or six hours was spent on mediation in order for cases to reach full agreement.[95] For cases reaching partial agreement, the average duration was similarly six hours.[96]

In terms of average costs for cases mediated in the CFI and reaching full agreement, costs were approximately HK$17,700.[97] For cases reaching partial agreement, the cost fluctuated from year to year, with an average of approximately HK$21,000.[98] Similarly, for mediated cases in the DC reaching full agreement, the average cost of mediation for each case was around HK$13,500.[99] For cases in the DC reaching partial agreement, the average cost was HK$16,800.[100]

4.5.1 Hong Kong's Civil Justice Rankings: Efficiency, Confidence and Perceptions of Justice

The voluntary mediation programme in Hong Kong can be examined within the larger context of its achievements in the areas of efficiency, confidence and perceptions of justice.

Table 4.1 shows positive movement over the past five years within Hong Kong in relation to its rankings in the areas of efficiency, confidence and perceptions of justice. Areas highlighted in grey indicate a positive movement in the rankings.

In terms of overall efficiency in the civil justice system, according to the *Global Competitiveness Report 2016–2017*,[101] Hong Kong ranked 2nd out of 138 countries in the efficiency of its legal framework in settling disputes. The accessibility and affordability of the civil justice system is 0.66[102] on a 1 point scale. Its score for 'no unreasonable delay' was 0.71[103] on a 1 point scale.

Confidence in court mediation systems can be examined in relation to the overall ranking of the civil justice system and ease of enforcement and impartiality and effectiveness of ADR. The overall rank for Hong Kong's

---

[94] *Ibid.*
[95] *Ibid.* 5, 7, 9, 11, 13, 15, 17, 19.
[96] *Ibid.*
[97] *Ibid.* 5, 9, 13, 17.
[98] *Ibid.*
[99] *Ibid.* 7, 11, 15, 19.
[100] *Ibid.*
[101] World Economic Forum, *Global Competitiveness Report 2016–2017*, pp. 196–7.
[102] World Justice Project, *Rule of Law Index 2016*, p. 84.
[103] See n. 101 above.

Table 4.1 Hong Kong rankings: developments in efficiency, confidence and perceptions of justice, 2011–2016*

	2011	2016
Efficiency		
• Efficiency of legal framework in settling disputes (rank)	5th/142	2nd/138
• Accessibility and affordability (percentile)	0.64	0.66
• No unreasonable delay (percentile)	0.7	0.71
Confidence		
• Civil justice (rank)	12th/66	12th/113
• Effective enforcement (percentile)	0.78	0.81
• Impartial and effective ADR (percentile)	0.7	0.81
Perceptions of justice		
• Rule of law (percentile)	0.91	0.95**
• No discrimination (percentile)	0.56	0.8

* Greyed rows indicate a positive trend in the rankings.
** World Bank Group, *Worldwide Governance Indicators 2015*, available at http://info.worldbank.org/governance/wgi/index.aspx#home.

civil justice in the *Rule of Law Index 2016*[104] was 12th out of 113 countries. Its scores for effective enforcement and impartial and effective ADR were both 0.81[105] on a 1 point scale.

Finally, with respect to perceptions of justice, Hong Kong's rule of law score was 95 on a 100 point scale in 2015.[106] The score for 'no discrimination' was 0.8.[107]

4.6 CONCLUSION

The Hong Kong court mediation programme has largely developed on the basis of the UK model, employing a robust encouragement of mediation by courts. Usage rates have increased over the past five years. Similarly, the percentage of cases reaching agreement has also increased. As can be

---

[104] See n. 102 above.
[105] See n. 102 above.
[106] World Bank Group, *Worldwide Governance Indicators 2015*, available at http://info.worldbank.org/governance/wgi/index.aspx#home.
[107] See n. 102 above.

seen above, Hong Kong's mediation programme has resulted in positive developments in the areas of efficiency, as measured by accessibility and affordability; reduction in delay; confidence, as measured by effective enforcement and impartial and effective ADR; and perceptions of justice, as measured by its percentiles in rule of law and absence of discrimination. This appears to indicate that the voluntary mediation programme as implemented in Hong Kong has resulted in significant successes in recent years.

5. Mediation in the French courts

5.1 GENERAL INTRODUCTION

While mediation has had a long history in France, it was only codified into law in the twentieth century. Under French law, both civil and criminal matters can be referred to mediation. However, mediation is most frequently used in domestic and small claims cases.[1] For judicial mediation, party consent is required to proceed with mediation[2] reflecting the importance of voluntariness in French mediation.

The French approach to voluntary mediation was significantly influenced by the European Union Directive on Mediation. On 21 May 2008, the European Parliament and the European Council issued Directive 2008/52/EC of the European Parliament and of the Council of 21 May 2008 on certain aspects of mediation in civil and commercial matters ('EU Directive'). This Directive sought to encourage the use of alternative dispute resolution (ADR), particularly mediation in cross-border civil and commercial disputes, and to ensure a balanced relationship between mediation and judicial proceedings.[3] It provided a general framework for mediation, including the definition, quality and accessibility of mediation, and the enforceability of settlement agreements.[4]

Giving effect to the EU Directive, on 16 November 2011, the French Ministry of Justice and Freedoms issued Ordonnance (Ordinance) No. 2011/1540 of 16 November 2011 (the 'Mediation Ordinance') transposing Directive 2008/52/EC. The Mediation Ordinance provided for confidentiality of mediation communications with some exceptions.[5] The Ordinance

---

[1] European e-Justice Portal, *Mediation in Member States: France* (27 September 2013), available at https://e-justice.europa.eu/content_mediation_in_member_states-64-fr-en.do?member51.

[2] Code of Civil Procedure (Code de procédure civile), art. 131-1.

[3] Directive 2008/52/EC of the European Parliament and of the Council of 21 May 2008 on certain aspects of mediation in civil and commercial matters, art. 1 [2008] OJ L136/3.

[4] *Ibid.*

[5] Ordonnance no. 2011-1540 du 16 novembre 2011 portant transposition de la directive 2008/52/CE du Parlement européen et du Conseil du 21 mai 2008

also confirmed that the court had the power to appoint a mediator, established the possibility for courts to give effect to settlement agreements, and specified that the provisions did not apply to criminal proceedings. Below, we will examine in greater detail the French approach to voluntary mediation in civil and commercial disputes.

5.2 LAW/POLICY BACKGROUND

Prior to the publication of the Mediation Ordinance,[6] judicial mediation in France was governed by Law No. 95-125 of 8 February 1995 on the organization of the courts and civil, criminal and administrative law ('Law of 8 February 1995'),[7] which was later amended by the Mediation Ordinance.

The EU Directive, which brought about the subsequent amendment of the French Mediation law, was issued on 21 May 2008. Article 12 of the Directive stated that, 'Member States shall bring into force the laws, regulations, and administrative provisions necessary to comply with this Directive before 21 May 2011'.[8] Since France did not transpose the Directive into its domestic legislation within the prescribed time-frame, on 22 July 2011, the European Commission sent a letter of formal notice to France and invited it to transpose the EU Directive.[9] This led to the issuance of the subsequent Ordinance No. 2011/1540.

On 16 November 2011, the Mediation Ordinance was issued to transpose the EU Directive into French law. Decree No. 2012-66 of 20 January 2012 on the amicable resolution of disputes was issued on 20 January

---

sur certains aspects de la médiation en matière civile et commerciale (Ordinance No. 2011/1540 of 16 November 2011 transposing Directive 2008/52/EC of the European Parliament and of the Council of 21 May 2008 on certain aspects of mediation in civil and commercial matters).

[6] Ministère de la Justice (Ministry of Justice), *Un nouveau cadre pour la médiation* [*A New Framework for Mediation*] (23 November 2011), available at www.justice.gouv.fr/le-ministere-de-la-justice-10017/direction-des-affaires-civiles-et-du-sceau-10023/un-nouveau-cadre-pour-la-mediation-23229.html.

[7] Loi no. 95-125 of 8 février 1995 relative à l'organisation des juridictions et à la procédure civile, pénale et administrative.

[8] Directive 2008/52/EC, art. 12.

[9] European Judicial Enforcement, Letter of formal notice sent by the European Commission to 9 Member States for failure to communicate the transposition measures of the Directive on mediation in civil and commercial matters, available at www.europe-eje.eu/en/actualite/letter-formal-notice-european-commission-9-member-failure-communicate-transposition-measur.

2012 to implement Ordinance No. 2011/1540 and incorporate it into the Code of Civil Procedure (Code de procédure civile).[10] It added Book V on amicable dispute resolution into the Code of Civil Procedure, which could be read together with Title VI on conciliation and mediation of Book I. It also amended relevant provisions in the Labour Code (Code du travail) and other related codes and laws.[11]

5.3 PURPOSE/RATIONALE BEHIND THE PROGRAMME

The aim of the EU Directive was to improve access to justice through the use of mediation and to maintain amicable relationships between parties in cross-border disputes.[12] France, as a Member State of the European Union, was obliged to abide by the Directive and to set a legal framework for mediation in cross-border disputes.

Nevertheless, despite efforts to encourage mediation, given the public's overall unfamiliarity and scepticism regarding the process, such efforts yielded limited results. Thierry Garby, the Vice-Chairman of the International Bar Association's Mediation Committee, noted that only a small proportion of commercial disputes in France went through mediation.[13] This view was shared by French scholar Arnaud Stimec who said, 'mediation seems to be still largely unknown or even worse misunderstood'.[14]

The limited use and understanding of mediation in France has been attributed to a number of factors, among them the public's relatively high level of trust in court proceedings, which have had a long history in France.[15]

---

[10] Décret no. 2012-66 du 20 janvier 2012 relatif à la résolution amiable des différends.
[11] *Ibid.*
[12] Directive 2008/52/EC, Preamble.
[13] T. Garby, 'The French Pledge for Mediation' (2006) 2 *Mediation Newsletter* (International Bar Association Legal Practice Division, April), as cited in A. Altman, 'Alternative Dispute Resolution in France' in F.P. Phillips, 'France: Current State of Arbitration and Mediation' *Business Conflict Blog* (4 June 2012), available at http://businessconflictmanagement.com/blog/2012/06/france-current-state-of-arbitration-and-mediation/.
[14] A. Stimec, 'Mediation Within or Between Organisations in France: State of Development, Barriers and Paths', paper presented at the 2001 International Association for Conflict Management Conference, 2001, as cited in Altman, 'Alternative Dispute Resolution in France' (n. 13 above).
[15] See n. 10 above.

Other factors include[16] distrust and scepticism of changes initiated by foreign bodies outside of France. Mediation was regarded as a foreign mechanism new to the French culture. Secondly, significant changes in the administration of justice, it was thought, should come about through legislative action rather than through the judiciary, which was seen as an arm of the government.[17] Thirdly, France, as a civil law system, saw the role of the courts as applying laws, rather than exploring party interests and engaging in problem solving processes.[18]

The adoption of the EU Directive helped mediation gain some degree of popularity among the French community. First, by transposing the Directive into French law, it became part of the French legal system. Secondly, as this legislative change was initiated by the Ministry of Justice and Freedoms, instead of by the courts, citizens could more easily accept the Directive as binding law. Ultimately, the issuance of Ordinance No. 2011/1540 assisted in overcoming some of the above-mentioned barriers in promoting the use of mediation.[19]

5.4 PROGRAMME FEATURES

The French Mediation Ordinance No. 2011/1540, along with other Acts and rules relating to mediation, introduced changes to the mediation landscape, including providing a definition, outlining mediation procedures, setting ground rules, ensuring confidentiality, and enforcing settlement agreements. Each of these elements will be discussed in greater detail below.

5.4.1 Definition of Mediation

Prior to the issuance of the Mediation Ordinance, there was no clear definition of 'mediation' in France. The Ordinance described the voluntary nature of mediation defined as:

> a structured process, however named, whereby two or more parties to a dispute attempt by themselves to reach an amicable agreement on the settlement of their dispute with the assistance of a neutral third party, the mediator, chosen by the parties, or with the parties' consent, named by the judge.[20]

---

[16] Altman, 'Alternative Dispute Resolution in France' (n. 13 above).
[17] *Ibid.*
[18] *Ibid.*
[19] Directive 2008/52/EC, Preamble, recital 30.
[20] Mediation Ordinance, art. 1.

This definition was subsequently included in article 21 of the Law of 8 February 1995. This relatively open definition of mediation allowed for a great deal of flexibility in practice.

5.4.2 Procedures and Scheduling of Mediation

The scheduling of court-based mediation is described in article 22 of the Law of 8 February 1995, as amended by Ordinance No. 2011/1540. Under this law, the judge, with the agreement of the parties, may in any court proceeding appoint a mediator to conduct mediation.[21] The procedures of judicial mediation are set out in articles 131-1 to 131-15 of the Code of Civil Procedure. Under this law, the judge has the power to direct parties to mediation for all or part of the dispute, subject to the agreement of the parties.[22] The duration of the mediation[23] may not exceed three months.[24] This term may be renewed[25] at the request of the mediator or by the judge.[26]

The mediation direction must indicate the agreement of the parties, the mediator, the duration of the initial mediation session and the date of the court hearing.[27] It must estimate the expected remuneration to the mediator and the contribution of each party.[28] If the mediation order is not properly executed, it will be rendered void and court proceedings will continue.[29]

Upon the issuance of the mediation order, the court registry notifies the parties and the mediator by delivering a copy of the decision through ordinary post.[30] The mediator must reply with his acceptance of the appointment[31] after which the mediator summons the parties to conduct mediation.[32]

The mediation may be terminated at the request of the parties or the mediator,[33] or where improper conduct is found in mediation after a

---

[21] Law of 8 February 1995, art. 22.
[22] Code of Civil Procedure, arts 131-1, 131-2.
[23] Law of 8 February 1995, art. 22-3.
[24] Code of Civil Procedure, art. 131-3.
[25] *Ibid.* art. 131-3.
[26] Law of 8 February 1995, art. 22-3.
[27] Code of Civil Procedure, art. 131-6.
[28] *Ibid.* art. 131-6.
[29] *Ibid.* art. 131-6.
[30] *Ibid.* art. 131-7.
[31] *Ibid.* art. 131-7.
[32] *Ibid.* art. 131-7.
[33] Law of 8 February 1995, art. 22-3.

hearing.[34] A decision to renew or terminate the mediation is not subject to appeal.[35] The mediator must keep the judge informed of any difficulties encountered during the course of mediation.[36] At the end of the mediation, the mediator must advise the judge of the outcome of the mediation.[37] In cases where an agreement is reached, the parties request the judge to approve the agreement and render it enforceable.[38]

With respect to mediation costs,[39] under article 22-2 of the Law of 8 February 1995, the prima facie rule is that parties are free to determine the distribution of costs. In cases where an agreement cannot be reached by the parties, the costs are to be borne equally by the parties, unless it would cause unfairness in light of the respective financial circumstances of the parties.[40]

5.4.3 Ground Rules

At present, there are no national rules governing the conduct of mediators nor the process of mediation. There is also no central authority regulating mediators. Each mediation service provider has its own rules and code of conduct. For example, the Centre de Médiation et d'Arbitrage de Paris (Paris Mediation and Arbitration Centre), and the Chambre arbitrale internationale de Paris (International Arbitration Chamber of Paris) each has its own distinct Rules of Mediation. In 2008, the Fédération Nationale des Centres de Médiation (National Federation of Mediation Centres) approved a code of ethics on the basis of the European Code of Conduct for Mediators.[41] The International Chamber of Commerce also has its own ICC Mediation Rules which have been in force from 2014.

Certain key features are included in most of France's mediation centre codes and rules. For example, the mediator must be neutral, independent and impartial. It is also of utmost importance that all information arising out of or in connection with the mediation should be kept confidential and not be disclosed to others without prior consent.

Mediator conduct is regulated under article 21-2 of the Law of 8 February 1995. According to this law, mediators must perform their duties

---

[34] Code of Civil Procedure, art. 131-10.
[35] *Ibid.* art. 131-15.
[36] *Ibid.* art. 131-9.
[37] *Ibid.* art. 131-11.
[38] *Ibid.* art. 131-12.
[39] *Ibid.* art. 131-13.
[40] Law of 8 February 1995, art. 22-2.
[41] See n. 1 above.

impartially, competently and expeditiously.[42] Article 131-5 of the Code of Civil Procedure provides guidance regarding the conditions that a mediator must satisfy.[43] First, he should not be under conviction, disability or forfeiture, and should not have a criminal record. Secondly, he must not have committed any dishonest or immoral act resulting in a disciplinary or administrative sanction. Thirdly, he must possess the necessary qualifications and competency to handle the dispute in question and must have proper training and experience in mediation practice. Fourthly, he must be independent and impartial. The French Code of Civil Procedure also clarifies that a mediator does not have investigative powers in conducting the mediation.[44]

5.4.4 Settlement Agreement and its Enforceability

With respect to the enforceability of mediation agreements, article 21–5 of the Law of 8 February 1995 stipulates that the agreement is subject to the judge's approval, and binding on parties.[45] Similarly, article 131–12 of the Code of Civil Procedure notes that settlement agreements may be recognized by the court at the request of the parties.[46] Under article 384 of the same Code, the judge is empowered to give legal force to the parties' agreement and to officially terminate legal proceedings.[47]

5.5 IMPLEMENTATION IN PRACTICE

French court cases heard subsequent to Ordinance No. 2011/1540 reflect the French courts' adoption of the Mediation Ordinance and the EU Directive. They also reaffirm the voluntary nature of court-referred mediation in France.

5.5.1 Court's Power to Refer Cases to Mediation

The court's power to refer cases to mediation subject to party agreement was affirmed in two recent cases.

Reaffirming the voluntary nature of court mediation, in case 13/04973,

---

[42] Law of 8 February 1995, art. 21-2.
[43] Code of Civil Procedure, art. 131-5.
[44] *Ibid.* art. 131-8.
[45] Law of 8 February 1995, art. 21-5.
[46] Code of Civil Procedure, art. 131-12.
[47] *Ibid.* art. 384.

one party requested that the court order mediation. However, the other party opposed the request. Since the court could not obtain agreement of the parties in accordance with article 131-1 of the Code of Civil Procedure, it did not order mediation as requested.[48]

In the divorce case 14/04022, the High Court judge suggested that the parties participate in mediation pursuant to the parties' agreement.[49] However, the mediation did not lead to a fruitful outcome and eventually the court proceedings continued.[50]

The procedures of judicial mediation were set out in case 13/02750.[51] In this case, the mediator was ordered to abide by article 131-4 of the Code of Civil Procedure which set out that a mediation must be completed within three months of the parties' agreement to mediation and could be renewed for another three months upon the mediator's request. Costs must be split on the basis of fairness and the final outcome must be reported to the court.

5.5.2 Effect of Mediation on Limitation Period

In relation to the effects of mediation on judicial limitation periods, the court gave effect to Article 8 of the EU Directive as adopted in the Civil Code. It ruled that participation in a mediation would suspend the limitation period, and would not prevent a party from initiating judicial proceedings or arbitration in relation to a dispute by the expiry of the limitation period.[52]

---

[48] Cour d'appel de Nîmes, 26 March 2015, 13/04973, available at www.legifrance.gouv.fr/affichJuriJudi.do?oldAction5rechJuriJudi&idTexte5JURITEXT000030417845&fastReqId51477121683&fastPos58.

[49] Cour d'appel de Rennes, 8 December 2015, 14/04022, available at www.legifrance.gouv.fr/affichJuriJudi.do?oldAction5rechJuriJudi&idTexte5JURITEXT000031617176&fastReqId51477121683&fastPos53.

[50] See Cour d'appel de Versailles, 13 July 2011, 09/03901, available at www.legifrance.gouv.fr/affichJuriJudi.do?oldAction5rechJuriJudi&idTexte5JURITEXT000024371613&fastReqId51532084963&fastPos52; see also Cour d'appel de Versailles, 11 May 2011, 10/01487, available at www.legifrance.gouv.fr/affichJuriJudi.do?oldAction5rechJuriJudi&idTexte5JURITEXT000024005761&fastReqId51532084963&fastPos54.

[51] Cour d'appel de Montpellier, 26 March 2014, 13/02750, available at www.legifrance.gouv.fr/affichJuriJudi.do?oldAction5rechJuriJudi&idTexte5JURITEXT000029200476&fastReqId51532084963&fastPos51; see also Cour d'appel de Versailles, 11 May 2011, 10/01487, available at www.legifrance.gouv.fr/affichJuriJudi.do?oldAction5rechJuriJudi&idTexte5JURITEXT000024005761&fastReqId51532084963&fastPos54.

[52] See Cour de cassation, civile, Chambre civile 1, 11 September 2013, 12-15103, Inédit, available at www.legifrance.gouv.fr/affichJuriJudi.do?oldAction5rechJuriJudi&idTexte5JURITEXT000027952260&fastReqId51257353088&fastPos51.

5.5.3 Court's Power to Monitor Organizations Providing ADR Services

With respect to a court's power to oversee the conduct of ADR service providers, in case 15-82429, the court ruled that an ADR service provider was criminally liable for deceptive trade practice.[53] In that case, the ADR provider advertised in leaflets that he could provide faster speed, lower cost, higher quality and more effective mediation services. It was ruled that the leaflet was likely to mislead an average consumer, who would likely be vulnerable when engaging the defendant's services, and would likely have been induced into the transaction due to the misleading statements.

5.5.4 Enforceability of Settlement Agreement

As stated in the Code of Civil Procedure, the court has the power to dismiss legal proceedings, approve settlement agreements and make them legally binding. In case 13/05058, the Court of Appeal of Rennes approved the agreement arising out of a domestic mediation and made it a legally enforceable document.[54] In another case 12/19285, the court relied on article 384 to enforce the party's mediation agreement and to discontinue legal proceedings.[55]

In case 10-14.992, the Court of Appeal enforced a settlement agreement, and the Supreme Court ruled that *'res judicata'*[56] applied in respect of the settlement agreement.[57] Hence, no claim could be raised based on the same cause of action in a later instance, as the agreement was binding between the parties.

---

[53] Cour de cassation, criminelle, Chambre criminelle, 22 March 2016, 15-82429, Inédit, available at https://www.legifrance.gouv.fr/affichJuriJudi.do?oldAction5rechJuriJudi&idTexte5JURITEXT000032311787&fastReqId51532084963&fastPos56www.legifrance.gouv.fr/affichJuriJudi.do?oldAction5rechJuriJudi&idTexte5JURITEXT000032311787&fastReqId51532084963&fastPos56.

[54] Cour d'appel de Rennes, 2 December 2014, 13/05058, available at www.legifrance.gouv.fr/affichJuriJudi.do?oldAction5rechJuriJudi&idTexte5JURITEXT000029860675&fastReqId5754179536&fastPos52.

[55] Cour d'appel de Paris, 25 September 2014, 12/19285, available at www.legifrance.gouv.fr/affichJuriJudi.do?oldAction5rechJuriJudi&idTexte5JURITEXT000029520667&fastReqId5754179536&fastPos53.

[56] A matter that has been adjudicated by a competent court and therefore may not be pursued further by the same parties.

[57] Cour de cassation, civile, Chambre sociale, 28 February 2012, 10-14.992, Inédit, available at www.legifrance.gouv.fr/affichJuriJudi.do?oldAction5rechJuriJudi&idTexte5JURITEXT000025437527&fastReqId5754179536&fastPos55.

5.6 ANALYSIS OF RESEARCH RESULTS

According to a report published by the Ministry of Justice in 2013, there were only 3,369 cases in the Tribunaux de grande instance (Courts of First Instance) in which parties engaged in mediation.[58] Overall, 593 civil cases were referred to mediation in 2013, 514 in 2012, and 277 in 2011.[59] Only in 46 cases did the court appoint a mediator in 2013, 46 in 2012, and 79 in 2011.[60] A settlement agreement was reached in only 5 per cent of cases in which a mediator intervened, as compared with a 3 per cent settlement rate when no mediator intervened.[61]

The number of applications intended to give effect to mediated agreements totalled 16 before the Court of Appeal and 1,158 before the Tribunaux de grande instance in 2013.[62] Most of these applications were to enforce settlement agreements reached by parties pursuant to mediation. The average cost of non-family mediation was estimated at between €1,500 and €2,000.[63]

For conventional mediation entered into by parties, usage rates appear higher overall. The Mediator of Economic and Financial Ministries received 2,197 applications for mediation in 2013, among which 1,865 were admissible.[64] Mediations led to satisfactory settlements in 63 per cent of cases.[65] The Club of Mediators for Public Service (Ce médiateur appartient au club des médiateurs de service au public) received 110,853 cases resulting in 46,536 mediations.[66] In 2013, the Inter-enterprises Mediator offered mediation in relation to extensive commercial disputes, handling a total of 850 cases with a success rate of 80 per cent.[67]

---

[58] Inspection Générale des Services Judiciaires (General Inspectorate of Judicial Services), *Rapport sur le développement des modes amiables de règlement des différends* [*Report on the Development of Amicable Dispute Settlement Modes*], No. 22–15 (April 2015) p. 19.
[59] *Ibid.*
[60] *Ibid.* 19.
[61] *Ibid.*
[62] *Ibid.* 17.
[63] *Ibid.* 21.
[64] *Ibid.* 23.
[65] *Ibid.*
[66] *Ibid.*
[67] *Ibid.*

Table 5.1 France's rankings: developments in efficiency, confidence and perceptions of justice, 2011–2016*

	2011	2016
Efficiency		
• Efficiency of legal framework in settling disputes (rank)	22nd/142	22nd/138
• Accessibility and affordability (percentile)	0.66	0.62
• No unreasonable delay (percentile)	0.44	0.6
Confidence		
• Civil justice (rank)	14th/66	23rd/113
• Effective enforcement (percentile)	0.56	0.7
• Impartial and effective ADR (percentile)	0.8	0.84
Perceptions of justice		
• Rule of law (percentile)	0.90	0.88**
• No discrimination (percentile)	0.59	0.7

* Greyed rows indicate a positive trend in the rankings.
** World Bank Group, *Worldwide Governance Indicators 2015*, available at http://info.worldbank.org/governance/wgi/index.aspx#home.

5.6.1 France's Civil Justice Rankings: Efficiency, Confidence and Perceptions of Justice

The voluntary mediation programme in France can be examined within the larger context of its achievements in the areas of efficiency, confidence and perceptions of justice.

Table 5.1 shows positive movement over the past five years within France's rankings in the areas of efficiency, confidence and perceptions of justice. Areas highlighted in grey indicate a positive movement in the rankings. As can be seen, over the past five years, France has experienced positive development in the areas of efficiency, as measured by reduction in delay; confidence, as measured by effective enforcement and impartial and effective ADR; and perceptions of justice, as measured by its percentile in absence of discrimination. This appears to indicate that the voluntary mediation programme as implemented in France has resulted in some significant contributions to the workings of its civil justice system in recent years.

In terms of overall efficiency in the civil justice system, according to the *Global Competitiveness Report 2016–2017*,[68] France ranks 22nd out of 138

---

[68] World Economic Forum, *The Global Competitiveness Report 2016–2017*, pp. 178–9.

countries in the efficiency of its legal framework in settling disputes. The accessibility and affordability of the civil justice system is 0.62 on a 1 point scale.[69] Its score for 'no unreasonable delay' was 0.6 on a 1 point scale.[70]

The overall rank for France's civil justice in the *Rule of Law Index 2016*[71] was 23rd out of 113 countries. Its scores for effective enforcement and impartial and effective ADR were 0.7 and 0.84 on a 1 point scale, respectively.[72]

Finally, with respect to perceptions of justice, the percentile for rule of law was 88 on a 100 point scale in 2015.[73] The score for 'no discrimination' was 0.7 on a 1 point scale.[74]

5.7 CONCLUSION

Despite general public scepticism toward ADR in France, the overall number of mediated cases has been increasing. This has largely been the result of efforts at public information in the civil and commercial sectors. Over the past five years, France has experienced positive development in the areas of efficiency, as measured by reduction in delay; confidence, as measured by effective enforcement and impartial and effective ADR; and perceptions of justice, as measured by its percentile in reduction of discrimination. This appears to indicate that the voluntary mediation programme as implemented in France has been associated with some significant contributions to the workings of its civil justice system in recent years.

---

[69] World Justice Project, *Rule of Law Index 2016*, p. 75.
[70] See n. 68 above.
[71] See n. 69 above.
[72] See n. 69 above.
[73] World Bank Group, *Worldwide Governance Indicators 2015*, available at http://info.worldbank.org/governance/wgi/index.aspx#home.
[74] See n. 69 above.

6. Mediation in the Dutch courts

6.1 INTRODUCTION

Since 2007, Dutch courts may make use of a voluntary mediation faculty in all courts of first instance and appeal.[1] While mediation processes in the Netherlands are unique in that they are not subject to legal controls, the uptake of mediation in the Netherlands has been lauded as a success. Governmental policy relating to court-connected mediation in the Netherlands has been to normalize the mediation process as a 'customizable' tool to be utilized where the needs of parties require it, as opposed to a cost-cutting measure aimed at relieving burdens on the judicial system. This chapter examines the operation of the mediation referral programme implemented by party agreement,[2] as piloted at the beginning of the twenty-first century, in the Dutch courts, qualitative and quantitative figures on its performance, and examination of the overall experience of efficacy, confidence and perceptions of justice.

Since the programme was introduced in 2007, the Netherlands has experienced positive development in the areas of efficiency, as measured by accessibility and affordability and reduction of delay; confidence, as measured by its overall civil justice ranking, effective enforcement and impartial and effective ADR; and perceptions of justice, as measured by its percentile in the reduction of discrimination.

6.2 LAW AND POLICY BACKGROUND

6.2.1 Pro-conciliation Legal Culture and Lack of Regulation

From the perspective of legal culture, the Dutch preference for extra-judicial negotiation of disputes, coupled with the role of lawyers in encouraging

---

[1] M. Pel, 'Regulation of Dispute Resolution in the Netherlands: Does Regulation Support or Hinder the Use of ADR?' in F. Steffek et al. (eds), *Regulating Dispute Resolution: ADR and Access to Justice at the Crossroads* (Oxford: Hart, 2013) p. 316.
[2] P. Albers, '27. The Netherlands' in G. De Palo and M.B. Trevor (eds), *EU Mediation Law and Practice* (Oxford University Press, 2012) p. 27.

111

settlement[3] and the general perception of judicial adjudication as a tool of last resort,[4] provides policy context for the introduction of voluntary court-connected mediation into the Dutch judiciary. Rather than aiming at alleviating an overburdened judicial system, the stated purpose of developing court-connected mediation services in the Dutch courts was to provide court users with a further option, in addition to the existing methods of judicial adjudication and court settlement, of alternate dispute resolution (ADR).[5]

Notwithstanding the policy to stimulate the development of ADR, it was believed that imposing regulations on mediation procedure could stymie its development.[6] In implementing the European Union (EU) Directive 2008/52/EC on certain aspects of mediation in civil and commercial matters (the 'Mediation Directive'), the relevant alterations relating to confidentiality of the mediation process, enforceability of the mediation agreement and the statute of limitations were made via amendments to the Civil Procedure Code (CPC), rather than a designated law.[7] Legislative additions on the regulation of particular aspects of mediation are currently under discussion.[8]

6.2.2 Development of the Dutch Mediation Programme

Mediation as a form of ADR first gained attention in the 1990s.[9] This led to the establishment by the Ministry of Justice in 1996 of an ADR committee, 'Platform ADR', with the purpose of investigating the possibility of developing ADR processes and consequently the court-connected media-

---

[3] Pel, 'Regulation of Dispute Resolution in the Netherlands' (n. 1 above) p. 315. Indeed, art. 3 of the Code of Conduct of the Dutch Bar Association stipulates that lawyers should operate on the principle and with consideration that an amicable settlement is preferable over litigation.

[4] Pel, 'Regulation of Dispute Resolution in the Netherlands' (n. 1 above) p. 315.

[5] M. Pel and L. Combrink, 'Referral to Mediation by the Netherlands Judiciary' in *Customized Conflict Resolution: Court-Connected Mediation in the Netherlands 1999–2009, Judicially Quarterly 2011* (The Hague: Sdu Uitgeverij, 2011) p. 25.

[6] Pel, 'Regulation of Dispute Resolution in the Netherlands' (n. 1 above) p. 310.

[7] Albers, '27. The Netherlands' (n. 2 above) p. 358.

[8] Pel, 'Regulation of Dispute Resolution in the Netherlands' (n. 1 above) p. 324.

[9] M.W. De Hoon and S. Verberk, 'Towards a More Responsive Judge: Challenges and Opportunities' (2014) 10(4) *Utrecht Law Review* 27, 29.

tion referral programme.[10] The discussions below provide an overview of the pilot, implementation and consolidation phases establishing the court referral programme.

In the pilot phase commencing in September 1999, the objective was to develop and operate voluntary referral to mediation services in at least four courts from 2000 to 2002, to determine whether such services were suitable for expansion on a nationwide basis.[11] The project commenced with the establishment of the Netherlands Court-Connected Mediation Agency (Landelijk bureau Mediation naast rechtspraak, LBM) to oversee the initiative.[12] By July 2000, six pilot projects including the Court of Appeal in Arnhem and five first-instance courts had established mediation referral services.[13] The data collected in the six projects was analysed by the Research and Documentation Centre of the Ministry of Justice (WODC), which concluded that a permanent mechanism for in-court mediation referrals within the judicial process was viable.[14] In 2002, the LBM completed a forecast study to determine the steps required to implement referral services in the Dutch judicial system, electing for phased implementation following consultation with the presidents of the courts.[15] In consultation with the Netherlands Mediation Institution (NMI), subsidized legal aid and judicial referral services were instituted.[16]

The national implementation of judicial referral services to mediation was announced by the Minister of Justice in April 2004.[17] The objective of the implementation phase was to establish referral services in all courts by April 2007, following a pre-determined schedule.[18] Each implementing court was provided with manuals, training courses, informational meetings and an LBM-allocated coach to instruct and provide common standards to all relevant personnel as to the goals and operation of the court-connected mediation service.[19] Mediators were invited to sign up to act as mediators for court-referred mediation.[20] May 2007 saw the entry

---

[10] *Ibid.* 29.
[11] Pel and Combrink, 'Referral to Mediation by the Netherlands Judiciary' (n. 5 above) p. 25.
[12] *Ibid.* 26.
[13] *Ibid.*
[14] *Ibid.*
[15] *Ibid.*
[16] *Ibid.*
[17] *Ibid.*
[18] *Ibid.* 27.
[19] *Ibid.*
[20] *Ibid.*

into the consolidation phase, which focused not only on the continued operation and consolidation of judicial referral service within Dutch courts, but on the normalization of court-referred mediation as a form of customized dispute resolution by members of the legal profession, judiciary and litigants.[21] Notably, court-referred mediation was viewed as an addition, rather than a blind replacement, of judicial adjudication.[22] While the LBM had played an integral role in the establishment and consolidation of the mediation referral system, it was succeeded by the Expert Group Customized Conflict Resolution programme in October 2009.[23]

6.3 PROGRAMME FEATURES

6.3.1 Referral to Mediation

Legal disputes may be referred to mediation by one of three processes: written referral, oral referral or self-referral.[24] In the early stages of the judicial process, *written referrals* are made upon positive determination by court staff that the case to be heard is suitable for mediation, at which point the option of mediation is proposed to the parties by letter.[25] An informational brochure and a 'self-test' are received with the letter, to help parties decide in light of the recommendation whether to opt for mediation.[26] The parties may then sign up for mediation by contacting the mediation officer at court.[27] Where mediation is considered a viable alternative during the trial, an *oral referral* presenting the option to the parties may be made by the judge.[28] Where the parties agree to mediate, the judge contacts the mediation officer at court.[29] Alternatively, *self-*

---

[21] *Ibid.*
[22] *Ibid.*
[23] *Ibid.* 28.
[24] Pel, 'Regulation of Dispute Resolution in the Netherlands' (n. 1 above) 317.
[25] Pel and Combrink, 'Referral to Mediation by the Netherlands Judiciary' (n. 5 above) p. 36.
[26] *Ibid.* 30. The 'self-test' consists of a list of possible considerations attached to the overarching question, 'Are you willing to cooperate in reaching a solution by mutual agreement?'. Where the answer to the question is affirmative, parties are encouraged to opt for mediation.
[27] *Ibid.* 53.
[28] *Ibid.* 30.
[29] *Ibid.* 31.

referral, in which the parties proactively agree to mediate by contacting the mediation officer, is a third avenue by which legal disputes may enter the mediation process.[30]

The mediation officer, the head of the mediation administrative office at all courts, plays an integral role in facilitating the parties' decision whether to refer their dispute to mediation, as he or she is the first port of call to address queries concerning the mediation process.[31] The mediation officer typically advises parties on mediation procedure, distinction from ordinary judicial procedure, expectations and obligations of both parties, as well as other key features, including its voluntary nature and confidentiality of proceedings.[32] Once referral to mediation is made, the case is stayed from judicial progress for three months, being the maximum time allocated to mediation.[33] Extensions may be sought where deemed necessary and with the agreement of all parties involved.[34]

6.3.2 Mediation Process

The mediation process, once commenced, is supervised by the mediation officer, whose duties include administering and keeping records of its progress, e.g. filing procedural steps taken by parties, or outcome of the session, in a 'mediation file'.[35] The mediation officer is responsible for encouraging the timely resolution of disputes by mediation.[36]

Once the parties decide to enter mediation, the mediation officer assists parties in selecting a mediator, by providing a list of qualified mediators and providing specific advice as to business experience, background and rates.[37] Where multiple parties are involved in the conflict, or the

---

[30] Pel, 'Regulation of Dispute Resolution in the Netherlands' (n. 1 above) p. 317.
[31] Pel and Combrink, 'Referral to Mediation by the Netherlands Judiciary' (n. 5 above) p. 31.
[32] *Ibid.* 31.
[33] *Ibid.* 30.
[34] Pel, 'Regulation of Dispute Resolution in the Netherlands' (n. 1 above) p. 319.
[35] Pel and Combrink, 'Referral to Mediation by the Netherlands Judiciary' (n. 5 above) p. 31.
[36] Pel, 'Regulation of Dispute Resolution in the Netherlands' (n. 1 above) p. 319.
[37] De Rechtspraak, *Procedure mediation naast rechtspraak*, available at www.rechtspraak.nl/Uw-Situatie/Onderwerpen/mediation-naast-rechtspraak/Procedure-mediation-naast-rechtspraak. Additionally, external mediators must comply with the quality requirements set by the Netherlands Mediation Institute (NMI) as well as any conditions set by the Council for the Judiciary. Such

dispute is complex in nature, more than one mediator may be engaged to address facets of the case or provide expertise.[38] The mediation officer also ensures that neither party has pre-existing personal or business relationships with the chosen mediator, so as to avoid conflicts of interest.[39] This may be the case where the parties are corporate entities seeking to engage their own in-house mediator.[40] Once the mediator is selected, the mediation officer schedules the first session between the parties and the external mediator.[41]

The first mediation session is generally scheduled to occur within two weeks of the referral, regardless of the method of referral.[42] In order to ensure full mediator impartiality, the mediator is not briefed on the dispute prior to the first meeting.[43] At the first meeting, the ground rules, procedure and proposed areas for mediation are decided and established by the parties, as facilitated by the mediator.[44] The mediator identifies the areas of dispute, existing impediments to resolution, and verifies that the persons present are the appropriate personnel to do so.[45] If preferred by the parties, a mediation agreement concretizing the agreements relating to the conduct of mediation, for instance, relating to time limits or confidentiality, and obligations of the participants may be signed by the parties.[46] During the subsequent course of mediation, the mediator considers all facets of the dispute, both legal and non-legal, to aid the parties in finding a solution which satisfies, as far as possible, the interests and concerns of all parties. At the close of each session, the mediator summarizes the progress made.[47] The parties may then make an appointment for a subsequent meeting as required.[48]

---

requirements include: ensuring that monitoring forms are completed; participation in the annual mediation evaluation on the basis of results recorded in the forms; taking out professional liability insurance. See Pel, 'Regulation of Dispute Resolution in the Netherlands' (n. 1 above) p. 317.

[38] De Rechtspraak, *Procedure mediation naast rechtspraak* (n. 37 above).
[39] *Ibid.*
[40] M. Pel, *Referral to Mediation: A Practical Guide for an Effective Mediation Proposal* (The Hague: Sdu Uitgevers, 2008) p. 4.
[41] Pel and Combrink, 'Referral to Mediation by the Netherlands Judiciary' (n. 5 above) p. 31.
[42] *Ibid.*
[43] De Rechtspraak, *Procedure mediation naast rechtspraak* (n. 37 above).
[44] *Ibid.*
[45] *Ibid.*
[46] *Ibid.*
[47] *Ibid.*
[48] *Ibid.*

6.3.3 Legal Representation

As mediation is generally conducted by the parties or their representatives, the mediation sessions are not usually attended by legal personnel.[49] However, where the parties agree, legal representatives may attend the meeting in person or by proxy to provide legal advice on the feasibility of a proposed solution.[50] Parties are encouraged to keep their legal representatives abreast of developments in the mediation process, and consult them for legal advice prior to signing any legally enforceable settlement agreement.[51]

6.3.4 Settlement and Conclusion of Mediation

Where parties come to partial or complete agreement, the mediator assesses whether the proposed solutions are feasible and practicable.[52] The parties may record the terms of their agreement in a settlement agreement, in line with article 279(4) of the CPC.[53] Where complete agreement is reached, settlement marks the end of the mediation procedure. Mediation agreements following court referral are enforceable via direct inclusion in the minutes of an oral hearing or written judgment.[54] The agreement is legally binding once countersigned by the parties, and in the event of default, may be directly enforced by engaging a bailiff.[55]

However, where agreement is partial, relates only to certain matters or has failed completely, the case may then return for judicial determination with respect to the unresolved matters.[56] The mediator provides instructions as to how to restart the legal proceedings, and any remaining discussions between the parties in the mediation session relate to the information and documents, if any, permitted to be adduced in subsequent proceedings.[57] At the same time, the mediation officer in charge of the case informs the referring judge (if any) and the court registry of the mediation

---

[49] *Ibid.*
[50] *Ibid.*
[51] *Ibid.*
[52] *Ibid.*
[53] Albers, '27. The Netherlands' (n. 2 above) p. 363.
[54] Pel, 'Regulation of Dispute Resolution in the Netherlands' (n. 1 above) p. 321.
[55] Albers, '27. The Netherlands' (n. 2 above) p. 363.
[56] De Rechtspraak, *Procedure mediation naast rechtspraak* (n. 37 above).
[57] *Ibid.*

outcome to determine when trial can be recommenced,[58] and if so, with respect to which issues.[59]

6.4 IMPLEMENTATION IN PRACTICE

6.4.1 Cost of Mediation

Beginning in April 2005, parties entitled to legal aid in judicial proceedings have been similarly entitled to apply for legal aid with respect to court-referred mediation services.[60] Since January 2011, subsidized fees are charged for the first two hours of mediation.[61]

6.4.2 Community Support for Mediation

Integral to the success of the Dutch mediation referral services has been the support of the judiciary, legal profession and parties to litigation.[62] This has led to a shift in the traditional role of the judge, from adjudicator to 'multi-tasking' facilitators of the dispute resolution process.[63] Increasing public awareness of mediation has led to an increase in mediators; at the end of 2011, of 4,493 registered mediators, 931 were certified.[64] However, of all registered mediators in 2011, only 9.8 per cent worked exclusively as a mediator, while 88.3 per cent undertook other non-mediation work.[65] The average number of mediations per year per registered mediator has steadily increased from 2004 (8.1) to 2011 (11.5).[66]

---

[58] Pel and Combrink, 'Referral to Mediation by the Netherlands Judiciary' (n. 5 above) p. 31.
[59] Pel, 'Regulation of Dispute Resolution in the Netherlands' (n. 1 above) p. 319.
[60] *Ibid.* 317.
[61] *Ibid.*
[62] De Hoon and Verberk, 'Towards a More Responsive Judge: Challenges and Opportunities' (n. 9 above) p. 30. Traditionally, such stakeholders may oppose mediation on the basis that such efforts are perceived as threatening their conventional roles or affect business.
[63] *Ibid.* 30.
[64] R.J.M. Vogels, *De stand van Mediation in Nederland* (2011) p. 5, available at https://mediatorsfederatienederland.nl/content/uploads/sites/2/2014/05/De_stand_van_Mediation_in_Nederland-2011-3.pdf.
[65] *Ibid.* 7.
[66] *Ibid.*

6.5 ANALYSIS OF RESEARCH RESULTS

6.5.1 Referral Rates

From April 2005 to December 2009, 14,250 cases pending judicial determination were referred to mediation.[67] In 2008 and 2009, approximately 3,700 and 4,200 were referred to mediation respectively.[68] Written referrals to court-based mediation are most frequently used in administrative cases involving a governmental agency.[69] In contrast, oral referrals to mediation are far more common in civil cases, with two-thirds of such referrals made by a judge.[70] Of the approximately 90 per cent of court-referred cases which entered the mediation process, 84 per cent proceeded to completion.[71]

6.5.2 Settlement Rates

From April 2005 to May 2009, 59 per cent of all court-referred mediations were settled by full (51 per cent) or partial (8 per cent) agreement.[72] Over the same period, administrative cases yielded a higher settlement rate, with 74 per cent of cases settled in full (69 per cent) or partial (5 per cent) agreement, in contrast with a lower rate of success in civil cases, with 54 per cent of cases settled fully (45 per cent) or partially (9 per cent).[73] Another factor influencing settlement rates was the method of referral, with written referrals leading to greater rates of success. In administrative cases, 75 per cent of written referrals reached some form of settlement, while 60 per cent of oral referrals reached settlement.[74]

---

[67] Pel and Combrink, 'Referral to Mediation by the Netherlands Judiciary' (n. 5 above) p. 35. These figures may be split into (i) initial implementation phase from April 2005 to December 2005, in which 830 cases were referred to mediation; and (ii) consolidation phase from January 2006 to December 2009, in which 13,420 cases were judicially referred.
[68] Ibid.
[69] Ibid. 36.
[70] Ibid. Pel explains this phenomenon by observing that as parties in civil cases have often entered into, without success, extra-judicial negotiations prior to the filing of the case in court, whether informally through legal representations, by non-judicial mediation or other means, the same parties are unlikely to accept a written referral for mediation.
[71] Ibid. 35.
[72] Ibid. 39.
[73] Ibid.
[74] Ibid. 40.

In 2011, a report prepared by the NMI indicated that of the last 10 mediations each conducted by a sample of mediators (n = 861), 69.8 per cent reached full settlement, 13.8 per cent reached partial settlement, and 16.4 per cent reached no settlement.[75] Such results mark a slight decrease from 2009, in which 70.3 per cent reached full settlement, 15.7 per cent reached partial settlement, and 14 per cent reached no settlement.[76]

6.5.3 Processing Time

A 2009 study by SEO Economic Research indicated that the processing time of judicial cases referred to court-connected mediation generally exceeded the processing time of comparable cases resolved solely through judicial procedure.[77] The extra time implications for court-referred cases (n = 1,099) ranged from an average of 61 days for administrative tax cases, 160 days for civil cases, to 205 days for administrative cases (excluding tax cases).[78] However, among the cases for which referral was made before trial, the average extra processing time decreased to just 33 days for administrative tax cases, 114 days for civil cases and 152 days for administrative cases (excluding tax).[79]

Extra processing time was also influenced by the eventual level of agreement; where the parties reached full agreement, this averaged 131 days for civil cases, 151 days for administrative cases, and 21 days for tax cases.[80] Where the parties did not reach agreement, an average of 187 days for civil cases, 256 days for administrative cases, and 55 days for tax cases were added to the processing time.[81] The longest additions to processing time generally occurred where the parties reached only partial agreement, with 209 days for civil cases, 328 days for administrative cases, and 55 days for tax cases.[82] Much of the extra processing time, however, may be attributed to administrative work processing and facilitating the mediation, as opposed to the mediation process itself, which yielded an average

---

[75] Vogels, *De stand van Mediation in Nederland* (n. 64 above) p. 14.
[76] *Ibid.* 7.
[77] 'Processing time' was defined as the time period spanning from commencement of judicial procedure (i.e. via the filing for a petition) to formal completion of the action (i.e. via judicial determination or case withdrawal). See Pel and Combrink, 'Referral to Mediation by the Netherlands Judiciary' (n. 5 above) p. 48.
[78] *Ibid.*
[79] *Ibid.*
[80] *Ibid.* 49.
[81] *Ibid.*
[82] *Ibid.*

processing time of 57 days for all cases, 65 days for civil cases[83] and 31 days in administrative cases.[84]

6.5.4 Resolution Time-frame

In 2009, the mean number of mediation sessions for all court-referred cases was three.[85] Administrative cases were generally resolved in fewer sessions, with almost 50 per cent of cases completed in a single session, and over 80 per cent in three sessions.[86] In contrast, fewer than 20 per cent of civil cases were resolved in a single session, and just over 50 per cent in three sessions.[87] The mean contact time between parties and the mediator was six hours for all court-referred mediations, almost seven hours for civil mediations, and slightly in excess of four hours for administrative cases.[88]

6.5.5 Average Costs

In 2009, the costs savings within the judiciary arising from cases utilizing court-referred mediation amounted to €53 in civil cases, €318 in administrative (excluding tax) cases, and €404 in administrative tax cases.[89] In addition, an average of €303 and €515 were saved in commercial and summary proceedings, respectively.[90] The cost-saving implications of court-referred mediation are less apparent where the parties do not reach agreement.[91] While an average of €63 is saved for administrative (excluding tax) cases that do not reach settlement, extra costs are incurred for civil and tax cases, at an average of €220 and €63, respectively.[92]

Figures from the Council of the Judiciary indicate that the labour costs attached to the mediation referral service averaged €41 per hour, for the

---

[83] *Ibid.* The discrepancy in mean processing time for civil and administrative cases is attributed to the number of divorce and separation cases in civil family disputes, the mediation of which often includes the testing of new family arrangements or other options that require time to ascertain.

[84] *Ibid.* 49 prefers the median values of processing time to avoid the inclusion of extreme values, namely, 35 days for all cases, 0 days (i.e. mediation completed on the same day) for administrative cases, and 46 days for civil cases.

[85] *Ibid.*
[86] *Ibid.* 50.
[87] *Ibid.*
[88] *Ibid.*
[89] *Ibid.* 51.
[90] *Ibid.*
[91] *Ibid.* 52.
[92] *Ibid.*

122   *Court mediation reform*

Table 6.1   The Netherlands' rankings: developments in efficiency, confidence and perceptions of justice, 2011–2016*

	2011	2016
Efficiency		
• Efficiency of legal framework in settling disputes (rank)	9th/142	12th/138
• Accessibility and affordability (percentile)	0.7	0.78
• No unreasonable delay (percentile)	0.66	0.83
Confidence		
• Civil justice (rank)	3rd/66	1st/113
• Effective enforcement (percentile)	0.81	0.88
• Impartial and effective ADR (percentile)	0.81	0.83
Perceptions of justice		
• Rule of law (percentile)	0.98	0.97**
• No discrimination (percentile)	0.8	0.92

*   Greyed rows indicate a positive trend in the rankings.
**   World Bank Group, *Worldwide Governance Indicators 2015*, http://info.worldbank.org/governance/wgi/index.aspx#home.

mediation officer spending an average of 4.6 hours on a referred case; and €29 per hour, for the staff member in the mediation administration office spending an average of 4.1 hours per case.[93] Considering such costs in tandem with the average costs saved or additionally expended as detailed above, the cost implications of court-referred mediation were an extra cost of €254 for civil cases, but costs savings of €97 for tax cases and €11 for administrative (excluding tax) cases. Thus, in 2009, the mediation referral system neared economic efficiency. It was projected that increasing trends in referral rates would bring the system closer to the same.[94]

6.5.6   Dutch Civil Justice Rankings: Efficiency, Confidence and Perceptions of Justice

The voluntary mediation programme in the Netherlands can be examined within the larger context of its achievements in the areas of efficiency, confidence and perceptions of justice, all of which indicate a strong and robust civil justice system.

---

[93]   *Ibid.*
[94]   *Ibid.*

Table 6.1 above shows positive movement over the past five years within the Netherlands' rankings in the areas of efficiency, confidence and perceptions of justice. Areas highlighted in grey indicate a positive movement in the rankings. As can be seen above, over the past five years, the Netherlands has experienced positive development in the areas of efficiency as measured by accessibility and affordability and reduction of delay, confidence as measured by its overall civil justice ranking, effective enforcement and impartial and effective ADR, and perceptions of justice as measured by its percentile in absence of discrimination. This appears to indicate that the voluntary mediation programme as implemented in the Netherlands has resulted in some significant contributions to the workings of its civil justice system in recent years.

In terms of overall efficiency in the civil justice system, according to the *Global Competitiveness Report 2016–2017*,[95] the Netherlands ranks 12th out of 138 countries in the efficiency of its legal framework in settling disputes. The accessibility and affordability of the civil justice system is 0.78 on a 1 point scale.[96] Its score for 'no unreasonable delay' was 0.83 on a 1 point scale.[97]

The overall rank for the Netherlands' civil justice in the *Rule of Law Index 2016*[98] was 1st out of 113 countries. Its scores for effective enforcement and impartial and effective ADR were 0.88 and 0.83 on a 1 point scale, respectively.[99]

Finally, with respect to perceptions of justice, the percentile for rule of law ranking was 97 on a 100 point scale in 2015.[100] The score for 'no discrimination' was 0.92 on a 1 point scale.[101]

6.6 CONCLUSION

The voluntary mediation programme in the Netherlands can be viewed within the context of a legal culture that values extra-judicial negotiation

---

[95] World Economic Forum, *The Global Competitiveness Report 2016–2017*, pp. 276–7.
[96] World Justice Project, *Rule of Law Index 2016*, p. 108.
[97] See n. 95 above.
[98] See n. 96 above.
[99] See n. 96 above.
[100] World Bank Group, *Worldwide Governance Indicators 2015*, http://info.worldbank.org/governance/wgi/index.aspx#home.
[101] See n. 96 above.

of disputes and views judicial adjudication as a tool of last resort.[102] Rather than aiming at alleviating an overburdened judicial system, the stated purpose of developing court-connected mediation services in the Dutch courts was to provide court users with a further option, in addition to the existing methods of judicial adjudication and court settlement, of alternate dispute resolution.[103] Since the programme was introduced in 2007, the Netherlands has experienced positive development in the areas of efficiency, as measured by accessibility and affordability and reduction of delay; confidence, as measured by its overall civil justice ranking, effective enforcement and impartial and effective ADR; and perceptions of justice, as measured by its percentile in the reduction of discrimination. This appears to indicate that the voluntary mediation programme as implemented in the Netherlands is associated with significant contributions to the workings of its civil justice system.

---

[102] Pel, 'Regulation of Dispute Resolution in the Netherlands' (n. 1 above) p. 315.
[103] Pel and Combrink, 'Referral to Mediation by the Netherlands Judiciary' (n. 5 above) p. 25.

7. Mediation in the Malaysian courts

7.1 GENERAL INTRODUCTION

In Malaysia, parties may voluntarily attempt mediation before commencing litigation. The Mediation Act 2012 was promulgated to facilitate the use of mediation prior to civil trials. Within the court system, mediation may only be initiated with the consent of all parties. Malaysia's robust voluntary court mediation programme has contributed to gains within the civil justice system in terms of both efficiency with respect to costs and time savings. Over the past five years, Malaysia has made progress in relation to its civil justice rankings in terms of levels of efficiency, as measured by reduction of delay; confidence, as measured by effective enforcement; and perceptions of justice, as measured by its rankings in the reduction of discrimination.

7.2 POLICY BACKGROUND

7.2.1 Historical Background

Malaysia is a multi-religious and multi-ethnic society comprised predominantly of Malays, Chinese and Indians.[1] Mediation in Malaysia finds its roots in the teachings of Islam, Hinduism, Buddhism, Christianity and Confucian principles of harmony.[2] Historical records also confirm early dispute resolution practices among the indigenous Malay people.[3] More recently, Western legal traditions have influenced the practice of contemporary mediation in Malaysia.

---

[1] Department of Statistics Malaysia, *Current Population Estimates, Malaysia, 2014–2016* (22 July 2016), available at www.statistics.gov.my/index.php?r5column/cthemeByCat&cat5155&bul_id5OWlxdEVoYlJCS0hUZzJyRUcvZEYxZz09&menu_id5L0pheU43NWJwRWVSZklWdzQ4TlhUUT09 (accessed 11 November 2016).

[2] M. Ishak Abdul Hamid and N. Azahani Nik Mohammad, 'Cross-Culture Jurisprudential Influence on Mediation in Malaysia' (2016) 4 *Malaysian Law Journal* xli, lix.

[3] *Ibid.*

While socio-political change has impacted traditional mediation practice, Malaysia has striven to conserve the concept of 'give and take', an underlying principle of its operative mediation landscape.[4] This has laid the foundation for the initiation of alternative dispute resolution (ADR) reforms.

In August 2010, the former Chief Justice Tun Zaki bin Tun Azim issued the Court's Practice Direction No. 5 of 2010 on Mediation to encourage parties to employ mediation in settling disputes. Since 2011, numerous court-annexed mediation centres have been established in major cities in Malaysia, including Kuala Lumpur, Kuantan and Johor Bharu.[5] The success rate of mediated cases in Kuala Lumpur was 28.3 per cent from January to December 2012.[6]

7.2.2 Rationale

Mounting case backlog has been a key driver of mediation reform in Malaysia. Following reports in the *New Straits Times* (18 June 2007) that more than 300,000 civil cases were pending in the Malaysian courts as of July 2006, followed by a report from the Prime Minister's Department in 2008 that there were more than 900,000 unresolved cases in the lower courts and more than 91,000 at the High Court,[7] several proponents suggested that ADR, including mediation, might assist in reducing the mounting backlog of civil cases nationwide.[8] In 2005, the Chairman of the Malaysian Mediation Committee of the Bar Council lent further support to the introduction of mediation in Malaysia.[9]

Since that time, Malaysia has promoted the development of mediation as an alternative to litigation.[10] In particular, court-connected mediation

---

[4] R.H.M. Leung, 'Chapter 12: Malaysia' in *Hong Kong Mediation Handbook* (2015) p. 196.

[5] Y.A.A. Tun Arifin bin Zakaria, Chief Justice of Malaysia, speech at the Opening of the Legal Year 2013 (Palace of Justice, Putrajaya, 12 January 2013), available at www.malaysianbar.org.my/speeches/speech_by_tun_arifin_bin_zakaria_chief_justice_of_malaysia_at_the_opening_of_the_legal_year_2013_palace_of_justice_putrajaya_12_jan_2013.html (accessed 25 October 2016).

[6] *Ibid.*

[7] T. Zaki Azmi, 'Overcoming Case Backlogs: The Malaysian Experience', paper presented at Asia Pacific Court Conference, Singapore, October 2010, pp. 4–8, available at http://app.subcourts.gov.sg/Data/Files/File/APCC2010/Slides/Session3_ZakiAzmi.pdf (accessed 12 November 2016).

[8] *New Straits Times*, 9 May 2008.

[9] *New Straits Times*, 18 June 2007.

[10] The former Chief Justice of the Federal Court, Tun Eusoff Chin, proposed the introduction of mediation to assist in disposal of cases (see *Star Newspaper*, 12 May 2000).

was introduced with a view to avoiding prolonged litigation proceedings and reducing the associated distress and anxiety caused from such delays.[11] It was also seen as a means of saving judicial time and costs[12] by assisting parties to reach either full or partial agreements.[13] However, despite judicial efforts to develop court-connected mediation, 'dispensing justice in civil and criminal litigation still remain[s] the core judicial function'.[14]

7.2.3 Terminologies and Definitions

As discussed below and provided for in Practice Direction No. 4 of 2016 on mediation, Malaysian courts can refer parties to voluntary mediation only with the consent of both parties. Court-referred mediation can take the form of court-annexed mediation, institutional mediation or judge-led mediation, collectively referred to as 'court-connected mediation'. Court-annexed mediation refers to mediation undertaken by a third party private mediator agreeable to all parties; institutional mediation refers to mediation conducted under the auspices of the Kuala Lumpur Regional Centre for Arbitration (KLRCA); finally, judge-led mediation refers to mediation conducted by a judge, usually a judge other than the presiding judge.[15]

7.3 PROGRAMME FEATURES

7.3.1 Scheduling: Timing, Costs, Duration

Prior to August 2010, court-connected mediation was conducted on an ad hoc basis in the Western Malaysian Penang High Court. Parties had the option of attempting mediation with the Malaysian Mediation Centre (MMC).[16] In managing cases, courts had the discretion to encourage mediation 'to ensure ... just, expeditious and economical disposal' as

---

[11] Justice Azahar bin Mohamed, Federal Court Judge, Malaysia, *Courts Reform Programmes: The Malaysian Experience* (1 December 2015) p. 5, available at http://sas-space.sas.ac.uk/6375/1/Azahar_bin_Mohamed_Court%20Reform_Programmes.pdf (accessed 26 October 2016).
[12] See n. 5 above.
[13] *Chief Justice Says Court Annexed Mediation a Free Programme* (26 August 2011), available at www.theborneopost.com/2011/08/26/chief-justice-says-court-annexed-mediation-a-free-programme/ (accessed 25 October 2016).
[14] See n. 9 above, p. 22.
[15] 'CJ: More cases being resolved through mediation', *Star Online*, 25 February 2011.
[16] Leung, 'Chapter 12: Malaysia' (n. 4 above) p. 202.

stipulated under Order 34 Rule 4 of the Rules of the High Court 1980 or under Order 19 Rule 1(1)(b) of the Subordinate Courts Rule 1980.

Following the introduction of Practice Direction No. 5 of 2010 on Mediation in August 2010, the former Chief Justice encouraged all levels of courts in Malaysia to facilitate the settlement of disputes. It was the first time civil courts were given a framework for exploring the amicable processes of dispute resolution before cases proceed to trial.

Effective from 15 July 2016, a new Practice Direction No. 4 on mediation (Mediation PD) came into force and replaced the previous Practice Direction No. 5 of 2010. The major innovation in the new Mediation PD was the additional option of institutionalized mediation under Annex B to the Mediation PD.[17]

The Mediation PD provides general guidelines for the initiation of court-connected mediation for cases that are brought to court. First, judges may suggest mediation to the parties to encourage them to settle at the pre-trial case management stage or at any stage in the proceedings, even after commencement of a trial.[18] The judge can request that parties meet in the presence of counsel for the purpose of suggesting mediation to the parties.[19] If a judge can identify the issues which may be amicably resolved, he/she may highlight those issues.[20] Parties, at their discretion, may select one of three modes of mediation, namely, judge-led mediation (Option A in the Mediation PD), institutional mediation under the auspices of the KLRCA (Option B in the Mediation PD), and mediation by a private mediator (Option C in the Mediation PD).[21] Upon agreeing to mediation, parties are given the freedom to opt for one mode, following the principle of party autonomy. Under the new Rules of Court 2012, the Mediation PD became formally incorporated into the civil justice system.[22]

The Mediation Act 2012 came into force on 1 August 2012 to promote and encourage mediation and facilitate the settlement of disputes in a fair, speedy and cost-effective manner. It is applicable to institutional and court-annexed mediation.[23] Section 6 of the Mediation Act 2012 provides that once parties agree to mediation, they must sign a written mediation agreement containing (i) an agreement to submit to mediation the disputes

---

[17] Mediation PD, para. 3.
[18] *Ibid.* para. 3.
[19] *Ibid.* para. 5.3.
[20] *Ibid.* para. 5.2.
[21] *Ibid.* para. 5.1.
[22] Rules of Court 2012, Order 34 Rule 2(2)(a).
[23] Mediation Act 2012, s.2(b) and (c).

concerned;[24] (ii) the appointment of a mediator;[25] (iii) the costs to be borne by the parties;[26] and (iv) the preservation of confidentiality of the mediation process.[27]

7.3.2 Judge-led Mediation

Parties to a dispute have the option of submitting their dispute to a judge-led mediation process. Judge-led mediation is a free mediation programme by which judges or court staff act as mediators to assist disputants in a litigation to find a solution without trial.[28] A panel of mediators consisting of judges, judicial commissioners or registrars may be selected.[29] The judge hearing the case must not be the mediating judge unless otherwise agreed by the parties.[30] The rationale for this rule is obvious: to avoid possible complaints of bias, prejudice or pre-judgment.[31] A mediation session is fixed no later than one month after parties agree to attempt mediation.[32]

Court-annexed mediation centres are set up within court complexes.[33] For instance, the Kuala Lumpur Court Mediation Centre contains three mediation caucus rooms and is furnished with sofas and armchairs to deliberately create a softer ambiance.[34] All the services and facilities provided by the centres are free of charge.[35] Parties maintain the right to proceed to trial if mediation fails.[36]

Given the convenience of this option, many parties select court-based

---

[24] *Ibid.* s.6(3).
[25] *Ibid.*
[26] *Ibid.*
[27] Mediation PD, Form 1.
[28] See n. 5 above.
[29] Mediation PD, para. 1.
[30] Mediation PD, Annex A, para. 1.
[31] See n. 5 above.
[32] See n. 5 above.
[33] See n. 5 above.
[34] Justice Audit Malaysia, *Courts* (2011), available at http://malaysia.justice mapping.org/?page_id523 (accessed 26 October 2016).
[35] Justice Mah Weng Kwai, 'Mediation Practices: The Malaysian Experience', speech given at High Court Kuala Lumpur, 18 February 2012, (2012) 5 *Malaysian Law Journal* clxvi, clxxiv.
[36] It has been suggested by R. French, *Perspectives on Court Annexed Alternative Dispute Resolution* (27 July 2009), available at www.hcourt.gov.au/assets/publica tions/speeches/current-justices/frenchcj/frenchcj27july09.pdf (accessed 12 November 2016), that this reflects a misconception of mediation where the formal authority of a judge in fact plays no function in it.

mediation over private mediation.[37] However, in spite of its convenience, concerns have been raised about the frequency of evaluative mediation practices,[38] the potential pre-judgment of a case[39] and lack of mediation training among court staff.[40]

7.3.3 Institutional Mediation under the KLRCA

In addition to free mediation services provide by court staff, parties may opt to attempt mediation through the KLRCA. The KLRCA is a non-profit, non-governmental and independent international body established under the auspices of the Asian-African Legal Consultative Organisation in 1978. It has developed a set of flexible rules for mediation.

There is no limitation as to the number of mediator(s) to be appointed, however, the default position is one.[41] Rule 10 of the KLRCA Rules of Mediation imposes a duty of independence and impartiality similar to that stipulated under section 7(7) of the Mediation Act 2012. This is a continuing duty and failing such duty may entitle the parties to appoint a new mediator.[42]

If the parties agree to institutional mediation in accordance with the KLRCA Rules of Mediation, the plaintiff's solicitor notifies the centre within seven calendar days.[43] Parties are required to participate in good faith in the mediation and have the authority to settle.[44] Mediation proceedings are held on KLRCA premises unless parties agree otherwise.[45]

7.3.4 Court-annexed Mediation

A third option open to litigants[46] is the selection of a mediator from a list of mediators empanelled by the Malaysian Mediation Centre (MMC).[47]

---

[37] U.A. Oseni Abu Umar Faruq Ahmad, 'Towards a Global Hub: The Legal Framework for Dispute Resolution in Malaysia's Islamic Finance Industry' (2016) 58(1) *International Journal of Law and Management* 10.
[38] Leung, 'Chapter 12: Malaysia' (n. 4 above) 202.
[39] *Ibid.* 203.
[40] *Ibid.* 202.
[41] KLRCA Rules of Mediation, Rule 9.
[42] *Ibid.* Rule 11.
[43] *Ibid.* Rule 8.
[44] *Ibid.* Rules 16 and 18.
[45] *Ibid.* Rule 22.
[46] See n. 37 above.
[47] Mediation PD, Annex C, para. 1.1.

The MMC handles commercial, civil and matrimonial disputes.[48] There is no monetary limit for claims coming under the MMC's jurisdiction.[49] The MMC requires its mediators to be practising members of the Malaysian Bar with at least seven years' standing, to have completed 40 hours of training under the MMC and to have passed a practical assessment conducted by the trainers.[50] Such mediators must 'possess the relevant qualifications, special knowledge or experience in mediation through training or formal tertiary education'.[51] There is no restriction as to the number of mediators appointed to resolve the dispute.[52] Section 9(3) of the Mediation Act 2012 establishes the duty of a mediator to act independently and impartially.[53]

Prior to the commencement of mediation, parties must sign a written mediation agreement. The agreement requires parties to act in good faith and have the authority to settle.[54] If the parties agree to be bound by the MMC Mediation Rules, the plaintiff's solicitor notifies the MMC within seven calendar days.[55] Where the parties fail to agree on the appointment of a mediator under the MMC, the Chairperson of the MMC must proceed to appoint one on the parties' behalf.[56]

The mediation session can be conducted in the mediator's office, the law society's premises or a function room.[57] A mediation session is usually fixed between one to two weeks from the date of request for mediation.[58]

---

[48] Asian Mediation Association, 'Malaysian Mediation Centre', available at www.asianmediationassociation.org/malaysian-mediation-centre/ (accessed 2 November 2016).

[49] Kuala Lumpur Legal Aid Centre, 'Don't Litigate – Mediate!', p. 2, available at www.kllac.com/PAMPHLETS%20inall/Don't%20Litigate%20Mediate%20verified/DON'T%20LITIGATE%20-%20MEDIATE!%20(english).pdf (accessed 2 November 2016).

[50] K. Zaman bin Bukhari, 'Arbitration and Mediation in Malaysia', paper presented at the 2003 8th General Assembly of the ASEAN Law Association, available at www.aseanlawassociation.org/docs/w4_malaysia.pdf (accessed 2 November 2016).

[51] Mediation Act 2012, s.7(2).

[52] Mediation PD, Annex C, para. 1.3, and Mediation Act 2012, s.7(4), (5).

[53] Mediation Act 2012, s. 7(7).

[54] *Ibid.* s.16.

[55] Mediation PD, Annex C, para. 2.

[56] Malaysian Bar Council, How Does One Go About Registering a Matter for Mediation', available at www.malaysianbar.org.my/How_does_one_go_about_registering_a_matter_for_Mediation_.html (accessed 2 November 2016).

[57] Mah Weng Kwai, 'Mediation Practices: The Malaysian Experience' (n. 35 above) clsvii.

[58] Mediation PD, Annex C, para. 2.

The length of mediation varies, depending on the complexity of the matter.[59] Mediation fees are shared by both parties and vary depending on the quantum of the claim.[60]

7.3.5 Legal Aid Department

The Legal Aid Department under the purview of the Legal Affairs Division of the Prime Minister's Department offers civil and Syariah mediation for domestic, motor vehicle and small consumer claims.[61]

7.4 GENERAL GROUND RULES

The voluntary nature of the mediation process in Malaysia is reiterated under section 3 of the Mediation Act 2012 which defines mediation as a voluntary process aimed at assisting parties to reach an agreement regarding a dispute. Further, mediation will not act as a stay of, or extension of, any proceedings which have already been commenced.[62] This allows mediation to be undertaken in parallel with litigation or arbitration proceedings. Mediation PD, paragraph 2.1 states that 'the benefit of settlement by way of mediation is that it is accepted by the parties'.[63]

7.4.1 Mediation Process

Mediators assume a multi-functional role in the mediation process, which includes: host and chair; guide, coach and educator; referee; assessor of reality; and protector of the process of mediation.[64] Once parties agree to voluntary mediation, they are asked to report to the court on the progress of the mediation.[65] All mediation must be completed within three months unless extended with leave of the court.[66]

---

[59] *Ibid.*
[60] *Ibid.*
[61] Malaysia Legal Aid Department, 'Mediation', available at www.jbg.gov.my/index.php?option5com_content&view5article&id573&Itemid5229&lang5en (accessed 26 October 2016).
[62] Mediation Act 2012, s.4(2).
[63] *Ibid.*
[64] L. Hop Bing, 'Mediation: The Way Forward, Challenges and Solutions', pp. 5–7, paper presented at Persidangan Tahunan Majlis Hakim-Hakim Malaysia, Grand Ballroom, Hotel JW Marriot, Kuala Lumpur, 12–15 December 2010.
[65] Mediation PD, para. 6.3(a).
[66] *Ibid.* para. 6.3(c).

(i) Judge-led mediation

For parties who select judge-led mediation under the Malaysian mediation scheme, the conduct of the mediation sessions is flexible.[67] The following description of the mediation process is extracted from the experience of Justice Mah Weng Kwai. Generally, the parties will first be introduced by their respective counsel and the judge-mediator will explain the objectives, ground rules and expectations of the mediation process.[68] The mediator will enter into a caucus meeting with the plaintiff or his/her representative who will be encouraged to state his/her case and expectations regarding an acceptable settlement.[69] Confidential information may also be disclosed to the mediator but not to the other side on this occasion. This is repeated for the defendant or his/her representative.[70] The judge-mediator may express his/her opinion on the strengths and weaknesses of each party's respective case.[71] Afterwards, both parties or their representatives will be present in the room again where they are encouraged to talk directly to each other, and if either party wishes to consult his/her counsel during the discussions, he/she may do so during a short break.[72]

If mediation is successful, parties will agree on the terms of the mediation settlement and once it is recorded as a consent order, there will be no right to appeal. If the settlement agreement includes withdrawal or dismissal of the action, parties file a notice of discontinuance. If mediation fails, either party has the right to proceed to trial where the case will revert to the original hearing judge for determination.[73]

(ii) Institutional mediation

For parties who select institutional mediation under Malaysia's voluntary mediation scheme, there is great flexibility in the conduct of mediation.[74] The parties may be required to participate in a preliminary conference before commencing formal mediation so as to clarify and agree upon the issues in dispute.[75]

---

[67] Secretariat of the Kuala Lumpur Court Mediation Centre, *Explanatory Note on Court-Annexed Mediation*, available at www.aseanlawassociation.org/11GAdocs/workshop5-malaysia.pdf (accessed 11 November 2016).
[68] Mah Weng Kwai, 'Mediation Practices: The Malaysian Experience' (n. 35 above) clxxii.
[69] *Ibid.*
[70] *Ibid.*
[71] *Ibid.*
[72] *Ibid.* clxxiii.
[73] Mediation PD, Annex A, para. 1.
[74] KLRCA Rules of Mediation, Rule 13.
[75] *Ibid.* Rule 15.

Once an agreement has been reached, the mediator will draw up the terms of the mediation settlement. If the settlement agreement includes withdrawal or dismissal of the action, parties will then file a notice of discontinuance with the court. If mediation fails, the case will be directed back to the court.[76]

(iii) Court-annexed mediation

For parties who select court-annexed mediation, a time is scheduled for the parties to meet where a brief statement of facts is presented.[77] The mediator may also request any party to submit additional information or documents as he/she deems appropriate.[78] Mediation can be conducted in English and/or Bahasa Malaysia or any other language upon request.[79] During the mediation process, the mediator will assume a facilitative role so as to enable the parties to reach a settlement.[80]

Once an agreement has been reached, the mediator will draw up the terms of the mediation settlement. If mediation fails, the case will be directed back to the court. The mediator, in addition to the parties, may also terminate the mediation if in his/her opinion 'further efforts at mediation would not contribute to a satisfactory resolution of the dispute'.[81]

7.4.2 Enforceability

Mediation is a non-binding process, unless the parties enter into an agreement stating that they are bound by the outcomes of a successful mediation. Agreements reached under court-referred mediation will be adopted as a judgment of the court or consent judgment binding on the parties.[82] *Chew Hon Keong* v. *Betterproducts Industries Sdn Bhd*[83] reaffirmed that a consent order made upon successful mediation is a judgment of the court which has every force of law and the fact that the terms of the court order were arrived at by consent was not relevant.[84]

---

[76] *Ibid.* Rule 25.
[77] The mediator has the power to request each party to submit a brief statement of facts supplemented by any supporting documents that the party deems fit, pursuant to Mediation Act 2012, s.10(1).
[78] *Ibid.* s.10(2).
[79] Malaysian Bar Council, 'Mediation Request Form' (26 July 2012), available at www.malaysianbar.org.my/index.php?option5com_docman&task5doc_view&gid 52387&Itemid5332 (accessed 2 November 2016).
[80] Mediation Act 2012, s.9(1).
[81] *Ibid.* ss.11(3) and 12(b).
[82] *Ibid.* s.14(1) and (2).
[83] [2013] 7 MLJ 196.
[84] *Chew Hon Keong* [2013] 7 MLJ 196, para. 20.

7.5 IMPLEMENTATION IN PRACTICE (CASE LAW)

The recent body of case law in Malaysia has further explored the meaning and ground rules of court-connected mediation, including the role of legal representatives, the voluntary nature of the settlement agreement, and the requirement of impartiality in the context of court-based mediation.

Sabah Forest Industries Sdn Bhd v. *Mazlan bin Ali*[85] stressed the importance of legal representation in a judge-led mediation session insofar as once a party's counsel has withdrawn from a session, that party would be left without legal representation.[86] The court in *Sabah Forest Industries Sdn Bhd* further reiterated the importance of the voluntary nature of any consensus reached under mediation, holding that '[i]n a mediation process, the resolution has to come from the parties and not from the third-party mediator. No order could be made by or come from the mediator'.

Further, consensus reached in mediation should not only be voluntary, but be crafted by the parties. It was held in *Chew Hon Keong* that the consent order was consistent with the chief rule of mediation that the decision-makers involved in the dispute must personally attend the mediation.

The issue of mediator neutrality was raised in *Dato' Dr Joseph Eravelly* v. *Dato Hilmi Mohd Nor*.[87] In that case, the defendants applied for the judge to recuse himself due to a danger of bias. The judge held that although the grounds raised were not sufficient to find bias on the part of the judge, the judge still agreed to recuse himself due to the perception of the defendants.[88]

7.6 ANALYSIS OF RESEARCH RESULTS

7.6.1 Mediation-related Statistics: Number of Cases that Accepted Mediation and Success Rate

There has been no formal study in Malaysia to measure the success of mediation except for statistics maintained by the courts.[89] Circumstantial

---

[85] [2012] 5 MLJ 382.
[86] *Sabah Forest Industries Sdn Bhd* (n. 85 above) held that 'the "mediation session" should have terminated once defendant's counsel withdrew from the session as withdrawal left the defendant without legal representation which put him at a high disadvantage. He was deprived of legal advice as to the "orders" imposed by the judge'.
[87] [2011] 3 CLJ 294.
[88] [2013] 5 AMR 363 HC.
[89] Leung, 'Chapter 12: Malaysia' (n. 4 above) p. 203.

Table 7.1 Successful mediated cases in various courts of Malaysia in 2011

Court	Total mediated cases	Successful mediation cases	Success rate
High Court	2,276	1,099	48.29%
Sessions Court	3,686	1,967	53.36%
Magistrates' Court	661	293	44.33%

observation has found that referral of cases to the MMC by courts was unpopular resulting in reconsideration of the practice.[90] This can be attributed to the view that court-based authority gives legitimacy to any settlement outcomes and is often preferred over outside service providers.[91]

(i) Judge-led mediation

For court-based mediation, the success rate ranged between 25–47 per cent depending on the State. For example, between January 2011 and December 2012, the success rate of mediated cases in the State of Johor Bahru was 47.6 per cent out of a total of 251 cases; in Kuala Lumpur, it was 28.3 per cent out of 571 cases; and in Kuantan, it was 25 per cent out of 80 cases.[92] The overall success rate of judge-led mediation in the High Court and subordinate courts in 2011 was approximately 50 per cent out of 2,276 and 4,347 cases, respectively (see Table 7.1).[93] Nevertheless, the formal mediation rate was still fairly low, perhaps due to limited public awareness about the mediation option.[94]

With respect to time savings, Justice David Wong highlighted in 2010 that the amount of judicial time saved as a result of the increased use of mediation was 3.38 years of hearing days, given the current success rate of 44 per cent.[95]

---

[90] Y.A.A. Tan Sri Arifin Zakaria, 'Responsibility of Judges under Practice Direction No. 5 of 2010', paper presented to Seminar on Mediation with Judge John Clifford Wallace, 2010.
[91] Leung, 'Chapter 12: Malaysia' (n. 4 above) p. 203.
[92] See above n. 4.
[93] Tan Sri Arifin Bin Zakaria, Chief Justice of Malaysia, Speech at the Opening of the Legal Year 2012, 19 January 2012), available at www.malaysianbar.org.my/speeches/speech_by_tan_sri_arifin_bin_zakaria_chief_justice_of_malaysia_at_the_opening_of_the_legal_year_2012_14_jan_2012.html (accessed 4 November 2016).
[94] *Ibid.*
[95] K. Lai and J. Chai, *MLC 2010: Mediation and the Courts – The Right Approach* (30 July 2010), available at www.malaysianbar.org.my/bar_news/berita_

(ii) Court-annexed mediation

From 2000 to September 2010, a total of 192 cases were referred to MMC, of which 109 were from the courts.[96] Only 54 cases (28 per cent) were successfully mediated out of the total mediated cases.[97] It is noteworthy that 86 cases (45 per cent) of the total were settled outside of court following the initiation of mediation.[98]

7.6.2 Malaysia's Civil Justice Rankings: Efficiency, Confidence and Perceptions of Justice

The voluntary mediation programme in Malaysia can be examined within the larger context of its achievements in the areas of efficiency, confidence and perceptions of justice.

Table 7.2 shows some modest positive movement over the past five years within Malaysia's rankings in the areas of efficiency, confidence and perceptions of justice. Areas highlighted in grey indicate a positive movement in the rankings. As can be seen, over the past five years, Malaysia has experienced positive development in levels of efficiency, as measured by reduction of delay; confidence, as measured by effective enforcement; and perceptions of justice, as measured by its percentile in the absence of discrimination.

In terms of overall efficiency in the civil justice system, according to the *Global Competitiveness Report 2016–2017*,[99] Malaysia ranks 19th out of 138 countries in the efficiency of its legal framework in settling disputes. The accessibility and affordability of the civil justice system is 0.5 on a 1 point scale.[100] Its score for 'no unreasonable delay' was 0.64 on a 1 point scale.[101]

Confidence in court mediation systems can be examined in relation to the overall ranking of the civil justice system and ease of enforcement and

---

badan_peguam/mlc_2010_mediation_and_the_courts_the_right_approach.html (accessed 26 October 2016).

[96] A. Abdul Wahab, *Court-Annexed and Judge-Led Mediation in Civil: Cases: The Malaysian Experience* (October 2013) p. 48, available at http://vuir.vu.edu.au/24331/1/Alwi%20Abdul%20Wahab.pdf (accessed 12 November 2016).

[97] S. Koshy, 'CJ Pushes Mediation Option', *Star Newspaper*, 29 October 2010, available at www.thestar.com.my/news/nation/2010/10/29/cj-pushes-mediation-option/ (accessed 11 November 2016).

[98] *Star Newspaper*, 29 October 2010.

[99] World Economic Forum, *The Global Competitiveness Report 2016–2017*, pp. 250–51.

[100] World Justice Project, *Rule of Law Index 2016*, p. 101.

[101] See n. 99 above.

Table 7.2 *Malaysia's rankings: developments in efficiency, confidence and perceptions of justice, 2011–2016**

	2011	2016
Efficiency		
• Efficiency of legal framework in settling disputes (rank)	17th/142	19th/138
• Accessibility and affordability (percentile)	0.53	0.5
• No unreasonable delay (percentile)	0.41	0.64
Confidence		
• Civil justice (rank)	47th/66	49th/113
• Effective enforcement (percentile)	0.5	0.57
• Impartial and effective ADR (percentile)	0.7	0.7
Perceptions of justice		
• Rule of law (percentile)	0.65	0.72**
• No discrimination (percentile)	0.47	0.51

*   Greyed rows indicate a positive trend in the rankings.
** World Bank Group, *Worldwide Governance Indicators 2015*, http://info.worldbank.org/governance/wgi/index.aspx#home.

impartiality and effectiveness of ADR. The overall rank for Malaysia's civil justice in the *Rule of Law Index 2016*[102] is 49th out of 113 countries. Its scores for effective enforcement and impartial and effective ADR were 0.57 and 0.7 on a 1 point scale, respectively.[103]

Finally, with respect to perceptions of justice, Malaysia's rule of law percentile was 72 on a 100 point scale in 2015.[104] The score for 'no discrimination' was 0.51 on a 1 point scale.[105]

7.7 CONCLUSION

Malaysia's robust voluntary court mediation programme has been characterized in recent years by high settlement rates. This has contributed to gains within the civil justice system in terms both of efficiency with respect

---

[102] See n. 100 above.
[103] See n. 100 above.
[104] World Bank Group, *Worldwide Governance Indicators 2015*, available at http://info.worldbank.org/governance/wgi/index.aspx#home.
[105] See n. 100 above.

to costs and time savings. Over the past five years, Malaysia has made some progress in relation to its civil justice rankings in terms of levels of efficiency, as measured by reduction of delay; confidence, as measured by effective enforcement; and perceptions of justice, as measured by the reduction of discrimination.

PART III

Mandated court mediation programmes

8. Mediation in the United States federal courts

8.1 GENERAL INTRODUCTION

In the United States, by 2012, 63 federal district courts authorized the required use of mediation, out of which 12 courts mandated the use of mediation for some or all civil cases.[1] Appellate courts have increasingly integrated alternate dispute resolution (ADR) methods into procedural rules.[2] This has included the development of mediation programmes based upon Rule 33 of the Federal Rules of Appellate Procedure.[3] While a federal mediation system exists, there is considerable variation in the regulation of mediation within the diverse states such that many state courts require parties 'to attempt to resolve their case by mediation before they can obtain a trial date'.[4] A diversity of models exist including mandatory assignment for all cases under a particular monetary amount or particular case types to court informal referrals or compelled orders to mediation after settlement conferences.[5] Stienstra has found that a presumption in favour of court referred mediation in the United States has been justified based on the unique legal, psychological and cultural characteristics

---

[1] United States Courts, 'Alternative Dispute Resolution Now an Established Practice in Federal Courts' (25 June 2012), available at www.uscourts.gov/news/2012/06/25/alternative-dispute-resolution-now-established-practice-federal-courts (accessed 28 January 2016); Donna Stienstra, *ADR in the Federal District Courts* (Federal Judicial Center, 2011), available at www.fjc.gov/public/pdf.nsf/lookup/adr2011.pdf/$file/adr2011.pdf (accessed 28 January 2016).
[2] See K.R. Casey, 'Time for Mandatory Mediation at Federal Circuit' (2005) *IP Law Bulletin* (March), available at www.stradley.com/articles.php?action5view&id5 146.
[3] *Ibid.*
[4] D.R. Hensler, 'Our Courts, Ourselves: How the Alternative Dispute Resolution Movement is Re-Shaping Our Legal System' (2003–2004) 108 *Pennsylvania State Law Review* 165.
[5] F. Steffek et al., 'Regulation of Dispute Resolution in the United States of America: From the Formal to the Informal to the "Semi-formal"' in *Regulating Dispute Resolution: ADR and Access to Justice at the Crossroads* (Oxford: Hart, 2013) p. 443.

within the country.[6] Low utilization of alternative procedures in the United States in the 1990s[7] was generally attributed to psychological and behavioural factors, including unfamiliarity with ADR, suspicion toward those suggesting the use of mediation, adversarialism, behavioural inertia, fear of appearing weak, and perceived economic self-interest.[8] For these reasons, a presumption in favour of court-based ADR programmes has been advocated.[9]

This chapter explains the law and policy background for the implementation of mandatory mediation programmes at the federal district court level in the United States. It illustrates the common features of mandatory mediation programmes supported by individual examples. It then examines important mediation cases involving the United States Justice Department, evaluates its performance, and finally explores the wider context of efficiency, confidence and perceptions of justice in the US system of civil justice. In particular, high rates of settlement have resulted in some cost and relational savings. Over the past five years, the United States' rankings in the areas of efficiency, confidence and perceptions of justice have all shown positive movement. In particular, the United States has made progress in its relative rankings in relation to efficiency, as measured by reduction of delay; confidence, as measured by effective enforcement and impartial and effective ADR; and perceptions of justice, as measured by its percentile in the reduction of discrimination.

8.2 LAW/POLICY BACKGROUND

In 1990, the United States Congress enacted the Judicial Improvements Act allowing federal district courts to refer cases for ADR, including mediation.[10] Under the Federal Rules of Appellate Procedure, all 13 federal courts of appeals have implemented appellate mediation or settlement programmes.[11] In 1994, the Judicial Conference of the United States

---

[6] D. Stienstra and T.E. Willging, *Alternatives to Litigation: Do They Have a Place in the Federal District Courts?* (Federal Judicial Center, 1995) p. 51.
[7] *Ibid.*
[8] *Ibid.* 52.
[9] *Ibid.* 52–3.
[10] A.H. Streeter-Schaefer, 'A Look at Court Mandated Civil Mediation' (2001) 49 *Drake Law Review* 367.
[11] US Supreme Court, *Advisory Committee Notes of the Federal Rules of Appellate Procedures*, Rule 33, provides that: 'The court may direct the attorneys,

put into effect an amended Rule 33. The amended rule permits courts to require clients to attend mediation sessions with their attorneys.[12]

The Alternative Dispute Resolution Act of 1998 (ADRA 1998)[13] requires every federal district court to implement a dispute resolution programme and authorizes the court to create mandatory mediation programmes so as to 'encourage and promote the use of alternative dispute resolution in [each] district'.[14] Under the Act, many states enacted some form of a mandatory mediation programme, by local rule or statute, to empower courts to compel participation by litigants.[15]

The implementation of mediation programmes in the federal courts arose out of the following four objectives:[16] first, the settlement of cases through helping parties communicate with each other; secondly, assisting litigants to develop creative and tailored solutions and mutually agreeable outcomes; thirdly, saving court and litigant resources and relieving

---

and in appropriate cases the parties, to participate in one or more conferences to address any matter that may aid in the disposition of the proceedings, including the simplification of the issues and the possibility of settlement. A conference may be conducted in person or by telephone and be presided over by a judge or other person designated by the court for that purpose. Before a settlement conference, attorneys must consult with their clients and obtain as much authority as feasible to settle the case. As a result of a conference, the court may enter an order controlling the course of the proceedings or implementing any settlement agreement'.

[12] Advisory Committee Notes of the Federal Rules of Appellate Procedures (2014), Rule 33.

[13] 28 USC ss. 651–58 (1998).

[14] United States Department of Justice, *Compendium of Federal District Courts' Local ADR Rules* (17 June 2014), available at www.justice.gov/olp/compendium-federal-district-courts-local-adr-rules (accessed 28 January 2016). (In the Civil Justice Reform Act of 1990, Congress authorized but did not require districts to implement ADR programmes as part of their plans to reduce civil justice expense and delay.) See also *Re African-American Slave Descendants' Litigation*, MDL No. 1491, Lead Case No. 02 C 7764, the motion to appoint a mediator was denied because the district had not adopted a local rule giving the court authority to compel mediation on an unwilling litigant, and the court could not, pursuant to 28 USCS s. 652 of the Alternative Dispute Resolution Act of 1998, have ordered mediation where one party objected.

[15] A.M. Pugh and R.A. Bales, 'The Inherent Power of the Federal Courts to Compel Participation in Nonbinding Forms of Alternative Dispute Resolution' (2003) 42 *Duquesne Law Review* 1, 10.

[16] R.J. Niemic, *Mediation and Conference Programs in the Federal Courts of Appeals: A Sourcebook for Judges and Lawyers* (Federal Judicial Center, 2006) pp. 5–6, available at www2.fjc.gov/sites/default/files/2012/MediCon2.pdf (accessed 28 January 2016). See also *Findings and Declaration of Policy*, Alternative Dispute Resolution Act of 1998 (1998), Pub. L. No. 105-315, ß 22, 112 Stat. 2993.

pressure on judges;[17] fourthly, addressing procedural efficiency by expediting court decisions.[18]

8.3 PROGRAMME FEATURES

The ADRA 1998 allows the federal district courts significant flexibility and discretion, 'including the ability to determine the extent of the court's ADR programme, [the] types [of ADR] used, [and] what disputes are covered'.[19]

8.3.1 Scheduling of Mediation

Rules governing referrals to mediation vary across the diverse federal mandatory mediation programmes. Some districts mandate mediation categorically while some select cases for mediation *sua sponte* or based on parties' consent, with a number of exceptions, such as where a judge determines that a case is unsuitable for mediation.[20] Some districts allow mandatory referrals with varying degrees of input from the judge assigned to the case, the parties, and an ADR administrator (e.g. District of Central California).

In general, the judge and a staff attorney review a given case and discuss mediation with the parties during an initial conference. Some districts require lawyers on both sides to discuss ADR with their clients and each other before the initial scheduling conference.[21] Parties then inform the court of the results of this discussion, at which time the assigning judge may require that the case be mediated. Parties are permitted to request a referral to mediation.[22]

Particular districts may opt for mandatory referral to mediation according to the type of claim. For example, the Southern District of New York allows mandatory mediation for claims involving issues regarding liability for damages. The Northern District of Illinois requires mandatory referral

---

[17] N.A. Welsh, 'The Thinning Vision of Self-Determination in Court-connected Mediation: The Inevitable Price of Institutionalization?' (2010) 6 *Harvard Negotiation Law Review* 1, 22–3.

[18] E. Ward, 'Transatlantic Perspectives on Alternative Dispute Resolution: Mandatory Court-Annexed Alternative Dispute Resolution in the United States Federal Courts: Panacea or Pandemic?' (2007) 81 *St John's Law Review* 77, 80–81.

[19] Stienstra (n. 1 above).

[20] Examples are Eastern District of Pennsylvania (PA), FL-S and IL-N for all cases filed under the Federal Trademark Act of 1946.

[21] Stienstra (n. 1 above) p. 241.

[22] *Ibid.* 271.

for all cases filed under the Federal Trademark Act of 1946. The Western District of Michigan requires certain tort cases to be mandatorily referred for mediation.

Parties may make an ad hoc appeal to the court for exclusion from mediation.[23] For example, the District of South California requires that all civil cases be subjected to mediation, yet parties can decline to participate by notifying the court. This notification can be given at the pre-trial scheduling conference where the judge, ADR administrator and counsel 'discuss whether mediation is appropriate for the case'.[24]

8.3.2 Mediation Process

Federal mandatory programmes are characterized by some common procedural elements. Parties may agree to modify certain procedures, except that they may not alter time limitations set by federal rules or order of the court (see Table 8.1).[25]

In most federal district courts, qualified mediators are appointed either by the court or the parties. The mediator schedules a mediation session with the parties prior to which each party must submit a memorandum outlining the case. For example, in the Northern District of Illinois, parties may be required by the mediator to submit a 'memorandum' addressing the strengths and weaknesses of the case and the terms that the party proposes for settlement. Some districts have detailed rules regarding the degree of formality of the memorandum, such as the Western District of New York. There must be a time buffer between the settlement conference and the final pre-trial conference.

Some districts require the physical presence of the parties or at least their representatives, including counsel, during the mediation session. Mediation sessions conducted through telephone are permitted in some districts, such as the Western District of North Carolina.

The rules of evidence do not usually apply to the mediation process. Thus, the testimony of a witness is not allowed. An exception may be that factual information having a bearing on the question of damages can be supported by documentary evidence whenever possible (e.g. Northern District of Indiana). A mediator can only provide an opinion on questions of fact and law on request.

---

[23] *Ibid.* 199.
[24] *Ibid.* 271.
[25] See District Court for the Eastern District of North Carolina, *Local ADR Rules* (2013), Rule 101.1g, available at www.nced.uscourts.gov/pdfs/localRules/ADRrules.pdf (accessed 28 January 2016).

Table 8.1 *Programme features of specific mandatory mediation programmes in 12 US federal districts*

District	Mediation referral processes
California Central[a]	• For judges participating in the district's Court-Directed ADR Programme, all eligible civil cases are automatically referred to the court's mediation programme or to private mediation. The judge will consider parties' written wishes in deciding whether to refer to the court's programme or private mediation. • Judges not participating in the Court-Directed ADR Programme may refer cases to the court programme *sua sponte*.
Florida Southern[b]	• Referral is mandatory by case type or track. Rule lists several exempt case types; all others are eligible. • The presiding judge may withdraw a case from mediation at any time at the request of a party or because the judge thinks the case is not suitable for mediation.
Illinois North[c]	• Referral is mandatory for all cases filed under the Federal Trademark Act of 1946, except that those under seal must not be referred while under seal.
Indiana North[d]	• Referral is mandatory by case type or track. Rule lists a number of exempt case types, including *pro se* cases. All other civil case types are eligible.
Michigan Western[e]	• Certain tort cases where the rule of decision is supplied by Michigan law are mandatorily referred unless the parties have agreed to use the court's mediation programme.
New York Western[f]	• The court expects that most cases that are referred to ADR will go to mediation, but makes a number of other ADR procedures available. Referral to ADR is mandatory, based on case type or track. • Judges may also refer cases *sua sponte*, or referral may be voluntary, based on consent of all parties. Referral to an ADR process other than mediation is upon stipulation of all parties.
North Carolina Eastern[g]	• Referral is mandatory based on case type or track for specified case types (e.g. contract, tort, civil rights). Referral may also be made based on consent of all parties.
North Carolina Middle[h]	• Referral is mandatory by case type or track for specified cases (e.g. contract, tort, civil rights). Judge may order on a case-by-case basis.

Mediation in the United States federal courts 149

Table 8.1 (continued)

District	Mediation referral processes
Missouri Western[i]	• Mandatory referral of all civil cases, except for several case types listed in the rule. Parties may ask for exemption in a written letter to the EAP administrator; appeals from the administrator's decision, while discouraged, may be made by motion to the assigned judge.
North Carolina Western[j]	• All civil cases must attend a mediated settlement conference unless otherwise ordered by the court. Parties may select another form of ADR, but if they do not they will be required to attend a mediated settlement conference. Rule lists a small number of exempt case types.
South Carolina[k]	• All civil cases are subject to mediation. Parties may, however, decline to participate by notifying the court.

a Central District of California, *Local Civil Rules* (2014), available at www.cacd.uscourts.gov/sites/default/files/documents/LocalRulesEffectiveJune21-2012-ChapterI.pdf (accessed 28 January 2016).
b Southern District of Florida, *Local Civil Rules* (2014), Rule 16.2, available at www.flsd.uscourts.gov/wp-content/uploads/2014/12/December-2014-Local-Rules.pdf (accessed 28 January 2016).
c Northern District of Illinois, *Procedures for Voluntary Mediation Programme* (2014), available at www.ilnd.uscourts.gov/LEGAL/generalr/GEN00142.HTM (accessed 28 January 2016).
d Northern District of Indiana, *Rules for Alternative Dispute Resolution* (2015), available at www.in.gov/judiciary/rules/adr/ (accessed 28 January 2016).
e Western District of Michigan, *Voluntary Facilitative Mediation Programme* (2014), available at www.miwd.uscourts.gov/sites/miwd/files/vfm_programme_desc.pdf (accessed 28 January 2016).
f Western District of New York, *ADR Plan* (2011), available at www.nywd.uscourts.gov/sites/default/files/ADRPlanRevisedJune242011.pdf (accessed 28 January 2016).
g Northern Carolina Court System, *Rules Implementing Mediation in Matters Before the Clerk of Superior Court* (2014), available at www.nccourts.org/Courts/CRS/Councils/DRC/Clerks/Rules.asp (accessed 28 January 2016).
h District Court for the Middle District of North Carolina, *Rules of Practice and Procedure* (2014), available at www.ncmd.uscourts.gov/sites/ncmd/files/CIV_LR.pdf (accessed 28 January 2016).
i Western District of Missouri, *Mediation and Assessment Programme* (2013), available at www.mow.uscourts.gov/district/map/MAPGeneralOrder_2013-08-01.pdf (accessed 28 January 2016).
j Western District of North Carolina, *Local Civil Rules* (2012), Local Rule 16, available at www.ncwd.uscourts.gov/sites/default/files/local_rules/LocalRulesMaster2011.Final_.pdf (accessed 28 January 2016).
k District Court of South Carolina, *Local Civil Rules* (2012), Local Rule 16, available at www.scd.uscourts.gov/Rules/2012/CivRules_Jan12.pdf (accessed 28 January 2016).

The entire mediation process is generally subjected to time limits set out by the district rules, such as the detailed time-frame set out in the local rules of the Eastern District of North Carolina. In some districts, like South Carolina, no extension of time is permitted unless for good reason.

8.3.3 Ground Rules that Should be Explained by Mediators at the Beginning of Mediation

At the beginning of a federal mediation session, mediators generally describe: (i) the nature and process of the mediation; (ii) the roles and responsibilities of the mediator and the parties; (iii) confidentiality of communications; (iv) costs; and (v) any other relevant issue as stated in the federal local rules.

(i) Nature and process of mediation
At the outset, the mediator must explain the differences between mediation and other forms of conflict resolution.[26] The mediation process must be described to the parties.[27] The mediator generally stipulates clearly the circumstances under which a mediator may meet alone with either of the parties or with any other person, so that the mediator may be seen to be impartial.[28]

(ii) Roles and responsibilities of the mediator and that of the parties
With regard to the duties and responsibilities of the mediator,[29] the differences between a mediator's role and a lawyer's role are set out.[30] The

---

[26] Middle District of Northern Carolina, *ADR Local Rules* (2012), Rule 83.9e, available at www.justice.gov/sites/default/files/olp/docs/nc-mid.pdf (accessed 28 January 2016).

[27] District Court for the Eastern District of North Carolina, *Local ADR Rules* (2013), Rule 101.1d, available at www.nced.uscourts.gov/pdfs/localRules/ADRrules.pdf (accessed 28 January 2016). See also District Court for South Carolina, *Local Civil Rules* (2013), Rule 16.10, available at www.scd.uscourts.gov/Rules/2013/LocalCivilRules-November2013.pdf (accessed 28 January 2016). See also Middle District of Northern Carolina, *ADR Local Rules* (2012), Rule 83.9e, available at www.justice.gov/sites/default/files/olp/docs/nc-mid.pdf (accessed 28 January 2016).

[28] District Court for South Carolina, *Local Civil Rules* (2013), Rule 16.10, available at www.scd.uscourts.gov/Rules/2013/LocalCivilRules-November2013.pdf (accessed 28 January 2016); District Court for the Eastern District of North Carolina, *Local ADR Rules* (2013), Rule 101.1d, available at www.nced.uscourts.gov/pdfs/localRules/ADRrules.pdf (accessed 28 January 2016).

[29] *Ibid.*

[30] Indiana Rules of Court, *Rules for Alternative Dispute Resolution* (2015), available at www.in.gov/judiciary/rules/adr/#_Toc428450678 (accessed 28 January 2016).

mediator (a) does not provide legal advice; (b) does not represent either party; (c) cannot discuss how the court would apply the law or rule in the parties' case, or what the outcome of the case would be if the dispute were to go before the court; and (d) must recommend that the parties seek or consult with their own legal counsel if they desire, or believe they need legal advice.[31] The mediator will make clear that he/she cannot advise any party what a party should do in a specific case, or whether a party should accept an offer.[32] Hence any agreement can only be reached by mutual consent of the parties.

The mediator may recess or suspend a mediation conference at any time. It is the duty of the mediator to determine if an impasse has been reached or if the mediation should be suspended or terminated.[33,34]

(iii) Costs

The costs of the mediation conference[35] and that of the mediated settlement conference[36] are made clear to the parties.

8.3.4 Conclusion of Processes

Within a specified time after the mediation conferences, the mediator submits a Mediation Report to the court or the ADR Programme Director. Some States have automated the final settlement process. For example, in the Central District of California, mediators electronically file a Mediation Report notifying the court that the mediation has concluded. Mediation Reports generally include information on attendance, settlement terms, case disposition, whether the case was settled (in full or in part) or was not settled (e.g. Southern District of Florida), whether the mediation was adjourned, and whether the mediator declared an impasse.[37]

If a settlement is reached (in full or in part), parties then promptly

---

[31] *Ibid.* See District Court for the Eastern District of North Carolina, *Local ADR Rules* (2013), Rule 101.1d, available at www.nced.uscourts.gov/pdfs/local Rules/ADRrules.pdf (accessed 28 January 2016). See also District Court for South Carolina, *Local Civil Rules* (2013), Rule 16.10, available at www.scd.uscourts.gov/Rules/2013/LocalCivilRules-November2013.pdf (accessed 28 January 2016).
[32] See n. 30 above.
[33] See n. 27 above.
[34] See n. 28 above
[35] See n. 28 above.
[36] See n. 27 above.
[37] For example, see Annexed Mediation of the Southern District of Florida, Rule 16.2. See also District Court for the Western District of Michigan, *Local Rules of Practice and Procedures.*

submit a notice to the court signed by all parties along with counsel within a specified period of time. Thereafter, the mediator and the parties determine if any follow-up actions are needed. Follow-up matters may include written reports, telephonic discussions or further mediation sessions (e.g. Western District of New York).

8.3.5 Procedures for Unresolved Cases

If mediation fails in a federal District Court, the case is then tried as originally scheduled. In the Eastern District of North Carolina, parties have the option of resolving the case through summary trial by a judge or a jury. The mediator is required to notify the court about the lack of agreement.

Generally, the proceedings of the mediation conference are kept confidential. Nevertheless, with the consent of the parties, the mediator's report may identify any outstanding issues which, if resolved, would facilitate a settlement. However, when inquiring into the question of whether the parties participated in mediation in good faith, most districts have substantially disregarded any recognition of mediation confidentiality, regardless of the existence of a confidentiality provision in local rules.[38]

8.3.6 Enforceability

At present, in the United States federal courts there are no special enforcement mechanisms for agreements reached in mediation.[39]

---

[38] See Western District of North Carolina, *Local Civil Rules* (2012), Local Rule 16, available at www.ncwd.uscourts.gov/sites/default/files/local_rules/LocalRulesMaster2011.Final_.pdf (accessed 28 January 2016).

[39] See J.R. Coben, 'Gollum, Meet Smeagol: A Schizophrenic Rumination on Mediator Values Beyond Self-Determination and Neutrality' (2004) 5 *Cardozo Journal of Conflict Resolution* 65, 73–4. (It provides that evidence suggests that mediation results in a high rate of compliance because parties are more accepting of a consensual solution than an imposed decision. Nonetheless, the amount of litigation over enforcement of mediated agreements indicates that some compliance problems do exist.) See E.E. Deason, 'Competing and Complementary Rule Systems: Civil Procedure and ADR: Procedural Rules for Complementary Systems of Litigation and Mediation – Worldwide' (2005) 80 *Notre Dame Law Review* 553, 582–92. (This gives an academic discussion proposing how to enforce mediated agreement, from applying contract principles to special enforcement rules.)

8.3.7 Challenges

Notwithstanding the contributions of federal mandatory mediation to overall efficiency and party satisfaction in many cases, some have suggested that mandatory mediation in the United States imposes financial barriers on those who wish to exercise their rights to a jury trial[40] through mandating expenditure at two points.[41] The first is when a party requires a ruling from a court indicating good faith participation,[42] and the second is in the legal preparation for the mediation session.[43] In addition to preparatory costs, mandatory mediation may delay compensation, placing added pressure on those requiring immediate financial liquidity. Additional questions have been raised with respect to the occurrence of coerced settlements.[44]

8.4 IMPLEMENTATION IN PRACTICE

Several recent federal cases demonstrate the frequency with which the US Justice Department uses mediation to resolve a wide range of cases.

In an Eastern District of California case brought under the Fair Housing Act,[45] the owner and manager of dozens of residential rental properties in Bakersfield was sued by the Department of Justice alleging that he sexually harassed women tenants and prospective tenants.

Subsequent to mediation, the case resulted in a consent decree, requiring the defendant to hire an independent manager to manage his rental properties and limiting his ability to have contact with current and future tenants. Furthermore, the defendant was obligated to pay more than US$2 million in monetary damages and civil penalties. This represents the largest monetary settlement ever agreed to in a sexual harassment lawsuit brought by the Justice Department under the Fair Housing Act.

---

[40] Coben, 'Gollum, Meet Smeagol' (n. 39 above) p. 56.
[41] *Ibid.* 57.
[42] *Ibid.*
[43] *Ibid.* 57–8.
[44] R.L. Wissler, *Trapping the Data: An Assessment of Domestic Relations Mediation in Maine and Ohio Courts* (Washington, DC: State Justice Institute, 1999).
[45] United States Department of Justice, *Justice News*, 11 September 2012, available at www.justice.gov/opa/pr/california-landlord-settles-sexual-harassment-lawsuit-213-million (accessed 28 January 2016).

In another case brought under the Fair Housing Act,[46] the Federal Court of South Carolina found that the defendant had violated the Fair Housing Act by discriminating against families with children. In August 2012, he agreed to pay US$25,000 to settle the lawsuit.

A third case, brought under the False Claims Act, illustrates the growing importance of mediation in settling complex disputes. In this case,[47] Abbott Laboratories Inc., B. Braun Medical Inc. and Roxane Laboratories Inc. were accused of engaging in a scheme to report false and inflated prices for pharmaceutical products, knowing that federal healthcare programmes relied on those reported prices to set payment rates.

The claims were first filed in the District of South Carolina and then handled cross-district in the Southern District of Florida and the District of Massachusetts. All defendants eventually agreed to pay US$421 million to settle the allegations.

8.5 ANALYSIS OF RESEARCH RESULTS

Recent studies of federal mandatory mediation programmes show that mandatory referral programmes result in higher settlement rates than those of non-mandatory programmes.[48] Settlement rates ranged from 21 to 60 per cent.[49] Trial rates in the federal courts have dropped despite a five-fold increase in the number of case filings.[50]

---

[46] United States Department of Justice, *Justice News*, 14 August 2012, available at www.justice.gov/opa/pr/justice-department-settles-lawsuit-against-south-carolina-landlord-discriminating-against (accessed 28 January 2016).

[47] United States Department of Justice, *Justice News*, 7 December 2010, available at www.justice.gov/opa/pr/pharmaceutical-manufacturers-pay-4212-million-settle-false-claims-act-cases (accessed 28 January 2016).

[48] Note that mandatory mediation is not required or was repealed in the local rules in the four sampled States.

[49] J.S. Kakalik et al., *An Evaluation of Mediation and Early Neutral Evaluation under the Civil Justice Reform Act* (RAND, 1996) p. 36, available at www.rand.org/content/dam/rand/pubs/monograph_reports/2007/MR803.pdf (accessed 28 January 2016).

[50] M. Galanter, 'The Vanishing Trial: What the Numbers Tell Us, What They May Mean' (2004) 10(4) *Dispute Resolution Magazine* 3, 3–4. See also R.W. Rack, Jr, 'Thoughts of a Chief Circuit Mediator on Federal Court-Annexed Mediation' (2002) 17 *Ohio State Journal on Dispute Resolution* 609, 614. (Federal judiciary statistics indicate that the percentage of district court civil cases that settled or were voluntarily dismissed has risen from 11.2 per cent in 1981 (the year the Sixth Circuit started its programme) to 48 per cent in 2000, and the number of federal civil trials has dropped approximately 36 per cent in the last five years.)

In a survey of judges and lawyers in the Northern District of California, which has long been a high functioning early initiator of federal mediation, 90 per cent of respondents stated that they had seen cases in which an 'ADR process helped produce a settlement even though one or more of the parties initially resisted or was reluctant to use ADR'.[51]

In addition, mandatory mediation programmes in the United States have resulted in some costs savings to parties. In a recent study, it was found that the highest total cost per case referred to mediation was US$490, a mere 3–10 per cent of the cost of litigation per litigant, which ranges from US$5,000 to US$17,000.[52] The average settlement rate was 47 per cent. Assuming an average litigation cost of US$10,510 per litigant, the districts saved US$1,776,190 per year. In cases that did not settle and proceeded to litigation, the court presumably expended an excess of US$490 dollars (on top of litigation costs per case).[53]

8.5.1 United States' Civil Justice Rankings: Efficiency, Confidence and Perceptions of Justice

The mandatory mediation programme in the United States can be examined within the larger context of its achievements in the areas of efficiency, confidence and perceptions of justice.

Over the past five years, as shown in Table 8.2, the United States' rankings in the areas of efficiency, confidence and perceptions of justice have all shown positive movement. Areas highlighted in grey indicate a positive movement in the rankings. As can be seen, over the past five years, the United States has experienced positive development in efficiency, as measured by reduction of delay; confidence, as measured by effective enforcement and impartial and effective ADR; and perceptions of justice, as measured by its percentile in the absence of discrimination.

In terms of overall efficiency in the civil justice system, according to the *Global Competitiveness Report 2016–2017*,[54] the United States ranks 21st out of 138 countries in the efficiency of its legal framework in settling disputes.

---

[51] Judge D.W. Nelson, 'ADR in the Federal Courts: One Judge's Perspective: Issues and Challenges Facing Judges, Lawyers, Court Administrators, and the Public' (2001) 17 *Ohio State Journal of Dispute Resolution* 1.
[52] *Ibid.* 39.
[53] T.K. Kuhner, 'Court-Connected Mediation Compared: The Cases of Argentina and the United States' (2005) 11 *ILSA Journal of International and Comparative Law* 519, 540–41.
[54] World Economic Forum, *Global Competitiveness Report 2016–2017*, pp. 356–7.

Table 8.2   *United States' rankings: developments in efficiency, confidence and perceptions of justice, 2011–2016**

	2011	2016
Efficiency		
• Efficiency of legal framework in settling disputes (rank)	36th/142	21st /138
• Accessibility and affordability (percentile)	0.47	0.41
• No unreasonable delay (percentile)	0.56	0.61
Confidence		
• Civil justice (rank)	21st/66	28th/113
• Effective enforcement (percentile)	0.65	0.66
• Impartial and effective ADR (percentile)	0.78	0.8
Perceptions of justice		
• Rule of law (percentile)	0.92	0.90**
• No discrimination (percentile)	0.43	0.46

*   Greyed rows indicate a positive trend in the rankings.
** World Bank Group, *Worldwide Governance Indicators 2015*, http://info.worldbank.org/governance/wgi/index.aspx#home.

The accessibility and affordability of the civil justice system is 0.41[55] on a 1 point scale, tied with non-OECD countries including Botswana and Pakistan. It is suggested that the extreme economic imbalance has favoured parties with the deepest pocket. The costs of obtaining quality counsel, trial discovery, witness preparation, jury research and appeal (if any) are so high that businesses and individuals without substantial financial resources simply cannot afford such costs.[56] There is also an absence of publicly administered fee schedules and the rejection of fee-shifting that leads to unpredictable outcomes and disproportionate legal costs.[57] The United States' score for 'no unreasonable delay' was 0.61[58] on a 1 point scale.

Confidence in court mediation systems can be examined in relation to the overall ranking of the civil justice system and ease of enforcement and impartiality and effectiveness of ADR. The overall rank for the United States' civil justice in the *Rule of Law Index 2016*[59] is 28th out of 113

---

[55] World Justice Project, *Rule of Law Index 2016*, p. 144.
[56] R. Sutton, 'With America's Poor Record on Civil Justice, Shouldn't We Encourage Litigation Finance?', *Inside Counsel*, 3 September 2015.
[57] *Ibid.*
[58] See n. 54 above.
[59] See n. 55 above.

countries. Its scores for effective enforcement and impartial and effective ADR were 0.66 and 0.8 on a 1 point scale, respectively.[60]

Finally, with respect to perceptions of justice, the United States' rule of law percentile was 90 on a 100 point scale in 2015.[61] The score for 'no discrimination' was 0.46.[62] The deep-rooted racial discrimination in the United States can explain this relatively low score.[63]

8.6 CONCLUSION

The United States federal mediation programme demonstrates the efficacy of high rates of settlement for mandatory referral programmes. Such high rates of settlement have also resulted in some costs and relational savings. Over the past five years, the United States' rankings in the areas of efficiency, confidence and perceptions of justice have all shown positive movement. In particular, it has made progress in its relative scores in relation to efficiency, as measured by reduction of delay; confidence, as measured by effective enforcement and impartial and effective ADR; and perceptions of justice, as measured by its percentile in the reduction of discrimination. Continued efforts, including safeguards to prevent bias and discrimination in mediation practice, are necessary to further advance court mediation programmes in the United States.

---

[60] See n. 55 above.
[61] World Bank Group, *Worldwide Governance Indicators 2015*, available at http://info.worldbank.org/governance/wgi/index.aspx#home.
[62] See n. 55 above.
[63] See e.g. M. Alexander, *The New Jim Crow: Mass Incarceration in the Age of Colorblindness* (New York: New Press, 2010).

9. Mediation in the Australian federal courts

9.1 GENERAL INTRODUCTION

Australia's programme of federal referral to court mediation has gained considerable traction in recent years with the majority of referred cases being finally settled. At the same time, over the past five years the quality of Australia's civil justice system has experienced positive development.

Australia adopts a federal law system which consists of three superior federal courts, namely, the High Court of Australia, the Federal Court of Australia, the Family Court of Australia, and the lower level Federal Circuit Court (known as the Federal Magistrates Court until 2013).[1] Mandatory mediation regimes of different degrees of compulsion are in place in the three superior federal courts.

At the federal level in Australian courts, both discretionary and categorical mandatory mediation approaches are adopted. The Federal Court has the power to order court-referred mediation pursuant to section 53A of the Federal Court of Australia Act 1976 (FCAA). Moreover, the legal aid policy for civil law proceedings also reflects the Australian trend of favouring alternative dispute resolution (ADR) rather than litigation. In particular, in Queensland, the conduct of the parties is a factor to be assessed in deciding whether a legal aid applicant will be granted legal aid.

This chapter will discuss the various mandatory mediation programmes at Australia's federal courts alongside its achievements in its civil justice system in relation to efficiency, confidence and perceptions of justice.

---

[1] J. Crawford and B. Opeskin, *Australian Courts of Law* (4th edn, Melbourne: Oxford University Press, 2004) p. 121. See also www.ag.gov.au/legalsystem/courts/Pages/default.aspx.

9.2 LAW/POLICY BACKGROUND

9.2.1 Mandatory Mediation in Australia

The mandatory mediation programme in Australia began in the 1980s, starting with the Victorian County Court Building Cases List. This programme made provision for matters to be referred to mediation for the resolution of building cases in 1983.[2] Thereafter, mandatory mediation programmes were introduced to the federal courts.

(i) Civil Dispute Resolution Act 2011

In 2009, the National Alternative Dispute Resolution Advisory Council (NADRAC) in its report *The Resolve to Resolve*, examined the possibility of stipulating pre-action requirements, with a view to encouraging greater use of ADR.[3] It looked to pre-action models whereby, when assessing costs, the courts may take into consideration the parties' conduct throughout the proceedings, including the pre-action stage.[4] The NADRAC recommended a quasi-compulsory system at the Australian federal court level.[5]

The Civil Dispute Resolution Act 2011 (CDRA) was enacted on 23 March 2011, with the object of 'ensur[ing] that, as far as possible, people take genuine steps to resolve disputes before certain civil proceedings are instituted'.[6] A 'genuine steps requirement', which requires parties to take genuine steps to resolve a dispute before certain proceedings can commence in the Federal Court or the Federal Magistrates Court, was introduced in the CDRA.[7] In *King Par LLC* v. *Brosnan Golf Pty Ltd*, Gordon J identified the object of the requirement was to 'prevent wastage of time and money'.[8]

---

[2] J. North, Law Council of Australia Ltd, speech given at the Malaysian Law Conference on 'Annexed Mediation in Australia: an Overview', 17 November 2005, available at www.lawcouncil.asn.au/lawcouncil/images/LCA-PDF/speeches/20051117CourtAnnexedMediationinAustralia.pdf (accessed 18 January 2016).

[3] National Alternative Dispute Resolution Advisory Council, 'Chapter 2: Encouraging Greater Use of ADR' in *The Resolve to Resolve: Embracing ADR to Improve Access to Justice in the Federal Jurisdiction* (NADRAC, September 2009).

[4] *Ibid.* 158, Annexe A.

[5] *Ibid.* 37, Recommendation 2.6.

[6] Civil Dispute Resolution Act (CDRA), s. 3.

[7] Australian Law Reform Commission, *Managing Discovery: Discovery of Documents in Federal Courts*, Report 115 (ALRC, 25 May 2011), available at www.alrc.gov.au/publications/1-introduction-inquiry/background-0 (accessed 18 January 2016).

[8] *King Par LLC* v. *Brosnan Golf Pty Ltd* [2013] FCA 640, para. 17.

(ii) Federal Court of Australia Act 1976

The Federal Court's Assisted Dispute Resolution programme was introduced in 1987, first as a pilot project in the Sydney Registry of the Federal Court.[9] In June 1991, section 11 of the Courts (Mediation and Arbitration) Act 1991 amended the FCAA, introducing section 53A(1).[10] Under section 53A(1), the Federal Court has the power to refer matters to ADR, including mediation.[11]

Mandatory mediation became possible under the Assisted Dispute Resolution programme when Schedule 8 to the Law and Justice Legislation Amendment Act 1997 was updated by section 53A(1A) of the FCAA.[12]

9.2.2 Legal Aid Policy in Australia Regarding Federal Civil Law

Since 1997, there has been an overall decline in federal legal aid funding in Australia. With a view to reducing legal aid cost, the Australian Commonwealth Government's policy relating to granting of legal aid is that 'civil law disputes should be resolved through alternative dispute resolution processes rather than through litigation, where appropriate'.[13]

Therefore, the current Commonwealth legal aid guideline is that:

> the [Legal Aid Commission of a State or Territory] must consider making a Grant of Legal Assistance for an applicant for assistance to participate in dispute resolution services [for civil law matters or FDR Services] before it considers making a Grant of Legal Assistance to that applicant for Litigation Services at any stage in the proceedings.[14]

Prior to 1997, cooperative funding arrangements were in place and 'each State and Territory LAC had responsibility for setting its own budget priorities and determining the amount of funding allocated to [these priorities]'.[15] This scheme was based on the principle of cooperative

---

[9] H. Astor and C. Chinkin, *Dispute Resolution in Australia* (Butterworths Australia, 1992) p. 163.
[10] D. Spencer and M. Brogan, *Mediation Law and Practice* (New York: Cambridge University Press, 2006) p. 272.
[11] Federal Court of Australia, 'Assisted Dispute Resolution', available at www.fedcourt.gov.au/case-management-services/ADR (accessed 18 January 2016).
[12] See n. 10 above.
[13] Commonwealth Legal Aid Service, *Priorities and Guidelines: General Principles*, available at www.lsc.sa.gov.au/cb_pages/commonwealth_guidelines.php#civilguidelines (accessed 14 January 2016).
[14] *Ibid*. Family Law Guidelines, Part 2 and Civil Law Guidelines, Part 4.
[15] R. Coates, 'A History of Legal Aid in Australia (Northern Territory Legal Aid Commission)', p. 13, paper presented at Fourth Annual Colloquium of the Judicial Conference of Australia, 'The 20th Century – A Century of Change',

federalism.[16] Legal aid in a State or a Territory had been provided by an independent statutory Legal Aid Commission established under State or Territory legislation.[17]

Since July 1997, Australia adopted a purchaser/provider funding arrangement for legal aid funding. Under the model, the Commonwealth government funding is exclusively used for funding matters arising from Commonwealth law, while States and Territories fund matters arising under their own law,[18] with some exceptions.[19]

After the change, the Legal Aid Commissions no longer had the responsibility for setting the guidelines and priorities for the granting of assistance relating to Commonwealth matters. This responsibility has been shifted to the Commonwealth bureaucracy.[20]

The change was a result of the Coalition government's promise to reform legal aid and reduce costs in the 1996 election campaign. One source of income for legal aid had been interest on solicitors' trust accounts, but income from these statutory interest schemes had been decreasing. Specifically, in '1991/92, Legal Aid Commissions received a total of $45.6 million from the statutory interest schemes. In 1998/99 that figure had declined to $25.6million'.[21] There were several reasons for the decline:

> [First,] interest rates [had] fallen in most jurisdictions [; secondly,] the amount of conveyancing conducted by solicitors [had] decreased [; and thirdly,] new banking technology [had] reduced the amount of time client's funds [stayed] deposited in solicitors trust accounts.[22]

2013, available at http://jca.asn.au/wp-content/uploads/2013/11/CoatesPaper.pdf (accessed 18 January 2016).

[16] *Ibid.*
[17] *Ibid.*
[18] M. Rix, 'Legal Aid, the Community Legal Sector and Access to Justice: What has been the Record of the Australian Government?' in *Proceedings of the International Symposium on Public Governance and Leadership: Managing Governance Changes Drivers for Re-constituting Leadership* (24–25 May 2007), available at http://ro.uow.edu.au/cgi/viewcontent.cgi?article51008&context5gsbpapers (accessed 18 January 2016). See also Legal Services Commission of South Australia, www.lsc.sa.gov.au/cb_pages/funding.php (accessed 12 January 2016).
[19] J. Murphy, *Legal Aid and Legal Assistance Services: Budget Review 2013–14* (May 2013). Exceptions include: '(i) the provision of early intervention legal education, information, advice, assistance and advocacy services; and (ii) legal representation of individuals whose legal problems involve a mixture of Commonwealth family law and state or territory law family violence and/or child protection issues (as described in the Commonwealth legal aid services)'.
[20] *Ibid.* 18.
[21] *Ibid.* 15.
[22] *Ibid.* 16.

As a result of the decline in income from statutory interest schemes, States had to significantly increase their share of Legal Aid Commission funding:

> For example in 1988/89 the Victorian Government only contributed $0.5 million to the Victorian Legal Aid Commission with the statutory interest scheme making up a further $18 million to account for the State share. In 1998/99 the Victorian State Government had to contribute $22 million to VLA with only $3.5 million being received from statutory interests accounts.[23]

With this background in mind, mandatory mediation was introduced for civil and family law legal aid cases.

9.3 PROGRAMME FEATURES

9.3.1 Civil Dispute Resolution Act 2011

Attempting an ADR process, including mediation, is a prerequisite to civil case filing in the Australian federal courts. Section 6 of the Civil Dispute Resolution Act 2011 requires that parties file a genuine steps statement before they can commence civil proceedings in an eligible court (including Federal Court and Federal Circuit Court). That statement must specify the steps taken in attempting to resolve the dispute, or the reasons why no such steps were taken.[24] Genuine steps include considering whether the dispute can be resolved by an ADR process.[25]

A genuine steps statement is not needed if the proceedings are wholly excluded proceedings.[26] If the proceedings are partly excluded, no genuine steps statement is needed for the excluded part.[27] A list of excluded proceedings is found in Part 4 of the CDRA, which includes appellant proceedings[28] and proceedings relating to the decisions of various tribunals, such as the Administrative Appeals Tribunal and the Copyright Tribunal.[29]

(i) Procedure

For the Federal Court, the procedures for filing a genuine steps statement are laid down in the Federal Court Rules 2011 and the Civil Dispute

---

[23] *Ibid.*
[24] CDRA, s.6(2).
[25] *Ibid.* s.4(1)(d).
[26] *Ibid.* s.6(3).
[27] *Ibid.* s.6(4).
[28] *Ibid.* s.15(d).
[29] *Ibid.* s.15(c).

Resolution Act. After the applicant has filed a genuine steps statement and a copy of that statement has been given to the respondent, the respondent must file his own genuine steps statement within a date specified in the application. In the respondent's statement, he must state whether he agrees with the applicant's statement or not. If he disagrees, either wholly or partly, he must state the reasons for disagreement.[30] Mediations are mostly conducted by the Registrars of the Court, but external mediators in Victoria and New South Wales are also available to conduct mediations.[31]

For the Federal Circuit Court, Division 4.2 of the Federal Magistrates Court Rules 2001 sets out specific rules in relation to the genuine steps obligations. The court takes into account the failure to take steps when exercising existing case management directions and costs powers. Family law proceedings are excluded from the genuine steps requirement as there are legislative pre-filing requirements which apply to parenting proceedings.

(ii) Enforceability

A failure to file a genuine steps statement in cases of non-excluded proceedings does not invalidate an application instituting civil proceedings.[32] However, non-compliance with the requirement is a relevant factor that judges take into account when awarding costs and exercising judicial power.[33] If a party does not participate in or delays participation in an ADR (including mediation) procedure, the court can order the obstructing party to bear procedural cost burdens, even in subsequent litigation.[34]

Under the Federal Court Rules, the court has power to make orders for the conduct of mediation. Examples of these orders include orders requiring minimum attendance requirements and the taking of appropriate ADR steps.[35]

In addition, a lawyer has the duty to advise his client of the genuine steps requirement and assist the client to comply with that requirement.[36]

---

[30] Federal Court Rules 2011 Rule 5.03; CDRA, s.7.

[31] T. Sourdin, 'Mediation in Australia: Impacts on Litigation' in D.K. Alexander, *Global Trends in Mediation* (The Hague: Kluwer Law International, 2006) p. 57.

[32] CDRA, s.10(2).

[33] *Ibid.* ss.11 and 12.

[34] *Ibid.* See also K.J. Hopt and F. Steffek, *Mediation: Principles and Regulation in Comparative Perspective* (Oxford University Press, 2012) p. 881.

[35] *Kilthistle No. 6 Pty Ltd and others (Receiver and Manager Appointed) v. Austwide Homes Pty Ltd and others*, BC9706608, Lehane J, Federal Court of Australia (unreported, 10 December 1997) at 6.

[36] CDRA, s.9.

Failure to fulfil such duties might result in the court ordering a cost order against the lawyer personally.[37] In *Superior IP International Pty Ltd* v. *Ahearn Fox Patent and Trade Mark Attorneys*[38] (discussed below), the lawyers of both parties were joined as parties in the proceedings because of their failure to advise their respective clients of the requirement.

9.3.2 Federal Court of Australia Act 1976

The Federal Court of Australia Act 1967 provides the court with the power to mandate pre-trial mediation. In particular, section 53A states:

> (1) The Court may, by order, refer proceedings in the Court, or any part of them or any matter arising out of them:
> (a) to an arbitrator for arbitration; or
> (b) to a mediator for mediation; or
> (c) to a suitable person for resolution by an alternative dispute resolution process;
> in accordance with the Rules of Court.

Such referrals may be made with or without the consent of the parties as stated in subsection 1A: 'Referrals under subsection (1) (other than to an arbitrator) may be made with or without the consent of the parties to the proceedings'. Moreover, it clarifies that 'this section does not apply to criminal proceedings'.[39]

9.4 IMPLEMENTATION IN PRACTICE

9.4.1 Civil Dispute Resolution Act 2011

Recent case law in Australia demonstrates the consequences of failing to comply with the genuine steps requirement in the Civil Dispute Resolution Act 2011. In *Superior IP International Pty Ltd* v. *Ahearn Fox Patent and Trade Mark Attorneys*,[40] Ahearn claimed a statutory demand on Superior IP for a relatively small debt of a total sum of only AUS$10,706.33. Superior IP made an application to set aside the statutory demand. No genuine steps statement had been filed in compliance with the CDRA and no attempt had been made by the lawyers of the parties to resolve the dispute.[41]

---

[37] *Ibid.* s.12(2) and (3).
[38] [2012] FCA 282.
[39] Federal Court of Australia Act 1976.
[40] [2012] FCA 282.
[41] *Ibid.* para. 4.

The court held that Superior IP had been wholly successful in its application and would ordinarily be entitled to an order for legal costs, based on the usual principle that costs follow the event.[42] However, in considering the factors affecting the cost of application, Reeves J referred to various provisions of the CDRA and FCAA, including section 12 of the CDRA[43] and section 37N(5) of the FCAA.[44] Reeves J allowed the parties to make submissions on the costs issue. In addition, he ordered the lawyers on both sides to join as parties to the proceedings for the determination of costs of proceedings. The basis of Reeves J's decision in refusing to award costs to Superior IP lies in section 12 of the CDRA and sections 37N and 43 of the FCAA.

Superior IP International Pty Ltd can be contrasted with *King Par LLC v. Brosnan Golf Pty Ltd* in which Gordon J held that the circumstances of the case did not warrant the award of costs on an indemnity basis.[45]

9.4.2 Federal Court of Australia Act 1976

Whether a court is to order a mandatory mediation depends on the facts of the case. There is no inflexible rule or principle categorizing cases in which such an order could or could not be ordered. Ultimately, the court needs to assess the utility of mediation and the particular circumstances of the case.[46]

In *Kilthistle No. 6 Pty Ltd and others (Receiver and Manager Appointed) v. Austwide Homes Pty Ltd and others*, Lehane J refused to make an order for mandatory mediation because mediation in the circumstances of the case would be costly and futile:

> In a case where a party to proceeding, particularly a party whose concurrence ultimately will be needed if any real progress is to be made, is adamantly opposed to mediation on the basis of a considered view, as to which it leads evidence, that it will be both costly and futile, the Court is likely, I think, to be slow to order a referral to a mediator. The number and nature of the issues in this case, the number of the parties, the course of the proceedings to date, the interlocutory matters remaining in dispute and the evidence of the applicants as to their attitude and its basis and as to their principal object in bringing these proceedings combine to convince me that mediation, at this stage, is unlikely to be either expeditious or effective.[47]

---

[42] *Ibid.* para. 30.
[43] *Ibid.* para. 40.
[44] *Ibid.* para. 43.
[45] *King Par LLC* v. *Brosnan Golf Pty Ltd* [2013] FCA 640, para. 17.
[46] *Australian Competition and Consumer Commission* v. *Collagen Aesthetics Australia Pty Ltd* [2002] FCA 1134.
[47] *Kilthistle No. 6 Pty Ltd and others* (n. 35 above) p. 6.

In *Collagen Aesthetics Australia*, a section 53A mediation order was declined given the unique circumstances of the case. The Australian Competition and Consumer Commission (ACCC) sued Collagen Aesthetics for publishing misleading and deceptive advertisements. Collagen Aesthetics sought an order for mediation under section 53A of the FCAA on the basis that the breach was only trivial and no serious harm was inflicted on the public by the advertisement. ACCC contended that mediation was unsuitable for the case because, first, the parties had attempted settlement between themselves but failed; secondly, it was unlikely that the matter would have settled because the parties could not agree on whether the breach was only trivial; thirdly, there were justifications to prosecute on the basis of public interest. Cooper J held that a court-ordered mediation would 'simply incur additional cost and delay without any reasonable prospect that the parties would by mutual agreement resolve the matters in dispute between them',[48] and as a result in that case no order for mediation was given.

The above two cases can be contrasted with *Australian Competition and Consumer Commission* v. *Lux Pty Ltd*,[49] in which mediation was ordered under section 53A of the FCAA. ACCC sought an injunction to prevent Lux from marketing its products to mentally disabled persons. Lux sought to set aside the section 53A order previously made by the court. The ACCC contended, inter alia, that it could not fulfil its function and objectives of ensuring compliance with the Trade Practices Act if it could not prosecute illegal conduct in contravention of the Act. The motion for discharge of the order was dismissed. It was held that it was possible that the ACCC's public interest obligations could be met through mediation, and there was a compelling interest in using mediation as a way of avoiding litigation. Moreover, there was a possibility that the parties could reach an agreement during mediation, and ascertain whether Lux was prepared to meet the ACCC's demands.

Similarly, *Jeray* v. *Blue Mountains City Council*[50] reflects the wide discretion of the court in exercising its power to order mediation. The Federal Circuit Court referred the parties to a debt dispute to mediation, but ordered that the scope of the mediation be limited to the timing and method of the payment. Jeray applied to extend the scope of mediation to the underlying alleged debt. The Federal Court upheld the Federal Circuit Court's decision, affirming the primary judge's power to limit the scope of mediation.

---

[48] *ACCC* v. *Collagen Aesthetics* (n. 46 above) para. 28.
[49] [2001] FCA 600.
[50] [2013] FCA 545.

9.5 ANALYSIS OF RESEARCH RESULTS

9.5.1 Civil Dispute Resolution Act 2011

Regarding the efficacy of the genuine steps requirements of the CDRA, Bowne commented that 'the issue of failure to file a genuine steps statement or to take genuine steps has been raised in only a handful of cases—and then only by parties'.[51]

9.5.2 Federal Court of Australia Act 1976

Despite the Federal Court's power to refer parties to any type of ADR, referrals are almost always to mediation. For example, in 2014–2015, 485 mediations and four conferences of experts in total were referred by different registries of the Federal Court. There were no arbitration, early neutral evaluation, court appointed experts or referees referrals.[52] Mediation referrals took up 11 per cent of the total filings and 19 per cent of the applicable filings (matters that are more commonly referred to mediation)[53] in that financial year.[54] Of the decided mediations, 53 per cent were fully or partly resolved.[55]

9.5.3 Australia's Civil Justice Rankings: Efficiency, Confidence and Perceptions of Justice

The mandatory mediation programme in Australia can be examined within the larger context of its achievements in the areas of efficiency, confidence and perceptions of justice.

Over the past five years, Australia's rankings in the areas of efficiency, confidence and perceptions of justice have all shown positive movement. As can be seen in Table 9.1, over the past five years, Australia has experienced positive development in efficiency, as measured by accessibility and affordability and reduction of delay; confidence, as measured by effective enforcement and impartial and effective ADR;

---

[51] A. Bowne SC, 'Reforms to Civil Justice: Alternative Dispute Resolution and the Courts' (2015) 39 *Australian Bar Review* 280.
[52] Federal Court of Australia, *Annual Report 2014–2015* (16 September 2015) p. 31, Table 3.5, available at www.fedcourt.gov.au/__data/assets/pdf_file/0006/29778/Annual-Report-2014-15.pdf (accessed 18 January 2016).
[53] *Ibid.* 275, 277.
[54] *Ibid.* 161, Appendix 5.
[55] *Ibid.* 163, Table A5.13.

Table 9.1 *Australia's rankings: developments in efficiency, confidence and perceptions of justice, 2011–2016**

	2011	2016
Efficiency		
• Efficiency of legal framework in settling disputes (rank)	14th/142	27th/138
• Accessibility and affordability (percentile)	0.5	0.57
• No unreasonable delay (percentile)	0.56	0.64
Confidence		
• Civil justice (rank)	13th/66	14th/113
• Effective enforcement (percentile)	0.66	0.82
• Impartial and effective ADR (percentile)	0.84	0.89
Perceptions of justice		
• Rule of law (percentile)	0.94	0.94**
• No discrimination (percentile)	0.53	0.65

*   Greyed rows indicate a positive trend in the rankings.
** World Bank Group, *Worldwide Governance Indicators 2015*, http://info.worldbank.org/governance/wgi/index.aspx#home.

and perceptions of justice, as measured by its percentile in the absence of discrimination.

In terms of overall efficiency in the civil justice system, according to the *Global Competitiveness Report 2016–2017*,[56] Australia ranks 27th out of 138 countries in the efficiency of its legal framework in settling disputes. The accessibility and affordability of the civil justice system was 0.57[57] on a 1 point scale. Its score for 'no unreasonable delay' was 0.64 on a 1 point scale.[58] This relatively low score could perhaps be explained by the fact that there is no upper limit of duration that can be identified at the start in most cases. In addition, interlocutory procedural disputes can delay the litigation as well.[59]

Confidence in court mediation systems can be examined in relation to the overall ranking of the civil justice system and ease of enforcement and impartiality and effectiveness of ADR. The overall rank for Australia's civil justice in the *Rule of Law Index 2016*[60] was 14th out of 113 countries.

---

[56] World Economic Forum, *The Global Competitiveness Report 2016–2017*, pp. 102–3.
[57] World Justice Project, *Rule of Law Index 2016*, p. 42.
[58] See n. 56 above.
[59] See n. 56 above.
[60] See n. 57 above.

Its scores for effective enforcement and impartial and effective ADR were 0.82 and 0.89 on a 1 point scale, respectively.[61] The score for impartial and effective ADR was particularly high as it is estimated that at least 90 per cent of civil disputes settle without a court hearing.[62]

Finally, with respect to perceptions of justice, Australia's rule of law percentile was 94 on a 100 point scale in 2015.[63] The score for 'no discrimination' was 0.65[64] on a 1 point scale. Australia ranks 10th out of 138 countries in judicial independence under the *Global Competitiveness Report 2016–2017*.[65]

9.6 CONCLUSION

Australia's programme of federal referral to court mediation has gained considerable traction in recent years with the majority of referred cases reaching final agreement. At the same time, over the past five years, Australia's civil justice system has experienced positive development in efficiency, as measured by accessibility and affordability and reduction of delay; confidence, as measured by effective enforcement and impartial and effective ADR; and perceptions of justice, as measured by its percentile in relation to reduction of discrimination.

---

[61] See n. 57 above.
[62] According to *The Costs and Funding of Civil Litigation*, this is an estimation made by the Law Society of New South Wales.
[63] World Bank Group, *Worldwide Governance Indicators 2015*, available at http://info.worldbank.org/governance/wgi/index.aspx#home.
[64] See n. 57 above.
[65] See n. 56 above.

10. Mediation in the Italian courts

10.1 INTRODUCTION

Due to a historical emphasis on litigation as a primary mode of dispute resolution, efforts at promoting conciliation and mediation in Italy had until the EU's 2008 Mediation Directive (Directive 2008/52/EC) been largely frustrated due to the 'voluntary' nature of such initiatives. However, as in other parts of Europe, increasing delays in case processing times and mounting backlogs of cases became symptomatic of increasing strain within the civil justice system. Efforts beginning with Legislative Decree No. 28 of 2010, and later amended by Legislative Decree No. 69 of 2013, instituted the first provisions for 'mandatory' mediation in Italian legal history.[1]

While the Italian legal community has exhibited resistance to the first introduction of mandatory mediation due to the intransigence of the judicial system,[2] the tendency to prefer court systems,[3] general suspicion of mediation,[4] the low cost of trial,[5] and the lack of willingness on the part of lawyers to face the prospect of competition in the business of dispute resolution,[6] efforts to engage lawyers in promoting mediation as key stakeholders of civil justice reform have begun to shift attitudes. Recent evidence shows positive results from an approach to 'mitigated mediation' in Italy.[7] When Italy adopted a 'mitigated' mandatory mediation system from March 2011 to October 2012, the number of mediations rose in number.[8] Since September 2013, litigants have been required to sit down

---

[1] G. De Palo and P. Harley, 'Mediation in Italy: Exploring the Contradictions' (2005) 21 *Negotiation Journal* 475.
[2] *Ibid.*
[3] *Ibid.*
[4] *Ibid.*
[5] *Ibid.* 476.
[6] *Ibid.*
[7] European Parliament Directorate-General for Internal Policies, *'Rebooting' the Mediation Directive: Assessing the Limited Impact of its Implementation and Proposing Measures to Increase the Number of Mediations in the EU* (2014) p. 8.
[8] *Ibid.*

with a mediator for a preliminary meeting at no cost in certain categories of cases.[9]

This chapter examines the operation of the mandatory mediation programme, as well as its recent reception within the context of developments within the Italian civil justice system. In particular, over the past five years, Italy has experienced some modest gains in its rankings in the areas of efficiency and confidence in the civil justice system.

10.2 LAW AND POLICY BACKGROUND

10.2.1 Italy's 'Pro-litigation' Legal Environment and Court Overload

Italy's historic emphasis on litigation meant that formalized judicial resolution of disputes was prioritized, on a societal level, to ADR mechanisms.[10] In addition, perhaps more than any other European Union Member State, Italy's judicial system was historically known for its lengthy and costly trial process.[11] Observers have noted, for instance, that it took typically over 10 years for a case to conclude.[12] Such threats to access to justice stemming from backlogs of civil cases and protracted judicial proceedings led to the recognition that the promotion of ADR mechanisms was needed to alleviate an overburdened justice system as early as the 1990s.[13] This prompted the passage of legislative measures promoting extra-judicial mediation.[14] The initial voluntary nature of the

---

[9] *Ibid.*
[10] G. De Palo and A.E. Oleson, 'Regulation of Dispute Resolution in Italy' in F. Steffek and H. Unberath (eds), *Regulating Dispute Resolution: ADR and Access to Justice at the Crossroads* (Oxford: Hart Publishing Ltd, 2013) p. 247.
[11] A. Niedostadek, '"Mediators Become Only Spectators. . .": Five Questions to . . . Carmine Oricchio / Italy', *Comparative Mediation* (26 August 2013), available at https://comparativemediation.wordpress.com/2013/08/26/mediators-become-only-spectators-five-questions-to-carmine-oricchio-italy/ (accessed 16 November 2015).
[12] *Ibid.*
[13] De Palo and Oleson, 'Regulation of Dispute Resolution in Italy' (n. 10 above) p. 247.
[14] Notably, Law No. 580 of 29 December 1993 required all Italian chambers of commerce to establish and promote arbitration and conciliation procedures for business disputes; further, Legislative Decree No. 5 of 17 January 2003 established an optional extra-judicial conciliation procedure for 'corporate cases' prior to registration of the dispute with the Ministry of Justice. See A. De Luca, 'Mediation in Italy: Features and Trends' in C. Esplugues and L. Marquis (eds), *New Developments in Civil and Commercial Mediation: Global Comparative Perspectives* (Switzerland: Springer International Publishing, 2015) p. 346.

extra-judicial options, however, meant that mediation remained underutilized as a form of ADR, with attendant implications for judicial workload.[15] Unsurprisingly, therefore, following the EU Mediation Directive of 2008, Italy became one of the few EU countries that ambitiously introduced mandatory mediation into national law in an effort to reform its justice system.

10.2.2 EU's Mediation Directive 2008/52/EC

The European Parliament's adoption of Directive 2008/52/EC on certain aspects of mediation in civil and commercial matters on 21 May 2008[16] created an impetus for the current mandatory mediation programme in the Italian courts. Noting the benefits of mediation as a form of ADR,[17] the Mediation Directive aimed to promote the use of mediation in settling civil and commercial cross-border disputes between EU nations.[18] The key provisions of the Mediation Directive provide for ensuring quality within the mediation process;[19] the right of courts to invite parties to mediate;[20] the enforceability of mediation agreements;[21] confidentiality;[22] and the general provision of information regarding mediation services.[23] Article 12 provides that all EU Member States[24] should pass legislation and administrative measures to comply with the Mediation Directive.[25]

Italy initially fulfilled her implementation obligations under article 12, via the issuance of Law No. 69 of 19 June 2009 by the Italian Parliament.[26]

---

[15] G. Matteucci, 'Mandatory Mediation: The Italian Experience' (2015) 16 *Revista Eletrônica de Direito Processual* 1.

[16] Directive 2008/52/EC of the European Parliament and of the Council of 21 May 2008 on certain aspects of mediation in civil and commercial matters [2008] OJ L136/3–8.

[17] In particular, recital 6 of the Preamble to the Mediation Directive notes benefits in time and cost, flexibility, voluntariness and ability to preserve cordial relationships between parties to the disputes. See [2008] OJ L136/3.

[18] Mediation Directive, art. 1(1)–(2).

[19] *Ibid.* art. 4.

[20] *Ibid.* art. 5.

[21] *Ibid.* art. 6.

[22] *Ibid.* art. 7.

[23] *Ibid.* arts 9 and 10.

[24] According to *ibid.* art. 1(3), all 'Member States' exclude Denmark, which opted out of the Directive.

[25] *Ibid.* art. 12.

[26] Disposizioni per lo sviluppo economico, la semplificazione, la competitività nonché in materia di processo civile (Law 69/2009), 19 June 2009, *Gazzetta Ufficiale*, no. 140, available at www.parlamento.it/parlam/leggi/09069l.htm.

Article 60 of Law 69/2009 conferred official recognition on mediation as an alternative dispute resolution (ADR) option in civil and commercial cases, and delegated authority to the Italian government to introduce a legislative decree implementing the Mediation Directive.[27] Accordingly, the Italian government introduced Legislative Decree No. 28 on 4 March 2010. The Decree became effective on 21 March 2011,[28] thereby incorporating the Mediation Directive into Italian law. The enactment of Ministry of Justice Decree No. 180 of 18 October 2010 (later amended by Ministry of Justice Decree No. 145 of 6 July 2011 and Ministry of Justice Decree No. 139 of 4 August 2014) further supplemented Decree 28/2010,[29] with specific provisions on mediation organizations, mediator qualification requirements and costs.[30]

10.2.3 Initial Mandatory Mediation Scheme under Decree 28/2010

Decree 28/2010, the predecessor to the current mandatory mediation programme, introduced mandatory mediation[31] for disputes relating to a wide range of civil and commercial matters, including[32] rights *in rem*; division of assets; inheritance; estates; leases; gratuitous loans; business leases; civil liability for medical malpractice; defamation; condominiums; and insurance and banking and financial contracts.[33] Negotiation and mediation were recognized as legitimate forms of dispute resolution, in addition to two forms of ADR specific to the financial and banking sector.[34] Further,

---

[27] Law 69/2009, art. 60. See also M. Marinari, '15. Italy' in G. De Palo and M.B. Trevor (eds), *EU Mediation Law and Practice* (Oxford University Press, 2012) paras 15.10–15.14.

[28] Attuazione dell'articolo 60 della legge 18 giugno 2009, no. 69, in materia di mediazione finalizzata alla conciliazione delle controversie civili e commerciali (Decree 28/2010), 5 March 2010, *Gazzetta Ufficiale*, no. 53, available at www.camera.it/parlam/leggi/deleghe/10028dl.htm.

[29] Regolamento recante la determinazione dei criteri e delle modalità di iscrizione e tenuta del registro degli organismi di mediazione e dell'elenco dei formatori per la mediazione, nonché l'approvazione delle indennità spettanti agli organismi, ai sensi dell'articolo 16 del decreto legislativo 4 marzo 2010, no. 28 (Decree 180/2010), 18 October 2010, available at www.mondoadr.it/cms/normativa/decreto-18-ottobre-2010-180-aggiornato-con-le-successive-modifiche-del-dm-14511-del-dm-13914.html.

[30] See Marinari, '15. Italy' (n. 27 above) para. 15.13.

[31] 'Mandatory mediation' refers to a requirement that parties must attempt dispute settlement via mediation, prior to pursuing court proceedings.

[32] Decree 28/2010, art. 5(1).

[33] Matteucci, *Mandatory Mediation: The Italian Experience* (n. 15 above) p. 5.

[34] These were, respectively, Arbitro Bancario e Finanziario and Camera Arbitrale e di Conciliazione, within two independent bodies. See *ibid.* 5.

judges adjudicating disputes were given the power to invite disputants, at any stage, to attempt mediation.[35] The entry into force of Decree 28/2010 in March 2011 culminated in a proliferation of mediation commissions and qualified mediators. Estimates suggest that in 2011, there were around 1,000 mediation bodies and 40,000 mediators.[36] While settlement rates in the second and third quarters of 2011 were between 51 and 59 per cent where all parties to a dispute where present, this amounted to settlement in just 15 per cent of all mediations.[37]

Despite a general upsurge in the number of qualified mediators in Italy, the mandatory mediation programme was faced with bitter opposition from a substantial portion of the legal community.[38] Immediately prior to the entry into force of Decree 28/2010 on 21 March 2011, Italy's national lawyers' union (Organismo Unitario dell'Avvocatura Italiana) launched an industrial action in opposition to mandatory mediation, halting judicial activity across the country for two days.[39] While proponents of the programme pointed to hefty financial costs caused by chronic delays in the Italian civil justice system,[40] a pro-litigation legal sector articulated concerns ranging from the lack of quality in services provided by mediation commissions, to potential violations of the constitutional right to defence in a trial.[41] Efforts to promote mediation were finally stalled on 24 October 2012, when the Constitutional Court struck down Decree 28/2010's provi-

---

[35] De Luca, 'Mediation in Italy: Features and Trends' (n. 14 above) p. 349.
[36] Matteucci, *Mandatory Mediation: The Italian Experience* (n. 15 above) p. 6.
[37] *Ibid.* 14, Table 8.
[38] P. Billiet, 'Refusing to Mediate: A Selection of Evolutions in Europe' in Association for International Arbitration (ed.), *European Mediation Training for Practitioners of Justice: A Gudie to European Mediation* (Maklu: Portland, 2012) p. 99.
[39] O. Bowcott, 'Compulsory mediation angers lawyers working in Italy's unwieldy legal system', *Guardian*, 23 May 2011, available at www.theguardian.com/law/butterworth-and-bowcott-on-law/2011/may/23/italian-lawyers-strike-mandatory-mediation.
[40] Italy's Central Bank estimated that delays in the civil justice system cost Italy approximately €16 billion, bringing to the fore the necessity of promoting alternative dispute resolution mechanisms to mitigate the backlog of cases and reduce case processing time. See G. Arosio et al., 'Ontology-driven Data Acquisition: Intelligent Support to Legal ODR Systems' in K.D. Ashley (ed.), *Legal Knowledge and Information Systems* (Amsterdam: IOS Press, 2013) p. 25.
[41] Matteucci, *Mandatory Mediation: The Italian Experience* (n. 15 above) p. 7. Some commentators further attribute the lawyers' opposition to mandatory mediation to protectionism in a traditionally pro-litigation society, particularly as legal representation is not a compulsory element of the mediation process. See Marinari, '15. Italy' (n. 27 above) para. 15.07.

sions for mandatory mediation as unconstitutional for 'over-delegation' (i.e. the state exceeded its mandate under Law 69/2009).[42]

10.2.4 Revival of the Mandatory Mediation Scheme under Decree 69/2013

Italy saw the reinstatement of mandatory mediation by the Italian government's passage of mediation regulations under Decree No. 69 of 2013, which amended Decree 28/2010, on 21 June 2013. This Decree entered into force three days later on 24 June 2013.[43] Decree 69/2013 was further supplemented and amended by the passage of Law No. 98 of 2013 by the Italian legislature, article 84 of which restored with modifications mandatory mediation with respect to certain classes of disputes.[44] Law 98/2013 came into force on 20 September 2013. Coupled with Decree 28/2010 (as amended by Decree 69/2013) and Decree 180/2010 (with associated amendments), these provisions form the cornerstone upon which Italy's mandatory mediation programme is currently based.

It should be noted that aside from the general requirement of mandatory mediation for civil and commercial disputes, specific mediation-related legislation for other areas of law exist.[45] For instance, mediation is required for disputes between telecommunications operators and end-users, by virtue of Law No. 249 of 31 July 1997. Similarly, Law No. 80 of 31 March 1998 rendered conciliation mandatory for labour disputes.[46] This chapter focuses on the features and implementation of the mandatory mediation programme introduced by Law 98/2013, Decree 69/2013 and Decree 180/2010.

---

[42] Matteucci, *Mandatory Mediation: The Italian Experience* (n. 15 above) p. 8. See also M.F. Corradi, 'ADR General Legal Framework in Italy' in S. Karkošková et al., *Resolving Disputes in the 21st Century* (Budapest: P.T. Muhely Ltd, 2013) p. 200. The judgment, Award No. 272 of 2012, is available at www.leggioggi.it/allegati/sentenza-corte-di-cassazione-n-2722012/.

[43] Disposizioni urgenti per il rilancio dell'economia, no. 69 (Decree 69/2013), 21 June 2013, available at www.gazzettaufficiale.it/eli/id/2013/06/21/13G00116/sg.

[44] Conversione, con modificazioni, del decreto-legge 21 giugno 2013, no. 69, Disposizioni urgenti per il rilancio dell'economia, no. 98 (Law 98/2013), 9 August 2013, available at www.bosettiegatti.eu/info/norme/statali/2013_0098.htm. See generally De Luca, 'Mediation in Italy: Features and Trends' (n. 14 above) pp. 350–51.

[45] De Luca, 'Mediation in Italy: Features and Trends' (n. 14 above) p. 351.

[46] *Ibid.* 351.

10.3 PROGRAMME FEATURES

10.3.1 New Scope of Mandatory Mediation under Decree 69/2013

Following amendments to Decree 28/2010 by Decree 69/2013, mandatory mediation is currently applicable to a narrower list of civil and commercial disputes, including those relating to: rights *in rem*; division of assets; inheritance; estates; leases; gratuitous loans; business leases; civil liability for medical malpractice; defamation and condominiums.[47] Notably, civil liability for motor vehicle and boat accidents is, by virtue of Decree 69/2013, exempted from mandatory mediation.[48]

Additionally, Decree 69/2013 extended the power of judges to compel mediation. Whereas the original provisions under Decree 28/2010 empowered judges to 'invite' disputants to mediate, the new provisions allow judges to suspend a case, actively 'order' mediation by establishing a 15-day deadline to file an application for mediation, and to fix dates for continuation of the trial following expiration of the time limit accorded to mediation.[49]

Another by-product of the amendments to Decree 28/2010 by Decree 69/2013 and Law 98/2013 is that legal representation is now compulsory for parties whose disputes fall under the categories to which the mandatory mediation requirement applies.[50] Legal assistance must be provided for the entirety of the mediation process, as well as beyond, should mediation fail. While no sanction is provided under legislation to enforce this requirement, this provision was likely included to garner support from the legal community.[51]

10.3.2 Mediation Procedure

At the beginning of the mediation process, parties to a dispute are required to file a request for mediation to a mediation institution, pursuant to article 4(1) of Decree 28/2010.[52] The chosen institution must be registered and authorized with Italy's Ministry of Justice.[53] The application form,

---

[47] Linklaters, 'Italy' in *Commercial Mediation: A Comparative Review* (2013) p. 23.
[48] De Luca, 'Mediation in Italy: Features and Trends' (n. 14 above) p. 350 (footnotes).
[49] Ibid. 349.
[50] Ibid. 356.
[51] Ibid. 356.
[52] Decree 28/2010, art. 4(1).
[53] Mediations administered by non-registered mediation bodies or private mediators are not considered 'mandatory mediation' as required by Decree

provided by the mediation institution, typically requires details including party names; addresses; contact details; details about the dispute; and the amount claimed.[54] While parties are technically free to select a mediation institution of their choosing, Law 98/2013 institutes a requirement that the request for mediation should be submitted to an institution in the same geographical jurisdiction as the judge presiding over the case.[55]

Following the initial mediation filing, the relevant mediation institution selects a mediator[56] in accordance with the institution's internal rules of procedure and professional competence requirements.[57] Where a dispute concerns highly technical details or specialist knowledge, co-mediators or experts may be appointed, with the relevant fees determined by the rules of the mediation institution.[58] Where parties are dissatisfied with the performance of their mediator, they are legally entitled to request a replacement mediator, utilizing procedures set out by the mediation institution.[59] In addition, the application and an initial meeting date (within 30 days of the filing) is arranged and communicated to all parties to the dispute.[60]

Law 98/2013 designates the first meeting as an information session intended to familiarize parties with the purpose and procedures of mediation.[61] This initial mediation session is typically provided free of charge.[62] The continuation of the process is contingent on the willingness of the disputants to mediate.[63] However, as attendance, even solely by legal representatives, of the first 'information' session is sufficient to satisfy

---

28/2010, art. 5(1). See De Luca, 'Mediation in Italy: Features and Trends' (n. 14 above) p. 352.

[54] For an example of a mediation request form, see the forms provided on Camera Arbitrale Milano's website: www.camera-arbitrale.it/en/Mediation/Rules%2C+Fees+and+Mediators.php?id5472.

[55] De Luca, 'Mediation in Italy: Features and Trends' (n. 14 above) p. 356.

[56] Decree 28/2010, art. 8(1). See De Luca, 'Mediation in Italy: Features and Trends' (n. 14 above) p. 353.

[57] Decree 28/2010, art. 3(2); Decree 180/2010, art. 7(5)(e). However, depending on the internal regulations and procedural rules adopted by the mediation institution, parties may be permitted to jointly designate a mediator to preside over the mediation. See De Luca, 'Mediation in Italy: Features and Trends' (n. 14 above) p. 353.

[58] Ibid. 354.

[59] Ibid. 354.

[60] Decree 28/2010, art. 8.

[61] De Luca, 'Mediation in Italy: Features and Trends' (n. 14 above) p. 355.

[62] Matteucci, *Mandatory Mediation: The Italian Experience* (n. 15 above) p. 8. Note that 'free of charge' applies to the mediation service; legal representatives are not exempt from remuneration during the first informational session.

[63] De Luca, 'Mediation in Italy: Features and Trends' (n. 14 above) p. 355.

the requirement of 'attempting' mediation set out in article 5 of Decree 28/2010, parties may simply choose not to mediate in favour of continuing the judicial process.[64]

10.3.3 Mediation Settlement

Once the mediation process has commenced, parties are free to undertake mediation sessions in the presence of all disputants, or through private sessions with the mediator. The principle of 'informality' in the mandatory mediation programme is reflected in article 8(3) of Decree 28/2010, which provides a great deal of flexibility with most matters left to the autonomy of the parties.[65] However, given the requirement of legal representation under Law 98/2013, it would seem that the sessions must be attended not only by parties, but by their counsel, who also play an instrumental role in the drafting and negotiation of mediation settlements.[66]

The mediator is under an obligation to assist parties in forging an agreement, in an informal and impartial manner.[67] In the event that the disputants are unable to reach a consensus, the mediator (compulsorily if requested by the parties) may advance a settlement proposal for consideration by the parties.[68] The mediator is under a duty to explain to the parties the potential consequences of non-acceptance of the mediator's proposal within seven days.[69] Article 13 of Decree 28/2010 provides for the situation in which a mediator's settlement proposal is refused by a party whose claim proceeds to succeed at court; if the award rendered by the judge equals the sum originally proposed, the party must cover all costs incurred after the proposal was suggested, as well as the costs of mediation.[70]

Once signed by the parties' legal representatives and validated in court, settlement agreements are directly enforceable as writs of execution, e.g. via specific performance.[71] Article 12 of Decree 28/2010 stipulates that a

---

[64] *Ibid.* 355.
[65] *Ibid.* 355. See also Decree 28/2010, art. 8(3).
[66] As settlement agreements are essentially contracts, the formal requirements required for valid contracts are necessary to ensure validity. De Luca, 'Mediation in Italy: Features and Trends' (n. 14 above) p. 356.
[67] Linklaters, 'Italy' (n. 47 above) p. 23.
[68] De Luca, 'Mediation in Italy: Features and Trends' (n. 14 above) p. 356; Linklaters, 'Italy' (n. 47 above) p. 23.
[69] A failure by either party to respond to the settlement proposal drawn up by the mediator will be deemed to operate as an implicit refusal. See De Luca, 'Mediation in Italy: Features and Trends' (n. 14 above) p. 356.
[70] *Ibid.* 356.
[71] Linklaters, 'Italy' (n. 47 above) p. 24.

party seeking to enforce the settlement agreement need not seek consent to do so from the other party.[72] The process of validation involves a judge ascertaining that the formal (e.g. the presence of all parties' certified signatures, registration status of the mediation institution) and substantive (e.g. compliance with public policy) requirements for the enforceability of the agreement are satisfied.[73] However, validation may be waived and the agreement automatically executed if all disputants are legally represented, and have signed the agreement.[74]

If mediation successfully results in agreement, the mediator appends the settlement agreement to the record of procedure.[75] Where agreement is ultimately not reached, or a party fails to participate fully in the mediation, the mediator makes a note as such in the record of procedure, which is signed by the parties and the mediator and retained by the mediation institution.[76] Sanctions associated with failure to participate in mediation without reasonable cause include fines to the sum of court costs.[77]

10.3.4 Mediators: Impartiality

Mediators must adhere to a general duty of impartiality and confidentiality, in accordance with Decree 28/2010.[78] The duty of impartiality requires mediators to sign declarations of impartiality, as well as prohibits mediators from receiving remuneration from the disputing parties directly.[79] The duty of confidentiality is similarly stringent, applying to all personnel employed by mediation institutions.[80] Statements made and information divulged during 'separate' meetings between one party and the mediator are confidential vis-à-vis the other party, unless expressly stated.[81] Further, due to the confidential nature of the mediation process, statements provided during the mediation process are, unless permitted by the party making the statement, inadmissible during any subsequent court proceedings.[82]

---

[72] Decree 28/2010, art. 12.
[73] De Luca, 'Mediation in Italy: Features and Trends' (n. 14 above) pp. 359–60.
[74] *Ibid.* 359–60.
[75] Decree 28/2010, art. 11. See De Luca, 'Mediation in Italy: Features and Trends' (n. 14 above) p. 356.
[76] *Ibid.* p. 356.
[77] *Ibid.* p. 356.
[78] *Ibid.* p. 354.
[79] *Ibid.* p. 354.
[80] Decree 28/2010, art. 9.
[81] *Ibid.* art. 9.
[82] *Ibid.* art. 10.

10.3.5 Time and Costs

A time limit of three months applies to the mandatory mediation process.[83] In the case of court-ordered mediation, disputes are generally suspended for a three-month period, to allow time for the mediation to take place.[84] The 'mediation period' is not calculated within compensatory claims for unreasonable delays during the judicial process.[85] Notwithstanding the above, parties may agree to continue to mediate following the expiration of the time limit.[86]

While the costs of mediation services vary depending on the rates set by individual mediation institutions, minimum and maximum rates have been statutorily established and adjusted with respect to public mediation providers.[87] Fees charged by mediation institutions are flat fees (i.e. they are fixed from the outset, regardless of the number of mediation sessions undertaken),[88] however, they do not include expert witness fees, if any. Parties receiving legal aid are entitled to have their mediation fees waived, provided that the substance of their dispute concerns matters to which mandatory mediation or court-ordered mediation applies.[89]

10.4 IMPLEMENTATION IN PRACTICE

Matteucci (2015) attributes the under-utilization of mediation tools to legal culture, noting that deeply ingrained habits by lawyers and judges alike mean that a shift towards wholesale adoption of mandatory mediation and its benefits will take time.[90] This is evident by the continuing suspicion of certain legal representatives toward the mediation process, as well as a judicial reluctance to overtly promote mediation.

---

[83] The original time limit provided for by art. 6 of Decree 28/2010 was four months; this was reduced to three months by Decree 69/2013, which amended Decree 28/2010 in reviving mandatory mediation in Italy. See De Luca, 'Mediation in Italy: Features and Trends' (n. 14 above) p. 355.
[84] *Ibid.* p. 349.
[85] *Ibid.* p. 355.
[86] *Ibid.* p. 355.
[87] *Ibid.* p. 360.
[88] *Ibid.* p. 361.
[89] *Ibid.* p. 360.
[90] Matteucci, *Mandatory Mediation: The Italian Experience* (n. 15 above) p. 11.

10.4.1 Initial Mediation Session

Despite the substantial legislative concessions made to the legal community by Decree 69/2013, the legal sector has reportedly remained somewhat aloof to an expanded role for mediation within the civil justice system.[91] Lawyers frequently fail to attend the first informative mediation session, or attend only to 'opt out' by expressing an intention not to mediate.[92] As a result, just 11 per cent of all registered mediation proceedings had full attendance in the first quarter of 2014.[93] Nonetheless, the judiciary has expressed opposition to such practices, noting that they frustrate the purpose of the mediation session.[94]

10.4.2 Court-ordered Mediation

While Decree 69/2013 permits judges to actively compel mediation in respect of 'mandatory mediation cases' by setting deadlines for filing a Request for Mediation form and staying proceedings, preliminary evidence suggests that the judicial power is not yet widely utilized.[95] It was reported that from June 2013 to June 2014, just 10 judges ordered mediation in relation to approximately 50 civil cases – a mere fraction of all the mediated cases filed during the same period.[96] While it is unclear as to whether the infrequent use of this power evidences a reluctance to compel mediation, or that such cases have already been covered by the legally 'mandatory' mediation cases, it is notable that judges have apparently not been utilizing this option with respect to non-mandatory cases.

10.5 ANALYSIS OF RESEARCH RESULTS

10.5.1 Acceptance Rates

The number of cases accepted for mediation has fluctuated in tandem with the establishment, suspension and re-establishment of mandatory

---

[91] *Ibid.* p. 9.
[92] *Ibid.* p. 9.
[93] *Ibid.* p. 9.
[94] *Ibid.* p. 11.
[95] *Ibid.* p. 11.
[96] *Ibid.* p. 11. However, it is noted that a portion of the period cited occurred during prior to the resumption of the mandatory mediation programme.

mediation reforms in 2011, 2012 and 2013, respectively.[97] 60,810 cases were accepted for mediation in 2011, increasing to 154,879 in 2012, before falling to just 41,604 cases in 2013, when the mandatory mediation regime was frozen following a determination of unconstitutionality by the Italian Constitutional Court.[98] The re-introduction of mandatory mediation in 2014 saw the number of cases accepted rise to a record high of 179,587.[99] In comparison, the total civil cases registered in Italian courts fell 8 per cent, from 228,870 to 195,273 between 2013 and 2014, following the re-establishment of its mandatory mediation programme.[100] Data from 2014 and the first quarter of 2015 indicate that most accepted mediations involved bank contract disputes (25.1 per cent), followed by property disputes (13.1 per cent) and leases (11.6 per cent).[101] Non-mandatory mediations accounted for 11.3 per cent of all mediations in 2014.[102]

10.5.2 Settlement Rates

In the first quarter of 2015, the settlement rate for all mediations was 22.2 per cent.[103] However, this figure includes the 52 per cent of cases in which parties attend the first mediation information session, without proceeding to mediate their dispute.[104] Participation has steadily risen from 27 per cent from the period spanning March 2011 to December 2012 to 32.4 per cent in 2013, 40.5 per cent in 2014, and 45 per cent in the first quarter of 2015.[105] The success rate almost doubles for parties who participate in mediation, with a 43.9 per cent settlement rate for all cases from March 2011 to December 2012, a 42.4 per cent settlement rate for all cases in

---

[97] Data presented from the Directorate-General of Statistics of the Ministry of Justice of Italy, updated of September 2015. F. De Paolis, 'The Controversial Issue of Mandatory Mediation: The Italian Experience', presentation given at the Seventh Asia Pacific Mediation Forum (APMF) Conference in Lombok, Indonesia, 10–12 February 2016.
[98] *Ibid.* slide 15.
[99] *Ibid.* slide 15.
[100] *Ibid.* slide 15.
[101] *Ibid.* slide 16.
[102] *Ibid.* slide 16.
[103] *Ibid.* slide 17. This settlement rate of 22.2 per cent in early 2015 is already higher than previous years; 9.912 per cent in 2011; 16.727 per cent in 2012; 6.365 per cent in 2013; and 17.958 per cent in 2014. See Matteucci, *Mandatory Mediation: The Italian Experience* (n. 15 above) p. 14, Table 8.
[104] De Paolis, 'The Controversial Issue of Mandatory Mediation: The Italian Experience' (n. 97 above) slide 17.
[105] *Ibid.* slide 17.

2013, and a 47 per cent settlement rate in 2014.[106] Interestingly, mediation elected by the parties consistently boasts a higher success rate as compared with mandated cases. Voluntary settlement rates were 65 per cent from the period spanning March 2011 to March 2012, 64 per cent in 2013, and 44 per cent in 2014.[107]

A recent study on the impact of Italian mediators' mediation approach on settlement rates found that evaluative mediations resulted in lower success rates than other styles.[108] The study also found a positive association between mediator post-graduate experience (particularly in negotiation) and successful outcomes.

10.5.3 Time-frame

Predictably, case processing times of civil cases are on average substantially longer, as compared to successfully mediated civil cases. While the mean time spent in mediation in successfully mediated cases has steadily increased from 2012 to the first quarter of 2015 (2012: 65 days; 2013: 82 days; 2014: 83 days; 2015 Q1: 98 days), the number of days required pales in comparison to the average of 844 days to complete a civil court case in 2013.[109] The increase in time required to process mediated cases may be attributable to the general increase in the number of cases being accepted for mediation through the mandatory mediation programme. In 2014, the average length of proceedings for mediations not resulting in a settlement agreement was 63 days.[110]

10.5.4 Italy's Civil Justice Rankings: Efficiency, Confidence and Perceptions of Justice

The mandatory mediation programme in Italy can be examined within the larger context of its achievements in the areas of efficiency, confidence and perceptions of justice.

---

[106] *Ibid.* slide 17. Note that the result in 2014 excludes mediations in which parties attended only the first information meeting.

[107] Matteucci, *Mandatory Mediation: The Italian Experience* (n. 15 above) p. 15, Table 13.

[108] L. Cominelli and C. Lucciari, 'Italian Mediators in Action: The Impact of Style and Attitude', paper presented at Law and Society Association Annual Meeting, New Orleans, 2016.

[109] Paolis, 'The Controversial Issue of Mandatory Mediation: The Italian Experience' slide 19.

[110] Matteucci, *Mandatory Mediation: The Italian Experience* (n. 15 above) p. 16, Table 15.

Table 10.1 Italy's rankings: developments in efficiency, confidence and perceptions of justice, 2011–2016*

	2011	2016
Efficiency		
• Efficiency of legal framework in settling disputes (rank)	133rd/142	136th/138
• Accessibility and affordability (percentile)	0.69	0.56
• No unreasonable delay (percentile)	0.25	0.35
Confidence		
• Civil justice (rank)	33rd/66	46th/113
• Effective enforcement (percentile)	0.38	0.42
• Impartial and effective ADR (percentile)	0.64	0.66
Perceptions of justice		
• Rule of law (percentile)	0.63	0.64**
• No discrimination (percentile)	0.63	0.59

*   Greyed rows indicate a positive trend in the rankings.
** World Bank Group, *Worldwide Governance Indicators 2015*, http://info.worldbank.org/governance/wgi/index.aspx#home.

Over the past five years, Italy has experienced some modest gains in its rankings in the areas of efficiency and confidence in the civil justice system. As can be seen above, over the past five years, Italy has experienced positive development in efficiency as measured by reduction of delay and confidence as measured by impartial and effective ADR.

In terms of overall efficiency in the civil justice system, according to the *Global Competitiveness Report 2016–2017*,[111] Italy ranks 136th out of 138 countries in the efficiency of its legal framework in settling disputes. The accessibility and affordability of the civil justice system is 0.56 on a 1 point scale.[112] Its score for 'no unreasonable delay' was 0.35 on a 1 point scale.[113]

Confidence in court mediation systems can be examined in relation to the overall ranking of the civil justice system and ease of enforcement and impartiality and effectiveness of ADR. The overall rank for Italy's civil justice in the *Rule of Law Index 2016*[114] was 46th out of 113 countries. Its

---

[111] World Economic Forum, *Global Competitiveness Report 2016–2017*, pp. 212–13.
[112] World Justice Project, *Rule of Law Index 2016*, p. 89.
[113] See n. 111 above.
[114] See n. 112 above.

scores for effective enforcement and impartial and effective ADR were 0.42 and 0.66 on a 1 point scale, respectively.[115]

Finally, with respect to perceptions of justice, Italy's rule of law percentile was 64 on a 100 point scale in 2015.[116] The score for 'no discrimination' was 0.59 on a 1 point scale.[117]

10.6 CONCLUSION

Italy's movement toward court-mandated mediation must be appreciated in the context of the role of domestic forces in Italy. For one, the country's notorious backlog and expensive litigation costs necessarily created momentum for embracing compulsory mediation. In addition, the influence of the EU Mediation Directive as part of a regional integration agenda, including Italy's attendant obligations in terms of recognition of cross-border mediated settlements, arguably created incentives to broaden reforms.[118] Finally, Italy's apparent success must also be viewed against the background of amendments, including those that were clearly designed to appease the legal fraternity by automatically qualifying all lawyers as mediators and requiring that they inform clients of mediation. This undoubtedly put lawyers at the centre of the success of the mediation programme in Italy. In addition, considering that lawyers were also frustrated by prolonged litigation, a mandatory mediation option premised on their substantial involvement benefited from strong buy-in. At the same time, over the past five years, Italy has experienced some modest gains in its rankings in the areas of efficiency and confidence in the civil justice system.

---

[115] See n. 112 above.
[116] World Bank Group, *Worldwide Governance Indicators 2015*, available at http://info.worldbank.org/governance/wgi/index.aspx#home.
[117] See n. 112 above.
[118] See n. 1 above.

11. Mediation in the Chinese courts

11.1 GENERAL INTRODUCTION

Mediation in China has experienced a gradual decline in recent years, while still accounting for a significant percentage of civil case disposition.[1] Such trends reinforce and provide nuance to the country's long socio-political history of 'tiao jie' in its various configurations.[2] The current mediation regime is governed by the People's Supreme Court that periodically issues guidelines and opinions on mediation binding on lower courts. The Civil Procedure Law also provides substantive law[3] outlining procedural requirements for mediation. It empowers the courts to initiate the mediation process and to ensure the enforceability of final agreements.[4] The courts are also allowed to invite experts to assist in the mediation process[5] or refer specialized cases out to relevant trade bodies.[6] Given the active role of judges in mediating nearly 50 per cent of civil disputes in China, the practice is generally considered to be de facto mandatory.[7]

Early studies of mediation in China examined its unique features,

---

[1] These findings are also discussed in S. Ali, 'Court Mediation in China in the Context of Global Mandatory and Voluntary Mediation Civil Justice Experience' in F. Hualing and M. Palmer (eds), *Mediation in Contemporary China: Continuity and Change* (London: Wildy, Simmonds and Hill, 2017).

[2] See generally, Wang Liming, 'Characteristics of China's Judicial Mediation System' (2009) 17 *Asia Pacific Law Review* 67; S. Lubman, 'Mao and Mediation: Politics and Dispute Resolution in Communist China' (1967) 55(5) *California Law Review* 1284.

[3] P.C.C. Huang, 'Court Mediation in China, Past and Present' (2006) 32(3) *Modern China* 275.

[4] *Ibid.*

[5] *Ibid.*

[6] M. Tai and D. Mcdonald, *Judicial Mediation in Mainland China Explained* (2012), available at https://hsfnotes.com/adr/2012/07/30/judicial-mediation-in-mainland-china-explained/.

[7] X. He and K.H. Ng, 'Internal Contradictions of Judicial Mediation in China', *Law and Social Inquiry*, 11 December 2012, available at https://ssrn.com/abstract52187880.

history and place within the civil justice system.[8] In recent times, the dynamics of mediation in the context of its impact on legal and social order in China[9] has been a rich area of scholarship.[10] Since the 1980s, studies of community and civil mediation in China have proliferated.[11] Most recently, research by Fu and Cullen has provided extensive insight into the transition from governmental emphasis on mediation in the 1950s to 1980s period, to increased attention on adjudication in the early 2000s, and then back to mediation beginning in 2006.[12] This transition has been associated with a reversal of judicial policies that were once hostile to mediation, such as prompt delivery of decisions, and replacement by minimum mediation quotas.[13] As judges take on the role of mediator, they are confronted by the interplay between state law and local customs.[14] China's recent resurgence

---

[8] See Lubman, 'Mao and Mediation: Politics and Dispute Resolution in Communist China' (n. 2 above); S. Lubman, 'Deng and Dispute Resolution: "Mao and Mediation" Revisited' (1997) 11 *Columbia Journal of Asian Law* 229.

[9] See M. Palmer, 'The Revival of Mediation in the People's Republic of China: 1. Extra-Judicial Mediation' in W.E. Butler (ed.), *Yearbook on Socialist Legal System* (Dobbs Ferry, NY: Transnational Books, 1987) pp. 219–77; H. Fu, 'Understanding People's Mediation in Post-Mao China' (1992) 6 *Journal of Chinese Law* 211.

[10] Fu Hualing and Palmer, *Mediation in Contemporary China* (n. 1 above); He and Ng, 'Internal Contradictions of Judicial Mediation in China' (n. 7 above); J. DeLisle, 'Law and China's Development Model' in P. Hsu, Y. Wu and S. Zhao, (eds), *In Search of China's Development Model: Beyond the Beijing Consensus* (London: Routledge, 2011) pp. 147–65.

[11] See D.C. Clarke, 'Dispute Resolution in China' (1992) 5 *Journal of Chinese Law* 245; Lubman, 'Deng and Dispute Resolution' (n. 8 above); S.G. Jiang, *Tiao Jie, Fa Zhi Yu Xian Dai Xing: Zhongguo Tiao Jie Zhi Du Yan Jiu* [*Mediation, Legality and Modernity: Mediation in China*] (Beijing: Zhongguo fa zhi chu ban she, 2001); X.B. Xu, *Mediation in China and the United States: Toward a Common Outcome* (Stanford University, JSD, 2003); S.E. Hilmer, *Mediation in the People's Republic of China and Hong Kong (SAR)* (The Hague: Eleven International, 2009).

[12] See H. Fu and R. Cullen, 'From Mediatory to Adjudicatory Justice: The Limits of Civil Justice Reform in China' in M.Y.K. Woo and M.E. Gallagher (eds), *Chinese Justice: Civil Dispute Resolution in Contemporary China* (Cambridge University Press, 2011) pp. 25–57; A. Halegua, 'Reforming the People's Mediation System in Urban China', available at http://papers.ssrn.com/sol3/papers.cfm?abstract_id51123283.

[13] *Ibid.*

[14] *Ibid.*; see also R. Peerenboom and H. Xin, *Dispute Resolution in China: Patterns, Causes and Prognosis*, La Trobe Law School Legal Studies Research Paper No. 2008/9; D. Ravenscroft, 'Mediation and Civil Justice Reform', *Hong Kong Lawyer* (2008), available at http://law.lexisnexis.com/webcenters/hk/Hong-Kong-Lawyer-/Mediation-and-Civil-Justice-Reform (accessed 28 November 2011).

in mediation has been viewed as an effort to increase access to courts and promote mediation as a mainstream dispute resolution mechanism, a reflection of growing dissatisfaction with adversarial litigation, and an effort to introduce a multi-door courthouse model in Chinese courts.[15]

In-court mediation in China refers to judicial mediation within the court system. While extensive out of court[16] mediation programmes[17] exist, in-court mediation is deemed part and parcel of the litigation process. This chapter will examine the nature of judicial mediation in China, relevant laws and policies and their implementation in practice. The wider context of China's achievements in efficiency, confidence and perceptions of justice in the civil justice system will be examined.

11.1.1 Differences Between Judicial Mediation and Settlement

Judicial mediation in China is an exercise of the adjudicative power of the people's courts. In other words, the power to mediate is an integral part of the jurisdiction of the courts. Settlement occurs where disputing parties exercise their litigation rights and substantive rights to settle without the facilitation of a third party.[18] The timing of judicial mediation and settlement is not identical: judicial mediation can only be conducted in the adjudication phase of the litigation proceedings while settlement can be reached at any time during the litigation.[19] Judicial mediation must be conducted in accordance with statutory procedures, yet no such procedures apply to settlement.[20] Any signed agreement reached during judicial mediation automatically ends the civil proceedings and is enforceable as

---

[15] See V. Waye and P. Xiong, 'The Relationship Between Mediation and Judicial Proceedings in China' (2011) 6(1) *Asian Journal of Comparative Law*, article 2.

[16] Constitution of the PRC, art. 111, states that, 'People's Mediation Committees are a working committee under grassroots autonomous organizations – Residents Committee, Villagers Committee – whose mission is to mediate civil disputes'.

[17] People's Mediation Law of the PRC, art. 5, provides that: 'The administrative department of justice under the State Council shall be responsible for guiding the people's mediation work of the whole nation, while the administrative departments of justice of the local people's governments at or above the county level shall be responsible for guiding the people's mediation work within their respective administrative regions. The grassroots people's courts shall provide guidance to the people's mediation commissions in their mediation of disputes among the people'.

[18] Chai Fabang et al. (eds), *Minshi Susong Faxue* 民事訴訟法學 [*The Studies of Civil Procedural Law*] (1995) pp. 247–8.

[19] *Ibid.* 248.

[20] Zhang Junhong et al. (eds), *Zhongguo Minshi Susongfa* 中國民事訴訟法 [*Civil Procedural Law of the PRC*] (1996) p. 187.

a court judgment, while agreement reached at settlement will only end the litigation proceedings upon approval of the court.[21]

11.1.2 Differences Between Judicial Mediation and Court-annexed Mediation

Unlike in many common law jurisdictions where court-annexed mediation is effectively an alternative dispute resolution (ADR) mechanism separate from the litigation process, judicial mediation in China is an integral part of the litigation process. It does not precede the trial hearing but occurs throughout the litigation process.[22] As a result, courts in China have significant involvement in judicial mediation, with judges typically assuming dual roles, acting both as a mediator and adjudicator in some cases.

The effects are also distinguishable: where judicial mediation fails, the evidence and submissions obtained by the judge may have continuous effect on the contemporaneous adjudication, whereas those attained in court-annexed mediation are usually not discoverable in subsequent litigation.

11.2 POLICY BACKGROUND

11.2.1 Historical Background

Judicial mediation in China, while evolving through diverse forms and objectives, has had a long history, finding roots in Confucian notions such as '以和为贵' ('harmony is to be prized'). Its development can be largely divided into four eras, including the revolutionary era, the pre-litigation era, the litigation era and the post-litigation era.

(i) Revolutionary Era
Before the founding of the People's Republic of China (PRC), Ma Xiwu developed a Trial Mode which combined mediation and arbitration during the Anti-Japanese War. He later assumed office as the presiding Judge of the East Tribunal of the High Court in Shanxi-Gansu-Ningxia

---

[21] *Ibid.* pp. 187–8.
[22] Yin Li, 'Fayuan Tiaojie Zhidu 第六章 法院調解制度' ['Judicial Mediation System'] ch. 6 in *Zhongguo Tiaojie Jizhi Yanjiu* 中國調解機制研究 [*The Studies on PRC Mediation System*] (2009) p. 109.

Border Region.[23] His success in resolving numerous complicated disputes using his trial method (later known as 'Ma Xiwu's Trial Mode'), combining mediation and adjudication, attracted wide public recognition.[24]

(ii) Pre-litigation Era (From the 1950s to the 1980s)
During the post-Mao era, civil disputes were classified as 'Internal Contradictions Among the People'. Civil mediation was emphasized in solving civil disputes.[25] The policy on adjudicating civil cases was succinctly expressed in the slogan, '依靠群众、调查研究、就地办案、调解为主' ('rely upon the masses, make investigations, try cases on the spot, and give priority to mediation').[26] The emphasis on the principle of 'giving priority to mediation' was maintained through the promulgation of the Civil Procedure Law (for Trial Implementation) 1982. In this Era, the mediation rate for first instance civil cases was as high as 75 to 80 per cent.[27]

Judicial mediation in China became formalized in 1951 with the Provisional Organic Regulations of the People's Courts of the People's Republic of China (人民法院暂行组织条例). Pursuant to article 12(2) and (5), prefecture-level courts were empowered to mediate civil as well as simple criminal cases. This power was reinforced in the first Organic Law of the People's Court (民法院组织法) enacted in 1954.

(iii) Litigation Era (1990s)
With the evolution of a national court system in China, trial became the major mode of civil dispute resolution with mediation being gradually marginalized. Due to the implementation of public trial and the tendency to emphasize judgment, the role of mediation was greatly weakened.[28] In this Era, there was a substantial rise in civil litigation cases from 3.21

---

[23] Wang Liming, 'Characteristics of China's Judicial Mediation System' (n. 2 above) p. 68.
[24] Ibid.
[25] Ibid.
[26] Hong Dongying, *Dangdai Zhongguo Tiaojie Zhidu Bianqian Yanjiu* 当代中国调解制度变迁研究 [*The Study on Changes of Mediation System in Contemporary China*] (2011) p. 91.
[27] Feng Xiaoguang, 'Tiaojie Zhidu Fazhan Jinchengzhong de Zhengzhi Dongyin 调解制度发展进程中的政治动因' ['Political Motives in the Process of Mediation System Development'], *People's Court Daily* 人民法院报, 20 April 2011, available at http://rmfyb.chinacourt.org/paper/html/2011-04/20/content_26131.htm?div5-1 (accessed 24 February 2016).
[28] Fu Hualing and Palmer, *Mediation in Contemporary China* (n. 1 above) p. 69.

million in 1990 to 6.23 million in 1999, amounting to an approximately 100 per cent increase in less than a decade.[29] This in turn triggered an increase in appeals and petitions.[30]

(iv) Post-litigation Era (Since the 2000s)
The twenty-first century has witnessed a great resurgence of ADR, with renewed emphasis on mediation encouraged in Chinese courts.[31] While adjudication still constitutes an important mode of resolution in China, at the same time, the judiciary is placing greater emphasis on mediation while endeavouring to overcome existing challenges, including prolonged mediation, coerced mediation and undue emphasis on mediation success rates.

The substantive law on judicial mediation is now mainly governed by four documents: the Civil Procedure Law of the People's Republic of China (2012 Amendment) (中华人民共和国民事诉讼法 (2012修正)) ('PRC Civil Procedure Law'); the Notice of the Supreme People's Court on Issuing Several Opinions on Further Implementing the Work Principle of 'Giving Priority to Mediation and Combining Mediation with Judgment' (最高人民法院印发《关于进一步贯彻 '调解优先、调判结合' 工作原则的若干意见》 的通知) ('SPC Several Opinions') promulgated in July 2010; the Several Opinions of the Supreme People's Court on Further Displaying the Positive Roles of Litigation Mediation in Building of a Harmonious Socialist Society (最高人民法院关于进一步发挥诉讼调解在构建社会主义和谐社会中积极作用的若干意见) ('SPC Opinion') promulgated on 6 March 2007; and the Provisions of the Supreme People's Court on Several Issues Concerning the Civil Mediation Work of the People's Court (最高人民法院关于人民法院民事调解工作若干问题的规定) ('SPC Provisions') promulgated on 16 September 2004. The SPC Provisions supplemented the SPC Opinion with additional rules governing mediation binding on lower courts.

11.2.2 Rationale/Initiating Legislation

Several specific advantages of judicial mediation have been cited in the Chinese context. First, the judiciary has noted that judicial mediation may assist in resolving conflicts while promoting social harmony, and enhancing

---

[29] Hong Dongying, *Dangdai Zhongguo Tiaojie Zhidu Bianqian Yanjiu* (n. 26 above) p. 92.
[30] *Ibid.*
[31] See Fu and Cullen, 'From Mediatory to Adjudicatory Justice' (n. 12 above) pp. 25–57.

mutual understanding and accommodation between disputants,[32] given the longstanding impact of Confucianism in China.[33]

Secondly, disputes are more likely to be resolved completely and finally by judicial mediation as compared to litigation (i.e. no mandatory execution by courts is needed to enforce a mediation agreement in most cases).[34] This is attributed to the role of the parties in mediation and the nature of agreements reached in contrast with the declaratory nature of court judgments.

Thirdly, mediation theoretically respects the will of the parties who generally are in the best position to know the truth behind a given dispute.[35] Some also argue that judicial mediation is more likely to achieve substantive justice.[36] However, this conclusion may not necessarily follow in the event of delay strategies, abuse of process and 'privatized' outcomes.

Fourthly, judicial costs may be reduced both horizontally and vertically. On the horizontal level, complicated issues of evidence and lengthy discovery processes may be streamlined.[37] Vertically, parties reaching agreement generally have no need for retrial or appeal. Therefore, judicial resources can be conserved.

11.3 PROGRAMME FEATURES

11.3.1 Scheduling: Stages, Scope, Initiation

(i) Judicial mediation in various phases of the civil litigation process
Judges and court staff in China are obliged to consider the suitability of mediation at all stages of the civil litigation life-cycle from filing to

---

[32] Fu Hualing and Palmer, *Mediation in Contemporary China* (n. 1 above) pp. 69–70.
[33] Chen Guo-Ming, 'Toward Transcultural Understanding: A Harmony Theory of Chinese Communication' in (2001) *Transcultural Realities: Interdisciplinary Perspectives on Cross-Cultural Relations* 55; Chen Guo-Ming and M.A. Ringo, *Chinese Conflict Management and Resolution: Advances in Communication and Culture* (Praeger Publishers, 2002).
[34] Fu Hualing and Palmer, *Mediation in Contemporary China* (n. 1 above) p. 70.
[35] Bai Jie, 'Fayuan Tiaojie Zhidu: Jiantao yu Chonggou 法院调解制度：检讨与重构' ['Judicial Mediation System: Criticism and Reflection'] in Society of Science (eds), *Xinjiang Daxue Xuebao* 新疆大学学报（社会科学版 (Xinjiang University, 2004) no. 9.
[36] Fu Hualing and Palmer, *Mediation in Contemporary China* (n. 1 above) p. 70.
[37] *Ibid.*

appeal, to re-trial and enforcement of judgments.[38] Judicial mediation for first instance cases can usually take place in three phases before the litigation process is concluded, namely, at the pre-trial, in-trial and post-trial stages.

Pre-trial mediation is conducted by court officials after acceptance of a case but prior to trial.[39] This may occur at the filing stage in the Case Filing Chamber. During this stage, a people's court may conduct mediation after the case is docketed but prior to the expiration of the defence period.[40] Alternatively, it can be undertaken by the case management staff.[41] Judicial mediation at this stage is subject to time limits to avoid prolonged mediation.[42]

If parties fail to reach a mediated agreement, non-controversial cases will be filtered and transferred to the designated court.[43] Court officials will conduct a preliminary review and arrange mediation before hearing. Applicable disputes include: (i) domestic; (ii) labour, home sites and adjacent relationship, and partnership disputes; and (iii) small claims cases or disputes over damages that result from traffic or work injury accidents.[44] Parties' consent to mediation is not necessary for these types of disputes.[45]

The people's court may, upon application of the parties, arrange for the exchange of evidence prior to court hearing.[46] At this stage, the judge formulates a preliminary view as to the controversial points, relevance of evidence and a way to resolve the dispute through mediation. Parties tend to agree to mediate to avoid further loss.[47]

Subsequently, in-trial mediation may also take place during the court hearing. Where parties still fail to reach agreement during the hearing

---

[38] SPC Several Opinions, art. 1.
[39] Interpretation of the Supreme People's Court on the Application of the Civil Procedure Law of the People's Republic of China (最高人民法院关于适用《中华人民共和国民事诉讼法》的解释), art. 142.
[40] SPC Provisions, art. 1.
[41] SPC Several Opinions, art. 1.
[42] D. McDonald and M. Tai, 'Judicial Mediation in Mainland China Explained' in Herbert Smith Freehills, *ADR Notes* (20 July 2012), available at http://hsfnotes.com/adr/2012/07/30/judicial-mediation-in-mainland-china-explained/ (accessed 15 March 2016).
[43] Yin Li, 'Fayuan Tiaojie Zhidu' (n. 22 above) p. 111.
[44] Several Provisions of the Supreme People's Court on the Application of Summary Procedures in the Trial of Civil Cases (最高人民法院关于适用简易程序审理民事案件的若干规定), art. 14.
[45] *Ibid.*
[46] Some Provisions of the Supreme People's Court on Evidence in Civil Procedures (最高人民法院关于民事诉讼证据的若干规定), art. 37.
[47] Yin Li, 'Fayuan Tiaojie Zhidu' (n. 22 above) p. 112.

process, a judge may advance a mediation proposal for reference of the parties or alternatively grant a time period for the parties to consider mediation on their own volition.[48]

(ii) Scope of application for judicial mediation
Most civil cases are suitable for mediation except for (i) cases which are not allowed to be mediated by law; (ii) cases which require further investigation; and (iii) complex and serious cases.[49] Cases not allowed to be mediated by law include 'cases that are governed by... special procedures, [including] procedures for urging debt repayment, procedures for public summons, and procedures for bankruptcy and debt repayment, cases confirming marriage and identity relationships as well as other civil cases that cannot be mediated, considering the nature of the cases'.[50]

(iii) Initiation of mediation
Judicial mediation can be initiated through one of two means: (i) by application of the parties, or (ii) at the initiative of the people's court.[51]

The court may invite outside parties to mediate, including relevant public institutions, social organizations or other organizations that have special connections with the parties or the case.[52] The settlement agreement may later be confirmed by the court, which will also respect the agreement after examining its legality.[53]

11.3.2 General Ground Rules

When trying civil cases, people's courts are required to conduct mediation on the basis of principles of free will, legality and by distinguishing between right and wrong based on clear facts.[54]

In law, mediation is a consensus-based process. Articles 93 and 96 of the PRC Civil Procedure Law stress the free will of the parties in both procedural and substantive aspects. The former refers to the conduct of judicial mediation, such that the parties should not be forced to participate in mediation. The SPC Provisions lay down detailed ground rules regard-

---

[48] Interpretation of the Supreme People's Court on the Application of the Civil Procedure Law of the People's Republic of China, art. 145.
[49] SPC Several Opinions, art. 9.
[50] SPC Provisions, art. 2.
[51] Yin Li, 'Fayuan Tiaojie Zhidu' (n. 22 above) p. 115.
[52] SPC Provisions, art. 3 and PRC Civil Procedure Law, art. 95.
[53] SPC Provisions, art. 3.
[54] PRC Civil Procedure Law, arts 9 and 93.

ing parties' freedom to determine the form of judicial mediation,[55] whether to reach an agreement,[56] the contents of the settlement agreement[57] and enforcement.[58] These rules afford substance and context to the principle of free will underlying the law of judicial mediation. Under the rules, judges may persuade parties to reach an agreement on the basis of mutual concessions but must not supplant their decision or compel them to compromise.[59]

Nevertheless in practice, observers note the existence of a tendency towards compulsion in the practice of mediation, contravening the principle of free will.[60] The incidence of coercion reflects a combination of heavy caseloads, and the fact that a judges' performance is appraised by reference to his/her case resolution rate, mediation rate and rate of appeal.[61] In turn, judges often exert political pressure on parties by inducing or coercing them to mediate, in order to achieve higher mediation rates.[62] Due to such political demands for settlements, judicial mediation has emerged as a 'far more adjudicatory, aggressive, and interventionist' process than described in law.[63] This process has been termed 'mediatory adjudication' reflecting the potential use of heavy-handed measures.[64] This has led to fairness concerns regarding agreements reached by virtue of the lack of genuine consent of the parties, especially as it is often the weaker party who compromises its interest to reach settlement.[65]

(i) Principle of Chinese mediation

In theory, all judicial conduct, including judicial mediation, must be carried out according to a number of principles. These include: the principle of legality, clarification of facts and priority to mediation. The principle

---

[55] SPC Provisions, arts 3, 4 and 7.
[56] SPC Provisions, art. 12.
[57] SPC Provisions, arts 9 and 12.
[58] SPC Provisions, art. 13.
[59] PRC Civil Procedure Law, art. 9.
[60] Wang Liming, 'Characteristics of China's Judicial Mediation System' (n. 2 above) p. 28; Fu Hualing and Palmer, *Mediation in Contemporary China* (n. 1 above) p. 71; He and Ng, 'Internal Contradictions of Judicial Mediation in China' (n. 7 above).
[61] SPC Several Opinions, art. 22.
[62] S.B. Lubman, *Bird in a Cage: Legal Reform in China After Mao* (Stanford, CA: Stanford University Press, 1999) p. 275.
[63] Huang, 'Court Mediation in China' (n. 3 above).
[64] P.C.C. Huang, 'Civil Justice in China: Representation and Practice in Late Qing' (1996) 32(3) *Canadian Journal of History* 498; Wang Liming, 'Characteristics of China's Judicial Mediation System' (n. 2 above) p. 28.
[65] *Ibid.* 28.

of legality embraces substantive and procedural facets. Procedurally, judicial mediation, despite being relatively flexible as compared with court litigation, must be conducted in compliance with procedural rules. The substantive content of settlement agreements must also comply with the law and reflect the genuine intention of the parties.[66] Within these baselines, judicial mediation possesses a certain degree of flexibility. For instance, the court may grant approval of a settlement agreement even if it exceeds the claims of the parties.[67]

The principle of 'facts being clear, and right being distinguished from wrong' means that people's courts must mediate on the basis of 'right and wrong premised on clear facts'.[68] The facts must be made clear during the course of the mediation process.[69] In addition, judicial mediation requires judges to follow the principle of 'giving priority to mediation, adjudicating without delay, and combining mediation with judgment to close a case'.[70] Finally, judicial mediation must be coordinated with other forms of mediation, such as civil mediation, industrial mediation and administrative mediation. For instance, the parties can request that the court entrust the People's Mediation Committee, relevant government departments or other social organizations to mediate on a coordinated basis.[71] Any settlement reached can then be confirmed by the court.[72]

(ii) Mediation process
Prior to initiating a mediation process, the people's court must inform the parties of the names of the presiding mediators and the court clerk, the right to apply for withdrawal and other litigation rights and obligations.[73]

Judicial mediation may be conducted by one judge or by the collegial bench.[74] The former is often applied in cases with relatively clear facts, rights and obligations, and few controversies; the latter is mainly used for complicated and significant first instance civil cases, and second instance

---

[66] SPC Provisions, art. 12(1)–(4).
[67] SPC Provisions, art. 9.
[68] PRC Civil Procedure Law, art. 93.
[69] Chang Yi et al. (eds), 'Renmin Fayuan Tiaojie 第十章 人民法院調解' ['Mediation by the People's Court'] ch. 10 in *Zhongguo Tiaojie Zhidu* 中国调解制度 [*The Mediation System of China*] (2013) p. 272.
[70] SPC Several Opinions, arts 2 and 3.
[71] SPC Provisions, art. 3(1); Fu Hualing and Palmer, *Mediation in Contemporary China* (n. 1 above) p. 72.
[72] SPC Provisions, art. 3(2).
[73] SPC Provisions, art. 5.
[74] PRC Civil Procedure Law, art. 94(1).

civil cases.⁷⁵ Alternatively, social organizations or political institutions may be invited to conduct mediation.⁷⁶

Judicial mediation is usually conducted in a private setting.⁷⁷ The presiding mediator may conduct mediation separately with each party to discuss the relative strengths and weaknesses of a case.⁷⁸ If a party cannot appear before the court, his/her authorized agent may participate⁷⁹ and sign the settlement agreement.⁸⁰ If a party to a divorce case cannot appear in court for mediation, he/she can present written opinions.⁸¹

Mediation may be concluded in one of three ways in China. First, where a settlement agreement has been reached through judicial mediation, the judge is responsible for ensuring that the terms are enforceable.⁸² The people's court prepares a consent judgment based on the settlement agreement.⁸³ The same judge is usually involved in both the preparation and execution of the consent agreement,⁸⁴ but will not simply render a judgment that mirrors a settlement reached by the parties themselves or through mediation.⁸⁵ The consent judgment should be affixed with the signature of the judges, court clerk and the people's court, and served on and signed by both sides before becoming legally binding.⁸⁶

Secondly, parties may reach a settlement agreement independently during the litigation process. The people's court may, upon the application of the parties, confirm the settlement agreement.⁸⁷

---

[75] Yin Li, 'Fayuan Tiaojie Zhidu' (n. 22 above) p. 115.
[76] SPC Provisions, art. 3(1).
[77] Interpretation of the Supreme People's Court on the Application of the PRC Civil Procedure Law, art. 146(1).
[78] SPC Provisions, art. 7(2); Hong Dongying, *Dangdai Zhongguo Tiaojie Zhidu Bianqian Yanjiu* (n. 26 above).
[79] According to PRC Civil Procedure Law, arts 59(1) and (2), the legal representative must submit to the people's court a power of attorney, stating the authorized matters and extent of authority.
[80] Interpretation of the Supreme People's Court on the Application of the PRC Civil Procedure Law, art. 147(1).
[81] *Ibid.* art. 147(2).
[82] Hong Dongying, *Dangdai Zhongguo Tiaojie Zhidu Bianqian Yanjiu* (n. 26 above).
[83] PRC Civil Procedure Law, art. 97(1).
[84] Hong Dongying, *Dangdai Zhongguo Tiaojie Zhidu Bianqian Yanjiu* (n. 26 above).
[85] SPC Provisions, art. 18; Interpretation of the Supreme People's Court on the Application of the PRC Civil Procedure Law, art. 148(1).
[86] PRC Civil Procedure Law, art. 97(2) and (3).
[87] SPC Provisions, art. 4.

Thirdly, where judicial mediation has failed to result in an agreement, or either party has retracted before the delivery and signature of the mediation agreement, the people's court will render judgment promptly to resolve the dispute.[88]

(iii) Post-mediation implications

Once a mediation agreement is reached and a settlement becomes legally binding, it has the following implications for the parties. First, the parties are not allowed to re-institute the same claim based on identical factual grounds.[89] Secondly, parties do not have a right of appeal since parties have a 'right of retraction' before the agreement becomes binding.[90] Thirdly, the substantive rights and obligations of the parties become clarified in accordance with the mediation agreement.[91]

11.3.3 Civil Mediation Paper (Consent Judgment)

The civil mediation paper (or consent judgment) is a formal court document detailing the claims, facts and outcome of the mediation.[92] The court ensures that the terms of the mediation paper comply with the law. The mediation paper may apply to only some of the claims with the other outstanding claims proceeding to trial.[93]

The parties' 'right of retraction' from unsigned civil mediation papers granted by article 99 of the PRC Civil Procedure Law has been heavily debated. Some supporters regard such a right as a right of relief, particularly if judges have applied undue authority, inducement or bias in the mediation process.[94] On the other hand, scepticism over such a right has been expressed because as soon as an agreement is reached, many believe it should be legally binding on both parties.[95] Otherwise,

---

[88] PRC Civil Procedure Law, art. 99.
[89] Yin Li, 'Fayuan Tiaojie Zhidu' (n. 22 above) p. 118.
[90] Chang Yi et al., 'Renmin Fayuan Tiaojie' (n. 69 above) p. 302.
[91] Yin Li, 'Fayuan Tiaojie Zhidu' (n. 22 above) p. 118.
[92] PRC Civil Procedure Law, art. 97(1).
[93] SPC Provisions, art. 17.
[94] Wu Hailong, 'Minshi Susong Tiaojie Kongquan Lunlue – Jiyu Benzhi de Gaige Silu he Sheji Chuangxin 民事诉讼调解控权论略—基于本质的改革思路和设计创新' ['Controlling Power on Mediation in Civil Litigation – Based on the Revolution and Design Innovation of its Nature'] in Cao Jianming (ed.), *Chengxu Gongzheng yu Susong Zhidu Gaige* 程序公正与诉讼制度改革 [*Procedural Justice and Reform of Litigation Process*] (2002).
[95] Han Chao and Lao Zijuan, 'Jingji Shenpan Fangshi Gaige Ruogan Wenti Yanjiu 经济审判方式改革若干问题研究' ['The Studies on the Reform of the

the principle of the 'sanctity of contract'[96] is undermined[97] and the principle of good faith in both substance and procedure is violated.[98] In addition, the respective rights and obligations of litigants remain unresolved with the resulting uncertainty undesirable for all parties.[99] Moreover, additional repercussions of the right of retraction include undermining the authority of the court, wasting judicial resources and inefficiency.[100]

If a party is of the view that the civil mediation paper is inconsistent with the intent of the settlement agreement, he may raise an objection to the court.[101] If such objection is deemed tenable, the people's court can supplement or correct the content of the civil mediation paper in accordance with the settlement agreement.[102] In other words, in case of inconsistencies between the mediation paper and the agreement, the agreement will prevail.[103] Any correction or supplement made by the court can only take the form of a ruling because the mediation paper is made in accordance with statutory procedures.[104]

Once the mediation paper becomes binding, it can be enforced by a court on the application of any party alleging breach.[105] If the mediation paper incorporates the terms of a separate settlement agreement which are subsequently breached, a separate court proceeding must be instituted to enforce it.[106]

Economic Judicial Modes'] in Jiang Ping (ed.), *Minshi Shenpan Fangshi Gaige yu Fazhan* 民事审判方式改革与发展 [*Reform and Development of the Civil Judicial Modes*] (1998) pp. 64–5.

[96] For instance, SPC Provisions, art. 10(1) stipulates that 'Where the mediation agreement stipulates that any party that does not perform the agreement shall assume civil liabilities, the people's court shall grant its approval'. This substantiates the contractual nature of settlement agreement once reached.

[97] Chang Yi et al., 'Renmin Fayuan Tiaojie' (n. 69 above) p. 299.

[98] *Ibid.* 300.

[99] Han and Lao, 'Jingji Shenpan Fangshi Gaige Ruogan Wenti Yanjiu' (n. 95 above).

[100] Chang Yi et al., 'Renmin Fayuan Tiaojie' (n. 69 above) p. 300.

[101] SPC Provisions, art. 16.

[102] *Ibid.*

[103] Yin Li, 'Fayuan Tiaojie Zhidu' (n. 22 above) p. 116.

[104] SPC Provisions, art. 16; Yin Li, 'Fayuan Tiaojie Zhidu' (n. 22 above) p. 116.

[105] SPC Provisions, art. 13.

[106] Hong Dongying, *Dangdai Zhongguo Tiaojie Zhidu Bianqian Yanjiu* (n. 26 above).

11.4 IMPLEMENTATION IN PRACTICE

Two high profile cases underscore the prominent role of mediation in court adjudication in China.[107]

The patent infringement case *Chint Group Corporation v. Schneider Electric Low Voltage (Tianjin) Co. Ltd*[108] (No. 276 Judgment (Zheminsanzhongzi) of the Zhejiang High People's Court (2007)) demonstrates the primacy of mediation in settling complicated civil claims. In this case, Schneider Electric SA filed lawsuits against one of its main Chinese competitors, Chint, for global patent infringements, including in China. Before all the cases were settled, Chint filed a counter-claim alleging that Schneider's mini circuit breaker had infringed Chint's utility model patent. After Schneider failed to invalidate Chint's patent, Wenzhou Intermediate People's Court ruled in favour of Chint, ordering Schneider to pay compensation of approximately RMB3.3 billion. Schneider appealed to the High People's Court of Zhejiang and the High People's Court of Beijing.

The High People's Court of Zhejiang, upon acceptance of the case, insisted on the principle of 'mediation first' and conducted a judicial mediation. In the mediation process, the court first asked both parties to devise and present multiple proposals from which an optimal global settlement might be adopted. In light of the global lawsuits between the parties worldwide and the numerous controversial issues, the court arranged each party to form a team of 10 individuals with background in technology, management and law. After the presiding judges identified mutually beneficial grounds to proceed, both parties formed a preliminary settlement agreement. Given that some of the key controversies were yet to be resolved, the court further called upon the Chairman and senior executives of the parties to attend mediation. Given the global nature of the dispute, the court rendered the process public and invited foreign delegations and media to attend the mediation. On 15 April 2009, both parties reached a global settlement, under which Schneider agreed to pay RMB157.5 million.

Similarly, the construction contract dispute of *Liu Ailong, Tang Shengming and others v. Fine Riding (Qinhuangdao) Tourism Development Co. Ltd*[109] (No. 214-220 Judgment (Shanminchuzi) of Shanhaiguan District People's Court

---

[107] 'Quanguo Fayuan Shida Tiaojie Anli 全国法院十大调解案例' ['Top 10 Mediation Cases in the National Courts'] (10 March 2012), available at www.chinacourt.org/article/detail/2012/03/id/474601.shtml (accessed 12 March 2016).

[108] 正泰集团股份有限公司诉施耐德电气低压(天津)有限公司、宁波保税区斯达电气设备 有限公司乐清分公司 (浙江省高级人民法院(2007)浙民三终字第276号).

[109] 刘爱龙、唐生明等诉有骏(秦皇岛)旅游开发有限公司 (河北省秦皇岛市山海关区人民法院(2010)山民初字第214–220号).

in Qinhuangdao City, Hebei Province (2010)) demonstrated the prominent role of judicial mediation. In this case, Fine Riding contracted with seven sub-contractors to build the Shanhaiguan National Park. Fine Riding later failed to pay the monthly instalments (totalling approximately RMB20 million), causing the construction work to be stalled and numerous migrant workers to be left without pay. In 2010, the seven sub-contractors raised claims in Shanhaiguan District People's Court against Fine Riding. All seven lawsuits were eventually resolved by judicial mediation.

The Court President became personally involved in the mediation process and actively communicated with both parties to attempt to rebuild trust. The Court President invited the participation of relevant third parties, including governmental departments and investment bodies to explore means of extending credit to the defendant. The loans granted by the state bodies and injection of funds by the investors eased the defendant company's cash flow problems and ensured that the workers could be paid and the work resumed.[110]

11.5 ANALYSIS OF RESEARCH RESULTS

11.5.1 Mediation-related Statistics

As can be seen from Table 11.1,[111] the number of judicial mediation cases at first instance court reflects both an overall and percentage wise

Table 11.1 Breakdown by types of disputes of judicial-mediated civil cases at the first instance level of the PRC courts

Type of dispute	Judicial mediation in 2011 (# of cases)	Judicial mediation in 2012 (# of cases)	Judicial mediation in 2013 (# of cases)	Judicial mediation in 2014 (# of cases)	Judicial mediation in 2015 (# of cases)
Contract-related tenure and infringement	1,199,000 697,940	1,426,117 774,943	1,385,334 692,219	1,295,072 653,108	1,420,597 627,618
Total	2,665,178	3,004,979	2,847,990	2,672,956	2,048,215

[110] 刘爱龙、唐生明等诉有騄(秦皇岛)旅游开发有限公司 (河北省秦皇岛市山海关区人民法院(2010)山民初字第214–220号).

[111] Extracted from the 'Statistical Tables on the Civil Cases Handled by First Instance Level of the PRC National Courts 全国法院审理民事一审案件情况统计表', published in the *Law Yearbook of China* 中国法律年鉴 for 2012–2016.

decline in recent years. While the percentage of contract-related disputes concluded by judicial mediation rose from 45 per cent in 2011 to 47.5 per cent in 2012, these numbers declined from 2013 onwards.

The data show an initially dwindling proportion of civil cases concluded by litigation with an approximately 9 per cent drop, from 36.4 per cent in 2008 to 27.5 per cent in 2012, followed by a resurgence in litigated cases in 2013 and 2014. From 2009 through 2013, the proportion of mediated cases surpassed that of litigated cases. Then from 2013 onward, judicial mediation has been on the decline. While many acknowledge that most of the cases that are withdrawn from court litigation can be attributed to successful mediation conducted by the court,[112] nevertheless, court statistics demonstrate the moderating role that judicial mediation is playing in contemporary China (see Table 11.2).[113]

11.5.2 Costs Incurred in Judicial Mediation

According to the PRC Civil Procedure Law and the Measures on the Payment of Litigation Costs (诉讼费用交纳办法), there are two types of mediation expenses, namely, the case acceptance fee and associated litigation expenses. The case acceptance fee is similar to a national tax which must be paid to the people's court. The rate is set according to the level of court handling the case and the nature of the dispute.[114] The fees are calculated as a percentage of the total amount claimed or a fixed sum based on the nature of the claim. No case acceptance fee is required for administrative compensation cases.[115] In the event that a case is withdrawn or resolved by mediation, the case acceptance fee is halved.[116]

Final mediation expenses are allocated according to a proportionate rate determined through negotiation between the parties.[117] If negotiation fails,[118] the court decides the allocation of mediation expenses.[119] In

---

[112] Yin Li, 'Fayuan Tiaojie Zhidu' (n. 22 above) p. 104.
[113] Extracted from the 'Statistical Tables on the Civil Cases Handled by First Instance Level of the PRC National Courts 全国法院审理民事一审案件情况统计表', published in the *Law Yearbook of China* 中国法律年鉴 for 2004–2016.
[114] The case acceptance fees for the various kinds of claims are stipulated under Measures on the Payment of Litigation Costs, art. 13.
[115] *Ibid.* art. 8.
[116] *Ibid.* art. 15.
[117] *Ibid.* art. 31.
[118] SPC Provisions, art. 14.
[119] Measures on the Payment of Litigation Costs, art. 31.

Table 11.2 Breakdown of civil cases closed at the first instance level of the PRC courts

Year	Total cases closed*	Cases with judgments handed down	Cases withdrawn	Cases mediated
2007	4,682,737	1,804,780 (38.54%)	1,065,154 (22.75%)	1,565,554 (33.43%)
2008	5,381,185	1,960,452 (36.43%)	1,273,767 (23.67%)	1,893,340 (35.18%)
2009	5,797,160	1,959,772 (33.81%)	1,494,042 (25.77%)	2,099,024 (36.21%)
2010	6,112,695	1,894,607 (30.99%)	1,619,063 (26.49%)	2,371,683 (38.80%)
2011	6,558,621	1,890,585 (28.83%)	1,746,125 (26.62%)	2,665,178 (40.64%)
2012	7,206,331	1,979,079 (27.46%)	1,906,292 (26.45%)	3,004,979 (41.70%)
2013	7,510,584	2,316,031 (30.84%)	1,887,191 (25.13%)	2,847,990 (37.92%)
2014	8,010,342	2,921,343 (36.47%)	1,895,743 (23.67%)	2,672,956 (33.37%)
2015	9,575,152	3,943,097 (41.18%)	2,174,041 (22.71%)	2,754,843 (28.77%)

* Including cases (i) with judgments handed down; (ii) dismissed; (iii) withdrawn; (iv) terminated; (v) mediated; (vi) transferred; and (vii) others.

practice, the court normally allocates mediation expenses depending on the respective financial situation of the parties and relative culpability.[120]

11.5.3 China's Civil Justice Rankings: Efficiency, Confidence and Perceptions of Justice

The mandatory mediation programme in China can be examined within the larger context of its achievements in the areas of efficiency, confidence and perceptions of justice.

Over the past five years, China has experienced some modest gains in its rankings in the areas of efficiency and confidence in its civil justice

---

[120] Chang Yi et al., 'Renmin Fayuan Tiaojie' (n. 69 above) p. 305.

Table 11.3 China's rankings: developments in efficiency, confidence and perceptions of justice, 2011–2016*

	2011	2016
Efficiency		
• Efficiency of legal framework in settling disputes (rank)	42nd/142	46th/138
• Accessibility and affordability (percentile)	0.62	0.59
• No unreasonable delay (percentile)	0.59	0.76
Confidence		
• Civil justice (rank)	44th/66	62nd/113
• Effective enforcement (percentile)	0.55	0.58
• Impartial and effective ADR (percentile)	0.59	0.62
Perceptions of justice		
• Rule of law (percentile)	0.43	0.44**
• No discrimination (percentile)	0.44	0.43

* Greyed rows indicate a positive trend in the rankings.
** World Bank Group, *Worldwide Governance Indicators 2015*, available at http://info.worldbank.org/governance/wgi/index.aspx#home.

system. As can be seen in Table 11.3, over the past five years, China has experienced positive development in efficiency, as measured by reduction of delay; and confidence, as measured by effective enforcement.

In terms of overall efficiency in the civil justice system, according to the *Global Competitiveness Report 2016–2017*,[121] China ranked 46th out of 138 countries in the efficiency of its legal framework in settling disputes. The accessibility and affordability of the civil justice system was 0.59.[122] Its score for 'no unreasonable delay' was 0.76[123] on a 1-point scale.

Confidence in court mediation systems can be examined in relation to the overall ranking of the civil justice system and ease of enforcement and impartiality and effectiveness of ADR. The overall rank for China's civil justice in the *Rule of Law Index 2016*[124] was 62nd out of 113 countries. Its scores for effective enforcement and impartial and effective ADR were 0.58 and 0.62 on a 1-point scale, respectively.[125]

---

[121] World Economic Forum, *The Global Competitiveness Report 2016–2017*, pp. 146–7.
[122] World Justice Project, *Rule of Law Index 2016*, p. 60.
[123] See n. 121 above.
[124] See n. 122 above.
[125] See n. 122 above.

Finally, with respect to perceptions of justice, China's rule of law percentile was 44 on a 100-point scale in 2015.[126] The score for 'no discrimination' was 0.43[127] on a 1-point scale.

11.6 CONCLUSION

China's court mediation programme accounts for a major share of global court mediation cases. With over 2.7 million mediated cases in 2015, no other country comes close to the significant usage of court mediation in China. Robust efforts to reform the programme have resulted in some modest gains not only to the mediation system but also to the wider experience of civil justice in China. Over the past five years, China has experienced some modest gains in its rankings in the areas of efficiency, as measured by reduction of delay; and confidence, as measured by effective enforcement.

---

[126] World Bank Group, *Worldwide Governance Indicators 2015*, available at http://info.worldbank.org/governance/wgi/index.aspx#home.
[127] See n. 126 above.

12. Mediation in the Indian courts

12.1 GENERAL INTRODUCTION

Largely motivated by a large backlog of cases, section 89 and Order X Rule 1A of the Code of Civil Procedure Act, 1908, gives Indian courts the jurisdiction, on consideration of the suitability of the case, to direct parties to mediation without requiring the consent of all parties.[1] In addition to mediation, the Civil Procedure Act also empowers courts to direct parties to four additional methods of alternative dispute resolution (ADR), including arbitration, conciliation, judicial settlement or Lok Adalat.

An important distinction to make is that the Indian Parliament treats mediation as distinct from conciliation: while the conciliator is 'proactive and interventionist', the 'mediator' is restricted to being a 'facilitator'.[2] Mediation is understood to be an informal process, not governed by the rules of evidence and formal rules of procedure; yet it is not 'extemporaneous or casual' as it is formally structured and has 'clearly identifiable stages'.[3] The goal of mediation, as practised in India, is to find a mutually acceptable solution that adequately and legitimately satisfies the needs, desires and interest of the parties.[4] In an effort to address a longstanding backlog of cases, courts (including the Supreme Court) may refer cases to mediation or if it is an uncomplicated case, it may be referred to Lok Adalat.[5]

Since the introduction of India's mandatory mediation programme, the majority of cases referred to mediation have settled. This high rate of settlement has contributed to efficiency and relational gains within the

---

[1] L.T. Ollapally, *Mandatory Court Referral for Mediation: Parties Retain the Right to Voluntary Decision*, 4 SCC J-27 (2011) pp. 1–2.

[2] J. Rao, *Concepts of Conciliation and Mediation and Their Differences* (2010) p. 1, available at http://lawcommissionofindia.nic.in/adr_conf/concepts%20med%20rao%201.pdf (accessed 10 November 2015).

[3] Ollapally, *Mandatory Court Referral for Mediation* (n. 1 above) p. 26, para 1.3.

[4] *Ibid.* 26, para. 1.4.

[5] *Ibid.*

country. At the same time, over the past five years, India has experienced modest gains in its civil justice rankings in the efficiency of its legal framework in settling disputes; confidence, as measured by effective enforcement; and perceptions of justice, as measured by its rule of law percentile.

12.2 POLICY BACKGROUND

12.2.1 Historical Background

The existence of mediation in India dates back to the pre-British era during which time a system was in place by which the Mahajans, 'prudent businessmen', would resolve disputes between merchants by conducting negotiations. By 1753, India was converted into a British Colony and British style courts were established by 1775. The British ignored local indigenous adjudication procedures and modelled court adjudication processes on those of British law courts of the period. The major conflict between British and Indian values became evident in that the former focused on a 'clear-cut decision', while the latter encouraged the parties to work out their differences through some form of compromise.[6]

Mediation in India also finds historic roots in the ancient Indian Panchayat system, where a village elder, 'Pancha' (mediator), would facilitate negotiations. However, the Panchayat system was focused on settling the 'community interest' rather than addressing the 'individual interest' of the parties.[7]

Both mediation and Lok Adalat find their roots in the 'Panchayat' system. The essence of mediation hinges on the fact that it is a 'confidential process' led by a mediator, while Lok Adalat is a 'public' process, 'presided over by a judge or panel of neutrals who propose monetary settlement after briefly hearing the factual background and claims involved in a dispute'.[8] Moreover, if a settlement is reached in Lok Adalat, 'an award is made and is binding on the parties, which can be enforced as a decree

---

[6] *Ibid.* 14.
[7] S.S. Huchannavar, 'In Search of True 'Alternative' to Existing Justice Dispensing System in India' (2013) 7(1) *NALSAR Law Review*, available at https://ssrn.com/abstract52558442.
[8] G. Relye and N.J. Bhatt, *Comparing Mediation and Lok Adalat: Toward an Integrated Approach to Dispute Resolution in India* (June 2009), available at www.mediate.com/articles/relyeaGbhattN1.cfm?nl5215 (accessed 10 November 2015).

of a civil court',[9] whereas a settlement under mediation is not enforceable unless decreed by the court.[10]

12.2.2 Initiating Legislation

Mediation was first legally recognized in India in the Industrial Disputes Act, 1947. Conciliators appointed under section 4 of the Act are 'charged with the duty of mediating and promoting the settlement of Industrial disputes'.[11] The Indian Parliament enacted the Arbitration and Conciliation Act in 1996.[12] Lok Adalat became a formalized mode of mediation under the Legal Services Authority Act, 1987.[13] Contemporary mediation gained recognition as a form of ADR in 1999 when the Indian Parliament passed the CPC Amendment Act of 1999, inserting section 89 in the Code of Civil Procedure, 1908. The amendment was brought into force with effect from 1 July 2002.[14] Order X Rules 1A, 1B and 1C, pertaining to the 'direction of the court' to opt for one of the five ADR modes under section 89, were added in 1999.[15]

(i) Relevant sections from the Code of Civil Procedure
The Civil Procedure Code (CPC) of India sets out the process by which a court may recommend mediation or another settlement process to the parties. In particular, where:

> it appears to the court that there exist elements of a settlement which may be acceptable to the parties, the court shall formulate the terms of settlement and give them to the parties for their observations and after receiving the observation of the parties, the court may reformulate the terms of a possible settlement and refer the same for . . . judicial settlement including settlement through Lok Adalat; or mediation.[16]

---

[9] V. Shroff and S. Parikh, 'India: a Conciliatory Approach' (2012) *International Financial Law Review* (September), available at www.iflr.com/Article/3083688/India-A-conciliatory-approach.html (accessed 10 November 2015).
[10] Presentation by S. Garg, *Emerging Trends in Mediation* (2015) p. 53 (on file with author).
[11] Ollapally, *Mandatory Court Referral for Mediation* (n. 1 above) p. 15.
[12] *Ibid.* 16.
[13] *Ibid.* 15.
[14] *Ibid.* 16.
[15] Garg, *Emerging Trends in Mediation* (n. 10 above) p. 53.
[16] Civil Procedure Code (CPC) 1908, s. 89, available at www.wipo.int/edocs/lexdocs/laws/en/in/in056en.pdf: '(1) Where it appears to the court that there exist elements of a settlement which may be acceptable to the parties, the court shall formulate the terms of settlement and give them to the parties for their observa-

Furthermore, Order X of the CPC highlights the directive nature of court mediation by stating under Rule 1A that:

> after recording the admissions and denials, the Court shall direct the parties to the suit to opt for either mode of the settlement outside the court as specified in sub-section (1) of section 89 . . . [and] the court shall fix the date of appearance before such forum or authority.[17]

12.2.3 Evolution of the Programme in India

The development and evolution of mediation in India[18] emerged with the holding of training sessions throughout India. The first training session was conducted in Ahmedabad (2000), by the US-based Institute for the Study and Development of Legal Systems (ISDLS).[19] In Ahmedabad, two senior lawyers started and developed a public charitable trust, Mediation Legal Education and Development.[20]

The Chief Justice of India formally inaugurated the Ahmedabad Mediation Centre in 2002, the first lawyer-managed mediation centre in India. In November 2002, he called a meeting of the Chief Justices of all the High Courts of the Indian States at New Delhi to 'impress upon them' the importance of mediation and the need to implement section 89 of the CPC.[21]

---

tions and after receiving the observation of the parties, the court may reformulate the terms of a possible settlement and refer the same for: (a) arbitration; (b) conciliation; (c) judicial settlement including settlement through Lok Adalat; or (d) mediation. (2) Where a dispute had been referred: (a) for arbitration or conciliation, the provisions of the Arbitration and Conciliation Act, 1996 shall apply as if the proceedings for arbitration or conciliation were referred for settlement under the provisions of that Act; (b) to Lok Adalat, the court shall refer the same to the Lok Adalat in accordance with the provisions of sub-section (1) of section 20 of the Legal Services Authority Act, 1987 and all other provisions of that Act shall apply in respect of the dispute so referred to the Lok Adalat; (c) for judicial settlement, the court shall refer the same to a suitable institution or person and such institution or person shall be deemed to be a Lok Adalat and all the provisions of the Legal Services Authority Act, 1987 shall apply as if the dispute were referred to a Lok Adalat under the provisions of that Act; (d) for mediation, the court shall effect a compromise between the parties and shall follow such procedure as may be prescribed'.

[17] Ibid.
[18] S. Purcell, *Dispute System Design: A Comparative Study of India, Israel, and California*, UC Hastings Research Paper No. 48 (2013).
[19] Ollapally, *Mandatory Court Referral for Mediation* (n. 1 above) p. 17.
[20] Ibid.
[21] Ibid.

In January 2003, the Institute for Arbitration Mediation Legal Education and Development (AMLEAD) and the Gujarat Law Society introduced a 32-hour Certificate Course for 'Intensive Training in Theory and Practice of Mediation'.[22] That same year, the US Educational Foundation in India (USEFI) organized training workshops in Jodhpur, Hyderabad and Bombay in June 2003.[23] The Chennai Mediation Centre was inaugurated on 9 April 2005 and started functioning in the premises of the Madras High Court as the first court-annexed mediation centre in India.[24]

The Delhi High Court Mediation and Conciliation Centre organized regular Mediation Awareness workshops and Advanced Mediation Training workshops.[25] In 2005, the Mediation and Conciliation Project Committee (MCPC), constituted by R.C. Lahoti J, initiated a pilot judicial mediation project in the Tis Hazari courts.[26] This endeavour led to the opening of a mediation centre in Karkardooma in 2006, and another in Rohini in 2009.[27]

In order to be formally trained as a mediator in India under the MCPC, an individual must undergo a 40-hour training programme and conduct 20 mediation sessions. Since the early 2000s,[28] 52 judicial mediation training programmes have been facilitated in various parts of the country. About 869 members of the judiciary have undergone the 40 hours of training.[29]

Court-annexed mediation centres have been opened in trial courts in Allahabad, Lucknow, Chandigarh, Ahmedabad, Rajkot, Jamnagar, Surat among other districts in India.[30] Such widespread community outreach has increased access to and understanding of the mediation process throughout India.[31]

(i) **Rationale**

Mediation was largely introduced in India as a result of a growing backlog of civil court cases. According to Shashank Garg, mediation was introduced largely due to a litigation explosion among a growing population

---

[22] *Ibid.*
[23] *Ibid.*
[24] *Ibid.*
[25] *Ibid.*
[26] *Ibid.*
[27] *Ibid.*
[28] *Ibid.*
[29] *Ibid.*
[30] *Ibid.* 18.
[31] *Ibid.*

of 1.3 billion people.[32] Liberalization and globalization also played a key role in increasing litigation rates in Indian courts, with about 30 million cases pending throughout the country. According to one estimate, at the current pace, courts will only be able to clear the existing backlog by 2330.[33]

(ii) Contributions of mediation in India

Among the contributions of mediation according to legal practitioners in India, is the autonomy given to parties 'over . . . the scope and outcome' of the process.[34] Its speed, efficiency and economy[35] stand in direct contrast with the slow pace of court litigation.[36] Fees range from Rs15,000 to 70,000[37] and parties do not need to pay mandatory court fees.[38]

12.3 PROGRAMME FEATURES

12.3.1 Mediation Process

Four important stages characterize the mediation process in India. These include the opening stage, the joint session, individual caucuses, and the final closing session. During the introductory stage, the mediator describes the overall mediation process in a 'language and manner understood by the parties and their counsel'. She explains the stages and ground rules of mediation along with roles of parties, mediator and advocates.[39] It is the mediator's duty to also highlight important aspects of the mediation process, confidentiality of communications, neutrality and finality.[40] At the outset, ground rules are established to ensure a respectful environment.[41]

The joint session aims to ensure that all parties develop a clearer understanding of the 'facts and issues' in dispute, the obstacles to resolution,

---

[32] Garg, *Emerging Trends in Mediation* (n. 10 above) p. 40.
[33] 'Forbes Welcome', www.forbes.com/forbes/welcome/ (accessed 16 November 2015).
[34] Ollapally, *Mandatory Court Referral for Mediation* (n. 1 above) p. 28, para. 1.1.
[35] *Ibid.* 28, para. 1.3.
[36] *Ibid.* 28, para. 1.1.
[37] *Ibid.*
[38] *Ibid.* 28, para. 1.16.
[39] Mediation and Conciliation Project Committee, Supreme Court of India, New Delhi, *Concept and Process of Mediation*, p. 7.
[40] *Ibid.* 7–8.
[41] *Ibid.* 8.

and potential solutions. The mediator ensures that each participant feels heard, and aims to maintain an open and respectful environment.[42] The focus at this stage is to gather information by permitting parties to 'narrate their case, explain perspectives, vent emotions and express feelings without interruption or challenge'.[43]

Mediators may stipulate the timing for the holding of a 'separate session' based on the 'productivity of the on-going joint session, silence by parties, loss of control, or at the request of . . . parties'.[44] Separate sessions aim to provide a venue to understand the dispute at a 'deeper level', 'provide a forum' for parties to 'vent emotions', 'disclose confidential information', and ultimately 'encourage parties to find terms that are mutually acceptable'.[45] In this stage, each party may talk to the mediator in confidence. This allows the mediator to gather more complete information.[46] The mediator may also explore sensitive or embarrassing issues. Common interests are identified, and the mediator formulates issues for resolution.

Once the parties have agreed upon the terms of settlement, the mediator 'orally confirms' the terms in front of the parties.[47] The terms are then written out, with the assistance of the mediator, and all parties to the litigation and their respective counsel sign the agreement. A copy is sent to the referral court for 'drawing up a decree in accordance with the agreement'.[48]

12.3.2 Court Referral to Mediation

Recent case law in India has addressed the question of the types of cases that can or cannot be referred to mediation.[49]

Under Order 1 Rule 8 of the CPC, suits involving 'public interest' or interests of 'numerous persons' who are not parties before the court cannot be referred to the mediation process.[50] Moreover, disputes pertain-

---

[42] *Ibid.* 9.
[43] *Ibid.* 8.
[44] Mediation and Conciliation Project Committee, *Concept and Process of Mediation* (n. 39 above).
[45] *Ibid.*
[46] *Ibid.*
[47] *Ibid.*
[48] *Ibid.* 14.
[49] *Afcons Infrastructure Ltd and another.* v. *Cherian Varkey Construction Co. (P) Ltd and others* (2010) 8 SCC 24, available at http://indiankanoon.org/doc/1875345/.
[50] *Ibid.* para. 18(i).

ing to the election to public offices, cases involving serious and specific allegations of fraud and fabrication of documents also may not be referred to mediation. The same goes for cases requiring the protection of the court (i.e. claims against minors and the mentally challenged) and cases involving prosecution of criminal offences.[51]

The types of cases that can be referred to mediation include most other pending suits in civil courts or other special tribunals/forums.[52] These include cases on contracts, imposition of specific performance, along with disputes between suppliers, builders, bankers and their customers, landlords and tenants, and insurers and the insured.[53] Cases relating to 'soured' or 'strained' relationships, including disputes relating to partnerships, can also be referred to mediation.[54] In addition, the courts have found that mediation is extremely helpful in cases where there is a 'need for continuation of the pre-existing relationship' such as disputes between neighbours, employers and employees, and members of societies.[55]

When referring a case to mediation, Lok Adalat or judicial settlement, the court will record its views 'having regard to the nature of the dispute' and mutual consent of the parties is not required. Under section 89 of the CPC, the court has to refer to the nature of the dispute and decide upon the appropriate ADR process. If the judge in charge of the case fails to arrive at a settlement, the case may be referred to another judge for judicial settlement. The court should keep track of the process by fixing a hearing date for the ADR Report. The period allotted for the process varies from one week to two months. No 'dragging' of proceedings is to be allowed.[56]

12.3.3 Enforceability

In terms of the enforceability of the mediated agreement, practitioners have observed that outcomes arrived at through mediation stand a greater chance of successful enforcement because all the parties concerned have perceived them to be in their mutual interest.[57] Furthermore,

---

[51] *Ibid.* para. 18(ii)–(vi).
[52] *Ibid.* para. 19.
[53] *Ibid.* para. 19(i).
[54] *Ibid.* para. 19(ii).
[55] *Ibid.* para. 19 (iii)–(v).
[56] *Ibid.*
[57] D.Y. Chandrachud, *Mediation: Realizing the Potential and Designing Implementation Strategies*, p. 10, available at http://lawcommissionofindia.nic.in/adr_conf/chandrachud3.pdf.

an award is enforceable as if it were a decree of the court.[58] The settlement therefore has the same force and effect as an arbitral award on agreed terms.[59]

12.4 IMPLEMENTATION IN PRACTICE

A number of recent Indian court cases have demonstrated the application of mediation law in matters arising before the judiciary, including commercial and property disputes.

While Indian courts have the power to mandate mediation, courts cannot impose the terms of a settlement. This was re-affirmed in the commercial case of *Salem Advocate Bar Association (II), Tamil Nadu v. Union of India*.[60] The court examined the issue of a court 'apply[ing] [its] mind so as to opt for one or the other of the four ADR methods . . . and if the parties do not agree . . . refer[ing] them to one or the other of the said modes'. It was decided in *Salem* that the term 'possible settlement' should be interpreted such that the court has the jurisdiction to 'formulate' a 'summary of [the] dispute' and not the actual 'terms of the settlement'.[61]

Similarly, in *Afcons Infrastructure Ltd and another v. Cherian Varkey Construction Co. (P) Ltd and others*,[62] the Supreme Court clarified that while reference to non-adjudicatory ADR processes such as mediation can be made without party consent, reference to adjudicatory ADR processes (including arbitration or conciliation) under section 89 can be made only with the consent of all parties. In this case, the appellant opposed arbitration, and as a result, the matter was remanded to the trial court to decide an appropriate non-adjudicatory ADR process. The main issue was the application of section 89 and whether it 'empower[ed] the court to refer parties to a suit to arbitration without the consent of both parties'.[63]

The Supreme Court held that 'a civil court exercising power under Section 89 of the CPC cannot refer a suit to arbitration unless all the

---

[58] *Ibid.*
[59] *Ibid.* 14.
[60] *Salem Advocate Bar Association (II), Tamil Nadu v. Union of India* (2005) 6 SCC 344, available at http://indiankanoon.org/doc/342197.
[61] R.V. Raveendran, *Alternate Dispute Resolution under Section 89 of the Code of Civil Procedure: Guidelines* (3 September 2011), available at www.legalblog.in/2011/09/alternate-dispute-resolution-under.html (accessed 16 November 2015).
[62] *Afcons Infrastructure Ltd v. Cherian Varkey Construction Co.* (n. 49 above).
[63] *Ibid.* para. 1.

parties to the suit agree to such reference'.[64] The court should 'record that the reference is by mutual consent', if the reference is to arbitration or conciliation.[65]

The court distinguished this case from domestic cases where the 'ideal stage for mediation is understood to be immediately after service of notice on the respondent and before the respondent files objections/ written statements' in order to 'avert the hostility' aggravated by 'counter-allegations'.[66] This is to be distinguished from civil suits such as *Afcons* where the appropriate stage for considering reference to ADR processes is after the completion of pleadings.

The judgment also provided an interpretation of section 89, elucidating how a court may ascertain which method of ADR to refer parties to. At first, 'consent for arbitration or conciliation' needs to be ascertained; if there is no consent, then Lok Adalat is to be specified for 'simple cases' and 'mediation' for all other cases, while reference to a 'Judge-assisted settlement' should only be called for in 'exceptional or special cases'.[67]

In the property dispute of *Moti Ram* v. *Ashok Kumar*, the court addressed the application of mediation confidentiality principles.[68] The court held that if mediation succeeds, the report to the court should not mention what transpired during the mediation proceedings. 'If the mediation is unsuccessful, then the mediator should only write one sentence in his report and send it to the Court stating that the "mediation has been unsuccessful"'.[69] Moreover, the mediator 'should not write anything discussed, proposed or done during the mediation proceedings' because the nature of mediation is based on 'offers and counter-offers' and confidentiality of the parties would be jeopardized.[70]

12.5 ANALYSIS OF RESEARCH RESULTS

Many contractual, commercial, and labour cases have been referred for mediation since the introduction of the mediation provisions in

---

[64] *Ibid.* para. 35(ii).
[65] *Ibid.* para. 32(i).
[66] *Ibid.*
[67] *Ibid.*
[68] *Moti Ram* v. *Ashok Kumar* (2011) 1 SCC 466, taken from Judicial Academy Jharkhand, *Case Law Booklet*, p. 8, available at available at http://jajharkhand.in/wp/wpcontent/uploads/2017/01/09_case_laws_on_mediation.pdf.
[69] *Ibid.*
[70] *Ibid.*

India. Since that time, 62 per cent of cases referred for mediation have settled within 60 days.[71]

Statistics show that mediation centres all across India report high mediation settlement rates. For example, 60 per cent of disputes heard in Delhi between 2005–2012 were resolved,[72] representing a 200 per cent increase in settlements between 2006 and 2007.[73] Statistics from the Bangalore Mediation Centre show similar results. Between January 2007 and 2014, the courts saw a total of 27,915 cases mediated out of 35,784 cases referred.[74] Some observers believe that this represents a significant advance in access and efficiency within the Indian judicial system since the introduction of its mediation programme.[75]

12.5.1 India's Civil Justice Rankings: Efficiency, Confidence and Perceptions of Justice

The mandatory mediation programme in India can be examined within the larger context of its achievements in the areas of efficiency, confidence and perceptions of justice.

Over the past five years, India has experienced some modest gains in its civil justice rankings in the areas of efficiency, confidence and perceptions of justice. As can be seen in Table 12.1, over the past five years, India has experienced positive development in the efficiency of its legal framework in settling disputes; confidence, as measured by effective enforcement; and perceptions of justice, as measured by its relatively higher rule of law percentile.

In terms of overall efficiency in the civil justice system, according to the *Global Competitiveness Report 2016–2017*,[76] India ranked 32nd out of 138 countries in the efficiency of its legal framework in settling disputes. The accessibility and affordability of the civil justice system was 0.31[77] on a 1

---

[71] Ollapally, *Mandatory Court Referral for Mediation* (n. 1 above) p. 1.

[72] Herbert Smith Freehills, 'Mediation Successful in 60% of Delhi Court Actions', *ADR Notes: India* (3 September 2012), available at http://hsfnotes.com/adr/2012/09/03/india-mediation-successful-in-60-of-delhi-court-actions/ (accessed 16 November 2015).

[73] Garg, *Emerging Trends in Mediation* (n. 10 above) p. 20.

[74] P. Yamini, *Mediation to Settle the Trouble in Family* (22 July 2014), available at www.dnaindia.com/bangalore/report-mediation-to-settle-the-trouble-in-family-2004308 (accessed 16 November 2015).

[75] Ollapally, *Mandatory Court Referral for Mediation* (n. 1 above).

[76] World Economic Forum, *Global Competitiveness Report 2016–2017*, pp. 202–3.

[77] World Justice Project, *Rule of Law Index 2016*, p. 86.

Table 12.1 *India's rankings: developments in efficiency, confidence and perceptions of justice, 2011–2016**

	2011	2016
Efficiency		
• Efficiency of legal framework in settling disputes (rank)	64th/142	32nd/138
• Accessibility and affordability (percentile)	0.44	0.31
• No unreasonable delay (percentile)	0.22	0.17
Confidence		
• Civil justice (rank)	48th/66	93rd/113
• Effective enforcement (percentile)	0.34	0.38
• Impartial and effective ADR (percentile)	0.62	0.57
Perceptions of justice		
• Rule of law (percentile)	0.52	0.56**
• No discrimination (percentile)	0.53	0.43

*   Greyed rows indicate a positive trend in the rankings.
** World Bank Group, *Worldwide Governance Indicators 2015*, available at http://info.worldbank.org/governance/wgi/index.aspx#home.

point scale. Its score for 'no unreasonable delay' was 0.17[78] on a 1 point scale.

The overall rank for India's civil justice in the *Rule of Law Index 2016*[79] was 93rd out of 113 countries. Its scores for effective enforcement and impartial and effective ADR were 0.38 on a 1 point scale and 0.57 on a 1 point scale, respectively.[80]

Finally, with respect to perceptions of justice, India's rule of law percentile was 56 on a 100 point scale in 2015.[81] The score for 'no discrimination' was 0.43[82] on a 1 point scale.

---

[78] See n. 77 above.
[79] See n. 77 above.
[80] See n. 77 above.
[81] World Bank Group, *Worldwide Governance Indicators 2015*, available at http://info.worldbank.org/governance/wgi/index.aspx#home.
[82] See n. 77 above.

12.6 CONCLUSION

Since the introduction of India's mandatory mediation programme, its high rate of settlement has contributed to the reduction of case disposition time and relational gains within the country, including giving parties greater autonomy over the scope and outcomes of disputes. At the same time, over the past five years, India has experienced modest gains in its civil justice rankings in the efficiency of its legal framework in settling disputes; confidence, as measured by effective enforcement; and perceptions of justice, as measured by its rule of law percentile.

PART IV

Empirical findings on court mediation

13. Insights and recommendations from a global mediation survey

13.1 INTRODUCTION

Building on an examination of country level case studies and time-series analysis of civil justice indicators in voluntary and mandatory mediation jurisdictions, this chapter explores the attitudes and perceptions of practitioners implementing court mediation programmes in five regions. The aim of the survey is to provide insights into the dynamics, challenges and lessons learned from the perspective of those directly engaged in the work of administering, representing and mediating civil claims. It aims to respond to calls for 'empirical studies of the effectiveness of ADR, especially outside of the United States'[1] and within and between alternative dispute resolution (ADR) programme types, including mandatory and voluntary programmes.

The principal finding of this chapter, based on survey data and follow up questions, is that from the perspective of the practitioner, both mandatory and voluntary mediation programmes are perceived with relatively equal levels of confidence, perceptions of fairness and efficiency (see Figure 13.1). While slight variations exist such that practitioners report higher levels of confidence in mandatory mediation programmes (70 per cent) as opposed to voluntary programmes (64 per cent), and higher perceptions of efficiency with respect to voluntary programmes (77 per cent) as opposed to mandatory programmes (68 per cent), both regard voluntary (81 per cent) and mandatory (82 per cent) mediation programmes with relatively equal perceptions of fairness.[2]

The findings of this chapter echo recent insights from scholars of civil mediation reform. In particular, the provision of high quality mediation coupled with contextual understanding will have a positive impact on

---

[1] L.B. Bingham et al., 'Dispute Resolution and the Vanishing Trial: Comparing Federal Government Litigation and ADR Outcomes' (2009) 24(2) *Ohio State Journal of Dispute Resolution* 1.
[2] No statistically significant variation exists with respect to such findings.

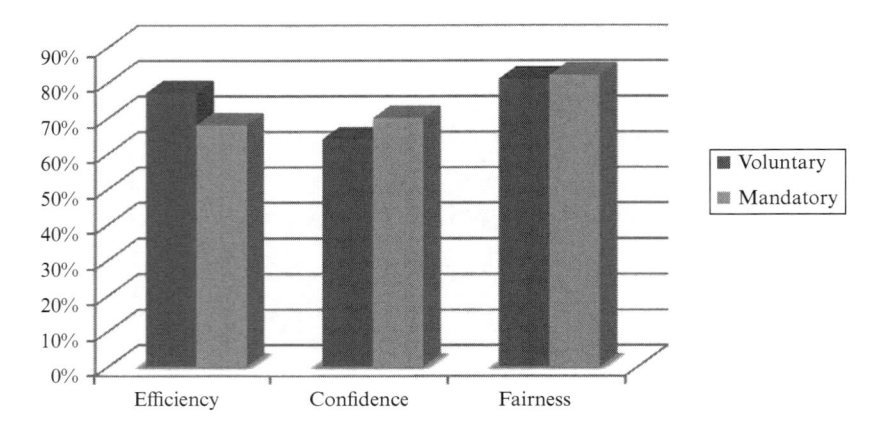

Figure 13.1 Percentage of practitioners rating very high/high perceptions of efficiency, confidence and fairness in court mediation by programme type

meaningful outcomes in increasingly complex forms of mediation.[3] Moreover, the relative advantages and disadvantages of mediation in a given jurisdiction vary according to the functioning of the underlying national civil litigation system.

The survey faces a number of limitations, including the fact that it represents a small-n sample, and as such, the findings cannot be considered generalizable. Also, as prior studies have noted, self-reported perceptions, particularly those reporting on self-efficacy, are subject to bias and statements may not always reflect actual practice.[4] In addition, varying judicial and cultural understandings of concepts of 'confidence', 'efficiency' and 'fairness' may also influence results.

13.2 SUMMARY OF FINDINGS

The findings of this chapter can be grouped into three areas. The first area reports on the correlation between mediation programme type and

---

[3] C. Menkel-Meadow, 'When Litigation is Not the Only Way: Consensus Building and Mediation as Public Interest Lawyering' (2002) 10 *Washington University Journal of Law and Policy* 37.

[4] J.A. Wall and K. Kressel, 'Research on Mediator Style: A Summary and Some Research Suggestions' (2012) 5(4) *Negotiation and Conflict Management Research* (November) 403.

perceptions of confidence, fairness and efficiency of the process. Here, the data suggests that while slight variation exists such that practitioners report higher levels of confidence in mandatory mediation programmes, and higher perceptions of efficiency with respect to voluntary programmes, both regard voluntary and mandatory mediation programmes with relatively equal perceptions of fairness. No statistically significant variation exists with respect to such findings.

The second section reports on insights from practitioners regarding the strengths and challenges of existing court mediation programmes by voluntary or mandatory programme type. The findings here indicate that practitioners working in mandatory court mediation programmes identify several key benefits of such programmes, including normalizing party-driven resolution, improved efficiency and speed through effective case screening and facilitating relational repair, while practitioners working in voluntary programmes identified key strengths of such programmes as the development of a well-established and supportive mediation culture, self-determined party engagement, simple procedures, high quality mediators, and ongoing monitoring and evaluation.

With respect to programme challenges, mandatory mediation practitioners noted that key challenges included limited party understanding of the mediation process; lawyer conflicts of interest; mediator quality; lack of good faith; inexperience in managing power imbalances; and resource limitations. Challenges within voluntary court mediation programmes included difficulties associated with encouraging party participation; limited resources; and mediator quality.

The final section of the chapter synthesizes practitioner suggestions for improving the overall court mediation process by programme type. Mandatory mediation practitioners had a number of useful suggestions for improving the quality of court mediation systems, including enhanced training; public education on the benefits of mediation; funding and organizational resources; mediator incentives; ongoing evaluation; and greater flexibility in settlement arrangements. Similar suggestions were identified by voluntary mediation programme practitioners, including enhanced training; greater financial resources; increased public education; improved facilities; and more directed encouragement of litigants' attempts of mediation. The findings of this chapter engage with the recent series of Global Pound Conference (GPC) sessions[5] suggesting

---

[5] For detailed analysis and country breakdowns, see International Mediation Institute, 'GPC Series Data', available at www.globalpoundconference.org/gpc-series-data/local-voting-results#.WTDnmhOGORs.

greater consideration may be given to the development of legislation supporting the enforcement of mediated settlements.[6]

13.3 SURVEY DATA COLLECTION METHOD

Survey data was collected from 83 practitioners in order to gain insight into the dynamics of mandatory and voluntary court mediation programmes and the impact of programme type, if any, on perceptions of confidence, fairness and efficiency among selected practitioners. The survey examined how practitioners working in voluntary and mandatory mediation programmes viewed existing strengths, challenges and lessons learned. However, it must be noted that given the small sample size (n = 83) the purpose of the survey is not to provide generalizable findings, but rather to supplement case studies by offering insights into how practitioners are learning to advance programme development in both mandatory and voluntary court mediation contexts.

The survey questionnaire contained a quantitative part asking for 'yes' 'no' answers and numerical responses in the form of percentage estimates or evaluations according to a 5 point scale, as well as a 'supplemental' part containing qualitative, open-ended questions asking for personal observations, judgements and proposals.

The first part of the survey asked participants for background information on their region of practice (see Figure 13.2), the nature of their court mediation system (whether voluntary or mandatory), and cost coverage of the programme. The second part of the survey examined the impact, if any, of court mediation programme type on participants' perceptions of confidence in the system, fairness and efficiency. The final part examined the strengths, challenges and suggestions for improving the overall functioning of both voluntary and mandatory court mediation programmes. These findings will be discussed in greater detail below.

The survey was conducted between September 2015 and January 2017. A total of 120 surveys were distributed in person and initiated via a weblink portal and 83 surveys were completed. The sample pool consisted of a convenience sample of voluntary and mandatory mediation practitioners selected from contacts made with members of professional court associations, including members of the ABA Young Lawyers Division, the ABA Section of Dispute Resolution, the Mediator Network, CPR Institute, National Centre for State Courts, Mediators Beyond Borders, Hong

---

[6] For detailed analysis and country breakdowns, see *ibid*.

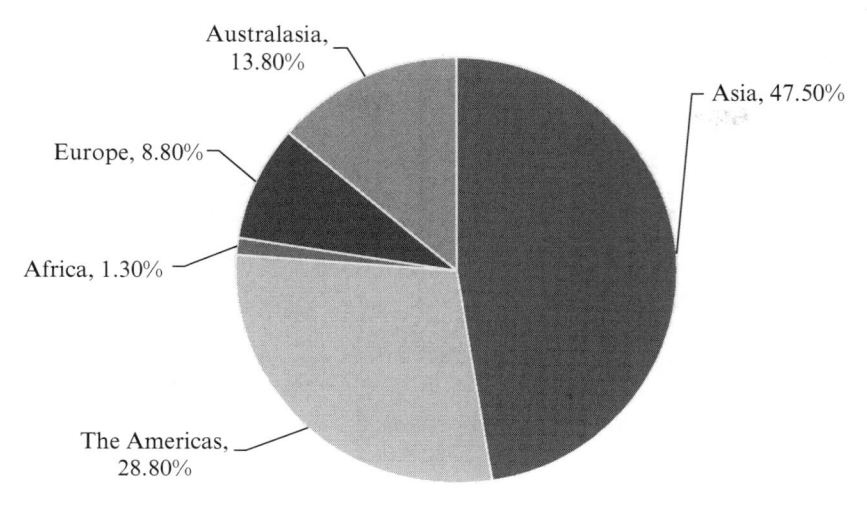

Figure 13.2   Region of practice

Kong Mediation Network, Resolution Systems Institute, the Asia Pacific Mediation Forum, the Court Annexed and Judicial Mediation Network and the Collaborative Justice Institute. In addition, the survey was distributed through contacts made at an Asia-Pacific UNCITRAL Conference on Harmonizing Trade Law, UC Hastings Centre for Negotiation and Conflict Resolution, the Singapore International Arbitration Forum, the Centre for International and Comparative Law, the Peace Chair at the University of Maryland, the UC Berkeley Centre for the Study of Law and Society, the Chiangmai Provincial Court Mediation Program, the Siam Legal ADR Group, the Knight Group Mediation Program, the ADR Unit of the US District Court, the Superior Court of California, the World Bank Group, the NY State Unified Court System, the Centre for Understanding Conflict, Shanghai Law School, Pepperdine Strauss Institute for Dispute Resolution, the Dubai International Court and the Japan Mediation Centre. Of the respondents, 6.3 per cent worked as an administrator of a court mediation programme, 37.5 per cent worked as a mediator, 28.8 per cent worked as a judge, 25 per cent worked as a lawyer, and 2.5 per cent were users of a court mediation programme (see Figure 13.3).

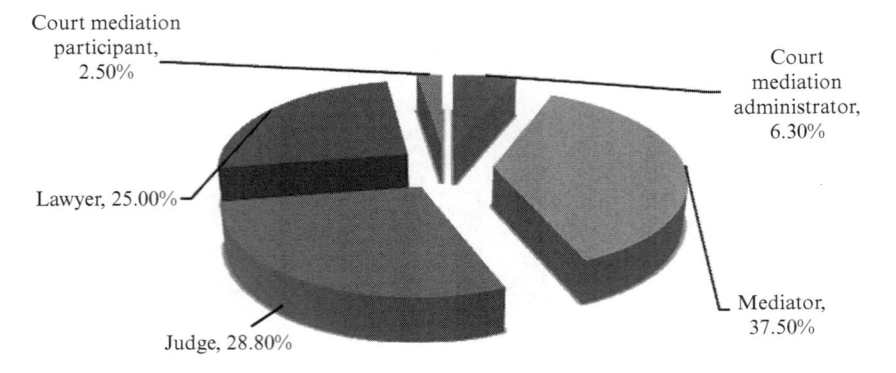

Figure 13.3   Experience with court mediation

13.4 COURT MEDIATION COSTS

Models of mediation financing vary by jurisdiction. The survey found that in terms of cost coverage, court mediation programmes employed a number of models ranging from either full to no financial support for mediation, reflecting the wide variation in current practice (see Figure 13.4).[7] For example, the Netherlands introduced the extension of legal aid funding to include mediation.[8] In Saskatchewan, Canada, compulsory mediation is free before a mediator selected by the Ministry of Justice. Some jurisdictions, such as Quebec, regulate the fees while others, such as Ontario, do not.[9]

The survey similarly found that in most cases, mediator fees are either borne by the court up to a certain number of hours or paid directly by

---

[7] Bingham et al., 'Dispute Resolution and the Vanishing Trial' (n. 1 above); E. Ward, *Mandatory Court-Annexed Alternative Dispute Resolution in the United States Federal Courts: Panacea or Pandemic?*, St John's University Legal Studies Research Paper Series 07-0077 (Jamaica, NY: St John's University School of Law, 2007); C. Menkel-Meadow, 'Empirical Studies of ADR: The Baseline Problem of What ADR Is and What It Is Compared To' in P. Cane and H. Kritzer (eds), *Oxford Handbook of Empirical Legal Studies* (Oxford University Press, 2009).

[8] A.J. De Roo and R.W. Jagtenberg, 'The Dutch Landscape of Court-Encouraged Mediation' in N.M. Alexander (ed.), *Global Trends in Mediation* (The Hague: Kluwer Law International, 2006) ch. 11, para. 11.9.

[9] A. Prujiner, 'Recent Developments in Mediation in Canada' in N.M. Alexander (ed.), *Global Trends in Mediation* (The Hague: Kluwer Law International, 2006) ch. 4, para. 4.3.2.

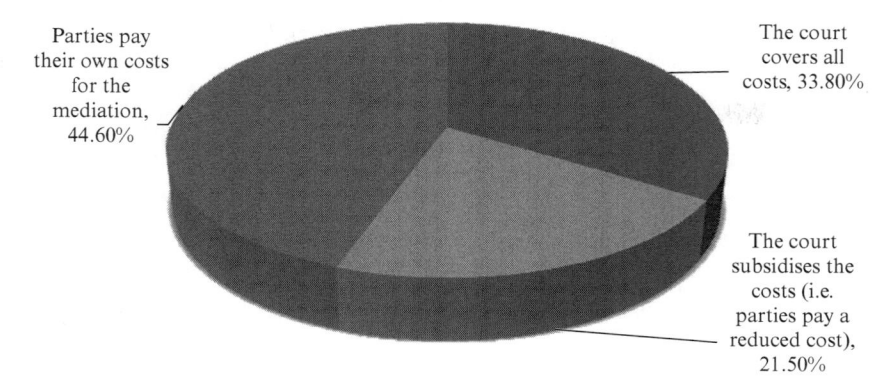

Figure 13.4   Court mediation cost coverage

the parties. Several practitioners noted that there is no fee for mandated mediation, particularly if the mediation is facilitated by the assigned judge. However, 'if [the] party choose[s] the mediator . . . then the party . . . pay[s] the mediator fee'.[10] Some other mandated court mediation programmes have a standard nominal fee for court mediation services. For example in the Philippines, parties are assessed a 'standard fee (Mediation fee) of P500 Philippine peso'.[11] In Florida, a sliding scale exists such that 'Florida subsidizes [a 2 hour] mediation for parties with joint income under $100k, $60/person if they make between $0–$50k jointly, and $120/person if between $50–$100k. After that, you have to use private mediation'.[12]

13.5   RATIONALE FOR INTRODUCING COURT MEDIATION PROGRAMMES

Scholarship has examined the varying rationales motivating courts to introduce mediation programmes.[13] As discussed earlier, existing intrinsic and extrinsic rationales for introducing court-based mediation in civil

---

[10]   Survey No. 4 (3 March 2016 7:57 a.m.).
[11]   Survey No. 16 (2 March 2016 12:41 p.m.).
[12]   Survey No. 30 (20 September 2015 3:18 a.m.).
[13]   D.R. Hensler, 'Our Courts, Ourselves: How the Alternative Dispute Resolution Movement is Re-Shaping Our Legal System' (2003–2004) 108 *Pennsylvania State Law Review* 165.

Table 13.1 Rationale for court mediation by programme type, 2015–2017

Response	Ranking by programme type	
	Voluntary	Mandatory
To reduce cost/time involved in litigation	1	1
To give parties a voice in the outcome	2	2
To improve court access	3	4
To improve the quality of outcomes/decisions	4	3

justice systems include efficiency,[14] reduction of case loads,[15] private and public sector cost reductions,[16] as well as extrinsic factors, including relational,[17] societal[18] and process-based[19] considerations.

This study compared motivating rationales behind the introduction of court mediation programmes from the perspective of practitioners by programme type (voluntary or mandatory) (see Table 13.1). It found an identity of rationales for the top two motivating factors, with primary importance placed on 'reduc[ing] costs/time involved in litigation (efficiency considerations) and secondary importance placed on 'giv[ing] parties a voice in the outcome' (relational and process-based considerations). For the motivating factors next in level of importance, practitioners in voluntary mediation programmes placed value on improving court access (#3) and improving the quality of outcomes/decisions (#4), while

[14] M. Dakolias, *Court Performance Around the World: A Comparative Perspective* (Washington, DC: World Bank, 1999) pp. 1–3.
[15] H. Foo Chee, *Civil Case Management in Singapore: Of Models, Measures and Justice* (ASEAN Law Association, 2016), available at www.aseanlawassociation.org/11GAdocs/workshop2-sg.pdf (accessed 14 January 2016).
[16] W. Maclons, *Mandatory Court Based Mediation as an Alternative Dispute Resolution Process in the South African Civil Justice System* (University of Western Cape, 2014) p. 85.
[17] Y. Shamir, *Alternative Dispute Resolution Approaches and Their Application* (UNESCO, 2003) p. 24.
[18] 'Engineering Peace: Achieving the Promise of Mediation in the World's Most Difficult Conflicts', available at www.mediate.com/articles/engpeace.cfm#_edn7 (accessed 19 January 2016).
[19] R. Zeinemann, 'The Characterisation of Public Sector Mediator' (2003) 24(2) *Environs Law* 51, available at http://environs.law.ucdavis.edu/volumes/24/2/articles/zeinemann.pdf; M. LeBaron and N.M. Alexander, *The Alchemy of Mediation, Essays in Mediation*, Singapore Management University School of Law Research Paper No. 11/2017 (2016).

mandatory programmes placed importance on improving the quality of outcomes/decisions (#3) and improving court access (#4).

13.6 SURVEY FINDINGS: CONFIDENCE, FAIRNESS AND EFFICIENCY

13.6.1 Confidence in Court Mediation Programme

While the survey findings show no statistically significant variation in the level of confidence in voluntary or mandatory court mediation programmes, the survey reflects a slightly higher level of confidence among practitioners in mandatory mediation programmes (see Table 13.2). Such programmes benefit from increased exposure, thereby offering parties a chance to observe possible beneficial results of mediation. Such benefits, scholars note, include an opportunity to tell one's side of the story, participate in the process and help craft the final outcome.[20] This echoes findings from recent studies showing that parties who entered mediation reluctantly nevertheless benefitted from the process[21] regardless of how the mediation was initiated.[22] This also correlates with findings that show higher compliance rates for judgments arrived at through mediation as compared with litigation.[23] Such beneficial perceptions alongside higher compliance rates may explain relatively higher levels of confidence in mandatory programmes.

---

[20] R.L. Wissler, 'Court-Connected Mediation in General Civil Cases: What We Know from Empirical Research' (2002) 17 *Ohio State Journal on Dispute Resolution* 641, 690; D. Quek Anderson, 'Mandatory Mediation: An Oxymoron? Examining the Feasibility of Implementing a Court-Mandated Mediation Program' (2010) 11(2) *Cardozo Journal of Conflict Resolution* (Spring), available at https://ssrn.com/abstract52843509.
[21] J. Pearson and N. Thoennes, 'Divorce Mediation: An Overview of Research Results' (1985) 19 *Columbia Journal of Law and Social Problems* 451; C. McEwen and T. Milburn, 'Explaining a Paradox of Mediation' (1993) 9 *Negotiation Journal* 23.
[22] F.E.A. Sander, 'Another View of Mandatory Mediation' (2007) *Dispute Resolution Magazine* (Winter) 16.
[23] C.A. McEwen and R.J. Maiman, 'Mediation in Small Claims Court: Achieving Compliance Through Consent' (1984) 18 *Law and Society Review* 11; N. Vidmar, 'An Assessment of Mediation in a Small Claims Court' (1985) 41 *Journal of Social Issues* 127.

Table 13.2 Confidence in mediation programme by programme type, 2015–2017*

Response	Programme type		
	Voluntary	Mandatory	Total
Highly confident/Confident	64%	70%	(55)
Somewhat/Not confident	36%	30%	(26)
Total	(31)	(50)	81

* The chi-square statistic is 0.264. The p-value is 0.607364. This result is not significant at p < .05.

13.6.2 Fairness

The survey results found no statistically significant difference in perceptions of outcome fairness among court mediation practitioners across voluntary and mandatory mediation programmes (see Table 13.3). Nearly an identical proportion of practitioners working in voluntary (81%) and mandatory (82%) programmes believed that outcomes arrived at through their court mediation programmes were either very fair or fair.[24] Such identity of response appears to indicate that the mechanism by which parties are introduced to court mediation has a limited impact on perceptions of fairness. It must be noted that the survey did not ask practitioners about perceptions of process fairness[25] requiring informed[26] participation; non-coercion;[27] absence of undue influence;[28] the

---

[24] Much of the ADR literature uses the terms 'fairness' and 'justice' interchangeably. See, for example, O. Shapira, 'Conceptions and Perceptions of Fairness in Mediation' (2012) 54 *South Texas Law Review* 281; J. Bercovitch, 'Mediation Success or Failure: A Search for the Elusive Criteria' (2006) 7 *Cardozo Journal of Conflict Resolution* 289, 291; J.M. Hyman, 'Swimming in the Deep End: Dealing with Justice in Mediation' (2004) 6 *Cardozo Journal of Conflict Resolution* 19; J.B. Stulberg, 'Mediation and Justice: What Standards Govern?' (2005) 6 *Cardozo Journal of Conflict Resolution* 213, 215 note 8.
[25] See generally, Shapira, 'Conceptions and Perceptions of Fairness in Mediation' (n. 24 above).
[26] J.M. Nolan-Haley, 'Informed Consent in Mediation: A Guiding Principle for Truly Educated Decisionmaking' (1999) 74 *Notre Dame Law Review* 775, 778 note 12.
[27] Cal. R. Ct. 3.857(b), available at www.courts.ca.gov/documents/title_3.pdf.
[28] See, e.g., Family Mediation Canada, *Members Code of Professional Conduct* (2013), available at www.fmc.ca/pdf/CodeProfessionalConduct.pdf.

Table 13.3   Fairness of mediation programme by programme type, 2015–2017*

Response	Programme type		
	Voluntary	Mandatory	Total
Very fair/fair	81%	82%	(67)
Somewhat/Not fair	19%	18%	(15)
Total	(32)	(50)	82

* The chi-square statistic is 0.0073. The p-value is 0.93171. This result is not significant at p < .05.

opportunity to terminate at any time;[29] absence of bias;[30] impartiality;[31] taking account of power differentials;[32] or providing an opportunity for a wide expression of views.[33] Rather, the focus on 'outcome fairness' as traditionally assessed by standards of equity;[34] legality;[35] beneficial impact on parties;[36] relational improvement;[37] and upholding of human

---

[29] Georgia Commission on Dispute Resolution, *Ethical Standards for Mediators* (2012) s. IV, p. 30, available at www.godr.org/files/APPENDIX%20C,%20CHAP%201,%206-1-2012.pdf.

[30] Sarah E. Burns, 'Thinking About Fairness and Achieving Balance in Mediation' (2008) 35 *Fordham Urban Law Journal* 39, 41.

[31] See, e.g., J. Dworkin and W. London, 'What is a Fair Agreement?' (1989) 7 *Mediation Quarterly* 3, 5.

[32] L. Boulle and M. Nesic, *Mediation: Principles, Process, Practice* (LexisNexis, 2001) pp. 454–5; T. Grillo, 'The Mediation Alternative: Process Dangers for Women' (1991) 100 *Yale Law Journal* 1545, 1550; R. Delgado et al., 'Fairness and Formality: Minimizing the Risk of Prejudice in Alternative Dispute Resolution' (1985) *Wisconsin Law Review* 1359, 1375–83.

[33] N.A. Welsh, 'Making Deals in Court-Connected Mediation: What's Justice Got to Do with It?' (2001) 79 *Washington University Law Quarterly* 787, 817.

[34] See, e.g., Bercovitch, 'Mediation Success or Failure: A Search for the Elusive Criteria' (n. 24 above) p. 291.

[35] See, e.g., J.W. Cooley, 'A Classical Approach to Mediation, Part I: Classical Rhetoric and the Art of Persuasion in Mediation' (1993) 19 *University of Dayton Law Review* 83, 130.

[36] See, e.g., J.B. Stulberg, 'Fairness and Mediation' (1998) 13 *Ohio State Journal on Dispute Resolution* 909; L. Susskind, 'Environmental Mediation and the Accountability Problem' (1981) 6 *Vermont Law Review* 1, 14–18.

[37] K.E. Menzel, 'Judging the Fairness of Mediation: A Critical Framework' (1991) 9 *Mediation Quarterly* 3, 6–16; and J.M. Hyman and L.P. Love, 'If Portia Were a Mediator: An Inquiry into Justice in Mediation' (2002) 9 *Clinical Law Review* 157, 186.

dignity,[38] appears to be independent of the mechanism by which parties arrive at mediation, whether voluntarily or though a mandatory process. The identity of perceptions of fairness across mandatory and mediation programme types appears to support suggestions that given the 'educative functions' of mandatory programmes, it is worthwhile 'to at least consider some form of dispute settlement procedure before trial'.[39]

13.6.3 Efficiency

Overall, the findings show no statistically significant difference in perceptions of efficiency between voluntary and mandatory court mediation programmes (see Table 13.4). However, surveyed practitioners regard voluntary mediation programmes as slightly more efficient than mandatory court mediation programmes. When examined from the court's operational cost perspective, voluntary mediation programmes generally place the burden of financing such services on the parties, and therefore overall voluntary mediation costs are lower as compared with mandatory programmes. From the perspective of the user, when mediation is successful, litigation expenses may be reduced. Several studies have identified a reduction in litigation costs when parties are successful in mediating their disputes.[40] However, when mediation is unsuccessful, overall costs

---

[38] Stulberg, 'Mediation and Justice: What Standards Govern?' (n. 24 above) 215 note 8.

[39] C. Menkel-Meadow, 'When Dispute Resolution Begets Disputes of its Own: Conflicts Among Dispute Professionals' (1997) 46(6) *UCLA Law Review*.

[40] For example, a study conducted by the International Finance Corporation in 2006 found that in more than 1,000 cases resolved through mediation in Serbia, Bosnia and Herzegovinia and Macedonia, direct costs of mediation averaged US$225 which represented about 50 per cent of the cost of litigation (about US$470). See I. Love, 'Settling Out of Court: How Effective is Alternative Dispute Resolution?' in *Viewpoint: Public Policy for the Private Sector*, IFC/World Bank Note No. 329 (October 2011), available at http://siteresources.worldbank.org/FINANCIALSECTOR/Resources/282044-1307652042357/VP329-Setting-out-of-court.pdf; see also, C.E. Jorquiera and G. Dabdoub Alvarez, *The Cost of Disputes in Companies and the Use of ADR Methods: Lessons from Nine Latin American Countries*, MIF Study (Washington, DC: Multilateral Investment Fund, 2005); J. Barkai and G. Kassebaum, *Hawaii's Court-Annexed Arbitration Program, Final Evaluation Report*, Program on Conflict Resolution Working Paper Series 1992-1 (Manoa: University of Hawaii, 1992); R. Hann and C. Baar, *Evaluation of the Ontario Mandatory Mediation Program (Rule 24.1): Executive Summary and Recommendations* (2001), available at www.attorneygeneral.jus.gov.on.ca/.

Table 13.4 *Efficiency of mediation programme by programme type, 2015–2017**

Response	Programme type		
	Voluntary	*Mandatory*	*Total*
Very efficient/efficient	77%	68%	(58)
Somewhat/Not efficient	23%	32%	(23)
Total	(31)	(50)	81

* The chi-square statistic is 0.835. The p-value is 0.360821. This result is not significant at p < .05.

of litigation generally go up.[41] In light of the impact of costs on overall efficiency, some mandatory mediation programmes provide an opt out mechanism for parties in the event that 'the costs of mediation would be higher than the requested relief'[42] and suggest that ongoing monitoring be required to ensure high quality mandatory court mediation programmes, particularly when parties are required to pay for mediation fees.[43] Original advocates of the multi-door courthouse have also cautioned that requiring that parties pay for court-annexed ADR may contradict the key idea of creating a justice system that provides parties with a range of options for dispute resolution.[44] Concerns have also been raised regarding the possibility that mandatory mediation systems in which users pay for mediation services may lead to satellite litigation and 'ultimately increase

---

[41] H. Genn et al., *Twisting Arms: Court Referred and Court Linked Mediation under Judicial Pressure*, Ministry of Justice Research Series 1/07 (London: Ministry of Justice Research Unit, 2007) (for cases that failed to settle through mediation, expenses were US$2,000–US$4,000 higher); J. Rosenberg and H.J. Folberg, 'Alternative Dispute Resolution: An Empirical Analysis' (1994) 46 *Stanford Law Review* 1487. (Similarly, ENE processes that did not result in settlement in California courts added about US$4,000 to the cost of litigation.) R. Wissler, 'The Effectiveness of Court-Connected Dispute Resolution in Civil Cases' (2004) 22 *Conflict Resolution Quarterly* 55 (reporting mixed results in cost savings); R.A. Posner, 'The Summary Jury Trial and Other Methods of Alternative Dispute Resolution: Some Cautionary Observations' (1986) 53 *University of Chichester Law Review* 366 (suggesting that there are no savings in costs).

[42] Colo. Rev. Stat. Ann. s. 13-22-311 (West 2009).

[43] Fla. R. Civ. P. 1.710(b). See also 'Florida's Court-Connected ADR History' in E. Reshard (ed.), *Florida Mediation and Arbitration Programs, A Compendium* (19th edn, Florida Dispute Resolution Centre, 2005–2006) p. 12, available at www.flcourts.org/gen_public/adr/bin/2006%20Compendium.pdf.

[44] F.E.A. Sander, 'Paying for ADR' (1992) 78 *ABA Journal* 105.

the costs for litigants and result in general inefficiency within the court system'.[45] For voluntary programmes, it is possible that because the decision regarding whether to proceed with mediation is left to the parties, once a decision is reached, a final agreement may be more likely. It is also important to recognize, as has been described by several mediation scholars, that a narrow focus on efficiency as measured by costs and time, while important, may nevertheless overlook the more important relational benefits of mediation.[46]

In addition to court and user costs, mediation programmes impact on court and user time. No doubt, mandatory mediation requires an additional time commitment on the part of disputing parties, which in some cases reduces overall disputing time if the mediation is successful.[47] However, when mediation fails to result in resolution, overall disputing time is extended.[48] Given mixed empirical findings,[49] there is no overall consensus on time savings in mediation.

---

[45] D. Quek Anderson, 'Mandatory Mediation: An Oxymoron? Examining the Feasibility of Implementing a Court-Mandated Mediation Program' (2010) 11(2) *Cardozo Journal of Conflict Resolution* (Spring), available at SSRN: https://ssrn.com/abstract52843509.

[46] See e.g., L.P. Love and E. Galton, *Stories Mediators Tell* (ABA Book Publishing, 2012); C. Menkel-Meadow, 'Alternative and Appropriate Dispute Resolution in Context: Formal, Informal, and Semiformal Legal Processes' ch. 50 in P.T. Coleman, M. Deutsch and E.C. Marcus (eds), *The Handbook of Conflict Resolution: Theory and Practice* (Wiley, 2014) pp. 1–28.

[47] See Rosenberg and Folberg, 'Alternative Dispute Resolution: An Empirical Analysis' (n. 41 above); Barkai and Kassebaum, *Hawaii's Court-Annexed Arbitration Program, Final Evaluation Report* (n. 40 above); Hann and Baar, *Evaluation of the Ontario Mandatory Mediation Program* (n. 40 above); Bingham et al., 'Dispute Resolution and the Vanishing Trial' (n. 1 above); A. Alvarez de la Campa, *The Private Sector Approach to Commercial ADR: Commercial ADR Mechanisms in Colombia* (Washington, DC: Investment Climate Department, World Bank, 2009), available at www.fias.net/index.cfm.

[48] See e.g., J.S. Kakalik et al., *An Evaluation of Mediation and Early Neutral Evaluation Under the Civil Justice Reform Act* (Santa Monica, CA: RAND Corporation, 1996) available at www.rand.org/pubs/monograph_reports/MR803.html. However, see also critiques of the study questioning the representativeness of the sample and other design flaws: T. Stipanowich, 'ADR and the "Vanishing Trial": The Growth and Impact of "Alternative Dispute Resolution"' (2004) 1(3) *Journal of Empirical Legal Studies* 843.

[49] See also Genn et al., *Twisting Arms* (n. 41 above) (showing no significant impact of mediation on case duration) and Wissler, 'The Effectiveness of Court-Connected Dispute Resolution in Civil Cases' (n. 41 above).

Table 13.5 Key achievements in mandatory and voluntary programmes, 2015–2017

Mandatory programmes	Voluntary programmes
• Normalizing party-driven resolution • Improved efficiency and speed through case-screening • Relational repair	• Well-established and supportive mediation culture • Self-determined engagement • High quality mediators • Ongoing monitoring and evaluation

13.7 SURVEY FINDINGS: STRENGTHS AND CHALLENGES OF COURT MEDIATION PROGRAMMES

Survey respondents shared what they believe is working well in both mandatory and voluntary mediation programmes (see Table 13.5). The responses are analysed in greater detail below.

13.7.1 Key Achievements in Mandatory and Voluntary Mediation Programmes

(i) Key achievements: mandatory programmes

For practitioners working in mandatory mediation programmes, the key areas of achievement were identified as:

- normalizing party-driven resolution;
- improved efficiency and speed through effective case screening; and
- facilitating relational repair.

A key benefit of mandated programmes is the normalization of a process of autonomous party-driven resolution. One practitioner noted that 'parties now expect that they will mediate – it is now a "normal" part of the legal process'.[50] While 'self referral is also encouraged',[51] a practitioner added:

> it helps that we are court mandated ... Many have never encountered this process and have no idea what to expect ... We draft our own agreements,

---

[50] Survey No. 26 (2 March 2016 9:12 a.m.).
[51] Survey No. 34 (13 September 2015 3:37 a.m.).

usually, which I personally feel makes them more neutral and accurate than if a non-professional or the more motivated attorney gets a chance to write it.[52]

In terms of both efficiency and efficacy, one practitioner noted that in her experience, mandatory programmes tend to be 'effective, [efficient], low cost, [and] fast'.[53] High settlement rates have been achieved in some mandatory programmes in spite of limited resources. One practitioner noted that the mandatory programmes he was involved with had achieved a 'high success ratio despite lack of facilities, low pay for mediators, and lack of office supplies'.[54]

Mandatory programmes work well when intake officers are vigilant in screening out inappropriate cases, for example, disputes involving domestic violence or post-traumatic stress disorder (PTSD). One practitioner noted the importance of 'the availability of exemptions for violence ... so that cases that are inappropriate or urgent come straight to court'.[55] Another practitioner agreed, observing that 'veteran mediations are compromised by PTSD issues'.[56] Another echoed the fact that 'domestic violence is an issue in 25% of our cases, regularly, but we have a screening questionnaire that is mailed with our order, and we always ask if people want to start together or separately, which helps'.[57] In sum, 'getting certain types of cases to mediation quickly ... saves a great deal of time and avoids hardening of positions'.[58]

The fact that mediation is 'less formal than court',[59] practitioners noted, provides opportunities for parties to 'talk together'[60] to get to the heart of issues and take ownership of resolution options. This is particularly effective when 'parties make their own plans, rather than having a judge make the decisions'.[61] The fact that such cases are 'court ordered' rather than discretionary was highlighted in providing 'parties ... an opportunity to resolve matters between them more effectively'.[62]

---

[52] Survey No. 30 (20 September 2015 3:18 a.m.).
[53] Survey No. 10 (3 March 2016 7:33 a.m.).
[54] Survey No. 16 (2 March 2016 12:41 p.m.).
[55] Survey No. 15 (2 March 2016 12:44 p.m.).
[56] Survey No. 31 (16 September 2015 6:21 p.m.).
[57] Survey No. 30 (20 September 2015 3:18 a.m.).
[58] Survey No. 38 (7 September 2015 9:49 p.m.).
[59] Survey No. 21 (2 March 2016 9:58 a.m.).
[60] Survey No. 36 (13 September 2015 3:00 a.m.).
[61] Survey No. 28 (14 October 2015 9:20 p.m.).
[62] Survey No. 32 (14 September 2015 9:50 a.m.).

(ii) Key achievements: voluntary programmes

For practitioners in voluntary mediation programmes, the key areas of achievement were identified as:

- the development of a well-established and supportive mediation culture;
- simple procedures and welcoming facilities creating robust engagement;
- high quality mediators; and
- ongoing monitoring and evaluation.

For voluntary programmes, a well-established and supportive mediation culture, including clear court rules, were cited as keys to its success. For example, one practitioner noted that 'the culture of mediation . . . is very strong'.[63] Supportive court rules are important. One practitioner noted that, 'what works well are the rules of court that encourage mediation, confidentiality, and parties' confidence in the process'.[64] Another practitioner added that the process, 'works better at an early stage of litigation'.[65]

In addition to a supportive formal infrastructure, informal support in the form of welcoming facilities and simple procedures were credited with positive voluntary mediation outcomes. One practitioner made positive reference to the fact that the 'court provid[es] coffee/tea and biscuits'.[66] Such informal support 'creat[es] an opportunity for parties to resolve disputes in an environment that supports parties to attempt resolution before further escalation and maintain (where applicable) important relationships'.[67] In addition, 'reducing of technicality in the process'[68] was cited as having a positive influence on voluntary outcomes.

Party engagement was also noted as a strength within voluntary programmes. A practitioner noted that once parties decide to try voluntary mediation, the programme 'works well'.[69] Another noted that the programme, 'gets rid of many small claims which would be financially inefficient to take to trial',[70] with 'outcomes [that] are mostly fair'.[71]

---

[63] Survey No. 4 (14 February 2016 11:44 a.m.).
[64] Survey No. 6 (13 January 2016 10:50 p.m.).
[65] Survey No. 23 (8 September 2015 1:07 p.m.).
[66] Survey No. 8 (7 December 2015 12:47 p.m.).
[67] Survey No. 13 (15 October 2015 1:56 a.m.).
[68] Survey No. 17 (13 September 2015 6:59 a.m.).
[69] Survey No. 22 (9 September 2015 12:53 p.m.).
[70] Survey No. 9 (13 November 2015 3:45 a.m.).
[71] Survey No. 11 (17 October 2015 6:38 p.m.).

Table 13.6   *Key challenges in mandatory and voluntary programmes, 2015–2017*

Mandatory programmes	Voluntary programmes
• Lack of good faith on the part of lawyers and parties • Limited party understanding of the mediation process • Lawyer conflicts of interest • Mediator quality • Managing power imbalance • Limited resources	• Encouraging party participation • Limited resources • Mediator quality

High quality mediators were credited with contributing to the success of voluntary mediation programmes. One practitioner noted that 'good mediators who are proactive'[72] are able to achieve positive results. Another noted that 'experienced mediators' ability to elicit objective information and evaluation, and collaborative negotiations'[73] have contributed to the success of the programme.

Ongoing reflection through data collection, monitoring and evaluation allow for continued refinement of voluntary programmes. As one practitioner noted, 'we have an excellent data collection system that allows us to monitor, evaluate and improve the program'.[74]

13.7.2 Key Challenges of Mandatory and Voluntary Programmes

Practitioners working in both mandatory and voluntary programmes shared some of the challenges facing their programmes (see Table 13.6). These will be examined in greater detail below.

(i) Key challenges: mandatory programmes

Practitioners working in mandatory mediation programmes described a number of challenges, including:

- a lack of good faith on the part of lawyers and parties;
- limited party understanding of the mediation process;
- lawyer conflicts of interest;

---

[72] Survey No. 10 (12 November 2015 3:39 p.m.).
[73] Survey No. 24 (7 September 2015 9:05 p.m.).
[74] Survey No. 19 (11 September 2015 8:05 p.m.).

- mediator quality;
- managing power imbalances; and
- resource limitations.

The challenge most frequently cited by practitioners in mandatory programmes was the generally low settlement rate due to a perception of a lack of good faith by lawyers and parties, many of whom saw the process as a step toward an ultimate court battle. According to one practitioner, 'in Indonesia based on a 2014 survey ... only 4% of cases that [are] submitted to court were able to reconcile [through] the court mediation program'.[75] This was partly attributable to the lack of 'good faith of both parties'.[76] One practitioner explained that 'the problem is that because it is compulsory, parties in dispute aren't putting their "heart" (effort and good faith) [in]to the mediation process. Mediation has a tendency to become just a "station" that must be "visited" on a "journey" and not as a destination'.[77] Another practitioner added that many parties 'just take it as an obligation in a court process'.[78]

Closely related to the issue of lack of good faith, is the issue of limited party understanding of the mediation process. One practitioner noted that 'when parties come to mediation, they've already been exposed to the combative nature of the court process and it takes a while sometimes to help them understand that they are empowered to make decisions collaboratively'.[79] Similarly, another practitioner noted, 'some times people want the court to solve their problem'.[80] Parties have unclear 'expectations of the outcome',[81] or simply 'want to make a consensus'.[82] Overall this points to a 'lack of awareness [among] people [of how] to solve their problems by mediation'.[83]

A related challenge in some mandatory court mediation programmes is the existence of conflicts of interest on the part of lawyers representing parties to court proceedings. As one practitioner noted, 'parties are represented by lawyer[s] and there [are] so many conflict of interest there'.[84]

---

[75] Survey No. 4 (3 March 2016 7:57 a.m.).
[76] Survey No. 4 (3 March 2016 7:57 a.m.).
[77] Survey No. 6 (3 March 2016 7:48 a.m.).
[78] Survey No. 22 (2 March 2016 9:46 a.m.).
[79] Survey No. 28 (14 October 2015 9:20 p.m.).
[80] Survey No. 9 (3 March 2016 7:35 a.m.).
[81] Survey No. 35 (13 September 2015 3:16 a.m.).
[82] Survey No. 1 (3 March 2016 8:03 a.m.).
[83] Survey No. 19 (2 March 2016 12:06 p.m.).
[84] Survey No. 2 (3 March 2016 8:01 a.m.).

Such conflicts include the perception that lawyers stand to lose hourly fees if the case settles quickly; the point at which cases are 'referred to mediation [is already a] very [costly stage] in the litigation process'.[85] In many cases, 'parties [will] not ... participate in the mediation process because they [are] represented by their lawyer'.[86]

Mediator quality was cited as a challenge among some practitioners working in mandatory programmes. One noted that the '[list] of mediators [and] quality of the mediators'[87] impeded the success of the programme. Another noted that it was difficult to find 'a mediator who understands the process and [who does] not impose ... [jargon] legalese'.[88] Another explained that 'because the mediation is free ... sometimes the mediator do[es] not [fulfil] their obligations'.[89]

Addressing power imbalances in the context of mandatory mediation also presented a challenge for many practitioners. One noted that it is 'challenging when dealing with people in different positions of power'.[90] Another observed instances in which 'an attorney representing one party push[ed] an unrepresented party to settle'.[91]

Resource limitations were cited as important challenges in mandatory programmes. One practitioner noted that although the programme in her court was 'work[ing] well ...the problem is [an] overload of cases'.[92] Another noted 'poor funding creates delay'.[93] Similarly, another practitioner observed that 'time is limited [in the mediation sessions] and parties [are] rushed to complete the session'.[94] A practitioner described that it was a matter of 'availability... we have three cases per day, sometimes we are slammed, sometimes we have no shows, but each of us staff members chews through hundreds of cases per year'.[95] In some cases, lack of support for execution of mediated settlements leads to the impression that 'the mediation [is] not effective, [since] some cannot be executed'.[96]

---

[85] Survey No. 17 (2 March 2016 12:35 p.m.).
[86] Survey No. 3 (3 March 2016 7:59 a.m.).
[87] Survey No. 14 (3 March 2016 7:20 a.m.).
[88] Survey No. 33 (13 September 2015 1:19 p.m.).
[89] Survey No. 18 (2 March 2016 12:20 p.m.).
[90] Survey No. 21 (2 March 2016 9:58 a.m.).
[91] Survey No. 29 (21 September 2015 1:57 p.m.).
[92] Survey No. 7 (3 March 2016 7:41 a.m.).
[93] Survey No. 15 (2 March 2016 12:44 p.m.).
[94] Survey No. 25 (2 March 2016 9:24 a.m.).
[95] Survey No. 30 (20 September 2015 3:18 a.m.).
[96] Survey No. 24 (2 March 2016 9:26 a.m.).

(ii) Key challenges: voluntary programmes

Practitioners working in voluntary court mediation programmes also shared a number of challenges facing such programmes. These included:

- encouraging party participation;
- limited resources; and
- mediator quality.

Among the most frequently cited challenges for practitioners working in voluntary mediation programmes was 'encouraging party participation'[97] given the dynamic of party entrenchment once cases enter the court system. One practitioner noted that 'parties are often more entrenched in [a] conflict due to court proceedings, [and they receive] . . .conflicting advice about mediation from legal representatives who would rather not lose clients'.[98] This view was shared by other practitioners who observed a 'resistance [on the part] of counsel in embracing the process'.[99] Others noted that once parties 'are already in the adversarial court system . . . it is not always [possible] to get [an] amicable outcome'[100] and it is 'hard to get cases in, [with] lawyers on board'[101] since 'it is voluntary'.[102]

In addition to party and counsel entrenchment, limited resources present another obstacle to quality mediation outcomes. As one practitioner noted, there are 'not enough resources to further engage neutrals (in program policy and planning, training, appreciation events, roster solicitation)'.[103] Another practitioner added that a major challenge is 'budget/funding, adequate resources, and the high supply of mediators in relation to demand'.[104] Limited time for mediation preparation presented a related challenge. According to one practitioner, 'we take case[s] with no time to prepare; often we go into mediation knowing that we have a very limited time frame in which to work'.[105] Such resource challenges limit 'accessibility'[106] of the system.

Finally, mediator quality was cited as an additional challenge facing voluntary programmes. One practitioner noted, 'the quality of the mediators

---

[97] Survey No. 19 (11 September 2015 8:05 p.m.).
[98] Survey No. 13 (15 October 2015 1:56 a.m.).
[99] Survey No. 17 (13 September 2015 6:59 a.m.).
[100] Survey No. 16 (13 October 2015 3:52 a.m.).
[101] Survey No. 22 (9 September 2015 12:53 p.m.).
[102] Survey No. 20 (10 September 2015 12:53 p.m.).
[103] Survey No. 5 (19 January 2016 9:18 p.m.).
[104] Survey No. 6 (13 January 2016 10:50 p.m.).
[105] Survey No. 15 (14 October 2015 8:02 p.m.).
[106] Survey No. 1 (2 March 2016 12:29 p.m.).

varies greatly, and since it is done by the mediators on a pro bono basis, the commitment of the mediators also varies'.[107] Another practitioner agreed, observing that 'the biggest challenge . . . [is] ensuring mediator quality'[108] in particular when 'judges act as mediators'.[109]

13.8 SURVEY FINDINGS: PRACTITIONER SUGGESTIONS FOR IMPROVING COURT MEDIATION PROGRAMMES

Practitioners working in both mandatory and voluntary mediation programmes identified a number of areas for continued improvement.

Practitioners working in both mandatory and voluntary mediation programmes had a number of suggestions for improving the court mediation system, including enhanced training; public education on the benefits of mediation; funding and organizational resources; mediator incentives; ongoing evaluation; and greater flexibility in settlement arrangements.

13.8.1 Enhanced Mediator Training

Perhaps the most commonly voiced suggestion for improving court mediation fell within the area of enhanced mediator training. Several practitioners noted an urgent need to 'give judges training'[110] as well as 'more

Table 13.7 Suggestions for improvement of mandatory and voluntary mediation programmes

Mandatory programmes	Voluntary programmes
• Enhanced training • Public education on mediation benefits • Funding/organizational resources • Quality mediator incentives • Ongoing evaluation • Flexibility in settlement arrangements	• Enhanced training • Financial resources • Public education • Improved facilities • Encourage greater party participation

[107] Survey No. 7 (12 December 2015 10:25 p.m.).
[108] Survey No. 19 (11 September 2015 8:05 p.m.).
[109] Survey No. 12 (15 October 2015 8:33 a.m.).
[110] Survey No. 1 (3 March 2016 8:03 a.m.).

training for mediator[s] so they can work efficiently and properly'.[111] Other practitioners noted a need for 'improv[ing] the soft skill[s] of mediator[s], especially the judge mediator',[112] 'to recruit more mediators from outside of the court'[113] and provide 'continu[ing] ... training'[114] in order 'to increase capacity building of mediator[s]'.[115] Some court mediation practitioners suggested that there is:

> [a] need [for] more professional opportunities ... for young mediators. Mediation is not seen as a start-off career choice for young attorneys. Most people come ... burned out at the end of their careers ... I believe mediation-oriented law clerkships would be a very valuable thing.[116]

Similarly, among voluntary mediation practitioners, the most frequently cited suggestion was the need for 'more mediator training'[117] as well as independent mediators who are not members of the judiciary. Several practitioners echoed the view that 'mediators need continued training and debriefing'.[118] Several believed that such mediators must be 'non-judge mediators with no KPI/agenda to force/achieve [settlement] at any cost'.[119] This view was echoed by others who suggested the need to 'use proper mediators, who are trained to mediate'.[120] The court could be encouraged to support such non-judge mediators 'with more referrals by judges to the process'.[121] Mediator quality could also be enhanced through 'us[ing] feedback ... to rate the mediators'[122] and 'improve autonomy and decreas[ing] evaluative outcomes'.[123] Evaluation and reflection, it was suggested, could improve the process by 'us[ing] the data we collect to change the program [and] implement mediator standards and peer review'.[124]

---

[111] Survey No. 2 (3 March 2016 7:59 a.m.).
[112] Survey No. 3 (3 March 2016 7:57 a.m.).
[113] Survey No. 6 (3 March 2016 7:41 a.m.).
[114] Survey No. 10 (3 March 2016 7:23 a.m.).
[115] Survey No. 22 (2 March 2016 9:26 a.m.).
[116] Survey No. 29 (20 September 2015 3:18 a.m.).
[117] Survey No. 1 (2 March 2016 12:29 p.m.).
[118] Survey No. 12 (15 October 2015 1:18 a.m.).
[119] Survey No. 2 (2 March 2016 12:25 p.m.).
[120] Survey No. 8 (13 November 2015 3:45 a.m.).
[121] Survey No. 10 (15 October 2015 8:33 a.m.).
[122] Survey No. 6 (12 December 2015 10:25 p.m.).
[123] Survey No. 9 (17 October 2015 6:38 p.m.).
[124] Survey No. 17 (11 September 2015 8:05 p.m.).

13.8.2 Public Education

In addition to the training of court mediation practitioners, enhancing general public education[125] was a frequently cited suggestion. Some mandatory mediation practitioners noted the need to better 'train people . . . to [understand the] benefits of the ADR program'[126] and to give more public 'education about mediation'.[127] Another observed that:

> because the mediation process mainly concerns . . . problems arising within the society – when the society itself has been exposed to retributive justice and mediation has been alienated, how can mediation be successfully implemented? I think . . . continuous legal counselling [for] society is paramount.[128]

In addition to general awareness, another noted the need for 'more effort in preparing people before they participate in mediation',[129] while another expressed a 'hope [that] in the future these individuals will realise that, it is not about just the money . . . but creating . . . [peace]'.[130] This require[s] 'education of lawyers as gatekeepers to be more involved and less resistant'.[131]

Similarly, voluntary mediation practitioners noted the need for 'judicial education [with] relevant law reform that encourages parties and legal professionals to promote mediation'[132] and 'changing the mind-set of lawyers and creating more awareness of the benefits of the process'.[133]

13.8.3 Financial and Organizational Resources

Many practitioners noted the need for additional financial and organizational resources. One practitioner suggested that the programmes be 'better funded to reduce delay'[134] and maintain 'better consistency between service providers'.[135] Another added that 'more time [should be] made available for the mediation'.[136] In addition to court mediation program-

---

[125] Survey No. 33 (13 September 2015 3:37 a.m.).
[126] Survey No. 3 (3 March 2016 7:57 a.m.).
[127] Survey No. 11 (3 March 2016 7:22 a.m.).
[128] Survey No. 5 (3 March 2016 7:48 a.m.).
[129] Survey No. 19 (2 March 2016 9:58 a.m.).
[130] Survey No. 9 (3 March 2016 7:27 a.m.).
[131] Survey No. 13 (2 March 2016 12:44 p.m.).
[132] Survey No. 11 (15 October 2015 1:56 a.m.).
[133] Survey No. 15 (13 September 2015 6:59 a.m.).
[134] Survey No. 13 (2 March 2016 12:44 p.m.).
[135] Survey No. 13 (2 March 2016 12:44 p.m.).
[136] Survey No. 35 (13 September 2015 3:00 a.m.).

matic support, some suggested a need for greater party-based support in the form of 'network support for people and their families [including those] with traumatic injuries'.[137] In addition, online resources in the form of mediation templates have been found to be helpful:

> in Florida, the standardized forms that are used state-wide . . . allow us to create a consistent process that helps us guide the parties to a satisfying, self-developed outcome. [As] it's on the court's public website . . . we treat is as information that can be shared, not legal advice. We have a state-wide ethics commission that produces advisory opinions that are guidance, not binding – but still a good fall back, and a resource for when we run into the need for external guidance.[138]

Voluntary mediation practitioners similarly suggested the need for greater financial and infrastructure resources for court mediation programmes. One noted the need for 'more funding – we have an established program with bench and bar support, the only thing we are lacking since 2009 is sufficient funding to maintain our programs'.[139] This view was echoed by other practitioners who noted the need for 'better funding, [and] more resources (i.e. staff, technology, equipment)'.[140] In addition to financial resources, improved facilities to support the mediation process was also highlighted. One noted that 'environment is crucial. [The] scheme [was less effective] when the court . . . just provided a room, [and] no dedicated staff and no refreshments'.[141] Others suggested the need for 'more time for mediation'.[142]

13.8.4 Rewards and Incentives

A system of rewards and incentives to enhance mediator and court practitioner quality, some believed, could improve programmes. One noted that 'successful . . . mediation [should be] reward[ed] [though] promotion'.[143] 'Regulations [are needed] to empower'[144] and support mediators.[145] Many identified a need to 'develop independent mediators'[146] who are not also

---

[137] Survey No. 30 (16 September 2015 6:21 p.m.).
[138] Survey No. 29 (20 September 2015 3:18 a.m.).
[139] Survey No. 4 (19 January 2016 9:18 p.m.).
[140] Survey No. 5 (13 January 2016 10:50 p.m.).
[141] Survey No. 7 (7 December 2015 12:47 p.m.).
[142] Survey No. 1 (2 March 2016 12:29 p.m.).
[143] Survey No. 18 (2 March 2016 10:04 a.m.).
[144] Survey No. 20 (2 March 2016 9:46 a.m.).
[145] Survey No. 31 (14 September 2015 9:50 p.m.).
[146] Survey No. 12 (3 March 2016 7:20 a.m.).

acting as judges.[147] As a corollary, practitioners suggested that 'lawyers should keep their legal opinions to themselves'[148] and 'provide parties with advice [regarding] realistic outcome[s] at mediation'.[149]

13.8.5 Flexible Settlement Arrangements

Greater flexibility in settlement arrangements was suggested by several practitioners. For example, 'allow[ing] for partial mediated settlement on some issues and reversion to court on others rather than [an] all or nothing [approach]: and expanded scope for referral'.[150] Other practitioners suggested expanding the types of cases open to mediation to empower people to resolve conflicts on their own.[151] Other practitioners suggested 'allowing judges to rule on settlements the day they are reached'[152] and 'hav[ing] a two-step mediation process, before discovery and then after discovery'.[153]

13.8.6 Access

Practitioners, particularly those working in voluntary programmes, suggested the need to 'encourage and enable access as early as possible in the process, encourage court buy-in and support, and dedicate resources to have well qualified, impartial mediators',[154] including 'more screening and funnelling of cases into mediation'.[155] Finally, some working in well-established voluntary programmes believed such programmes could be improved if they were made mandatory and the scope of eligible cases widened. Several suggested 'mak[ing] this a court mandated process'[156] and 'widen[ing] [the scope beyond] small claims'.[157]

13.8.7 Ongoing Evaluation

Finally, practitioners suggested that ongoing qualitative and quantitative evaluation could enhance the development of court mediation guidelines

---

[147] Survey No. 23 (2 March 2016 9:24 a.m.).
[148] Survey No. 32 (13 September 2015 1:19 p.m.).
[149] Survey No. 34 (13 September 2015 3:16 a.m.).
[150] Survey No. 16 (2 March 2016 12:20 p.m.).
[151] Survey No. 27 (14 October 2015 9:20 p.m.).
[152] Survey No. 28 (21 September 2015 1:57 p.m.)
[153] Survey No. 37 (7 September 2015 9:49 p.m.).
[154] Survey No. 20 (7 September 2015 9:05 p.m.).
[155] Survey No. 5 (13 January 2016 10:50 p.m.).
[156] Survey No. 16 (13 September 2015 6:27 a.m.).
[157] Survey No. 18 (10 September 2015 12:53 p.m.).

and best practices. One noted the need to 'mov[e] from purely quantitative measures to qualitative measures to ensure party decision making and self determination'.[158] This process could be supported through '[revision] of mediation guidelines'.[159] In terms of supporting the court mediation process, another suggested 'limiting the time between mediation orders and the deadline to complete mediation'.[160]

Such findings engage with the recent series of Global Pound Conference (GPC) series[161] suggesting that greater consideration may be given to the development of legislation supporting the enforcement of mediated settlements.[162]

13.9 CONCLUSIONS

Building on an examination of statistics and case studies exploring the dynamics of voluntary and mandatory mediation programmes in diverse regions, the attitudes and perceptions of practitioners implementing court mediation programmes in five regions provides insights into the dynamics, challenges and lessons learned from the perspective of those directly engaged in the work of administering, representing and mediating civil claims. The principal finding, based on survey data and follow up questions, is that from the perspective of the practitioner, both mandatory and voluntary mediation programmes are perceived with relatively equal levels of confidence, perceptions of fairness and efficiency. While slight variations exist, such that practitioners report higher levels of confidence in mandatory mediation programmes, and higher perceptions of efficiency with respect to voluntary programmes, both regard voluntary and mandatory mediation programmes with relatively equal perceptions of fairness. No statistically significant variation exists with respect to such findings.

Practitioners working in mandatory court mediation programmes identified several key benefits of such programmes, including normalizing party-driven resolution, improved efficiency and speed through effective case screening and facilitating relational repair, while practitioners working in voluntary programmes identified the key strengths of voluntary

---

[158] Survey No. 15 (2 March 2016 12:35 p.m.).
[159] Survey No. 14 (2 March 2016 12:41 p.m.).
[160] Survey No. 26 (19 October 2015 7:16 p.m.).
[161] For detailed analysis and country breakdowns, see International Mediation Institute, 'GPC Series Data', available at www.globalpoundconference.org/gpc-series-data/local-voting-results#.WTDnmhOGORs.
[162] See *ibid*.

programmes as the development of a well-established and supportive mediation culture, self-determined engagement, simple procedures, high quality mediators and ongoing monitoring and evaluation.

Practitioner suggestions for improving the overall court mediation process included enhanced mediator training; expanded public education, funding and organizational resources; mediator incentives; ongoing evaluation; and greater flexibility in settlement arrangements.

14. Conclusions

This book has explored initial comparative findings examining the association of judicial voluntary and mandatory mediation structure with perceptions of justice, efficiency and confidence in courts. Building on a growing body of empirical cross-jurisdictional research examining mediation reform and policy,[1] and scholarship that has examined the varying intrinsic and extrinsic rationales motivating courts to introduce mediation

---

[1] See F. Steffek et al., *Regulating Dispute Resolution: ADR and Access to Justice at the Crossroads* (Oxford: Hart, 2013); Schonewille & Schonewille, *Variegated Use of Mediation: A Comparative Study of Mediation Regulation and Practices in Europe and the World* (The Hague: Eleven International Publishing, 2014); D. Stienstra and T.E. Willging, *Alternatives to Litigation: Do They Have a Place in the Federal District Courts?* (Washington, DC: Federal Judicial Center, 1995); R.L. Wissler, 'Mediation and Adjudication in the Small Claims Court: The Effects of Process and Case Characteristics' (1995) 29 *Law and Society Review* 323; C. Menkel-Meadow, 'Regulation of Dispute Resolution in the United States of America: From the Formal to the Informal to the "Semi-formal"' in F. Steffek et al. (eds), *Regulating Dispute Resolution: ADR and Access to Justice at the Crossroads* (Oxford: Hart, 2013); T. Stipanowich, 'The International Evolution of Mediation: A Call for Dialogue and Deliberation' (2015) 46 *Victoria University of Wellington Law Review* 1191; S.I. Strong, 'Realizing Rationality: An Empirical Assessment of International Commercial Mediation' *Washington and Lee Law Review* (forthcoming); H. Genn et al., *Twisting Arms: Court Referred and Court Linked Mediation Under Judicial Pressure* Ministry of Justice Research Series 1/07 (London: Ministry of Justice Research Unit, 2007); G. De Palo and P. Harley, 'Mediation in Italy: Exploring the Contradictions' (2005) 21 *Negotiation Journal* 469; J. Macfarlane, 'Experiences of Collaborative Law: Preliminary Results from the Collaborative Lawyering Research Project' (2004) *Journal of Dispute Resolution* 179; T.C.W. Farrow, 'Negotiation, Mediation, Globalization Protests and Police: Rights Processes; Wrong System, Issues, Parties and Time' (2002) 28 *Queen's Law Journal* 665; L. Blomgren Amsler et al., 'The State of Dispute System Design' (2015) 33 *Conflict Resolution Quarterly* S7; A. Kupfer Schneider, 'Foreword: The Future of Court ADR: Mediation and Beyond' (2012) 95(3) *Marquette Law Review* (Spring); T. Sourdin and A. Zariski, *The Multi-Tasking Judge: Introduction to Comparative Judicial Dispute Resolution* (Thomson Reuters Australia, 2013); D. Quek Anderson and J. Lee, 'The Global Pound Conference: A Conversation on the Future of Dispute Resolution' (2016) *Asian Journal on Mediation* 70.

programmes,[2] including reduction of caseloads,[3] private and public sector cost reductions,[4] as well as extrinsic factors including relational,[5] societal[6] and process-based[7] considerations, this book narrows its focus to the question of regional engagement in court mediation and the resulting impact, if any, on user experience.

As examined in the book, and responsive to diverse domestic circumstances, significant variation in the implementation of court mediation reforms currently exists. Avenues toward voluntary or mandatory mediation to some extent reflect varying underlying concepts of individual and collective justice. Given that 'public means available for financing dispute resolution are not unlimited', a balancing of individual process choices and social efficiency is required.

Global soft law policy-making, including Model Laws drafted by the UNCITRAL Working Group II, has generally left open the question of voluntary or mandatory mediation programme design to reflect domestic circumstance.[8] The scope of application of the law is expanded to all contexts 'irrespective of the basis upon which the conciliation is carried out, including agreement between the parties whether reached before or after a dispute has arisen, an obligation established by law,

---

[2] D.R. Hensler, 'Our Courts, Ourselves: How the Alternative Dispute Resolution Movement is Re-Shaping Our Legal System' (2003–2004) 108 *Pennsylvania State Law Review* 165.

[3] H. Foo Chee, *Civil Case Management in Singapore: Of Models, Measures and Justice* (ASEAN Law Association, 2016), available at www.aseanlawassociation.org/11GAdocs/workshop2-sg.pdf (accessed 14 January 2016).

[4] W. Maclons, *Mandatory Court Based Mediation as an Alternative Dispute Resolution Process in the South African Civil Justice System* (University of Western Cape, 2014) p. 85; and questioning the impact of mediation on cost reductions, see D.R. Hensler, *A Research Agenda: What We Need to Know About Court-Connected ADR* (Santa Monica, CA: RAND Corporation, 2000), available at www.rand.org/pubs/reprints/RP871.html.

[5] Y. Shamir, *Alternative Dispute Resolution Approaches and Their Application* (UNESCO, 2003) p. 24.

[6] 'Engineering Peace: Achieving the Promise of Mediation in the World's Most Difficult Conflicts', available at www.mediate.com/articles/engpeace.cfm#_edn7 (accessed 19 January 2016).

[7] R. Zeinemann, 'The Characterisation of public sector mediator' (2003) 24(2) *Environs Law* 51, available at http://environs.law.ucdavis.edu/volumes/24/2/articles/zeinemann.pdf.

[8] See generally, E. Van Ginkel, 'The UNCITRAL Model Law on International Commercial Conciliation' (2004) 21(1) *Journal of International Arbitration* 1; P. Binder and J. Sekolec, *International Commercial Arbitration and Conciliation in UNCITRAL Model Law Jurisdictions* (London: Sweet & Maxwell, 2005).

or a direction or suggestion of a court, arbitral tribunal or competent governmental entity'.[9] The provisions in the Model Law governing mediation are designed to accommodate differences in procedure while leaving parties free to carry out the mediation process as deemed appropriate.[10]

In responding to calls for expanded empirical research exploring the operation[11] and experience of civil justice reforms, and building on an important foundation of rich scholarship examining the extension[12] and usage[13] of court-mandated mediation; investigation of efficiency claims;[14] impacts on the quality and means[15] of access;[16] social justice and minority impacts;[17]

---

[9] UNCITRAL Model Law, Art. 8.
[10] *Ibid.* Explanatory Notes, para. 12.
[11] See C. Tobias, 'Civil Justice Delay and Empirical Data: A Response to Professor Heise' (2000) 51(2) *Case Western Reserve Law Review* 235; M. Heise, 'Justice Delayed? An Empirical Analysis of Civil Case Disposition Time' (2000) 59(4) *Case Western Reserve Law Review* 813.
[12] C. Menkel-Meadow, 'Pursuing Settlement in an Adversary Culture: A Tale of Innovation Co-Opted or the Law of ADR' (1991) 19 *Florida State Law Review* 1; J. Resnik, 'Many Doors? Closing Doors? Alternative Dispute Resolution and Adjudication' (1995) 10 *Ohio State Journal of Dispute Resolution* 211; E.E. Deason, 'Procedural Rules for Complementary Systems of Litigation and Mediation – Worldwide' (2004) 80 *Notre Dame Law Review* 553.
[13] See T.C.W. Farrow, *Civil Justice, Privatization and Democracy* (2011), available at http://papers.ssrn.com.eproxy1.lib.hku.hk/sol3/papers.cfm?abstract_id51795407 (accessed 28 November 2011).
[14] Hensler, *A Research Agenda* (n. 4 above); T.J. Stipanowich, 'ADR and the "Vanishing Trial": The Growth and Impact of Alternative Dispute Resolution' (2004) 1(3) *Journal of Empirical Legal Studies* 843; K. Kressel D.G. Pruitt, 'Themes in the Mediation of Social Conflict' (1985) 41 *Journal of Social Issues* 179; J. Kakalik et al., *Just, Speedy and Inexpensive? An Evaluation of Judicial Case Management Under the Civil Justice Reform Act* (Santa Monica, CA: RAND Corporation, 1997).
[15] See H. Genn, *Paths to Justice: What People Do and Think About Going to Law* (Oxford: Hart Publishing, 1999); H. Genn, *Judging Civil Justice* (Cambridge University Press, 2000).
[16] H. Genn, 'What is Civil Justice For? Reform, ADR, and Access to Justice' (2013) 24 *Yale Journal of Law and the Humanities* 397.
[17] R. Delgado et al., 'Fairness and Formality: Minimizing the Risk of Prejudice in Alternative Dispute Resolution' (1985) *Wisconsin Law Review* 1359; G. LaFree and C. Rack, 'The Effects of Participants' Ethnicity and Gender on Monetary Outcomes in Mediated and Adjudicated Civil Cases' (1996) 30 *Law and Society Review* 767; S. Press, 'Court-Connected Mediation and Minorities: Has Any Progress Been Made?' (2013) *ABA Dispute Resolution Magazine* (Summer) 36.

settlement outcomes;[18] cultural factors;[19] and experience of procedural justice,[20] the 10 longitudinal country case studies presented in this book, supplemented by survey research about the perceptions, observations and experiences of court mediation practitioners from diverse regions, provides insight into the dynamics, strengths and challenges of mandatory and voluntary court mediation programmes.

For any comparative study, key limitations must be acknowledged. In particular, it must be noted that given the small sample size of the country case studies (n = 10) and survey research (n = 83) and lack of policy uniformity in some cases, the results cannot be considered generalizable but rather aim at offering initial insights into the efficacy of diverse civil mediation policy approaches. In addition, correlation of changes in civil justice systems and perceptions of justice over time, or even in the aggregate, are not a sign of a causal relationship. A diversity of external, exogenous and intervening variables, including court financing, cultural factors and political environment, also impact programme outcomes, and mediation programme design and civil justice quality indicators in many cases mutually influence one another. This being the case, and confident that future studies will continue to refine and develop increasingly more accurate approaches to the analysis of such relationships, the aim of the research is to glean insights from practice that can assist in outlining directions for further study with the wider objective of developing a court system responsive to user needs.

Cognizant of the study's limitations, the key finding of the 10 country case studies, survey research and longitudinal analysis of aggregate civil justice indicators suggest that while both voluntary and mandatory mediation programmes demonstrate unique programmatic strengths and are associated with positive gains in the advancement of civil justice quality over a five-year period since implementation, sampled voluntary mediation programmes are associated with a slightly higher proportion of longitudinal advancement in levels of efficiency, confidence and perceptions of

---

[18] J.M. Brett, Z.I. Barsness and S.B. Goldberg, 'The Effectiveness of Mediation: An Independent Analysis of Cases Handled by Four Major Service Providers' (1996) 12(3) *Negotiation Journal* 259; M. Galanter and M. Cahill, 'Most Cases Settle: Judicial Promotion and Regulation of Settlements' (1994) 46 *Stanford Law Review* 1339.

[19] See Heise, 'Justice Delayed?' (n. 11 above).

[20] J. Thibaut and L. Walker, 'A Theory of Procedure' (1978) 66(3) *California Law Review* 541; D. Stienstra et al., *Report to the Judicial Conference Committee on Court Administration and Case Management: A Study of Five Demonstration Programs Established Under the Civil Justice Reform Act of 1990* (Washington, DC: Federal Judicial Center, 1997).

Conclusions 253

justice, with an identical proportion of voluntary and mandatory regions experiencing positive advancement in the sub-categories of effective enforcement, rule of law, and impartial and effective alternative dispute resolution (ADR). These findings generally appear to support insights from behavioural economics and political theory that positive reinforcement or 'nudges' encouraging mediation are at least as effective as directions issued through legislation and that in some contexts, 'facilitation and encouragement together with selective and appropriate pressure are likely to be more effective and possibly more efficient than blanket coercion to mediate'.[21] At the same time, the provision of high quality mediation coupled with contextual understanding will have a positive impact on meaningful outcomes in increasingly complex forms of mediation.[22] In circumstances of higher reported discrimination, effective corrective measures, including adequate training, will be required to address the possibility for lax civil rights[23] and procedural justice compliance.[24]

At the same time, from the perspective of the 83 court mediation practitioners surveyed, practitioners report slightly higher levels of confidence in mandatory mediation programmes, higher perceptions of efficiency with respect to voluntary programmes, and regard voluntary and mandatory mediation programmes with relatively equal perceptions of fairness.[25]

With regard to confidence in mediation programmes, survey findings reflect a slightly higher level of confidence among practitioners in mandatory mediation programmes (70 per cent) as opposed to voluntary programmes (64 per cent).[26] Such programmes benefit from increased exposure, thereby offering parties a chance to observe possible beneficial results of mediation. Such benefits, scholars note, include an opportunity

---

[21] Genn et al., *Twisting Arms* (n. 1 above); See also: R. Thaler and C. Sunstein, *Nudge* (Penguin Books, 2008); S. Ali, *Nudging Civil Justice: Examining Voluntary and Mandatory Court Mediation Experience in Diverse Regions*, forthcoming.

[22] C. Menkel-Meadow, 'When Litigation is Not the Only Way: Consensus Building and Mediation as Public Interest Lawyering' (2002) 10 *Washington University Journal Law and Policy* 37.

[23] See L. Edelman, 'Legal Ambiguity and Symbolic Structures: Organizational Mediation of Civil Rights Law' (1992) 97(6) *American Journal of Sociology* 1531; M. Feeley, *The Process is the Punishment: Handling Cases in a Lower Criminal Court* (New York: Russell Sage Foundation, 1979); C. Albiston, 'The Rule of Law and the Litigation Process: The Paradox of Losing by Winning' (1999) 33(4) *Law and Society Review* 869; Genn, *Paths to Justice* (n. 15 above); Genn, *Judging Civil Justice* (n. 15 above).

[24] Feeley, *The Process is the Punishment* (n. 23 above); Albiston, 'The Rule of Law and the Litigation Process' (n. 23 above).

[25] Such findings are not statistically significant.

[26] Results are not statistically significant.

to tell one's side of the story, participate in the process, and help craft the final outcome.[27] This echoes findings from recent studies showing that parties who entered mediation reluctantly nevertheless in some cases benefitted from the process,[28] regardless of how the mediation was initiated.[29] This also correlates with findings that show higher compliance rates for judgments arrived at through mediation as compared with litigation.[30] Such beneficial perceptions, alongside higher compliance rates, may explain relatively higher levels of confidence in mandatory programmes.

In addition, nearly an identical proportion of practitioners working in voluntary programmes (81 per cent) and mandatory programmes (82 per cent) believed that outcomes arrived out through respective court mediation programmes were either very fair or fair.[31] Such identity of response appears to indicate that the mechanism by which parties are introduced to court mediation has a limited impact on perceptions of fairness given that, regardless of the form of entry, the nature of party participation and substantive outcomes remain in the hands of participants. Outcome fairness as traditionally assessed by standards of equity;[32]

---

[27] R.L. Wissler, 'Court-Connected Mediation in General Civil Cases: What We Know from Empirical Research' (2002) 17 *Ohio State Journal on Dispute Resolution* 641, 690; D. Quek Anderson, 'Mandatory Mediation: An Oxymoron? Examining the Feasibility of Implementing a Court-Mandated Mediation Program' (2010) 11(2) *Cardozo Journal of Conflict Resolution* (Spring), available at SSRN: https://ssrn.com/abstract52843509.

[28] J. Pearson and N. Thoennes, 'Divorce Mediation: An Overview of Research Results' (1985) 19 *Columbia Journal of Law and Social Problems* 451; C. McEwen and T. Milburn, 'Explaining a Paradox of Mediation' (1993) 9 *Negotiation Journal* 23.

[29] F.E.A. Sander, 'Another View of Mandatory Mediation' (2007) *Dispute Resolution Magazine* (Winter) 16.

[30] C.A. McEwen and R.J. Maiman, 'Mediation in Small Claims Court: Achieving Compliance Through Consent' (1984) 18 *Law and Society Review* 11; N. Vidmar, 'An Assessment of Mediation in a Small Claims Court' (1985) 41 *Journal of Social Issues* 127.

[31] Much of the ADR literature uses the terms 'fairness' and 'justice' interchangeably. See e.g., O. Shapira, 'Conceptions and Perceptions of Fairness in Mediation' (2012) 54 *South Texas Law Review* 281; J. Bercovitch, 'Mediation Success or Failure: A Search for the Elusive Criteria' (2006) 7 *Cardozo Journal of Conflict Resolution* 289, 291; J.M. Hyman, 'Swimming in the Deep End: Dealing with Justice in Mediation' (2004) 6 *Cardozo Journal of Conflict Resolution* 19; J.B. Stulberg, 'Mediation and Justice: What Standards Govern?' (2005) 6 *Cardozo Journal of Conflict Resolution* 213, 215 note 8.

[32] See e.g., Bercovitch, 'Mediation Success or Failure: A Search for the Elusive Criteria' (n. 31 above).

legality;[33] beneficial impact on parties;[34] relational improvement;[35] and upholding of human dignity,[36] as distinct from 'process fairness';[37] requiring informed[38] participation; non-coercion;[39] absence of undue influence;[40] the opportunity to terminate;[41] absence of bias;[42] impartiality;[43] accounting for power differentials;[44] and free expression,[45] appears to be independent of the mechanism by which parties arrive at mediation – whether voluntarily or though a mandatory process. This appears to support suggestions by scholars that given the 'educative functions' of mandatory programmes, it is worthwhile 'to at least consider some form of dispute settlement procedure before trial'.[46]

---

[33] See e.g., J.W. Cooley, 'A Classical Approach to Mediation, Part I: Classical Rhetoric and the Art of Persuasion in Mediation' (1993) 19 *University of Dayton Law Review* 83, 130.

[34] See e.g., J.B. Stulberg, 'Fairness and Mediation' (1998) 13 *Ohio State Journal on Dispute Resolution* 909; L. Susskind, 'Environmental Mediation and the Accountability Problem' (1981) 6 *Vermont Law Review* 1, 14–18.

[35] K.E. Menzel, 'Judging the Fairness of Mediation: A Critical Framework' (1991) 9 *Mediation Quarterly* 3, 6–16; and J.M. Hyman and L.P. Love, 'If Portia Were a Mediator: An Inquiry into Justice in Mediation' (2002) 9 *Clinical Law Review* 157, 186.

[36] Stulberg, 'Mediation and Justice: What Standards Govern?' (n. 31 above) 215 note 8.

[37] See generally, Shapira, 'Conceptions and Perceptions of Fairness in Mediation' (n. 31 above).

[38] J.M. Nolan-Haley, 'Informed Consent in Mediation: A Guiding Principle for Truly Educated Decisionmaking' (1999) 74 *Notre Dame Law Review* 775, 778 note 12.

[39] Cal. R. Ct. 3.857(b), available at www.courts.ca.gov/documents/title_3.pdf.

[40] See e.g., Family Mediation Canada, *Members Code of Professional Conduct* (2013), available at www.fmc.ca/pdf/CodeProfessionalConduct.pdf.

[41] Georgia Commission on Dispute Resolution, *Ethical Standards for Mediators* (2012) s. IV, p. 30, available at www.godr.org/files/APPENDIX%20C,%20CHAP%201,%206-1-2012.pdf

[42] S.E. Burns, 'Thinking About Fairness and Achieving Balance in Mediation' (2008) 35 *Fordham Urban Law Journal* 39, 41.

[43] See e.g., J. Dworkin and W. London, 'What is a Fair Agreement?' (1989) 7 *Mediation Quarterly* 3, 5.

[44] L. Boulle and M. Nesic, *Mediation: Principles, Process, Practice* (Butterworths South Africa, 2001) pp. 454–5; T. Grillo, 'The Mediation Alternative: Process Dangers for Women' (1991) 100 *Yale Law Journal* 1545, 1550; R. Delgado et al., 'Fairness and Formality: Minimizing the Risk of Prejudice in Alternative Dispute Resolution' (1985) *Wisconsin Law Review* 1359, 1375–83.

[45] N.A. Welsh, 'Making Deals in Court-Connected Mediation: What's Justice Got to Do with It?' (2001) 79 *Washington University Law Quarterly* 787, 817.

[46] C. Menkel-Meadow, 'When Dispute Resolution Begets Disputes of its Own: Conflicts Among Dispute Professionals' (1997) 46(6) *UCLA Law Review*.

With respect to efficiency, surveyed practitioners regard voluntary mediation programmes (77 per cent) as slightly more efficient than mandatory court mediation programmes (68 per cent).[47] When examined from a judiciary's operational cost perspective, voluntary mediation programmes generally place the responsibility of financing such services on the parties, and therefore overall voluntary mediation costs are lower as compared with mandatory programmes. From the perspective of the user, when mediation is successful, litigation expenses may be reduced.[48] However, when mediation is unsuccessful, overall costs of litigation generally go up.[49] In light of the impact of costs on overall efficiency, some mandatory mediation programmes provide an opt-out mechanism for parties in the event that 'the costs of mediation would be higher than the requested relief'[50] and suggest that ongoing monitoring be required to ensure high quality mandatory court mediation programmes, particularly when parties are required to pay for mediation fees.[51] Original advocates

---

[47] Nevertheless, such results are not statistically significant.

[48] For example, a study conducted by the International Finance Corporation in 2006 found that in more than 1,000 cases resolved through mediation in Serbia, Bosnia and Herzegovinia and Macedonia, direct costs of mediation averaged US$225 which represented about 50 per cent of the cost of litigation (about US$470). See I. Love, 'Settling Out of Court: How Effective is Alternative Dispute Resolution?' in *Viewpoint: Public Policy for the Private Sector*, IFC/World Bank Note No. 329 (October 2011), available at: http://siteresources.worldbank.org/FINANCIALSECTOR/Resources/282044-1307652042357/VP329-Setting-out-of-court.pdf; see also C.E. Jorquiera and G. Dabdoub Alvarez, *The Cost of Disputes in Companies and the Use of ADR Methods: Lessons from Nine Latin American Countries*, MIF Study (Washington, DC: Multilateral Investment Fund, 2005); J. Barkai and G. Kassebaum, *Hawaii's Court-Annexed Arbitration Program, Final Evaluation Report*, Program on Conflict Resolution Working Paper Series 1992-1 (Manoa: University of Hawaii, 1992); R. Hann and C. Baar, *Evaluation of the Ontario Mandatory Mediation Program (Rule 24.1): Executive Summary and Recommendations* (2001), available at www.attorneygeneral.jus.gov.on.ca/.

[49] Genn et al., *Twisting Arms* (n. 1 above) (for cases that failed to settle through mediation, expenses were US$2,000–US$4,000 higher); J. Rosenberg and H.J. Folberg, 'Alternative Dispute Resolution: An Empirical Analysis' (1994) 46 *Stanford Law Review* 1487. (Similarly, ENE processes that did not result in settlement in California courts added about US$4,000 to the cost of litigation.) R. Wissler, 'The Effectiveness of Court-Connected Dispute Resolution in Civil Cases' (2004) 22 *Conflict Resolution Quarterly* 55 (reporting mixed results in cost savings); R.A. Posner, 'The Summary Jury Trial and Other Methods of Alternative Dispute Resolution: Some Cautionary Observations' (1986) 53 *University of Chichester Law Review* 366 (suggesting that there are no savings in costs).

[50] Colo. Rev. Stat. Ann. s. 13-22-311 (West 2009).

[51] Fla. R. Civ. P. 1.710(B). See also 'Florida's Court-Connected ADR History' in E. Reshard (ed.), *Florida Mediation and Arbitration Programs, A Compendium*

of the multi-door courthouse have cautioned that requiring that parties pay for court-annexed ADR may contradict the key idea of creating a justice system that provides parties with a range of options for dispute resolution,[52] or lead to satellite litigation and 'ultimately increase the costs for litigants and result in general inefficiency within the court system'.[53] Consistent with previous empirical findings,[54] there is no overall consensus on cost[55] or time savings in voluntary or mandatory mediation. It is for this reason that many scholars look beyond a narrow focus on court backlog reduction and cost and time savings, to wider extrinsic spill-over benefits in preserving relationships, engaging individuals in a process of crafting and implementing solutions and developing long-term skills to address ongoing and future conflicts.

With respect to advancing programme quality, survey findings provide insights into the dynamics, challenges and lessons learned from the perspective of those directly engaged in the work of administering, representing and mediating civil claims. In particular, the findings indicate that practitioners working in mandatory court mediation programmes identify several key benefits, including normalizing party-driven resolution; improved efficiency and speed through effective case screening; and contributing to relational repair, while practitioners working in voluntary programmes identified the key strengths of such programmes as the development of simple procedures; self-determined engagement; high quality mediators; and ongoing monitoring and evaluation. With respect to programme challenges, mandatory mediation practitioners noted that key challenges included limited party understanding of the mediation process; lawyer conflicts of interest; mediator quality; lack of good faith; inexperience in managing power imbalances; and resource limitations, while challenges within voluntary court mediation programmes included difficulties associated with encouraging party participation; and limited resources. Practitioner suggestions for improving the overall court mediation process ranged from enhanced training; public education;

(19th edn, Florida Dispute Resolution Centre, 2005–2006) p. 12, available at www.flcourts.org/gen_public/adr/bin/2006%20Compendium.pdf.

[52] F.E.A. Sander, 'Paying for ADR' (1992) 78 *ABA Journal* 105.

[53] Quek Anderson, 'Mandatory Mediation: An Oxymoron?' (n. 27 above).

[54] See also Genn et al., *Twisting Arms* (n. 1 above) (showing no significant impact of mediation on case duration) and Wissler, 'The Effectiveness of Court-Connected Dispute Resolution in Civil Cases' (n. 49 above).

[55] D. Hensler, 'In Search of Good Mediation' in J. Sanders and V. Lee Hamilton (eds), *Handbook of Justice Research in Law* (New York: Springer, 2001).

organizational resources; to ongoing evaluation and greater flexibility in settlement arrangements.

The question of voluntary or mandatory programme design is highly context dependent and as such the book does not purport to offer a unitary conclusion but rather to reflect on the achievements of such programmes and what has led to success. The relative advantages and challenges of mediation in a given jurisdiction vary according to the functioning of the underlying national civil litigation system. As noted in an earlier study, 'the differences in the structure and court environments of ... programs mean that each program ... is unique: they cannot simply be lumped together and viewed generically'.[56] While the study reports on the programme's correlation with the same measures, including efficiency, confidence and perceptions of justice, the results must be seen as reflecting the unique conditions of each particular programme and 'any cross-program comparisons must therefore take into account the impact of programmatic and environmental differences on these results'.[57] Given the primary focus of the study on general civil claims, it must be noted that court referral of family cases to well trained mediation staff resulting in well documented benefits to parties, is not the focus of the study and is therefore beyond the scope of interpretation.

On the whole, whether voluntary or mandatory, it can be suggested that at an early stage, small scale pilot mediation programmes can provide a useful base of experience to develop culturally specific programmes and train a growing pool of capable mediators, engage in a collective process of learning and advance programme design. At the mid-stage, as experience is gained, public information programmes can assist with the diffusion and expansion of such programmes in a given region. At an advanced stage, as high quality mediation services are developed and mediators receive adequate training in avoiding implicit bias, preventing the abuse of power imbalances, and public funds are available to support such programmes, then movement towards more targeted encouragement of mediation in appropriate cases can further enhance options for resolution. In all stages, ongoing learning though collaborative reflection on challenges and best practices will assist in the advancement of court mediation practices and inform policy reform. Such ongoing learning, coupled with the provision of accessible public information on the mediation process, will contribute to enhanced efficacy. In all cases, as recent research has found,

---

[56] H. Anderson and R. Pi, *Evaluation of the Early Mediation Pilot Programs* (Judicial Council of CA Administrative Office of the Courts, 2004).
[57] *Ibid.*

'innovations intended to reduce costs and delay should not do so at the expense of those qualities of the judicial process that are more important to litigants'.[58] Institutions involved in the provision of court mediation services must be mindful of benchmarking success beyond measures of 'settlement' to actual resolution of issues through an impartial, just and principle-based process.[59] Success will largely depend on the quality and skill of the mediators, institutional support, party education and preparation, and engagement with local needs and conditions.

Given the complexity of surrounding civil justice dynamics, much remains to be examined, including the need for more in-depth qualitative studies examining intra-mediation programme variation, and how mediator and participant training[60] including programmes directed toward the cultivation of impartiality and equity contributes to the development of surrounding mediation culture and the advancement of social justice and cohesion. Future studies by a growing number of researchers will no doubt contribute insights to the advancement of such understanding.

---

[58] E.A. Lind et al., *The Perception of Justice: Tort Litigants' Views of Trial, Court-Annexed Arbitration, and Judicial Settlement Conferences* (Santa Monica, CA: RAND Corporation, 1989).

[59] See Genn, 'What is Civil Justice For?' (n. 16 above); M. Mironi, 'Mediation v. Case Settlement: The Unsettling Relations Between Court and Mediation – A Case Study' (2014) 19 *Harvard Negotiation Law Review* 173.

[60] Empirical studies indicate that nearly 30 per cent of court mediators believe that further training is needed to effectively conduct mediations. See S. Purcell and J. Martinez, 'Mediators in the Field: Experiences Around the Globe' (2014) *Dispute Resolution Magazine* (Winter).

Select bibliography

Albiston, C. (1999) 'The Rule of Law and the Litigation Process: The Paradox of Losing by Winning' 33(4) *Law and Society Review* 869

Alexander, N.M. (2001) 'What's Law Got to Do with It? Mapping Modern Mediation Movements in Civil and Common Law Jurisdictions' 13(2) *Bond Law Review*, article 5

— (2006) *Global Trends in Mediation*. Alphen aan den Rijn: Kluwer Law International

— (2009) *International and Comparative Mediation: Legal Perspectives*. The Hague: Kluwer Law International

— (2010) *The New Jim Crow: Mass Incarceration in the Age of Colorblindness*. New York: New Press

Ali, S. (2011) *Resolving Disputes in the Asia Pacific Region: International Arbitration and Mediation in East Asia and the West*. Abingdon: Routledge

Ali, S. and Lee, F. (2011) 'Lessons Learned from a Comparative Examination of Global Civil Justice Reforms' 53(4) *International Journal of Law and Management* 262

Alkon, C.J. (2016) 'The Modern Problem-Solving Court Movement: Taking Stock After 25 Years', paper presented at Association of American Law Schools Annual Conference

Amsler, L.B. (2008) 'Designing Justice: Legal Institutions and Other Systems for Managing Conflict' 24(1) *Ohio State Journal on Dispute Resolution* 1

Amsler, L.B., Martinez, J.K., Smith, S.E. and Merchant, C. (2015) 'The State of Dispute System Design' 33(S1) *Conflict Resolution Quarterly* S7

Anderson, D.Q. (2010) 'Mandatory Mediation: An Oxymoron? Examining the Feasibility of Implementing a Court-Mandated Mediation Program' 11(2) *Cardozo Journal of Conflict Resolution* 479

Anderson, D.Q. and Lee, J. (2016) 'The Global Pound Conference: A Conversation on the Future of Dispute Resolution' 70 *Asian Journal on Mediation* 1793

Anderson, H. and Pi, R. (2004) *Evaluation of the Early Mediation Pilot Programs*. San Francisco, CA: Judicial Council of California

Aragaki, H.N. (2009) 'Deliberative Democracy as Dispute Resolution:

Conflict, Interests, and Reasons' 24(3) *Ohio State Journal on Dispute Resolution* 406

Barkai, J. and Kassebaum, G. (1992) *Hawaii's Court-Annexed Arbitration Program, Final Evaluation Report*, Program on Conflict Resolution Working Paper Series 1992-1. Manoa: University of Hawaii

Bergin, P.A. (2012) *Objectives, Scope and Focus of Mediation Legislation in Australia.* New South Wales Judicial Scholarship, article 24

Binder, P. and Sekolec, J. (2005) *International Commercial Arbitration and Conciliation in UNCITRAL Model Law Jurisdictions.* London: Sweet & Maxwell

Bingham, L.B., Nabatchi, T., Senger, J. and Jackman, M.S. (2009) 'Dispute Resolution and the Vanishing Trial: Comparing Federal Government Litigation and ADR Outcomes' 24(2) *Ohio State Journal of Dispute Resolution* 1

Birke, R. and Teitz, L.E. (2002) 'US Mediation in 2001: The Path that Brought America to Uniform Laws and Mediation in Cyberspace' *American Journal of Comparative Law* 181

Blake, S., Browne, J. and Sime, S. (2011) *A Practical Approach to Alternative Dispute Resolution.* Oxford University Press

Bowne, A. (2015) 'To Civil Justice: Alternative Dispute Resolution and the Courts' 39 *Australian Bar Review* 275

Brazil, W. (2007) 'Hosting Mediations as a Representative of the System of Civil Justice' 22 *Ohio State Journal on Dispute Resolution* 227

Brett, J.M., Barsness, Z.I. and Goldberg, S.B. (1996) 'The Effectiveness of Mediation: An Independent Analysis of Cases Handled by Four Major Service Providers' 12(3) *Negotiation Journal* 259

Bruni, A. (2010) 'Mediation in Italy' 2 *Revista Forumul Judecatorilor* 96

Bryan, P.E. (1992) 'Killing Us Softly: Divorce Mediation and the Politics of Power' 40 *Buffalo Law Review* 441

Burns, S.E. (2008) 'Thinking About Fairness and Achieving Balance in Mediation' 35 *Fordham Urban Law Journal* 39

Bush, R.A.B. and Folger, J.P. (2004) *The Promise of Mediation: The Transformative Approach to Conflict.* John Wiley & Sons

Callister, R.R. and Wall, J.A. (1997) 'Japanese Community and Organizational Mediation' 41(2) *Journal of Conflict Resolution* 311

Campbell, D. and Cotter, S. (1994) *Dispute Resolution Methods.* London: Graham & Trotman

Charles, W.E. (1996) 'Confidentiality, Privilege and Rule 408: The Protection of Mediation Proceedings in Federal Court' 60 *Louisiana Law Review* 91

Clark, B. (2012) 'Lawyers and Mediation' 31 *Berlin Heidelberg, Springer Legal Studies* 162

Clarke, D.C. (1992) 'Dispute Resolution in China' 5 *Journal of Chinese Law* 245
Coben, J.R. (2004) 'Gollum, Meet Smeagol: A Schizophrenic Rumination on Mediator Values Beyond Self-Determination and Neutrality' 5 *Cardozo Journal of Conflict Resolution* 65
Cohen, A.J. (2011) 'Revisiting Against Settlement: Some Reflections on Dispute Resolution and Public Values' 78 *Fordham Law Review* 101
Cominelli, L. and Lucciari, C. (2016) *Italian Mediators in Action: The Impact of Style and Attitude*, Law and Society Association Annual Meeting New Orleans
Cornes, D. (2008) 'Mediation Privilege and the EU Mediation Directive: An Opportunity?' 74(4) *Arbitration, the Journal of the Chartered Institute of Arbitrators* 395
Crawford, J. and Opeskin, B. (2004). *Australian Courts of Law*. Melbourne: Oxford University Press
Damaska, M. (1986) *The Faces of Justice and State Authority: A Comparative Approach to the Legal Process*. New Haven, CT: Yale University Press
Davies, E., Fenn, P. and O'Shea, M. (2005) *Dispute Resolution and Conflict Management in Construction: An International Perspective*. Abingdon: Routledge
De la Campa, A.A. (2008) *The Private Sector Approach to Commercial ADR: Commercial ADR Mechanisms in Colombia*. Investment Climate Department of the World Bank Group
De Luca, A. (2015) 'Mediation in Italy: Feature and Trends' in C. Esplugues Mota and L. Marquis (eds), *New Developments in Civil and Commercial Mediation*. Springer International Publishing
De Paolis, F. (2011) 'Italy Responds to the EU Mediation Directive and Confronts Court Backlog: The New Civil Court Mandatory Mediation Law' 4(1) *New York Dispute Resolution Lawyer* 44
Deason, E.E. (2004) 'Procedural Rules for Complementary Systems of Litigation and Mediation – Worldwide' 80 *Notre Dame Law Review* 553
Delgado, R., Dunn, C., Brown, P., Lee, H. and Hubbert, D. (1985) 'Fairness and Formality: Minimizing the Risk of Prejudice in Alternative Dispute Resolution' *Wisconsin Law Review* 1359
DeLisle, J. (2011) 'Law and China's Development Model' in P. Hsu, Yu-shan Wu and Suisheng Zhao (eds), *In Search of China's Development Model: Beyond the Beijing Consensus*
Denzin, N.K. (1978) *The Research Act: A Theoretical Introduction to Sociological Methods*. New York: McGraw-Hill
Dickey, M.P. (2010) 'ADR Gone Wild: Is It Time for a Federal Mediation Exclusionary Rule?' 25 *Ohio State Journal on Dispute Resolution* 713

Diessner, R. (2000) 'Action Research' in 1:1 *Converging Realities*. Switzerland: Landegg Academy

Esplugues, C. (2014) 'Civil and Commercial Mediation in the EU after the Transposition of Directive 2008/52/EC' in C. Esplugues (ed.), *Civil and Commercial Mediation in Europe, II Cross-border Mediation*. Cambridge: Intersentia

Feeley, M. (1979) *The Process is the Punishment: Handling Cases in a Lower Criminal Court*. New York: Russell Sage Foundation

Feldman, E.A. (2014) *No Alternative: Resolving Disputes Japanese Style*, Faculty Scholarship Paper 1551, available at http://scholarship.law.upenn.edu/faculty_scholarship/1551

Ficks, E. (2009) 'Models of General Court-Connected Conciliation and Mediation for Commercial Disputes in Sweden, Australia and Japan' 13(1) *Journal of Japanese Law* 25

Fiss, O. (1979) *The Forms of Justice*, Faculty Scholarship Series Paper 1220, available at http://digitalcommons.law.yale.edu/fss_papers/1220/

— (1984) 'Against Settlement' 93(6) *Yale Law Journal* 1073

Folberg, J. (2005) *Resolving Disputes: Theory, Practice, and Law*. Aspen Law & Business

Fu, H. (1992) 'Understanding People's Mediation in Post-Mao China' 6 *Journal of Chinese Law* 211

— (2009) *Access to Justice in China: Potentials, Limits and Alternatives*, available at https://papers.ssrn.com/sol3/papers.cfm?abstract_id51474073

Fu, H. and Cullen, R. (2007) 'From Mediatory to Adjudicatory Justice: The Limits of Civil Justice Reform in China' in M.Y.K. Woo and M.E. Gallagher (eds), *Chinese Justice: Civil Dispute Resolution in Contemporary China*. Cambridge University Press [2011]

Fu, H. and Palmer, M. (eds) (2017) *Mediation in Contemporary China: Continuity and Change*. London: Wildy, Simmonds and Hill

Fuller, L.L. (1970) 'Mediation – Its Forms and Functions' 44 *Southern California Law Review* 305

— (1978) 'Forms and Limits of Adjudication' 92(2) *Harvard Law Review* 353

Galanter, M. (1974) 'Why the 'Haves' Come Out Ahead: Speculations on the Limits of Legal Change' 9(1) *Law and Society Review* 95

— (2004) 'The Vanishing Trial: What the Numbers Tell Us, What They May Mean' 10(4) *Dispute Resolution Magazine* 3

Galanter, M. and Cahill, M. (1994) 'Most Cases Settle: Judicial Promotion and Regulation of Settlements' 46 *Stanford Law Review* 1339

Galanter, M., Garth, B., Hensler, D.R. and Zemans, F. (1994) 'How to Improve Civil Justice Policy' 77 *Judicature* 185

Garg, S. (2015) *Emerging Trends in Mediation*, available at www.inadr.org/wp-content/uploads/2014/10/Emerging-trends-in-Mediation-1.pptx

Genn, H. (1999) *Paths to Justice: What People Do and Think About Going to Law*. Oxford: Hart Publishing
— (2009) *The Hamlyn Lectures: Judging Civil Justice*. Cambridge University Press
— (2010) *Judging Civil Justice*. Cambridge University Press
— (2013) 'What is Civil Justice For? Reform, ADR, and Access to Justice' 24 *Yale Journal of Law and the Humanities* 397
Genn, H. and Beinart, S. (1999) *Paths to Justice: What People Do and Think About Going to Law*. Oxford: Hart Publishing Publishing
Genn, H., Fenn, P., Mason, M., Lane, A., Bechai, N., Gray, L. and Vencappa, D. (2007) *Twisting Arms: Court Referred and Court Linked Mediation under Judicial Pressure*. London: Ministry of Justice
Ginsburg, T., Monateri, P.G. and Parisi, F. (2014) 'Classics in Comparative Law: An Introduction' in T. Ginsburg, P.G. Monateri and F. Parisi (eds), *Classics in Comparative Law*. Cheltenham: Edward Elgar
Goodman, J.W. (2003) 'The Pros and Cons of Online Dispute Resolution: An Assessment of Cyber-Mediation Websites' 2(1) *Duke Law and Technology Review* 1
Gordon, E.E. (1998) 'Why Attorneys Support Mandatory Mediation' 82 *Judicature* 224
Gregory, A. and Litt, N. (2000) 'No Confidence: The Problem of Confidentiality by Local Rule in the ADR Act of 1998' 78 *Texas Law Review* 1015
Grillo, T. (1991) 'The Mediation Alternative: Process Dangers for Women' 200 *Yale Law Journal* 1545
Halegua, A. (2008) *Reforming the People's Mediation System in Urban China*, available at https://ssrn.com/abstract51123283
Hamilton, J.W. (1999) 'Protecting Confidentiality in Mandatory Mediation: Lessons from Ontario and Saskatchewan' 24 *Queen's Law Journal* 574
Hanks, M. (2012) 'Perspectives on Mandatory Mediation' 35(3) *University of New South Wales Law Journal* 929
Hann, R. and Baar, C. (2001) *Evaluation of the Ontario Mandatory Mediation Program (Rule 24.1): Executive Summary and Recommendations*. Ontario: Ministry of the Attorney General
Harman, J. (2014) *From Alternate to Primary Dispute Resolution: The Pivotal Role of Mediation in (and in Avoiding) Litigation*, available at www.federalcircuitcourt.gov.au/wps/wcm/connect/fccweb/reports-and-publications/speeches-conference-papers/2014/speech-harman-alternate-to-primary-dispute-resolution
He, Xin and Ng, Kwai Hang (2012) 'Internal Contradictions of Judicial Mediation in China', *Law and Social Inquiry*, 11 December

Heise, M. (2000) 'Justice Delayed? An Empirical Analysis of Civil Case Disposition Time' 50(4) *Case Western Reserve Law Review* 813

Hensler, D.R. (1993) 'Studying Gender Bias in the Courts: Stories and Statistics' 45(6) *Stanford Law Review* 2187

— (1994) *Why We Don't Know More About the Civil Justice System – and What We Could Do About It*. USC Law

— (2000) *A Research Agenda: What We Need to Know About Court-Connected ADR*. Santa Monica, CA: RAND Corporation

— (2001) 'In Search of Good Mediation' in J. Sanders and V.L. Hamilton (eds), *Handbook of Justice Research in Law*. New York: Springer

— (2003) 'Our Courts Ourselves: How the Alternative Dispute Resolution Movement is Reshaping Our Legal System' 108(1) *Pennsylvania State Law Review* 165

Hilary, A. and Christine, C. (1992) *Dispute Resolution in Australia*. Butterworths Australia

Hilmer, S.E. (2009) *Mediation in the People's Republic of China and Hong Kong (SAR)*. Eleven International

Hodson, D. (2008) 'The EU Mediation Directive: The European Encouragement to Family Law ADR' 209 *International Family Law* 16

Hopt, K.J. and Steffek, F. (2012) *Mediation: Principles and Regulation in Comparative Perspective*. Oxford University Press

Huang, P.C.C. (2006) 'Court Mediation in China, Past and Present' 32(3) *Modern China* 275

Huchannavar, S. (2013) 'In Search of True "Alternative" to Existing Justice Dispensing System in India Shivaraj' 7(1) *NALSAR Law Review* 1

Hyman, J.M. and Love, L.P. (2002) 'If Portia Were a Mediator: An Inquiry into Justice in Mediation' 9 *Clinical Law Review* 157

Idei, N. (2012) 28 *Japan Commercial Arbitration Association Newsletter* 1, available at www.jcaa.or.jp/e/arbitration/docs/newsletter28.pdf

Iwai, N. (1990–1991) 'Alternative Dispute Resolution in Court: The Japanese Experience' 6 *Ohio State Journal on Dispute Resolution* 201

Iwasaki, K. (1994) 'ADR: Japanese Experience with Conciliation' 10(1) *Arbitration International* 91

Izumi, C. (2010) 'Implicit Bias and the Illusion of Mediator Neutrality' 34 *Washington University Journal of Law and Policy* 71

Jacobs, P. (2005) 'A Recent Comparative History of Mandatory Mediation vs. Voluntary Mediation in Ontario, Canada', *International Bar Association Mediation Newsletter*

Jiang, S.G. (2001) *Tiao Jie, Fa Zhi Yu Xian Dai Xing: Zhongguo Tiao Jie Zhi Du Yan Jiu* [*Mediation, Legality and Modernity: Mediation in China*]. Beijing: Zhongguo Fazhi Chu Ban She

Jorquiera, C.E. and Alvarez, G.D. (2005) *The Cost of Disputes in Companies*

and the Use of ADR Methods: Lessons from Nine Latin American Countries*, MIF Study. Washington, DC: Multilateral Investment Fund
Kagan, R. (2001) *Adversarial Legalism: The American Way of Law*. Cambridge, MA: Harvard University Press
Kakalik, J.S. (ed.) (1996) *An Evaluation of Mediation and Early Neutral Evaluation Under the Civil Justice Reform Act*. Santa Monica, SA: Rand Corporation
Kakalik, J.S., Dunworth, T., Hill, L.A., McCaffrey, D.F., Oshiro, M., Pace, N.M. and Vaiana, M.E. (1996) *An Evaluation of Mediation and Early Neutral Evaluation Under the Civil Justice Reform Act*. Santa Monica, CA: RAND Corporation
— (1997). *Just, Speedy and Inexpensive? An Evaluation of Judicial Case Management Under the Civil Justice Reform Act*. Santa Monica, CA: RAND Corporation
Kakiuchi, J.S. (2013) *Regulating Dispute Resolution, ADR and Access to Justice at the Crossroads*. London: Bloomsbury Professional
— (2015) 'Regulating Mediation in Japan: Latest Development and Its Background' in *New Developments in Civil and Commercial Mediation*. New York: Springer
Keet, M. (2005) 'The Evolution of Lawyers' Roles in Mandatory Mediation: A Condition of Systemic Transformation' 68(2) *Saskatchewan Law Review* 313
Kressel, K. and Pruitt, D.G. (1985) 'Themes in the Mediation of Social Conflict' 41 *Journal of Social Issues* 179
Krygier, M. (2015) *Legal Pluralism and the Value of the Rule of Law*. Sydney: HKU-UNSW Research Symposium
Kuhner, T.K. (2005) 'Court-Connected Mediation Compared: The Cases of Argentina and the United States' 11 *ILSA Journal of International and Comparative Law* 540
LaFree, G. and Rack, C. (1996) 'The Effects of Participants' Ethnicity and Gender on Monetary Outcomes in Mediated and Adjudicated Civil Cases' 30 *Law and Society Review* 767
LeBaron, M. and Alexander, N.M. (2016) 'The Alchemy of Mediation' in *Essays in Mediation*. Singapore Management University School of Law
Liming, W. (2009) 'Characteristics of China's Judicial Mediation System' 17 *Asia Pacific Law Review* 67
Lind, E.A., MacCoun, R.J., Ebener, P.A., Felstiner, W., Hensler, D.R., Resnik, J. and Tyler, T.R. (1989) *The Perception of Justice: Tort Litigants' Views of Trial, Court-Annexed Arbitration, and Judicial Settlement Conferences*, Santa Monica, CA: RAND Corporation
Love, I. (2011) 'Settling Out of Court: How Effective is Alternative

Dispute Resolution?' in *Viewpoint: Public Policy for the Private Sector*, IFC/World Bank Note No. 329

Love, L.P. and Galton, E. (2012) *Stories Mediators Tell*. ABA Book Publishing

Low, J. and Quek D. (2012) 'Introducing a "Presumption of ADR" for Civil Matters in the Subordinate Courts' 22 *Law Gazette*

Lubman, S. (1967) 'Mao and Mediation: Politics and Dispute Resolution in Communist China' 55(5) *California Law Review* 1284

— (1997) 'Deng and Dispute Resolution: "Mao and Mediation" Revisited' 11 *Columbia Journal of Asian Law* 229

MacCoun, R.J., Lind, E. and Hensler, D.R. (eds) (1989) *The Perception of Justice: Tort Litigants' Views of Trial, Court-Annexed Arbitration, and Judicial Settlement Conferences*. Santa Monica, CA: RAND Corporation

Macfarlane, J. and Keet, M. (2005) 'Civil Justice Reform and Mandatory Civil Mediation in Saskatchewan: Lessons from a Maturing Program' 42(3) *Alberta Law Review* 677

McAdoo, B. (2006) 'All Rise, the Court is in Session: What Judges Say About Court-Connected Mediation' 22(2) *Ohio State Journal on Dispute Resolution* 337

McEwen, C.A. and Maiman, R.J. (1984) 'Mediation in Small Claims Court: Achieving Compliance Through Consent' 18 *Law and Society Review* 11

McEwen, C. and Milburn, T. (1993) 'Explaining a Paradox of Mediation' 9 *Negotiation Journal* 23

McHale, J.Q.C. (2012) 'Access to Justice: A Government Perspective' 63 *University of New Brunswick Law Journal* 352

McHale, J.Q.C. and Farrow, T.C.W. (2013) 'Mandatory Dispute Resolution and the Question of Resources'. *Slaw*

Menkel-Meadow, C. (1991) 'Pursuing Settlement in an Adversary Culture: A Tale of Innovation Co-Opted or the Law of ADR' 19 *Florida State Law Review* 1

— (1996) 'Introduction: What Will We Do When Adjudication Ends – A Brief Intellectual History of ADR' 44 *UCLA Law Review* 1613

— (1997) 'When Dispute Resolution Begets Disputes of Its Own: Conflicts Among Dispute Professionals' 46 *UCLA Law Review*, article 6

— (2002) 'When Litigation is Not the Only Way: Consensus Building and Mediation as Public Interest Lawyering' 10 *Washington University Journal of Law and Policy* 37

— (2006) 'Peace and Justice: Notes on the Evolution and Purpose of Legal Process' 94 *Georgetown Law Journal* 553

— (2015) Alternative and Appropriate Dispute Resolution in Context

Formal, Informal, and Semiformal Legal Processes, available at https://ssrn.com/abstract52584188

Menkel-Meadow, C. and Garth, B. (2010) 'Process, People, Power and Policy: Empirical Studies of Civil Procedure and Courts' in P. Cane and H. Kritzer (eds), *Oxford Handbook of Empirical Legal Research*. Oxford University Press

— (2010) 'The Baseline Problem of What ADR is and What It is Compared To' in P. Cane and H. Kritzer (eds), *Oxford Handbook of Empirical Legal Research*. Oxford University Press

Mironi, M.M. (2014) 'Mediation v. Case Settlement: The Unsettling Relations Between Court and Mediation, a Case Study' 19 *Harvard Negotiation Law Review* 173

Mistelis, L. (2003) 'ADR in England and Wales: A Successful Case of Public Private Partnership' 6(3) *ADR Bulletin*, Article 6

Moberly, R.B. and Levine, L.E. (2009) 'The New Arkansas Appellate Mediation Program' 61 *Arkansas Law Review* 429

Nelson, D.W. (2001) 'ADR in the Federal Courts: One Judge's Perspective: Issues and Challenges Facing Judges, Lawyers, Court Administrators, and the Public' 17 *Ohio State Journal of Dispute Resolution* 1

Nolan-Haley, J.M. (1999) 'Informed Consent in Mediation: A Guiding Principle for Truly Educated Decisionmaking' 74 *Notre Dame Law Review* 775

— (2007) 'Consent in Mediation' 14 *Dispute Resolution Magazine* 4

— (2010) 'Mediation Exceptionality' 78 *Fordham Law Review* 1247

— (2011) 'Is Europe Headed Down the Primrose Path with Mandatory Mediation' 37 *North Carolina Journal of International Law* 981

— (2012) 'Mediation: The New Arbitration' 17 *Harvard Negotiation Law Review* 61

— (2014) 'Mediation: The Best and Worst of Times' 16 *Cardozo Journal of Conflict Resolution* 731

Nolan-Haley, J.M. and Annor-Ohene, J.K. (2014) 'Procedural Justice Beyond Borders: Mediation in Ghana' *Harvard Negotiation Law Review Online* 1

Nottage, L.R. (2004) 'Civil Procedure Reforms in Japan: The Latest Round' 22 *Ritsumeikan University Law Review* 81

Ollapally, L. (2011) *Mandatory Court Referral for Mediation: Parties Retain the Right to Voluntary Decision*, available at campmediation.in/images/articles/Mandatory_Court_Referral.doc

Palmer, M. (1987) 'The Revival of Mediation in the People's Republic of China: 1. Extra-Judicial Mediation' in W.E. Butler (ed.), *Yearbook on Socialist Legal System*

Pearson, J. and Thoennes, N. (1985) 'Divorce Mediation: An Overview of Research Results' 19 *Columbia Journal of Law and Social Problems* 451

Peckham, R.F. (1984) 'Judicial Response to the Cost of Litigation: Case Management, Two-Stage Discovery Planning and Alternative Dispute Resolution' 37 *Rutgers University Law Review* 253

Peerenboom, R. and Xin, H. (2008) *Dispute Resolution in China: Patterns, Causes and Prognosis*, La Trobe Law School Legal Studies Research Paper No. 2008/9

Pham, H.T. (2004) 'Developing Countries and the WTO: The Need for More Mediation in the DSU' 9 *Harvard Negotiation Law Review* 331

Plapinger, E. and Stienstra, D. (1996) *ADR and Settlement in the Federal District Courts: A Sourcebook for Judges and Lawyers*. Federal Judicial Centre and the CPR Institute for Dispute Resolution

Press, S. (2013) 'Court-Connected Mediation and Minorities: Has Any Progress Been Made?' *ABA Dispute Resolution Magazine* (Summer) 36

Pryles, M.C. (2006) *Dispute Resolution in Asia*. Alphen aan den Rijn: Kluwer Law International

Pugh, A.M. and Bales, R.A. (2003) 'The Inherent Power of the Federal Courts to Compel Participation in Nonbinding Forms of Alternative Dispute Resolution' 42 *Duquesne Law Review* 1

Purcell, S. (2013) *Dispute System Design: A Comparative Study of India, Israel, and California*, UC Hastings Research Paper No. 48

Purcell, S. and Martinez, J. (2014) 'Mediators in the Field: Experiences Around the Globe' *Dispute Resolution Magazine* (Winter)

Rack, R.W. (2002) 'Thoughts of a Chief Circuit Mediator on Federal Court-Annexed Mediation' 17 *Ohio State Journal on Dispute Resolution* 609

Radford, M.F. (2000) 'Advantages and Disadvantages of Mediation in Probate, Trust, and Guardianship Matters' 1 *Pepperdine Dispute Resolution Law Journal* 241

Rao, J. (2015) *Concepts of Conciliation and Mediation and Their Differences*, available at http://lawcommissionofindia.nic.in

Raveendran, R.V. (2011) *Alternate Dispute Resolution Under Section 89 of the Code of Civil Procedure: Guidelines*, available at Legalblog.in

Resnik, J. (1995) 'Many Doors? Closing Doors? Alternative Dispute Resolution and Adjudication' 10 *Ohio State Journal of Dispute Resolution* 211

Reuben, R.C. (2010) 'How ADR Can Foster the Rule of Law: Beyond the Fundamental Tension', paper presented at Symposium on 'ADR and the Rule of Law: Making the Connection' Missouri School of Law

— (2010) 'ADR and the Rule of Law: Making the Connection' 16(4) *Dispute Resolution Magazine* 4

Rosenberg, J. and Folberg, H.J. (1994) 'Alternative Dispute Resolution: An Empirical Analysis' 46 *Stanford Law Review* 1487

Ross, L. (1990) 'The Changing Profile of Dispute Resolution in Rural China: The Case of Zouping County, Shandong, China' 26 *Stanford Journal of International Law* 15

Sanchez, V.A. (1996) 'Towards a History of ADR: The Dispute Processing Continuum in Anglo-Saxon England and Today' 11 *Ohio State Journal on Dispute Resolution* 1

Sander, F.E.A. (1979) 'Varieties of Dispute Processing' in A. Levin and R. Wheeler (eds), *The Pound Conference: Perspectives on Justice in the Future*. Eagan, MN: West Publishing

— (2007) 'Another View of Mandatory Mediation' 13(2) *Dispute Resolution Magazine* 16

Saposnek, D.T. (1992) 'Clarifying Perspectives on Mandatory Mediation' 39(4) *Family Court Review* 490

Schneider, A.K. (2012) 'Foreword: The Future of Court ADR: Mediation and Beyond' 95(3) *Marquette Law Review* 799

Shroff, V. and Parikh, S. (2012) 'India: A Conciliatory Approach' *International Financial Law Review*

Slapper, G. and Kelly, D. (2015) *The English Legal System: 2015–2016*. Abingdon: Routledge

Smith, G. (1998) 'Unwilling Actors: Why Voluntary Mediation Works, Why Mandatory Mediation Might Not' 36 *Osgoode Hall Law Journal* 847

Solomon, V.E. (2015) 'Divorce Mediation: A New Solution to Old Problems' 16(4) *Akron Law Review* 5

Sourdin, T. (2006) 'Mediation in Australia: Impacts on litigation' in N. Alexander (ed.), *Global Trends in Mediation*. Alphen aan den Rijn: Kluwer Law International

Sourdin, T. and Zariski, A. (2013) *The Multi-Tasking Judge: Introduction to Comparative Judicial Dispute Resolution*. Thomson Reuters Australia

Spencer, D. (2013) 'Case Notes: Mandatory Mediation for Only Part of a Dispute; Costs Awarded for an Unreasonable Act; and Mediation Media Watch' 24 *Australasian Dispute Resolution Journal* 203

Spencer, D. and Brogan, M. (2006) *Mediation Law and Practice*. New York: Cambridge University Press

Stienstra, D. (2011) *ADR in the Federal District Courts*. Federal Judicial Center

Stienstra, D., Johnson, M., Lombard, P. and Pecherski, M. (1997) *Report to the Judicial Conference Committee on Court Administration and Case Management: A Study of Five Demonstration Programs Established Under the Civil Justice Reform Act of 1990*. Washington, DC: Federal Judicial Center

Stipanowich, T. (1996) 'Beyond Arbitration: Innovation and Evolution in the United States Construction Industry' 31 *Wake Forest L. Rev.* 169

— (2004) 'ADR and the "Vanishing Trial": The Growth and Impact of "Alternative Dispute Resolution"' 1(3) *Journal of Empirical Legal Studies* 843
— (2015) 'The International Evolution of Mediation: A Call for Dialogue and Deliberation' 46 *Victoria University of Wellington Law Review* 1191
— (2016) 'Insights on Mediator Practices and Perceptions' *Disp. Resol. Mag.*, Winter 2016, at 4
Streeter-Schaefer, H.A. (2001) 'A Look at Court Mandated Civil Mediation' 49 *Drake Law Review* 367
Strong, S.I. (2016) 'Realizing Rationality: An Empirical Assessment of International Commercial Mediation' *Washington and Lee Law Review* 1973
Stulberg, J.B. (1981) 'Theory and Practice of Mediation: A Reply to Professor Susskind' 6 *Vermont Law Review* 85
— (1998) 'Fairness and Mediation' 13 *Ohio State Journal on Dispute Resolution* 909
Susskind, L. (1981) 'Environmental Mediation and the Accountability Problem' 6 *Vermont Law Review* 1
Taivalkoski, P. and Pynnä, A. (2015) 'The Courts and Bar Association as Drivers for Mediation in Finland' in *New Developments in Civil and Commercial Mediation*. New York: Springer
Thompson, P.N. (2011) 'Codifying Mediation 2.0: Good Faith Mediation in the Federal Courts' 26 *Ohio State Journal on Dispute Resolution* 363
Tjersland, O., Gulbrandsen, W. and Haavind, H. (2015) 'Mandatory Mediation Outside the Court: A Process and Effect Study' 33 *Conflict Resolution Quarterly* 19
Tobias, C. (2000) 'Civil Justice Delay and Empirical Data: A Response to Professor Heise' 51(2) *Case Western Reserve Law Review* 235
Van Ginkel, E. (2004) 'The UNCITRAL Model Law on International Commercial Conciliation' 21(1) *Journal of International Arbitration* 1
Ver Steegh, N. (2002) 'Yes, No, and Maybe: Informed Decision Making About Divorce Mediation in the Presence of Domestic Violence' 9 *William and Mary Journal of Women and the Law* 145
Vidmar, N. (1985) 'An Assessment of Mediation in a Small Claims Court' 41 *Journal of Social Issues* 127
Vindeløv, A.V. (2003) 'Mediation in Danish Law: In Retrospect and Perspective' in N. Alexander (ed.), *Global Trends in Mediation*. Alphen aan den Rijn: Kluwer Law International
Wang, G. and Yang, F. (2013) *Mediation in Asia-Pacific: A Practical Guide to Mediation and its Impacts on Legal Systems*. The Hague: Kluwer
Ward, E. (2007) 'Transatlantic Perspectives on Alternative Dispute Resolution: Mandatory Court-Annexed Alternative Dispute Resolution

in the United States Federal Courts: Panacea or Pandemic?' 81 *St John's Law Review* 77

Waye, V. and Xiong, P. (2011) 'The Relationship between Mediation and Judicial Proceedings in China' 6(1) *Asian Journal of Comparative Law*, article 2

Welsh, N.A. (2001) 'Making Deals in Court-Connected Mediation: What's Justice Got to Do with It?' 79 *Washington University Law Quarterly* 787

— (2010) 'The Thinning Vision of Self-Determination in Court-Connected Mediation: The Inevitable Price of Institutionalization?' 6 *Harvard Negotiation Law Review* 22

Weston, M.A. (2003) 'Confidentiality's Constitutionality: The Incursion on Judicial Powers to Regulate Party Conduct in Court-Connected Mediation' 8 *Harvard Negotiation Law Review* 29

Winston, D.S. (1996) 'Participation Standards in Mandatory Mediation Statutes: You Can Lead a Horse to Water' 11 *Ohio State Journal on Dispute Resolution* 187

Wissler, R.L. (1997) 'The Effects of Mandatory Mediation: Empirical Research on the Experience of Small Claims and Common Pleas Courts' 33 *Willamette Law Review* 565

— (2002) 'Court-Connected Mediation in General Civil Cases: What We Know from Empirical Research' 17 *Ohio State Journal on Dispute Resolution* 641

— (2004) 'The Effectiveness of Court Connected Dispute Resolution in Civil Cases' 22 *Conflict Resolution Quarterly* 55

Xu, X.B. (2003) *Mediation in China and the United States: Toward Common Outcome*, JSD available at Stanford University Libraries

Yasui, A. (2003) *Alternative Dispute Resolution in Japan*, available at www.iadcmeetings.mobi/assets/1/7/18.2_-_Yasui ADR_System_in_Japan.pdf

Zekoll, J., Bälz, M. and Amelung, I. (2014) *Formalisation and Flexibilisation in Dispute Resolution*. The Hague: Martinus Nijhoff

Zhang, Y. (2015) 'Mediation Model Differences Between China and Australia and Their Possible Collaboration' 1(1) *Journal of Interdisciplinary Conflict Science* 46

Zylstra, A. (2001) 'Road from Voluntary Mediation to Mandatory Good Faith Requirements: A Road Best Left Untraveled' 17 *Journal of the American Academy of Matrimonial Lawyers* 69

Index

access to justice
  accessibility 31
    France 110
    Hong Kong 86
    India 216
    Malaysia 137
    The Netherlands 111
    United Kingdom 82, 84
    United States 156
  affordability 31–4
    France 110
    Hong Kong 86
    India 216
    Malaysia 137
    The Netherlands 111
    United Kingdom 82, 84
    United States 156
  human rights considerations 45–6
  impartial justice *see* impartiality
  improvement of 228, 246
  inconsistency with institutionalized court-based settings 44–5
  rise of court-based mediation, scholarly critiques 43–8
Access to Justice (*Interim* and *Final Reports*,1995 and 1996) 66
adjudication 16
administrative cases 119, 196
ADR *see* Alternative Dispute Resolution (ADR)
Afcons Infrastructure Ltd and another v. Cherian Varkey Construction Co. (P) Ltd and others (2010), India 212, 214
African countries 54–5
Ahmedabad Mediation Centre, India 209
AIJA (Australian Institute of Judicial Administration) 38
Alternative Dispute Resolution (ADR) 49, 66
  see also Alternative Disputes Resolution Act 1998, US; Alternative Disputes Resolution Act 2010, Ghana; arbitration; arbitrators; conciliation; court-based mediation; mediation; National Alternative Dispute Resolution Advisory Council, Australia
  Australia 158, 160, 163, 164
  China 189
  France 99, 106
  global context of court mediation reform 25, 27, 31, 32
  global mediation survey 221
  Hong Kong 85, 86
  impartiality and effectiveness 96, 138, 156, 168, 184, 204
  India 206
  Italy 173, 174
  Malaysia 126
  The Netherlands 112, 113
  organizations providing ADR services, monitoring 107
  Platform ADR 113
  United States 45, 143, 144, 145, 146, 155
Alternative Disputes Resolution Act 1998, US 146
Alternative Disputes Resolution Act 2010, Ghana 55
arbitration 55, 106, 132, 171, 189
  see also Arbitration and Conciliation Act 1996, India; Institute of Arbitration and Mediation (IIAM), India; Kuala Lumpur Regional Centre for Arbitration
  Australia 164, 167
  awards 214
  India 206, 209, 214, 215

Arbitration and Conciliation Act 1996, India 208, 209
Assisted Dispute Resolution programme, Australia 160
Australia 158–69
  Alternative Dispute Resolution (ADR) 158, 160, 163, 164
  arbitration 164, 167
  Assisted Dispute Resolution programme 160
  Civil Dispute Resolution Act 2011 (CDRA) 159, 162–5, 167
  civil justice ranking 167–9
  civil justice system 158, 168, 169
  court-annexed mediation 28
  Courts (Mediation and Arbitration) Act 1991 160
  District Court Act 1967 (Queensland) 30
  Federal Circuit Court (Magistrates Court) 158, 162
  Federal Court 158, 162
  Federal Court of Australia Act 1976 158, 160, 164, 167
  Federal Court Rules 2011 162
  High Court 158
  Institute of Judicial Administration (AIJA) 38
  Law and Justice Legislation Amendment Act 1997 160
  law/policy background 159–62
  Legal Aid Commissions 161, 162
  legal aid policy 160–62
  mandatory mediation in 28, 37–8, 52, 159–60
  National Alternative Dispute Resolution Advisory Council (NADRAC) 38, 159
  New South Wales 28, 29, 30, 37–8, 47
  practical implementation of ADR policies 164–6
  programme features 162–4
  Requirement to Attend Mediation Orientation Session 30
  research results, analysis 167–9
  South Australia 30
  tribunals 162
  Victoria 28, 30, 159, 162

Australian Competition and Consumer Commission v. *Collagen Aesthetics Australia Pty Ltd* (2002) 165, 166

backlogs of cases *see* case backlogs
Bangalore Mediation Centre 216
Bosnia and Herzegovina 33, 232
Bradford v. *James* (2008) 73
Brazil 27
Burchell v. *Bullard* (2005) 72

California 147, 148, 153, 155
Camp David mediation 42
CAMS *see* Court of Appeal Mediation Scheme (CAMS), UK
Canada
  mandatory mediation 30, 37
  Public Service Staff Relations Board 40
  Quebec 226
  Saskatchewan province 56, 226
Carter, President Jimmy 42
case backlogs 257
  global context of court mediation reform 26, 29, 36
  India 35, 206, 210, 211
  Italy 170, 171–2, 174, 185
  Malaysia 126–7
  programme design 55, 58
caseload reduction rationale, court mediation reform 3, 18, 67, 228, 250, 257
  global context of court mediation reform 26, 27, 29, 34–5, 37, 38, 43, 48
CDRA *see* Civil Dispute Resolution Act 2011 (CDRA), Australia
CEDR Solve (mediation provider), UK 69, 70
Central London County Court (CLCC)
  Automatic Referral to Mediation pilot scheme 30
  county court trial centre 32
  voluntary mediation scheme (VOL) 66, 67–8, 79–80
Centre for Effective Dispute Resolution (CEDR), UK 81
CFI (Court of First Instance), Hong Kong 85, 95, 96

Champion Concord Ltd v. *Lau Koon Foo (No. 2)* FACV16/2010; (2011), Hong Kong 92
Chennai Mediation Centre, India 210
Chew Hon Keong v. *Betterproducts Industries Sdn Bhd* (2013), Malaysia 134, 135
China 186–205
  civil justice ranking 203–5
  civil justice system 187, 188, 204
  civil mediation paper (consent judgment) 198–9
  Civil Procedure Law, PRC 186, 190, 194, 198, 202
  Confucianism 189
  contracts 199, 200–201, 202
  costs issues 202–3
  early studies of mediation in 185–6
  fees 202
  ground rules 194–8
  initiating legislation 191–2
  initiating of mediation 194
  judicial mediation 188–9, 191–4
    advantages, Chinese context 191–2
    costs incurred 202–3
    scope of application for 194
    in various phases of civil litigation process 192–4
  legality principle 195–6
  litigation era (1990s) 190–91
  mediation process 196–8
  People's Mediation Committee 196
  policy background 189–92
  post-litigation era (post-2000s) 191
  post-mediation implications 198
  practical implementation 200–201
  pre-litigation era (1950s to the 1980s) 190
  principles of Chinese mediation 195–6
  programme features 192–9
  rationale for mediation 191–2
  research results, analysis 201–5
  revolutionary era 189–90
  scheduling of mediation sessions 192–4
  scope of application for judicial mediation 194

  statistics, mediation-related 201–2
  in-trial mediation 193–4
Chint Group Corporation v. *Schneider Electric Low Voltage (Tianjin) Co. Ltd* (2007), China 200
'*chotei*,' Japan 54
Civil Dispute Resolution Act 2011 (CDRA), Australia 159, 162–5, 167
  enforceability 163–4
  practical implementation 164–5
  procedure 162–3
civil justice
  see also justice
civil justice rankings
  Australia 167–9
  China 203–5
  Hong Kong 96–7
  India 27
  Italy 183–5
  Malaysia 137–8
  The Netherlands 122–3
  United Kingdom 82–4
  United States 155–7
civil justice reform
  see also reform of court mediation
  Hong Kong Civil Justice Reform (CJR) 85, 86, 88, 91, 93
  Italy 170
  United States 145
civil justice systems 9, 12, 26, 31–2, 37, 252
  Australia 158, 168, 169
  China 187, 188, 204
  France 109
  Hong Kong 96
  India 216
  Italy 170, 171, 174, 181, 184, 185
  Malaysia 125, 128, 137, 138
  The Netherlands 110, 122, 123, 124
  United Kingdom 67, 82, 83
  United States 155, 156
civil law
  see also commercial disputes
  contracts *see* contracts
  employment 27, 42, 47, 65
  family cases *see* family law
  property 182, 214, 215
Civil Mediation Online Directory, UK 67

civil mediation paper (consent judgment) 198–9
Civil Procedure Act, India 206
Civil Procedure Code (CPC), The Netherlands 112
Civil Procedure Rules (CPR), Hong Kong 29
Civil Procedure Rules (CPR), UK 44, 68, 70, 74–6, 78
CLCC *see* Central London County Court (CLCC)
Code of Civil Procedure, France 101, 103, 105, 107
Code of Civil Procedure, India 35, 208–9, 212
coercion to mediate 13, 30, 195, 253
see also mandatory mediation
global context of court mediation reform 44, 46
non-coercive mediation 230, 255
Colombia 36
commercial disputes
France 100, 101
India 214, 215
Italy 172, 173, 175, 176
Malaysia 131
community-based mediation 41–2
conciliation 79, 101, 250
India 206, 209, 214, 215
Italy 170, 171, 175
mandatory 36
versus mediation 206
Model Law on International Commercial Conciliation, UNCITRAL 60, 61
programme design 54, 60, 61
traditional 10
confidence in mediation 252–3
Australia 168–9
China 203, 204
France 109
global mediation survey 229–30
Hong Kong 86, 96–7
India 207, 216
Malaysia 137–8
mandatory mediation 221, 253–4
measures 9
The Netherlands 111, 122
United Kingdom 82, 83–4
United States 144, 155

confidentiality in proceedings
France 99, 102
India 215
Italy 152, 179
Malaysia 129
The Netherlands 112, 115, 116
programme design 55, 61
conflicts of interest 15, 19, 239–40, 257
avoiding 91, 116
Confucianism, China 189
consent for meditation
agreement 197
all parties 125, 148, 206, 214
both parties 69, 127, 214
decrees 153
delay in 73
France 102
global context of court mediation reform 39
judgments 134, 197, 198–9
judicial mediation 99
lack of 6, 30, 179, 193, 213, 214, 215
Malaysia 127
mutual 151, 213, 215
orders 76, 133, 134, 135
programme design 50, 51, 57
United Kingdom 69, 71
United States 146, 151, 152
written 91
contracts 27
China 199, 200–201, 202
Hong Kong 92, 94
India 213, 215
Italy 173, 178, 182
United Kingdom 69, 76
United States 152
costs issues
see also fees
awards 71, 72, 74, 163, 165
China 202–3
France 103
global mediation survey 226–7
Hong Kong 94–5
Italy 180
judicial mediation 202–3
The Netherlands 118, 121–2
reduction of cost rationale for court-based mediation 18, 26, 31–4, 48, 192, 228, 232, 250, 257
United Kingdom 77

United States 151
unreasonable failure to engage in mediation 94–5
voluntary mediation 232–4
Court of Appeal Mediation Scheme (CAMS), UK 67
    see also United Kingdom
    pre-settlement 69–70
    post-settlement 70
    statistics 80
Court of First Instance (CFI), Hong Kong 85, 95, 96
Court of Justice of the European Union (CJEU) 45, 58
court procedures, complexities 27
court-annexed mediation
    Australia 28
    data collection 7
    India 35–6, 210
    Malaysia 126, 129, 130–32, 134, 137
    The Netherlands 36
court-based mediation
    see also mediation; reform of court mediation
    confidence in programmes see confidence in mediation 229–30
    costs 226–7
    in-court mediation 113, 188
    court-annexed mediation see court-annexed mediation
    court-ordered mediation 181
    efficacy issues 25
    extrinsic factors 2, 26, 39–43, 249–50
    improvement strategies 242–7
    intrinsic policy justifications 2, 26–43, 249–50
    judge-led 129–30, 133, 136
    pre-trial 128, 147, 164, 193
    process considerations 40–41
    public policy 46–7
    rationales for see rationales for court-based mediation
    reform aims, global context 25–48
    regional implementation of 29
    scholarly critiques of rise in access to justice 45–6
        inconsistency with institutionalized court-based settings 44–5

public policy 46–7
response to 48
unsuitability for particular case types 47
scholarly critiques of rise of 43–8
strengths and challenges 235–42
time reduction 38
in-trial 53, 193–4
court-ordered mediation, Italy 181
Courts (Mediation and Arbitration) Act 1991, Australia 160
Courts and Legal Services Act 1990, UK 31
CPC Amendment Act, India 208
criminal law
    Australia 164
    China 190
    France 99, 100, 105, 107
    global context of court mediation reform 28, 36
    India 213
    Malaysia 127
    programme design 56
    United Kingdom 67
cross-border law 58, 61
CY Foundation Group Ltd v. *Leonora Yung and others* (2011), Hong Kong 93

data collection
    methodology 7–10
    survey data collection method 224–6
Dato' Dr Joseph Eravelly v. *Dato Hilmi Mohd Nor* (2011), Malaysia 135
delay reduction, as rationale for court-mediation reform
    Australia 167, 169
    China 204, 205
    France 109, 110
    global context of court mediation reform 19, 26, 30, 34–9
    Hong Kong 86, 96, 98
    Italy 184
    Malaysia 125, 137, 139
    The Netherlands 111, 123, 124
    United Kingdom 65, 82, 84
    United States 144, 155, 157
Delhi High Court Mediation and Conciliation Centre 210

Denmark 53–4
discrimination reduction rationale 19, 86, 110, 111, 124, 169
  Malaysia 125, 139
  United States 144, 157
dispute settlement
  cultural and societal approaches to 53
  dispute types 55–6
District Courts (DCs), Hong Kong 85, 95
divorce law 106, 121, 197
domestic violence cases 236
Dunnett v. Railtrack plc (2002), UK 69, 71–2, 80

economic development 27
effectiveness of ADR 96, 138, 156, 168, 184, 204
efficiency factors 252–3
  Australia 167, 168
  China 203, 204
  economic development and judicial efficiency 27
  France 109–10
  Hong Kong 86, 96
  India 207, 216
  Italy 184
  Malaysia 137
  measures 9
  The Netherlands 111, 122, 123
  programme design 232
  rationales for mediation 51
  and rise of court-based mediation 26–30
  Singapore as role model 27–8
  United Kingdom 82
  United States 144, 155
  voluntary mediation 253, 256
employment 27, 42, 47, 65
  labour disputes 56, 175
enforcement of mediated agreements
  Australia 163–4
  Civil Dispute Resolution Act 2011 (CDRA), Australia 163–4
  cross-border 61
  France 105
  Hong Kong 92
  India 213–14
  Malaysia 134

  mediation award 213–14
  settlement agreements 75–6
  United Kingdom 75–6
  United States 152–3
EU Mediation Directive 2008/52/EC 45
  and France 99, 100, 101, 102, 106
  and Italy 170, 172–3, 185
  and The Netherlands 112
  voluntary and mandatory mediation 57–8
European Convention on Human Rights (ECHR) 45, 59
European Council 99
European Court of Human Rights (ECtHR) 58
European Parliament 172
expenses *see* costs issues; fees
Expert Group Customized Conflict Resolution program, The Netherlands 114
extrinsic factors, court-based mediation 2, 26, 39–43, 249–50
  process considerations 40–41
  relational justifications 39–40
  societal considerations 41–3

family law
  divorce 106, 121, 197
  domestic violence cases 236
  matrimonial law 131
Federal Circuit Court, Australia 158, 162
Federal Court of Australia 158, 162
Federal Court of Australia Act 1976 158, 160, 164, 167
fees
  calculating 202
  cancellation 70
  case acceptance 202
  China 202
  contingent 91
  court 34, 211
  expert witness 180
  fixed 69
  free or discounted 53
  global mediation survey 226–7, 233, 240
  Hong Kong 91

hourly 240
India 211
Italy 177, 180
Malaysia 132
mandatory mediation 257
The Netherlands 118
paid for by parties 257
subsidized 118
United Kingdom 31, 68, 69, 70, 71, 81, 82
venue 82
waiver 180
Finland 42
Fiss, Owen 15, 46
Florida 148, 151, 154, 227
France 99–110
  civil justice system 109
  Club of Mediators for Public Service 108
  Code de procédure civile (Code of Civil Procedure) 101, 103, 105, 107
  commercial disputes 100, 101
  court powers to monitor organizations providing ADR services 107
  Decree 2012/-66 of 20 January 2012 100–101
  effect of mediation on limitation period 106
  and EU Mediation Directive 99, 100, 101, 102, 106
  ground rules, ADR programmes 104–5
  Inter-enterprises Mediator 108
  International Arbitration Chamber of Paris 104
  Law No. 95-125 of 8 February 1995 100, 103, 104, 105
  law/policy background 100–101
  Mediation Ordinance No. 2011/1540 99–100, 102
  Mediator of Economic and Financial Ministries 108
  Ministry of Justice and Freedoms 100, 102
  National Federation of Mediation Centres 104
  Paris Mediation and Arbitration Centre 104
  practical implementation of ADR policies 105–7
  procedures and scheduling of mediation 103–4
  programme features 102–5
  purpose/rationale behind mediation programme 101–2
  referral for mediation 105–6
  research results, analysis 108
  settlement agreements, enforceability 105, 107
  voluntary mediation 99, 102, 110
free will 51, 195
Fuller, Lon 1, 15, 16

Garby, Thierry 101
Garg, Shashank 210
Garritt-Critchley v. Ronnan (2014), UK 77
general public polling (GPP) 8
Genn, H. 79
Ghana 54–5
Global Competitiveness Report 2016–2017
  Australia 169
  France 109–10
  Hong Kong 96
  India 216
  Italy 184
  Malaysia 137
  The Netherlands 123
  United Kingdom 83
  United States 155
global mediation survey 221–48
  confidence in court mediation programmes 229–30
  court mediation costs 226–7
  efficiency 232–5
  fairness 230–32
  fees 226–7, 233, 240
  findings 229–35, 242–7
  improvement strategies, mediation programmes 242–7
  limitations 222
  rationale for introducing at mediation programmes 227–9
  strengths and challenges of court mediation programmes 223, 235–42
  summary of findings 222–4

survey data collection method 224–6
Global Pound Conference (GPC) 223–4
Golden Eagle International (Group) Ltd v. *GR Investment Holdings Ltd* (2010), Hong Kong 94, 95
'good faith' requirements 51
Grillo, T. 47
Group of Friends of Mediation, United Nations 42
Gujarat Law Society, India 210

Hak Tung Alfred Tang v. *Bloomberg LP and Another* (2010), Hong Kong 94
Halsey v. *Milton Keynes General NHS Trust* (2004), UK 45, 72, 77, 94–5
hearings 27, 70
Her Majesty's Courts Service (HMCS) Small Claims Mediation Scheme, UK 67, 68, 70, 80
HMCS (Small Claims Mediation Scheme), UK 67, 68, 70, 80
Hong Kong 85–98
  Alternative Dispute Resolution (ADR) 85, 86
  civil justice ranking 96–7
  Civil Justice Reform (CJR) 85, 86, 88, 91, 93
  civil justice system 96
  Civil Procedure Rules 29
  Construction and Arbitration List 87
  contracts 92, 94
  Court of First Instance 85, 95, 96
  court power to resolve points of difference in mediation proposals 93–4
  court-based mediation 29
  District Courts (DCs) 85, 95
  duration of case 95–6
  Governmental 2007–2008 Policy Address 87
  initiating legislation 88–9
  Joint Mediation Helpline Office 86
  Lands Tribunal 87
  law/policy background 86–9
  Mediation Certificate, filing 89–90
  Mediation Code 90, 91–2
  Mediation Co-ordinators' Offices 85
  Mediation Council 42
  Mediation Minute 90
  Mediation Notice 90
  Mediation Ordinance (MO) 91–2
  Mediation Response 90
  New Insurance Mediation Pilot Scheme (NIMPS) 88
  pilot programmes 42, 86, 87–8
  practical implementation of ADR policies 93–4
  Practice Direction 3.3 88
  Practice Direction 6.1 87
  Practice Direction 31 29, 85, 88, 89, 92, 93
  programme features 89–95
  Proposal 64 29
  Proposal 68 86–7
  referral for mediation 86
  research results, analysis 95–7
  Rules of the High Court (Amendment) Rules 2008 88–9, 95
  settlement agreements 92
  voluntary mediation 29
  webpage, mediation-dedicated 86
  Working Party on Mediation 29, 86, 87, 91
human rights considerations 26
  critique of court-based mediation 45–6
  mandatory or voluntary mediation 58, 59

Illinois 146–7, 148
impartiality 26, 179
  of ADR 96, 138, 156, 168, 184, 204
  of mediators 116, 130, 179
implementation of ADR policies
  Australia 164–6
  China 200–201
  France 105–7
  Hong Kong 93–4
  India 214–15
  Malaysia 135
  The Netherlands 118
  United Kingdom 76–8
  United States 153–4
improvement strategies, court mediation programmes

Index

access to justice 246
  enhanced mediator training 242–3
  financial and organizational resources 244–5
  flexible settlement arrangements 246
  ongoing evaluation 246–7, 256–7
  public education 244
  rewards and incentives 245–6
in-court mediation 113, 188
indemnity basis, costs paid on 77
independence, duty of 130
India 206–18
  Ahmedabad Mediation Centre 209
  arbitration 206, 209, 214, 215
  Arbitration and Conciliation Act 1996 208, 209
  Bangalore Mediation Centre 216
  British style courts in 207
  case backlogs 35, 206, 210, 211
  Chennai Mediation Centre 210
  civil justice ranking 27, 216–17
  civil justice system 216
  Civil Procedure Act 206
  Code of Civil Procedure (CPC) 35, 208–9, 212
  commercial disputes 214, 215
  conciliation 206, 209, 214, 215
  contracts 213, 215
  contributions of mediation in 211
  court-annexed mediation 35–6, 210
  CPC Amendment Act 208
  Delhi High Court Mediation and Conciliation Centre 210
  enforcement 213–14
  evolution of mediation in 209–11
  fees 211
  Gujarat Law Society 210
  historical background 207–8
  Industrial Disputes Act 1947 208
  initiating legislation 208–9
  Institute for Arbitration Mediation Legal Education and Development (AMLEAD) 210
  Institute for the Study and Development of Legal Systems (ISDLS) 209
  Institute of Arbitration and Mediation (IIAM) 42
  Legal Services Authority Act 1987 35, 208
  Lok Adalats (specialized courts) 35, 206, 207, 208, 209, 213
  Madras High Court 210
  mandatory mediation 206, 216, 217
  Mediation and Conciliation Project Committee (MCPC) 210
  mediation process 211–12
  Pancha 207
  Panchayat system 207
  policy background 207–11
  practical implementation of ADR policies 214–15
  programme features 211–14
  rationale for mediation 210–11
  referral for mediation 212–13
  research results, analysis 215–17
  US Educational Foundation in India (USEFI) 210
Indiana 147, 148, 150
Industrial Disputes Act, India 208
industrial mediation 196
Institute for Arbitration Mediation Legal Education and Development (AMLEAD), India 210
Institute for the Study and Development of Legal Systems (ISDLS), India 209
Institute of Arbitration and Mediation (IIAM), India 42
institutional mediation
  inconsistency with institutionalized court-based settings 44–5
  Malaysia 133–4
Inter-American Commission on Human Rights (IACHR) 59
Inter-American Court of Human Rights 58
International Arbitration Chamber of Paris 104
International Chamber of Commerce 104
in-trial mediation 53, 193–4
intrinsic policy justifications 2, 26–43, 249–50
Israel 56
Italy 170–85
  acceptance rates 181–2
  case backlogs 170, 171, 174, 185
  civil justice ranking 183–5

civil justice system 170, 171, 174, 181, 184, 185
commercial disputes 172, 173, 175, 176
conciliation 170, 171, 175
Constitutional Court 174–5, 182
contracts 173, 178, 182
court-ordered mediation 181
Decree 28/2010 170
  entry into force 174
  impartiality of mediators 179
  initial mandatory mediation scheme under 173–5
  mediation settlement 177–9
Decree 180/2010 173, 175
Decree 145/2011 173
Decree 69/2013 170
  court-ordered mediation 181
  initial mediation session 181
  new scope of mandatory mediation under 176
  revival of mandatory mediation scheme under 175
and EU Mediation Directive 170, 172–3, 185
fees 177, 180
impartiality of mediators 178, 179
initial mediation session 181
Law 580/1993 171
Law 249/1997 175
Law 80/1998 175
Law 69/2009 172–3
Law 98/2013 175, 177
mandatory mediation 52, 170, 173–5, 176, 178–9
mediation procedure 176–8
mediation settlement 178–9
practical implementation of ADR policies 180–81
programme features 176–80
'pro-litigation' legal environment and court overload 171–2
research results, analysis 181–5
settlement rates 182–3
time and costs of mediation 180
trial length 27

Japan 54
Jeray v. *Blue Mountains City Council* (2013) 166

Johor Bharu, Malaysia 126
judge-led mediation
  see also judicial mediation
  China 188–9, 192–4
  versus court-annexed mediation 189
  Malaysia 127, 129–30, 133, 136
  scope of application for 194
  versus settlement, 188–9
Judicial Improvements Act, US 144
judicial mediation
  see also court-based mediation; judge-led mediation
  advantages, Chinese context 191–2
  China 188–9, 191–4
  France 106
  and litigation 189, 192–4
  versus settlement 188–9
  signed agreement reached during 188–9
  versus court-annexed mediation 189
justice
  access to *see* access to justice
  civil *see* civil justice
  impartial 26
  perceptions of *see* perceptions of justice
  procedural 47
justifications for court-based mediation *see* rationales for court-based mediation

Kenya 55
Kilthistle No. 6 Pty Ltd and others (Receiver and Manager Appointed) v. *Austwide Homes Pty Ltd and others* (1997), Australia 163, 165
King Par LLC v. *Brosnan Golf Pty Ltd* (2013), Australia 159, 165
Kuala Lumpur, Malaysia 126, 136
Kuala Lumpur Court Mediation Centre 129
Kuala Lumpur Regional Centre for Arbitration 127, 128
  institutional mediation under 130
  KLRCA Rules of Mediation 130
Kuantan, Malaysia 126, 136

Landelijk bureau Mediation naast rechtspraak (Dutch Court-Connected Mediation Agency) 113, 114
'landing and building leases mediation,' Japan 54
Law and Justice Legislation Amendment Act 1997, Australia 160
Law Society of New South Wales 29
LBM *see* Landelijk bureau Mediation naast rechtspraak (Dutch Court-Connected Mediation Agency)
Legal Aid Commissions, Australia 161, 162
legal aid policy
　Australia 160–62
　Italy 180
　Malaysia 132
　United Kingdom 31, 67
legal culture 111, 123, 180
　local 25
Legal Services Authority Act 1987, India 35, 208
limitation periods, France 106
litigation
　Italy, 'pro-litigation' legal environment and court overload 171–2
　judicial mediation 189, 192–4
　litigation era, China (1990s) 190–91
　versus mediation 126, 229, 236
　post-litigation era, China (post-2000s) 191
　pre-litigation era, China (1950s to the 1980s) 190
　satellite 233, 257
Liu Ailong, Tang Shengming and others v. Fine Riding (Qinhuangdao) Tourism Development Co. Ltd (2010), China 200–201
Lok Adalats (specialized courts), India 35, 206, 207, 208, 209, 213
longitudinal analysis 8, 10, 252
Luban, D. 46–7

Ma Xiwu, Trial Mode 189, 190
Macedonia 232
Malaysia 125–39

ADR terminologies and definitions 127
case backlogs 126–7
civil justice ranking 137–8
civil justice system 125, 128, 137, 138
commercial disputes 131
court-annexed mediation 126, 129, 130–32, 134, 137
diversity in 125
enforceability of agreements 134
fees 132
ground rules 132–4
historical background 125–6
institutional mediation 133–4
judge-led mediation 129–30, 133, 136
Kuala Lumpur Court Mediation Centre 129
Kuala Lumpur Regional Centre for Arbitration 127, 128
KLRCA Rules of Mediation 130
Legal Aid Department 132
Mediation Act 2012 128–9
Mediation Centre 127, 130–31
Mediation Committee of the Bar Council 126
mediation process 132–4
policy background 125–7
practical implementation of ADR policies 135
Practice Direction No. 4 on mediation 126, 128
Practice Direction No. 5 on mediation 126, 128
programme features 127–32
rationale for mediation 126–7
research results, analysis 135–8
Rules of the High Court 1980 128
scheduling of mediation sessions 127–9
Subordinate Courts Rule 1980 128
voluntary mediation 125, 133, 138
Malmesbury (James Carleton, Seventh Earl of Malmesbury) and others v. Strutt & Parker (a Partnership) (2008) 72
mandatory mediation
　see also voluntary mediation
　access to justice 46

appropriate, where 236
Australia 28, 37–8, 52, 159–60
Canada 30, 37
characterization of jurisdictions practising 6
conceptual divide between voluntary and mandatory mediation 50–57
confidence in 221, 253–4
cost considerations 33–4
direct court supervision 51
efficiency factors 232
improvement strategies 223
India 206, 216, 217
Italy 52, 170, 173–5, 176, 178–9
versus judicial determination 47
jurisdictional selection 52, 53
key achievements 223, 235–6, 252
key challenges 153, 223, 238–40
power imbalances, managing 240
programme design 49–61
regional and international approaches to 57–61
resource limitations 240
settlement rates 236
United States 143–4, 148–9, 154, 155
voluntary versus mandatory mediation 232–3
Massachusetts 154
matrimonial law 131
mediation
see also costs issues; court-based mediation; efficacy of global court mediation reform, assessing; fees; judge-led mediation; judicial mediation; mandatory mediation; mediation processes; mediators; perceptions of justice; referral for mediation; *respective countries*; voluntary mediation
adaptability across jurisdictions 49, 50
administrative 119, 196
coercion 13, 30, 44, 46, 195, 253
conceptual divide between voluntary and mandatory mediation 50–57
versus conciliation 206

conclusion of 117–18
consent for see consent for mediation
cross-border law 45
defining 60, 102–3
degree of movement along voluntary/mandatory spectrum 5
EU Mediation Directive see EU Mediation Directive 2008/52/EC
industrial 196
institutional 133–4
judicial see judicial mediation
jurisdictional selection of mandatory or voluntary systems 52–7
lawyers, engagement with trial programmes 52–3
versus litigation 126, 229, 236
online 57
opt-in/opt-out rules 5–6, 256
practical implementation see mediation, practical implementation
public acceptance 181–2
regional and international approaches to 57–61
rejection of 71–2, 76, 77, 94–5
reports 151
satisfaction with 17
success of 232–3
telephone-based 70
theory 15–18, 221–2
timing of see time frames/timing of mediation
unreasonable failure to engage in/ unreasonable refusal 71–2, 77, 94–5
voluntary nature of 72–3
voluntary versus mandatory 232–3
Mediation and Conciliation Project Committee (MCPC), India 210
Mediation Code, Hong Kong 90
ground rules 91–2
Mediation Council, Hong Kong 42
Mediation Ordinance (MO), Hong Kong 91–2
Mediation Ordinance No. 2011/1540, France 99–100
mediation, practical implementation

Index

Australia 164–6
China 200–201
France 105–7
Hong Kong 93–5
India 214–15
Italy 180–81
Malaysia 135
The Netherlands 118
United Kingdom 65, 76–8
United States 153–4
mediation processes
   China 196–8
   India 211–12
   Italy 176–8
   Malaysia 131, 132–4
   The Netherlands 115–16, 120–21
   normative and public policy expectations 51
   processing time 120–21
   rationales for court-based mediation 39, 40–41
   United Kingdom 74–5
   United States 147–50
mediation rationales *see* rationales for court-based mediation
mediators
   Club of Mediators for Public Service, France 108
   conduct 104–5
   duties 104–5
      confidentiality 91
      impartiality 116, 130, 178, 179
      independence 130
   European Code of Conduct for Mediators 104
   ground rules, explaining 150–51
   Mediator of Economic and Financial Ministries, France 108
   multi-functional role 132
   qualifications 174
   quality of 240, 241–2
   reporting obligations 51–2
   training of 210, 242–3
Mediators Without Borders group 43
mediatory adjudication 195
methodology, research
   see also Global Competitiveness Report 2016–2017; Rule of Law Index 2016

correlation 11, 12, 20, 222–3, 252, 258
data collection 7–10
Global Competitiveness Report (GCR) 8, 9
improvement of overall court mediation process by program type 223–4
judicial and governance indicators 8, 9, 10
longitudinal analysis 5, 8, 252
Rule of Law Index (ROI) 8, 9
strengths and challenges 10–11, 252
survey data collection method 224–6
t-test 11
Michigan 147, 148, 151
Ministry of Justice and Freedoms, France 100, 102
Missouri 149
MMC (Malaysian Mediation Centre) 127, 130–31
   Mediation Rules 131
Model Law on International Commercial Conciliation, UNCITRAL 60, 61, 251
Moti Ram v. *Ashok Kumar* (2011), India 215
multi-door courthouse 2, 233, 257
Murray v. *Bernard* (2015), UK 78

NADRAC (National Alternative Dispute Resolution Advisory Council), Australia 38, 159
National Alternative Dispute Resolution Advisory Council, Australia 38
National Alternative Dispute Resolution Advisory Council (NADRAC), Australia 38, 159
National Federation of Mediation Centres, France 104
National Mediation Helpline, UK 66–7, 71, 81
Netherlands, The 111–24
   administrative cases 119
   civil justice ranking 122–3
   civil justice system 110, 122, 123, 124
   Civil Procedure Code (CPC) 112

community support for
    mediation 118
conclusion of mediation 117–18
costs issues 118, 121–2
Council of the Judiciary 121–2
court-annexed mediation 36
Court-Connected Mediation Agency
    (LBM) 113, 114
development of Dutch mediation
    programme 112–14
and EU Mediation Directive 112
Expert Group Customized Conflict
    Resolution program 114
fees 118
law/policy background 111–14
legal representation 117
Mediation Institution (NMI) 113,
    120
mediation process 115–16
Ministry of Justice 112, 113
pilot programmes 113
Platform ADR 113
practical implementation of ADR
    policies 118
processing time 120–21
pro-conciliation legal culture and
    lack of regulation 111–12
programme features 114–18
referral for mediation 111, 114–15,
    119
Research and Documentation
    Centre, Ministry of Justice 113
research results, analysis 119–23
resolution time frame 121
settlement 117–18
    settlement rates 119–20
voluntary mediation 112, 122,
    123–4
New Insurance Mediation Pilot
    Scheme (NIMPS), Hong Kong 88
New South Wales, Australia 28, 29, 30,
    37–8, 47
New York 146, 147, 148, 152
Nigel Witham Ltd v. *Robert Lesley
    Smith and Jacqueline Isaacs*
    (2008) 73
NIMPS (New Insurance Mediation
    Pilot Scheme), Hong Kong 88
non-coercive mediation 230, 255
North America 32

North Carolina 34, 147, 148, 149, 150,
    152
*Northrop Grumman Mission Systems
    Europe Ltd* v. *BAE Systems (Al
    Diriyah C4I) Ltd* (2014), UK 78
nudge theory 12, 253

OECD (Organisation for
    Economic Co-operation and
    Development) 27
ongoing evaluation 246–7, 256–7
online mediation 57
oral referral for mediation 114
orders, court-ordered mediation 181

Pancha, India 207
Panchayat system, India 207
Paris Mediation and Arbitration
    Centre 104
party entrenchment 241
People's Republic of China (PRC) 186
    see also China
    Civil Procedure Law 186, 190, 194,
        198, 202
    Mediation Law 188
    Provisional Organic Regulations 190
perceptions of justice 252–3
    Australia 169
    China 205
    France 109, 110
    Hong Kong 89, 96, 97, 98
    India 207, 216
    Italy 185
    measures 9, 10
    The Netherlands 111, 122, 123
    United Kingdom 82
    United States 144, 155, 157
PGFII SA v. *OMFS Company I Ltd*
    (2013), UK 76, 77
Philippines 227
pilot programmes 258
    Canada 37
    Hong Kong 42, 86, 87–8
    The Netherlands 113
    United Kingdom 30, 66, 67, 68
post-litigation era, China (post-
    2000s) 191
post-traumatic stress disorder
    (PTSD) 236
post-trial mediation 193

Index

power imbalances, managing 15, 20, 21, 47, 223, 240, 257, 258
PRC *see* People's Republic of China (PRC)
pre-litigation era, China (1950s to the 1980s) 190
pre-trial mediation 128, 147, 164, 193
process considerations, court-based mediation 40–41
process pluralism 17
programme design 49–61
  see also mandatory mediation; voluntary mediation
  case backlogs 55, 58
  conciliation 54, 60, 61
  confidentiality in proceedings 55, 61
  consent for mediation 50, 51, 57
  context dependant 258
  criminal law 56
  efficiency factors 232
  mixed methods of mandatory and voluntary mediation 6
property law 182, 214, 215
public education 242, 244
public policy
  critique of court-based mediation 46–7
  mediation settlement 179
  voluntary and mandatory mediation, conceptual divide 51, 52
Public Service Staff Relations Board, Canada 40

qualified respondent questionnaires (QRQs) 8
Quebec, Canada 226

rationales for court-based mediation
  see also court-based mediation; efficiency factors; impartiality; mediation
  caseload reduction *see* caseload reduction rationale, court mediation reform
  cost reduction *see* costs issues
  court access *see* access to justice
  delay reduction *see* delay reduction, as rationale for court-mediation reform
  effectiveness and efficiency 26–30

  extrinsic 2, 26, 39–43, 249–50
  harmony 41, 87, 125, 189, 191
  impartiality 26
  India 210–11
  intrinsic 2, 26–43, 249–50
  Malaysia 126–7
  outcome fairness 230–32, 254–5
  process considerations 40–41
  quality of outcomes/decisions 228, 229, 254
  relational justifications 39–40
  self-determination 17, 44
  societal considerations 41–3
  United Kingdom 67–8
  voice in outcome, giving to parties 228
  workplace relations, improving 40
RDC (Rules of the District Court (Amendment) Rules 2008, Hong Kong 88–9, 95
referral for mediation
  automatic 6
  categorical 30, 158
  discretionary 6, 30, 158
  France 105–6
  Hong Kong 86
  India 212–13
  The Netherlands 111, 114–15, 119
  oral 114
  self-referral 114–15, 235
  written 114, 119
reform of court mediation
  aims, global context 25–48
  assessing efficacy of global court mediation reform 1–22
  civil case administration 2
  data collection methods 7–10
  empirical studies 25
  findings, summary of 11–15
  global mediation survey 232–5
  limitations 10–11
  programme quality 257–8
  spill-over benefits 257
  theoretical background 15–18
relational justifications, court-based mediation 39–40
res judicata 107
Research and Documentation Centre of the Dutch Ministry of Justice 113

research results, analysis
    see also methodology, research;
        statistics, research
    Australia 167–9
    China 201–5
    France 108
    Hong Kong 95–7
    India 215–17
    Italy 181–5
    Malaysia 135–8
    The Netherlands 119–23
    United Kingdom 79–81
    United States 154–7
Resource Development Ltd v.
    Swanbridge Ltd (2009), Hong
    Kong 93–4
resources
    financial and organizational 244–5
    limitations 240, 241
revolutionary era, China 189–90
rewards and incentives 245–6
rule of law
    Hong Kong 86, 98
    India 217
    United Kingdom 82, 84
Rule of Law Index 2016
    Australia 168
    China 204
    India 217
    Italy 184
    The Netherlands 123
    United Kingdom 84
    United States 156–7
Rules of the High Court (Amendment)
    Rules 2008, Hong Kong 88–9,
    95

Sabah Forest Industries Sdn Bhd
    v. *Mazlan bin Ali* (2012),
    Malaysia 135
Salem Advocate Bar Association (II),
    Tamil Nadu v. *Union of India*
    (2005), India 214
Sander, F.E.A. 6
Saskatchewan province, Canada 56,
    226
satellite litigation 233, 257
scheduling of mediation sessions
    China 192–4
    France 103–4

Malaysia 127–9
United States 146–7
self-determination 17, 44
self-referral for mediation 114–15,
    235
Serbia 232
settlement
    case settlement 5
    enforceability of agreements
        see settlement agreements,
        enforceability
    flexible arrangements 246
    versus judicial mediation 188–9
    The Netherlands 117–18
    out of court 47
    partial agreement 117–18
    rates of *see* settlement rates
    wakai (judicial settlement), Japan
    54
settlement agreements, enforceability
    France 105, 107
    Hong Kong 92
    Malaysia 134
    United Kingdom 75–6
settlement rates
    see also settlement agreements,
        enforceability
    India 206–7
    Italy 182–3
    mandatory mediation 236
    The Netherlands 119–20
    relational and commercial
        disputes 55–6
    United States 154, 155
silence 76, 77, 212
Singapore, as role model 27–8
Small Claims Mediation Scheme
    (HMCS), UK 67, 68, 70, 80
soft law 6, 30, 250
South Carolina 149, 150, 154
statistics, research
    see also research results, analysis
    China 201–2
    Hong Kong 95–6
    Malaysia 135–7
    United Kingdom 79–81
Stienstra, D. 143–4
Stimec, Arnaud 101
Stipanowich, T.J. 6, 7
sub-Saharan Africa 54–5

*Superior IP International Pty Ltd
v. Ahearn Fox Patent and
Trade Mark Attorneys* (2012),
Australia 164, 165
Supreme People's Court, China
see also China; People's Republic of
China (PRC)
ground rules laid down by 194–5
Notice of the Supreme People's
Court on Issuing Several
Opinions on Further
Implementing the Work
Principle of "Giving Priority
to Mediation and Combining
Mediation with Judgment" 191
Provisions on Several Issues
Concerning the Civil Mediation
Work of the People's Court 191
Several Opinions on Further
Displaying the Positive Roles
of Litigation Mediation in
Building of a Harmonious
Socialist Society 191

telephone-based mediation 70
time frames/timing of mediation
data collection 8
Italy 180, 183
The Netherlands 120–21
processing time 120–21
resolution time frame 121
United Kingdom 73
voluntary versus mandatory
mediation 234
Tomlin orders, UK 76
triangulation of research 7, 8
t-test 11
Turkey 42

UNCITRAL (United Nations
Commission on International
Trade Law) 6
Conciliation Rules 60
Model Law on International
Commercial Conciliation 60,
61, 251
Working Group 250
United Kingdom 65–84
Automatic Referral to Mediation
pilot scheme 30

CEDR Solve (mediation
provider) 69, 70
Central London County Court
Automatic Referral to Mediation
pilot scheme 30
county court trial centre 32
voluntary mediation scheme 68
Centre for Effective Dispute
Resolution (CEDRI) 81
civil justice ranking 82–4
civil justice review (1990s) 31
civil justice system 67, 82, 83
Civil Mediation Online
Directory 67, 71
Civil Procedure Rules (CPR) 44, 68,
70, 74–6, 78
consent for mediation 69, 71
contracts 69, 76
cost reduction 31
Court of Appeal (Civil
Division) 67–8
Court of Appeal Mediation Scheme
(CAMS) 67, 69–70, 80
court-based ADR initiatives for non-
family civil disputes 79–80
Courts and Legal Services Act
1990 31
encouragement of ADR 30, 32
fees 31, 68, 69, 70, 71, 81, 82
government mediation 81–2
ground rules, mediation 71–3
historical background 66–7
Interim Report 1995 32
Legal Aid Board 67
mediation process 74–5
National Mediation Helpline 66–7,
71, 81
non-family cases 69, 79–80
paths to justice survey 79
policy background 66–8
practical implementation of
mediation policies 76–8
pre-action protocols 74
programme features 68–71
rationale for VOL pilot scheme 67–8
research statistics 79–81
settlement agreements 75
Small Claims Mediation Scheme
(HMCS) 67, 68, 70, 80
Tomlin orders 76

voluntary mediation 68, 79–84
Woolf Reforms 32, 66
United Nations
　see also UNCITRAL (United Nations Commission on International Trade Law)
　General Assembly 43, 61
　use of mediation by 42–3
United Nations Commission on International Trade Law see UNCITRAL (United Nations Commission on International Trade Law)
United States 143–57
　Alternative Dispute Resolution (ADR) 45, 143, 144, 145, 146, 155
　Alternative Disputes Resolution Act 1998 145, 146
　budget allocation 32
　California 147, 148, 153, 155
　challenges regarding mandatory mediation 153
　civil justice ranking 155–7
　civil justice system 155, 156
　conclusion of processes 151–2
　Congress 144, 145
　consent for mediation 146, 151, 152
　contracts 152
　costs issues 151
　court-based mediation 143–4
　enforcement 152–3
　Fair Housing Act 153, 154
　Federal Rules of Appellate Procedure 143, 144
　Federal Rules of Civil Procedure 27
　Federal Trademark Act 1946 147
　Florida 148, 151, 154, 227
　ground rules, explaining by mediators 150–51
　Illinois 146–7, 148
　Indiana 147, 148, 150
　introduction of mediation in (1983) 27
　Judicial Conference 1994 144–5
　Judicial Improvements Act 144
　Justice Department 144, 153
　law/policy background 144–6
　mandatory mediation 143–4, 148–9, 153, 154, 155
　Massachusetts 154
　mediation process 147–50
　Mediation Reports 151
　Michigan 147, 148, 151
　Missouri 149
　nature and process of mediation 150
　New York 146, 147, 148, 152
　North Carolina 34, 147, 148, 149, 150, 152
　objectives for implementation of mediation programmes 145–6
　practical implementation of ADR policies 153–4
　programme features 146–53
　research results, analysis 154–7
　roles and responsibilities of mediators and parties 150–51
　scheduling of mediation sessions 146–7
　South Carolina 149, 150, 154
　unresolved cases 152
　Virginia 30
US Educational Foundation in India (USEFI) 210

Victoria, Australia 28, 30, 162
　County Court Building Cases List 159
Virginia, United States 30
voluntary mediation
　see also mandatory mediation
　characterization of jurisdictions practising 6
　conceptual divide between voluntary and mandatory mediation 50–57
　costs issues 232–4
　efficiency factors 232, 256
　France 99, 102, 110
　free will assumption 51
　Hong Kong 29
　jurisdictional selection 52, 53
　key achievements 223, 237–8, 252
　key challenges 223, 241–2
　Malaysia 125, 133, 138
　The Netherlands 112, 122, 123–4
　programme design 49–61
　regional and international approaches to 57–61
　United Kingdom 68, 79–84

voluntary nature of mediation 65, 72–3
voluntary versus mandatory mediation 232–3

wakai (judicial settlement), Japan 54
WODC (Research and Documentation Centre of the Dutch Ministry of Justice) 113
women's interests, undermining 16
Woolf Reforms, UK 32, 66

World Bank 27, 28
   Worldwide Governance Indicators (WGIs) 8, 9
World Economic Forum 8, 9, 28
World Justice Project 8
World Trade Organization (WTO), Dispute Settlement Body 58
written referrals for mediation 114, 119
written settlement agreements 75–6
Wu Yim Kwong Kindwind v. *Manhood Development Ltd* (2012) 95